Foodways and Empathy

Person, Space and Memory in the Contemporary Pacific

Series editors: Prof. Jürg Wassmann (University of Heidelberg, Institute of Anthropology), Dr. Verena Keck (Goethe University Frankfurt, Institute of Anthropology)

Advisory board: Prof. Pierre R. Dasen (University of Geneva, Department of Anthropology of Education and Cross-Cultural Psychology), Prof. Donald H. Rubinstein (University of Guam), Prof. Robert Tonkinson (The University of Western Australia, Department of Anthropology), Prof. Peter Meusburger (University of Heidelberg, Department of Economic and Social Geography), Prof. Joachim Funke (University of Heidelberg, Department of Psychology)

The many different localities of the Pacific region have a long history of transformation, under both pre- and post-colonial conditions. More recently, rates of local transformation have increased tremendously under post-colonial regimes. Yet, until now, research has concentrated on the macro- or culturally specific aspects of globalization, while neglecting actual actors and their perspectives of social change. This series supplements earlier work through the integration of cultural research with psychological methodologies, linguistics, geography and cognitive science.

Foodways and Empathy
Relatedness in a Ramu River Society, Papua New Guinea

Anita von Poser

berghahn
NEW YORK • OXFORD
www.berghahnbooks.com

First published in 2013 by

Berghahn Books

www.berghahnbooks.com

©2013 Anita von Poser

Library of Congress Cataloging-in-Publication Data

Poser, Anita von.
 Foodways and empathy: relatedness in a Ramu River society, Papua New Guinea / Anita
von Poser.
     pages cm. — (Person, space and memory in the contemporary pacific; volume 4)
 Includes bibliographical references and index.
 ISBN 978-0-85745-919-0 (hardback : alk. paper) — ISBN 978-0-85745-920-6
 (institutional ebook)
 1. Bosmun (Papua New Guinean people)—Food—Social aspects. 2. Bosmun (Papua
New Guinean people)—Kinship. 3. Bosmun (Papua New Guinean people)—Social life
and customs. 4. Food—Social aspects—Papua New Guinea—Ramu River Valley.
5. Kinship—Papua New Guinea—Ramu River Valley. 6. Ramu River Valley (Papua New
Guinea)—Social life and customs. I. Title.
 DU740.42P68 2013
 305.899'12—dc23

                                                                            2012037865

British Library Cataloguing in Publication Data

A catalogue record for this book is available from the British Library

Printed in the United States on acid-free paper.

ISBN: 978-0-85745-919-0 Hardback
ISBN: 978-0-85745-920-6 Institutional EBook

In Memory of Ndombu and Kose

Contents

List of Illustrations

Acknowledgments

Several people were instrumental in the creation of this book, contributing their thoughts, their time, their ideas, their support, and their valuable criticism.

First of all, I am indebted to many Bosmun and to the Rom in particular:

Dia olgeta lain long ples,
mi laik tok tenkyu tru long yupela olgeta. Fes taim mi kam na stap, mi no bin save wanem ol lain stret bai stap na bai soim wanem kain pasin long mi. Asples bilong mi long Germany i bin stap longwe tru long wara Ramu na mi no bin save wanem kain pasin stret bai stap long dispela hap. I go go go go nau—em nau—mi skelim pinis: Ol gutpela lain tasol i stap! Pasin bilong ai i stap! Yumi kaikai wantaim, yumi wokabaut wantaim, yumi krai lap wantaim, yumi tok gudbai long yumi yet. Yumi tok helo gen long yumi yet. Na olsem na, em dispela tupela ples, ples Bosmun na ples Germany, ol i muv kam klostu nau long tupela yet. Vut bilong mi i pulap long amamas tasol. Dispela wok mi pinisim pinis, em bikos ol gutpela tingting tasol yupela i salim i kam long mi i bin strongim mi stret. Olsem na, mi tok: nda yaaoŋ!

I am deeply grateful to Jürg Wassmann and Verena Keck. Both, in their individual ways, encouraged me to travel to Papua New Guinea. They were my teachers, and a lot of what I heard from them while studying anthropology in classrooms became true as I set out on my own path with Bosmun. Their concern and support have been of a personal and cordial kind that went well beyond their role as academic instructors. I would also like to express my appreciation to Holger Jebens for spontaneously consenting to read through an earlier version of this book.

My research was made possible with the generous and structural support of several institutions and persons in charge: I conducted fieldwork at the Lower Ramu River in 2004/05 and 2006 as part of the project *Person, Space and Memory in the Contemporary Pacific* (see Wassmann & Stockhaus 2007) started by Jürg Wassmann and funded by the German Volkswagen Foundation. A teaching grant from the German Academic Exchange Service (DAAD) allowed me to return to Papua New Guinea in 2008 on a project on *Subject-Related Partnerships with Institutions of Higher Education and Developing Countries*; I am glad to have participated in a promising collaboration between the Department of Anthropology in Heidelberg and the Faculty of Arts at the Divine Word University in Madang (see Keck et al. 2008). In 2008, I was also given a grant by The Society for Endangered Languages (GBS) in Germany for the purpose of returning my linguistic data to Bosmun. As a doctoral fellow of the Marsilius-Kolleg (2008/09), an Initiative of Excellence of the University of Heidelberg, I was able to fully concentrate on writing the first version of Bosmun ethnography. Here, I would like to especially thank Thomas Fuchs. Günther Schlee of the Max Planck Institute for Social Anthropology in Halle / Saale and Mirko Sporket of the Max Planck Institute for Demographic Research in Rostock supported my plans to conduct research in Papua New Guinea in 2010 as a postdoctoral fellow of the Max Planck International Research Network on Aging. Upon this return, I had the opportunity to discuss my findings with the people of Daiden. I would also like to express my appreciation to Birgitt Röttger-Rössler for taking me on as part of her team at the Institute of Social and Cultural Anthropology, Free University of Berlin, and for giving me all the freedom that is needed to combine teaching, motherhood, and the preparation of a book.

The way this book has taken shape was influenced, to a large degree, by the many valuable comments and critiques I received from my anonymous Berghahn reviewers. I highly benefited from their clarifications and suggestions, and I hope that my attempts to overcome obvious shortcomings are reflected in my narrative. Many thanks, of course, also go to Marion Berghahn, Ann Przyzycki DeVita, Elizabeth Berg, and Melissa Spinelli of Berghahn Books.

Douglas Hollan and C. Jason Throop triggered my interest in the anthropology of empathy. I thank them for giving me the opportunity to join the sessions on "empathy" in 2007 and 2008 that they organized at the annual meetings of the Association for Social Anthropology in Oceania (ASAO). The comments and theoretical issues raised in this session, especially by Roger Lohmann and Thomas Ernst and by Alan Rumsey, who discussed the paper that I presented, have been very helpful.

Teachers, colleagues, and / or friends at the University of Heidelberg gave valuable advice regarding methodology and medical precautions prior to fieldwork, among them Thomas Widlok, Don Gardner, and Angella Meinerzag. Angella and Franziska Herbst sacrificed their time to give useful comments on earlier drafts. Sabine Hess shared with me the intricate problems that kinship diagrams can provoke and how to solve them. General discussions on Papua New Guinea with Martin Maden have been enlightening in many ways. Bettina Ubl shared with me experiences in Daiden and memories of Daiden once we were back in Germany. Bettina and Andreas Mayer gave useful comments from the background of psychology with regard to empathy and theory of mind research.

I also wish to acknowledge my colleagues Jutta Turner and Bettina Mann at the Max Planck Institute for Social Anthropology in Halle / Saale for the kind permission to use in this book the map of the Lower Ramu area that Jutta drew for me while I was working there.

When I began writing down my Bosmun data in English, David Valpey and Barbara Zipser were very helpful. My cordial thanks go to Ron Beier for his proofreading of the draft on which this book is based and for his many thoughtful comments. I am very glad that we met in Rostock. If there are any mistakes left they are, of course, my own.

My initial contact with Bosmun was facilitated by John Hickey, a former Australian and now Papua New Guinean citizen and politician who has been living in the Bosmun area since 1972. Greg Murphy, Director of the Madang Open Campus of UPNG (University of Papua New Guinea) introduced Jürg, Verena, and me to John. During my stays at the Ramu River, I did not see him often due to his time-consuming profession. He took the time, however, to travel with me to the Ramu and to introduce me to the people of Rom. Jürg, Verena, and Greg went with us, and I am very grateful for their company during this first initiation of mine into Bosmun life. In 2005, John and I had a longer conversation. He gave me important hints with regard to historical orientation, self-baked bread, and brewed, ground coffee in his generator-driven house at the Ramu.

During my stays in Madang, I met several people who supported me in many ways: Sam Mbamak (John's adopted son) and his wife Anna helped organize my travels to the Ramu. Catherine Levy gave linguistic expertise when she came to visit me in Daiden. Diane and Mike Cassell gave me a warmhearted reception whenever I needed a rest. At Divine Word University, Meri Armstrong, Monika Rothliesberger, and Cindy Lola provided help as I searched the university library. Mark Solon, Patrick Gesch, Anastasia Sai, Samuel Roth, and Jerry Semos created a cooperative atmosphere at the Department of PNG Studies. Discussions with students of the PNG Studies Department, especially with Gloria Nema, Mary Daure, Heni Aisi, Peter Topura, and Joyce Maragas, helped me to become more aware of the role of anthropologists working and teaching in Papua New Guinea. Nicolas Hamny of the Madang Planning Office provided me with census information for the Lower Ramu area. In Port Moresby, I greatly benefited from meeting Jim Robins at the National Research Institute, Don Niles at the Institute of Papua New Guinea Studies, and Elias Masuali at the National Archives. Gabriele Schwind was very helpful when I visited the Library of the Anthropos Institute in Sankt Augustin in Germany.

I also wish to acknowledge my friends who provided me with the sense of the home that I had before adding Daiden to my personal list of familiar places: Melanie Bretscher and Herbert Kölzer called me whenever I was in Madang. In motivating me they simply ignored the conventional limitations of long-distance calls. Suntka Müller kept sending me letters, some of which even reached me while I was in Daiden. A particularly great flow of memories came over me when I received a package from her that contained a tiny silver spoon, some tea, and East Frisian "Kluntje."

I am deeply grateful to my family for their support. My parents, Jelena and Gerhard Stadler, gave me what only parents can give—their love and compassion, and their faith in all the projects I ever started. They also gave financial support while I studied, and they generously cofunded my travels to Papua New Guinea. Without them, I would hardly have taken the paths that I did. My niece Suzana Nećakov always reminds me of our common "Šiaćki" heritage that has provided me and, I guess, her, with something not easy to explain. She gave me a notebook that returned with many notes. Suzana and her parents, Milovan and Dušica, also provided me with IT facilities when I visited Serbia, my mother's home country. Before my husband and I moved to Berlin, Nicola von Albrecht and Boris von Poser kindly put us up whenever we came to visit archives and when we needed an alternative space while in the process of writing and reflection. Cornelia von Poser-Hirche also played a great role in the current project. We met in Papua New Guinea, in an atmosphere of instant mutual sympathy that later turned not only into an in-law relation but also into friendship.

Last but not least, I wish to thank Alexis von Poser, my husband and colleague, for the life and the passions that we share. Apart from reading various drafts and helping me with computer problems, he has provided humor and the patience that I needed in coming to terms with Bosmun ethnography. I have been fortunate that our paths crossed at the very right moment—somewhere between Kayan and Bosmun. I hope that we will return to Papua New Guinea together with our son Arthur who has been with us since we left.

Annotations to the Text

Tok Pisin (Melanesian Pidgin) terms are italicized. With the exception of personal names and place names, terms in the Bosmun vernacular are italicized and underlined. I have translated these terms directly in text; translations are marked by single quotation marks. The local terms also reoccur in a glossary. In quoting people, I have included the verbatim accounts in Tok Pisin. This may be of interest to readers familiar with this common language, which is widely spoken in the northern part of Papua New Guinea. As for the Tok Pisin terms, I recommend *The Jacaranda Dictionary and Grammar of Melanesian Pidgin* by Mihalic (1986), originally published in 1971, as well as the *Papua New Guinea Tok Pisin English Dictionary* recently released by Oxford Press (2008). I should note, however, that Bosmun sometimes abbreviate the following words: *save* turns into *sa, yupela* into *yutla, mitupela* into *mitla,* and *dispela* into *disela* or *disla.*

Instead of using the phonetic alphabet, for which a computer would be indispensable, I have decided to use a kind of written form that in my view is most practicable for preserving a language in a rural area that still relies mostly on typewriters. Shorter vowels are indicated by a single letter (*a, e,* and *o*), longer vowels by a double letter (*aa, ee,* and *oo*). *X* is pronounced similarly to the "ch" used in the Scottish word "loch." The phonetic symbols *i, ŋ,* and *ŋg* were already part of an alphabet introduced by the Summer Institute of Linguistics (SIL). Bosmun accept these symbols, and they regularly modify *i, n,* and *ng* in texts by hand. The SIL's suggestion to differentiate the vowels and the phonemes that I present as *x* by using symbols with bars appeared confusing to my informants and to me. Therefore, my presentation of Bosmun phonemes in this book is:

    a as in "cut"
    oo as in "ought"
    ŋ as in "tongue"
    aa as in "laugh"
    mb as in "wombat"
    ŋg as in "finger"
    i as in "the"
    nd as in "reprimand"
    x as in "loch"
    o as in "oppose"
    nz as in "benzene"

In indicating kinship terms, I shall apply a set of standard abbreviations as suggested in the reader *Kinship and Family* edited by Parkin and Stone (2004):

F: father
M: mother
P: parent
B: brother
Z: sister
G: sibling
H: husband
W: wife
E: spouse
S: son
D: daughter
C: child
e: elder
y: younger
os: opposite-sex
ss: same-sex

Introduction

Mi kaikai saksak ya ('I am eating sago') or *mi tanim saksak nau* ('I am stirring sago now') are two of the phrases I heard most often while I was living and working in the Bosmun area. Whenever I visited people or passed households on my way to other destinations, the residents would use food-related phrases almost like expressions of standard greeting. I was consistently welcomed by being given information about a household's current food situation. Even if no one was preparing or consuming a meal at the moment I passed by, I would receive greetings such as: *Mi no kaikai yet* ('I haven't eaten yet'), *Mi kaikai pinis ya* ('I've finished eating'), or *Mi wok saksak pinis na mi kam* ('I just returned from sago making'). Also, when listening to conversations in the beginning, I repeatedly heard the phrase *No ken hait na kaikai* ('Don't eat in secret'). As my fieldwork proceeded, I realized that Bosmun use food-related statements such as these to enact a kind of "transparent personhood" that is at the heart of local configurations of relatedness and empathy. My book aims to cover the conceptual convergence of food sharing and empathy by illustrating how Bosmun engage in "empathetic foodways" in order to keep or sever kin-ties and social relationships in general. With the ethnographic example of Bosmun, I hope to be able to offer a novel contribution to the emerging variety of "local cultures of relatedness" (Carsten 2000: 1) that have come to the fore in recent theorizing about kinship.

The present account is based on my twenty-three month experience in northeast Papua New Guinea. Bosmun live alongside the banks of the Lower Ramu River, in a region belonging to the Madang Province. The Ramu River, locally called Xoaam (the Bosmun generic term for any larger river), rises in the highlands of the Eastern Bismarck Range and flows into the Bismarck Sea between Cape Purpur and Venus Point. With a length of 720 kilometers, it is Papua New Guinea's fifth largest river (Rannells 2001: 149). Bosmun territory lies approximately fifteen kilometers south of the Ramu estuary, in the vicinity of a tributary named Mbur, which flanks the main river on its western side (see map 0.1). My first fieldwork was carried out from September 2004 to October 2005. John Hickey[1] had asked the people of Daiden, a Bosmun place situated directly at the banks of the Ramu, whether they would take me in, which they fortunately did. Shortly after my return to Germany, I had the chance to take another six-week trip to Papua New Guinea on an interdisciplinary project, and so I returned to Daiden in April 2006. This time I was accompanied by the psychologist Bettina Ubl who was interested in exploring children's

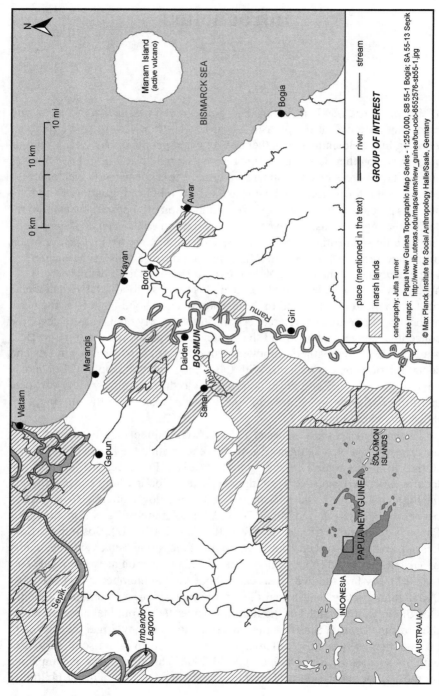

Map 0.1: Lower Ramu River.

perspective-taking and the development of a "theory of mind" (Ubl 2007; A. von Poser & Ubl forthcoming). In 2008, my husband and colleague Alexis and I stayed in the town of Madang for four months, teaching anthropology at Divine Word University. Although our academic work took up a fair amount of time, there were still opportunities for shorter trips to the Ramu and for people to visit us in town. My last visit to Papua New Guinea was in 2010.

Personally, "going back to the field" in 2006 was certainly more crucial to me than the other returns, since I had to find out what kind of imprints I had left on people's lives. Upon my arrival, I was delighted to see that our bond was still strong. Even though I had left the people of Daiden just a short while before, our reunion was marked by jointly remembering and narrating the experiences that we had shared during my first fourteen months there. We recalled bright as well as sad or trying moments, including one particular incident I was explicitly told to write about. One day, as Kopri, my *saate yap* ('father's younger brother') said, this incident would become a *raarŋanini,* an 'ancestral story.' As I had initially declared a particular interest in people's lives and their present and ancestral customs, he and several others felt that I should be the one to write down the incident and that this detail should not be missing in my book. This was also the point in time at which I began to comprehend what food-related action meant to the people of this place. Below, after recounting this incident, I outline the theoretical body of my book, introduce my conversation partners, and describe my research methods.

Sharing Bananas after a Raging Fire

About four weeks after my arrival, a fire broke out in Daiden and within less than fifteen minutes seven households, two partially completed buildings, and a recently built birth-house were destroyed by the flames. A single household consists of a cooking-house, a sleeping-house, a resting platform and one or more utility buildings where tools and firewood are stored. All of the inhabitants were at work or visiting relatives when the fire took place, so nobody was injured. Nevertheless, the damage left thirty-nine former residents suddenly homeless. Because the wind blew from another direction, my house survived undamaged despite being close to the point of origin of the fire. This was particularly important as all my equipment was stored in this building. Otherwise, I do not know whether I would have continued doing my research.

It was a strange situation. I was relocated unexpectedly without actually having moved myself. The fire had turned my location into a part of the periphery, whereas before it had been situated adjacent to a densely populated part of Daiden. Now I had to face a sudden void instead of the lively spot it had been before. Still, I think the fire marked the time when the people of Daiden and I formed a relationship of mutual concern beyond formal friendliness. Before I describe the situation after the fire, let me share a few impressions that always come to mind whenever I reflect on my initial time in Daiden.

Right from the beginning the people of Daiden gave me a house to live in by myself. They had agreed that Seres, a young unmarried man who later became my *nduaŋ* ('brother'), would provide the house and, during my presence, would live with another brother of ours next door to me. Having "my house" was indeed reassuring since going into the field was a new experience for me and the first weeks were really overwhelming, if not arduous at times. I had to cope not only with hundreds of eyes following me all the time, but also with how quickly people spoke Tok Pisin. In addition, the people of Daiden had a clear picture of what a *waitmeri* ('white woman') was. When I went to a household, for instance, as I did to introduce myself to each family and to survey the residential structure, people would often say that I should come back another day. When I asked if they were busy at the moment, they answered that they did not have a chair for me to sit on. They would have to find a chair first in order to make me feel comfortable in the way they presumed would be appropriate "for people like me."

People constantly worried about my physical and emotional well-being. There was, for instance, regular talk about my loss of weight using startling descriptions, of which Tok Pisin has many (I never got badly ill during fieldwork and losing weight was a natural adaption to the tropical climate). People usually said to me: *Bifo yu save karim as na nau yu kamap bun* ('At the time of your arrival, you carried your bottom and now you look like a bone'). When I add the detail that in everyday Bosmun speech such comments are usually accompanied by much laughter, such a portrayal might appear impolite to outsiders. From Bosmun perspectives, however, it is quite common to identify people by means of their physical traits without insulting them. Let me give another example that shows the emotional support I was offered. I once received a letter from my parents and suddenly started crying. Nothing serious had happened. They just wrote to me about what was going on at home and that they missed me. Once this episode of self-pity was over, I heard three women sitting on the platform next to my house crying. When I asked them why they were crying, they answered that my pain would fade away if I were not crying alone. A shared feeling would relieve my sadness, they anticipated.

I appreciate people's commitment to welcoming me into their lives. In some ways, however, their care for me was going to restrict my independence regarding the work I had come to do. It took me a while to convince the people of Daiden that I had enough strength to walk the distances required to reach other Bosmun places, which I considered important for getting a broader perspective on things. Moreover, I had to communicate that "white people" do not only like canned food and that I would instead be looking forward to tasting local and fresh foods. Nevertheless, I have to admit that in the beginning, people's desire to avoid overwhelming me with their normal way of life suited my moods to some degree. Frequently they suggested that I should go back to my house to have a rest. Of course, I also sensed that they were not quite ready to let me come closer. They did not really know who I was or what I expected from them. In a similar manner, I kept myself somewhat distanced because of some challenging distractions like adapting myself to the tropical environment and managing the initial intense flow of information. Thus, I did not hesitate to take the recommended breaks.

After a month of the people of Daiden and I cautiously coming closer to one another, a fire flared up in the early afternoon, dragging us into a short, distressing scenario. A woman had dried fish on a grill over an oil-drum, and while she was occupied with something else, the flames in the drum shot up, passed over to the sago roof of her kitchen, and spread to the other houses. Due to the searing heat, most of the people, including myself, became petrified with shock. We just stood and stared. The fire disappeared as promptly as it had appeared and came suddenly to a halt before reaching another house standing nearby. The fire's destructive force had left behind a field of glowing embers that would not cool off until the next day, granting an eerie light that lasted throughout the night until dawn. As the anxiety lessened, people started to walk around the remains of their dwelling sites hoping to find anything important that might have survived. Some of them did so in silence, some of them in tears. Around sunset, people finally sat down and I joined them. Meanwhile, the news had spread and relatives living elsewhere were coming by to emotionally support those affected by the fire. The loss of a house is not only a material but also an emotional loss for Bosmun since it evokes memories of the deceased who had once contributed in some way to the house. An older woman, for example, mourned over the wooden plates that her father, a skilled carver, had once made for her during her childhood. She had used these plates from adulthood onward, and they had been a significant part of her cooking-house.

Above all I remember two laments. The first was from a woman of Ndenekaam, another Bosmun place about half an hour's walk from Daiden. She had come to look after her daughter, who had become a widow only recently. A year before, the daughter's husband had been killed by a crocodile. The woman mourned for her daughter's children, who had lost first their father and now the house that their father had built. She expressed her grief by calling out all the names of her beloved in a sad, melodic way. Over and over, she repeated her pity and everyone listened. I spent the night outside with them, listening to these expressions of grief. Looking back, this was the beginning of a deeper tie between the people of Daiden and me. I did not want to leave and nobody told me to leave.

The second lament that I bear in mind was from the father of the man who had died in the crocodile attack. The older man had gone to Madang and was supposed to come back the next day. During the night some people talked about his probable reaction, predicting that he would turn up in rage. No one took special notice of me. I turned into a listener, as did the others who had come to see the tragedy with their own eyes. The next morning, we heard the man's voice from afar. His weeping combined with expressions of anger silenced everyone. He did not immediately approach the area where his household had stood. As he came nearer, he stopped moving, just staring at what was left and then called his dead son's name. Many times he pointed at the burned house posts, declaring that it was his son who had provided the wood and had shaped the posts for his parents' home. After more than an hour, the man came closer and ultimately joined his wife, who had already taken a seat next to the now empty plot.

Three days and nights the people simply sat beside their burned homes. Eventually, I went back to my house, but I did not feel good being alone. I sat on the floor and glanced at a huge bunch of bananas, a gift a woman had brought me some days before. Suddenly I felt ashamed. I had so many bananas, too many for me alone, whereas those people outside had lost almost everything. I began thinking about giving them the bananas, but felt awkward because those bananas were far from being sufficient for thirty-nine individuals and their accumulated relatives. Finally, I decided to walk over and share the bananas anyway. Moving from family to family, I distributed two or three bananas to each without saying anything. In view of the disaster, I had nothing to say. A week later, when all those who had lost their homes had been taken in by relatives and had started to clear up the burned ground, I had a conversation with Seres about the incident. He told me that people were talking about my behavior and had come to the conclusion that I possess a personal trait, which they call *ramkandiar,* that is, looking after others and helping them if they are in need, but—and this is crucial—without asking them.

I refer to the phenomenon of *ramkandiar,* which appeared to me to be the most fundamental moral value in Daiden, as 'watching others and being watched.' In Bosmun understandings, "watching" is not confined to the visual sense alone. "Watching" correlates with drawing one's own conclusions about one's observations. The term *vaas,* which Bosmun use to say that they 'see' or 'watch' something or someone, implies that they 'think-feel' of / into something or someone and that they reflect on something or someone. To 'think-feel' can be glossed by the Bosmun phrase *vut moŋ.* My interviewees also described it as 'to think of someone who is worried' or 'to feel sorry for someone,' since this is what "good people" should always do. The locus of one's intentionality and one's actions are the intestines, called *moŋ.* As a verb, *moŋ* also means 'to do / to act.' The term *vut* denotes heart palpitations as well as all other pulsations that people feel in the human body. A woman, for instance, pointed to her temples, her neck, her hands, and the part between her ankle and heel to explain *vut* to me. Thus, it is the whole body that is 'thinking-feeling'—with the belly at its center. *Ndiar* ('the willingness to make peace / to mediate') refers to any positive behavioral quality in Bosmun moral theory. More than anything else, it is expressed through the sharing of food. Someone with *ndiar* is said to perform *tip yaaoŋ* ('virtuous / sociable behavior'). Someone who lacks *ndiar* is said to perform the opposite, referred to as *tip yaakak* ('bad / unsociable behavior'). *Ramak* (from which *ramka-* in *ramkandiar* derives) literally means 'eye' and implies that people should use their eyes to watch others and sociably respond to them if they see them in troubled states. That was what I had done, Seres concluded: I had anticipated that people must be suffering from hunger—and without asking anybody—had shared the bananas among them. I expressed my doubts regarding the insufficient amount of my food distribution. Seres smiled and declared that this was not what had mattered. It was the first time that I heard of *ramkandiar*. In retrospect, this dialogue with Seres paved my way for understanding the grounds of Bosmun sociality and how, in general, the sharing of food may relate to empathy in a place such as Daiden.

Making Kin through Foodways and Empathy

This section introduces three theoretical themes in order to build the conceptual framework in which my ethnographic data is anchored: *kinship / relatedness, foodways,* and *empathy.*

Kinship / Relatedness

Based on his observations among the Reite on the Rai coast of Papua New Guinea, where "[p]eople share substance, and are therefore kin, because they have grown in the same land," Leach (2003: 30) dismisses the conventional genealogical model upon which so much of anthropology's study of kinship has rested. He contends that to map links between individuals in a kinship diagram and "say that this is a kinship connection is meaningless" (Leach 2003: 30) in terms of understanding Reite relationships. Rather, kinship comes into being through creativity as manifested in the relations between persons and places. Bamford (2007, 2009), too, draws on a non-genealogical approach to explain kin conceptions among the Kamea of Papua New Guinea. She writes that, despite her "repeated attempts to anchor intergenerational relations in a procreative bond, Kamea were quite insistent that parents do not share any kind of physical connection with their offspring. Kamea do have a means of tracing social relationships through time, but this is not seen to rest upon genealogical connections; instead, it eventuates from the ties that people form with the land" (Bamford 2007: 6).

Relating in a more general way to the shift in recent theorizing about kinship, Leach says: "whereas in the past one might have looked for the structure of society in kinship categories, now it is the life-cycle, and particularly the ascription of identity and relatedness through activities, which takes narrative prominence.... One way of understanding this move is to say [that] this is because the agentive, creative aspect of people's interactions seemed to be missing from earlier understandings of kinship" (2003: 23).

Carsten (1997) makes a similar point about the dynamics of kinship in *The Heat of the Hearth,* her ethnographic case study on the Langkawi in West Malaysia. She argues that people do not consider each other kin because of notions of shared blood—as assumed in Euro-American folk understandings of procreation. Rather, Langkawi "become kin to each other through living and eating together" (1997: 27). Based on the data of how Langkawi themselves build and recognize relations, Carsten takes a fresh conceptual approach to the study of kinship "as a process." This approach might also be paraphrased with what Weismantel has described as "making kin" among the Zumbagua of Ecuador, where "[e]very adult seemed to have several kinds of parents and several kinds of children" (1995: 689), depending on how many ties he or she had built through particular experiences of feeding and caring. Carsten, in particular, draws her inspiration from the work of Schneider (1984). In *A Critique of the Study of Kinship,* Schneider showed that a distinction between the biological and the social had been set a priori in the anthropological study of kinship, leading to the reproduction of "the ethnoepistemology of European culture" (1984: 175) in the representation of other societies. In pointing to the idea that people elsewhere may not give primacy to relationships as resulting from sexual reproduction, Schneider triggered a general rethinking of classic kinship analysis (Carsten 2004: 19–20). To convey her approach, Carsten advocates the use of the term "relatedness" in order to indicate "an openness to indigenous idioms of being related" (2000: 4) and suggests that, as ethnographers, we should, first of all, ask ourselves: "how do the people we study define and construct their notions of relatedness and what values and meaning do they give to them?" (1997: 290).

My ethnography is concerned with exactly these questions: how is kinship made known in Daiden, how is it emergent from specific social practices, why and in what ways are ties kept or undone? Bosmun do acknowledge ties in genealogical terms, but these ties may easily become hollow if they are not "activated" in the right way. In order to convey how the "making of" kin works in Daiden, I need to analyze people's foodways as they relate to the phenomenon of empathy.

Foodways

In an anthology about food and gender, Counihan (1998: 1) states that "food-ways" are "an effective prism through which to illuminate human life." She defines foodways as the "behaviors and beliefs surrounding the production, distribution, and consumption of food" (Counihan 1999: 6). In my definition of the term, I wish to stress that foodways also implies the emotional assessments that people make of food-related behaviors and practices. I assume that foodways offer vital clues to personhood. Much has been written about personhood in anthropology—ranging from Mauss's ([1938] 1985) classic essay published in 1938 to more recent theoretical reflections and ethnographic illustrations.[2] Bosmun personhood, as I explore it, conflates aspects that have been split conceptually, for instance, by Harris (1989), who splits these aspects into three distinct analytical categories. She claims that we should differentiate between the social, psychic, and biophysical aspects of our existence as social actors, which she terminologically translates as "person," "self," and "individual"; yet, she admits that these components can be interrelated differently in different localities (Harris 1989: 599–604).[3] In Bosmun subjectivity, social, psychic, and physical states are held to be deeply interwoven. The medium through which such putatively distinct categories such as "person," "self," and "individual" are articulated is food. Of course, food (_aamarees_ for 'cooked food,' _ximir_ for 'raw food') is recognized for its nutritional importance and seen as vital to maintaining people's bodies. However, as we shall see, this biophysical necessity is so deeply linked to the social and emotional realm that feelings of hunger may be ignored or downplayed in situations in which different codes of conduct need to be acknowledged.

The role of food has been a rewarding topic in anthropology for decades, in approaches ranging from structuralist (e.g., M. Douglas 1966, 1997; Lévi-Strauss [1964] 1969, 1997) and symbolic (e.g., Kahn 1986) to more experiential and phenomenological approaches (e.g., Eves 1998), and it continues to be an issue of anthropological interest (Alexeyeff, James & Thomas 2004; Counihan & van Esterik 1997; Manderson 1986b; Mintz & Du Bois 2002; Watson & Caldwell 2005; Whitehead 2000). This may certainly be traced back to the fact that "[n]ext to breathing, eating is perhaps the most essential of all human activities, and one with which much of social life is entwined" (Mintz & Du Bois 2002: 102). Scholars have analyzed how people's foodways relate to politics and to power on local levels (e.g., Young 1971) and global levels (e.g., Watson & Caldwell 2005), how they relate to the subject of gender (e.g., Counihan & Kaplan 1998; Kahn 1986), to the body (e.g., Counihan 1999; Meigs 1984), to memory (e.g., Holtzman 2006; Sutton 2001) and to socialization (Tietjen 1985), how food taboos express status in kinship relations (Paulsen 2003), how food words become person-referring avoidance terms

(Stasch 2002: 338–339), how food is classified in and across cultures (e.g., Pollock 1986; Wassmann 1993), and how food marks cultural boundaries and their transcendence (Haines & Sammells 2010).

Bosmun foodways are not just political, economic or social. They also entail emotional and intentional meanings and might therefore be understood as what Mageo (2011: 76) calls "enacted empathy." The way Bosmun perceive action bears resemblance to the Lelet of New Ireland in Papua New Guinea where "actions display intentionality" (Eves 1998: 36). This holds true elsewhere in Papua New Guinea (e.g., Fajans 1997: 119; Kahn 1986: 1, 39; Manderson 1986a: 13, 17; Schieffelin 1976: 47–48) and in other parts of the Pacific (e.g., Alexeyeff 2004). Barlow (2001: 86–91), for instance, writes about the food-based empathetic communication in the mother-child relationship among the Murik in northwest Papua New Guinea, where mothers enthusiastically respond to their children's efforts to assist in procuring food and thus give them social recognition. Furthermore, Murik children "repair hurt feelings and relationships by offering food" (Barlow 2001: 90). A similar meaning is ascribed to action, and more particularly to the gestures of giving among the Sabarl in the Louisiade Archipelago of Papua New Guinea. Battaglia (1990: 56) talks of "enactments of emotion." Sabarl exchanges of food and other gifts are "statements of trust and sentiment"; the "giving of oneself emotionally generates many of the 'unofficial texts' of social relationship: the perennial small gestures of 'empathy,' ... the shows of tolerance for and sensitivity to the moods and 'soul searchings' ... of others, the expressions of sincerity and gestures of politeness—all of which are taken as serious measures of the person as someone worth 'remembering'" (Battaglia 1990: 56).

What makes the Bosmun case of particular interest for a discussion about food and empathy is not only that the sharing of food expresses people's tolerance for and sensitivity to the states of others, but that people who share food feel justified in inquiring into their consociates' lives, on the one hand, and that they allow their consociates to inquire into their own lives, on the other.

Empathy

Fundamental to the notion of empathy is the assumption that one is able to comprehend the "subjective experience of another from a quasi-first person perspective" (Hollan & Throop 2008: 387). The term is derived from the German word *Einfühlung* (literally: 'feeling into') made prominent, especially by Vischer (1873), in nineteenth-century philosophical debates on aesthetics. *Einfühlung* became the intellectually recognized way to contemplate an art object and thus to detect its ultimate soul and beauty (see Jahoda 2005: 154). Apart from *Einfühlung*'s importance in the sphere of art, Lipps (1903a, 1903b, 1906), its other major proponent, also prompted its significance for interpersonal and psychological processes. Psychologist Titchener (1909) translated it into English as 'empathy' in his lectures on experimental psychology (see Jahoda 2005: 154–159, 161). According to Strauss, psychologists have basically argued that empathy consists of a cognitive and an affective component. Cognitively, empathy is the "awareness of another person's feelings," whereas affectively, empathy is "an emotional reaction to another's feelings" (Strauss 2004: 434). While it is theoretically intriguing to distinguish the cognitive and the affective aspects of empathy, one should not think that there are separate processes at work (see Engelen & Röttger-Rössler 2012; Walter 2012).[4] I believe that the attempt to arrive at a genuine awareness of another's feelings (via cognitive empathy) cannot succeed without emotionally acting and reacting (via affective empathy) in appropriate ways.[5]

Whereas considerable attention has been paid to food as an anthropological category, this has not been the case with "the ethnography of empathy" (Hollan 2012: 70). Hollan and Throop (2008: 385, 388–391, 396) argue that this may be partly ascribed to Geertz's (1984) critique of anthropologists who, in claiming to be empathetic, were instead actually projecting their own ideas onto observed social phenomena (see Robbins & Rumsey 2008: 416–417).[6] Indeed, drawing the line between projection and empathy is not that easy. As Lohmann critically remarks, "projection is often, and arguably always, a part of empathetic experience, and one that can improve as well as diminish the accuracy of empathy. Though projection of our own thoughts and feelings onto others typically creates inaccurate impressions, it is only through knowing our own volition, motives, and reactions that we are able to model what these must be like for others" (2011: 109). Yet, projection is subjective and static, whereas empathy is intersubjective and processual. Empathizer and empathizee engage in an "ongoing dialogue" (Hollan 2008: 476) that allows them to gain an accurate perception of another's states. This also means that one has to continually revise and reformulate one's own assessments of the other. As Hollan points out, "[t]his concern with accuracy, the willingness, indeed the necessity, to alter one's impression of another's emotional state as one engages with the other and learns more about his or her perspective, is what distinguishes empathy from simple projection—the attribution of one's own emotional reactions and perspectives to another" (2008: 476).[7]

Geertz's unmaking of empathy, as suggested by Hollan and Throop (2008: 385), has had its effects. In their 1986 review on the anthropology of emotions, Lutz and White, for instance, only briefly address empathy. Drawing on R. Rosaldo's (1988) claim that understanding of others is created through experiencing similarities,[8] they conclude that empathetic sensitivity becomes possible by "walking in the other person's shoes" (Lutz & White 1986: 415). In another anthropological collection that focuses specifically on ethnopsychologies in the Pacific (White & Kirkpatrick 1985), discussions of empathy seem to be equally muted. Only Black (1985: 249–253) pays explicit attention to it, seeking, in his contribution, to explore an attempted suicide within the context of a Micronesian's psychological world. Local concepts of empathy are not analyzed, however, as the parties involved in the empathetic encounter are taken to be the ethnographer and the people "investigated." Black notes that:

> [A]s ethnographers, we are heirs to a long tradition of fieldwork in which the ability to comprehend (intuit may be a better word) the emotional life of people is virtually taken for granted. I am referring here to the notion of "empathy" which is widely regarded as a prerequisite for successful participant observation. Whatever else is meant by this very slippery term, it always connotes an identification between ethnographer and "native." This identification is built on past learnings at the same time that it is used to develop further learnings. And most if not all of these learnings have to do with feelings. (1985: 249)

Black's notion of empathy is basically in line with that of Halpern (2001), a bioethicist, who critically reexamines the early twentieth-century rise of objectivism in medicine that led to a condemnation of judgments as based on emotional assessments. Halpern situates herself in the following way: "Writers on empathy either base empathy in detached reason or sympathetic immersion. Against these models I describe empathy in terms of a listener using her emotional associations to provide a context for imagining the distinct experiences of another person. Therefore, empathy is a form of *emotional reasoning*" (2001: xv; emphasis added). In praising the cognitive potential of emotion, Halpern (2001: 11, 41, 50) defines emotional reasoning as "emotion-guided activity of imagination" that involves the process of "associational linking." Black and Halpern both distinguish empathy as mutual sensitivity occurring between at least two individuals (Black 1985: 292; Halpern 2001: 41). Moreover, both relate empathy to the realm of imagination or association and to the accumulation of emotional knowledge. Thinking of it as evolving out of continual learning and interaction, Black (1985: 252–253) situates empathy theoretically between the Freudian psychoanalytic tradition and hermeneutics. Thus, empathy emerges primarily as a method applied by the sensitive fieldworker to produce successful intersubjective encounters and scholarly outcomes—the method whose feasibility Geertz once contested.[9]

Hollan and Throop (2008: 389–390) claim, however, that anthropologists should not only be aware of empathy's role in a fieldwork situation but should also pay attention to how empathy is marked and articulated cross-culturally. What about empathy in local "hermeneutic circles" and what about the variety of peoples' interpretive modes? To my surprise, Bosmun daily discourse turned out to be a hermeneutic circle, encouraging multiple voices to overlap

and to coconstruct social reality and subjectivity ever anew. This is a fact I me-
thodically had to take into account, a point that I elucidate later. What kinds of
feelings, intentions, or desires to associate with whom, why, when, and where
is not the same everywhere. In Bosmun subjectivity, the realm of imagination and association is layered with meanings that are inextricably linked to
people's foodways. Moreover, as several scholars have recently shown, the
assumption of being able to gain an accurate understanding of other people's
states does not hold sway everywhere: there are people who doubt that empathy is possible, and there are people who, although not doubting it, are not
allowed to either speculate about the states of others or reveal their states
to others because of sociocultural proscription (e.g., Feinberg 2011; Groark
2008; Lepowsky 2011; Lohmann 2011; Mageo 2011; Throop 2011). This
assumption has recently been referred to as "the doctrine of 'the opacity of
other minds'" by Robbins and Rumsey (2008: 408). Although I often heard
people in Daiden say, *Mi no save long tingting bilong em* ('I do not know what
he / she thinks'), I did not interpret such statements as a credo for a generally assumed "opacity of other minds." For I realized that achieving others'
quasi–first person perspective is deemed possible among persons who have
built mutual trust—the prerequisite for developing openness to others (Mageo 2011: 86)—through long-standing food-related experiences. Partners in
commensality commonly make efforts to understand the other and commonly
show approval of "being understood" (Hollan 2008) by the other. Moreover,
Bosmun anchor positive and negative empathy in social space and thus create
a "landscape" (Hirsch 1995a) of familiar and unfamiliar places: partners in
commensality expect benevolent empathy to define interpersonal life in the
familiar places of shared households, whereas negative empathy is thought to
prevail in places unfamiliar to them.[10]

Indeed, empathy is not only about "understanding others," but also about
"being understood," referred to by Hollan (2008: 481) as the "flip side of what
we normally think of as empathy." Even if I try to walk in the other person's
shoes and even if the other and I have shared some crucial experiences, my
empathetic attempt will only succeed if the other provides me with the "appropriate cues for understanding" (Hollan 2008: 484) and if he or she is open
to engage in the actions and discourses that I consider central (see Wikan
1992: 471). Therefore, anthropologists should also explore "the ways in which
people in different times and places promote or discourage understanding of
themselves" (Hollan 2008: 475). What about the "appropriateness and possibility" (Throop 2008: 406) of empathetic self-expression according to prevailing cultural rules? On Yap in Micronesia, for instance, a person who fails in
self-governance is called a "papaya" that has "ripened" (Throop 2008: 414).
The papaya's exterior skin and color mirror its interior state. People know
from the exterior whether the fruit is ripe or unripe. A critical Yapese virtue

is to conceal one's interiority and instead show an "opaque exterior." If someone is described as a "papaya that ripened," it is meant in a pejorative sense (Throop 2008: 414, 415).

Although Bosmun do not use the image of a papaya, this transparency would perfectly suit their notion of a virtuous person. Concealing one's interior—a Yapese ideal of self-management—is what renders a person in Daiden highly suspicious and malevolent. One is expected to show transparency, even if this means to express, for instance, states of anger or jealousy which, at least according to other ethnopsychologies (including Western psychology), are interpreted as rather negative feelings. Also, to pretend that one is detached in view of another's turmoil, as among the Toraja in Indonesia, where people only turn to the other once the other has calmed down (Hollan 2011: 201), does not correspond to the Bosmun ideal of a good person. Rather, as among the Sabarl, "an openness to exchanges of feeling and thought is the precondition of meaningful social interaction. ... The channeled person—one who is physically, intellectually, and emotionally 'open' to engaging in the flow of relations ... reflects health in society itself" (Battaglia 1990: 57). Such a model of the relational person or the "relational self" (Kirmayer 2008: 461), as one may alternatively call it, is based on the primacy many Melanesian societies give to the value of relationality in shaping cultural imperatives (see Robbins 2004: 13) and in defining personal identities (see Stasch 2002: 347). The idea of the person as evolving out of social connections was prompted probably most significantly by M. Strathern, who proposed what since has been taken up repeatedly because of its persuasive point of view: "Indeed, persons are frequently constructed as the plural and composite site of the relationships that produced them. The singular person can be imagined as a social microcosm" (1988: 13).[11] According to the specific relational order of living together in Daiden and according to my interpretations of *ramkandiar*, emotions and intentions are to be seen less as inner bodily states, as propagated by Western psychology (Lutz & White 1986: 429), than they are seen to result from people's engagements with others. People in Daiden consider themselves related to many others and acknowledge that those who belong to the same familiar place coshape their feelings and thoughts by engaging in the premise of "watching others and being watched."

Coming back to how notions of empathy and food merge conceptually in Daiden, I finally need to address the question of how well-being is defined in Daiden. Concerning general discussions about empathy beyond the particularities of a single ethnographic case, one of course also needs to ask how well-being is defined elsewhere. Only by answering this question may we know how to successfully and (ideally) positively empathize with others in Daiden and elsewhere. To answer briefly for the moment: it is the foodways that I describe in this book that cause or spoil well-being in Daiden and that have to be taken into account when pondering people's empathethic approximations of others' states.

Encountering Bosmun Relationality

I now describe the context in which I conducted my ethnographic fieldwork. I first present those people who are usually called the anthropologist's "informants," "interlocutors," or "friends in the field," followed by a discussion of methods, ethical considerations, and limits that evolved during my time in the field. In this section, I call people by their real personal names. I think everyone in the Bosmun area knew whom I met on the most regular basis and thus there is no need for anonymity when introducing them in a very general way. However, in the remaining parts of the book, when it comes to more detailed knowledge and to individual opinions, I have opted for anonymization. I feel compelled to do this since I cannot really anticipate people's reactions when reading their names in descriptions that deal with rather personal scenes of their lives.

People "Looking through Bamboo"

Ethnographers' informants, also called "interlocutors" or "friends" according to the situation of engagement, are sometimes addressed with kinship terms too, if a family has decided to care particularly for the visiting anthropologist and if the anthropologist has agreed to it. This was the case with me, as the wider Bosmun community obviously felt more comfortable being able to identify me concretely in the web of their local, intra- and interfamilial relationships. According to Bosmun perspectives, one must have a social identity, and therefore I became socially integrated.

After two months in Daiden, people of other households started to talk about me as the "daughter of Nuŋgap and Samar" (see figure 0.1 and figure 0.2). Their son Seres had provided me with a house and they lived next door.

Figure 0.1: Nuŋgap. The photograph was taken by my husband Alexis during one of his visits to Daiden. Note in the background that the wall of the house is made of bark, a material that is rarely seen these days.

It is interesting to note that none of
them referred to me in this way at the
beginning; rather, "outsiders," that
is, people outside this nuclear family
core, were the first to refer to me as
such. Nuŋgap himself, who eventually became my *saate* ('father'), only
became ready to talk with me as the
fourth month of my stay with him
and his family began. A cautious yet
friendly and socially well-respected
man, he later explained to me that he
did not want to disturb my conversations with those "people who came
knocking at my door right from the
start." I think maybe it was due to his
unintrusive behavior that I personally
attuned to him as a paternal figure.

Figure 0.2: Samar. Samar kneading sago
fibers.

In my affirming response to people's suggestions that I should become
a *ŋgaŋgir* ('adopted child') of Nuŋgap and Samar, a core group of "consociates"—in Geertz's sense—emerged in due course. "'Consociates' are individuals who actually meet, persons who encounter one another somewhere in the
course of daily life. They thus share, however briefly or superficially, not only
a community of time but also of space. They are 'involved in one another's
biography' at least minimally; they 'grow older together' at least momentarily,
interacting directly and personally as egos, subjects, selves" (Geertz 1973:
365). For convenience, I refer to the people central to my understanding of
Bosmun life as informants, conversation partners, or consociates, or I call
them "brothers," "sisters," and so on. Yet, these terms appear either too technical or inadequate to aptly describe the individuals with whom I interacted and
the quality of our interactions. Even if people classed me as a "daughter," for
example, everybody knew that due to my profession I would ask questions a
"more typical daughter" probably would not. Likewise, to call those people
"friends" seems difficult to me since, as I suppose, there were differences in
the ways we perceived each other and our relations. There were some people
whom I considered friends and some I did not, though I met with both in a
polite manner. How would they perceive me? In rethinking the idea of friendship cross-culturally, Bell and Coleman have pointed to the social situatedness
of ethnographic fieldworkers:

> After all, the development of some form of friendship is inherent within anthro-
> pological practice. Fieldworkers usually have to establish cordial and even close

relations with informants if they are not to become like ethologists, observing interactions while remaining aloof from close social contact. The ambiguity and complexity of the fieldwork relationship offer us, however, some initial clues to the questions to be posed by any comparative study of friendship: Do both sides of the cultural "divide" understand the relationship in compatible ways? (1999: 2)

Apart from the subjective and experiential level of interpersonal contacts, there are cultural directives that may not be disregarded (see A. Strathern 1996: 90). In the Bosmun context, friendship is connected to the issue of gender. To speak of Bosmun males as my friends would fail to capture real local life. In their view, to develop a bond of "spontaneous and unconstrained sentiment or affection" (Carrier 1999: 21) without becoming sexually attracted in some way is said to be impossible between members of the opposite sex. A male's *xue* ('friend') is male and a female's *xue* is female. Male and female are always considered potential spouses or at least sexually active and generative partners. A display of friendship is only allowed between opposite-sex members who are either related by kinship or who are separated by a fact such as a major age difference so that sexual engagement is unlikely.

To avoid any misunderstandings and to best comprehend the people who let me learn along with them, I wish to think of them in a way that can also be read as my personal tribute to each of them. According to a Bosmun saying, I introduce them as the people who were inclined to "look through bamboo" for me. Such a person is referred to as *rongo maankat mot / mes* (*rongo* stems from *rone,* which means 'a type of bamboo' of which public flutes are made, *maankat* translates as 'to visually permeate,' and *mot* and *mes* denote 'man / male' and 'woman / female'). When Bosmun say that one "looks through bamboo," they have in mind that one is able to visually permeate the diaphragms of a bamboo. A bamboo's so-called diaphragms are its inner walls, which have to be removed first in order to make proper use of its tube-like shape as a water container, a cooking device, or a musical instrument. This metaphor is a common expression to refer to knowledgeable, sociable people, to people of great renown. It is a metaphor on wisdom but hints also at a notion Bosmun have about human perceptibility in general. At certain stages or situations in life, people are believed to be capable of broadening their perceptual spectrum and transcending the given borders of time and space. A person can be in one place but he or she might also hear what is talked about in another place or at another point in time. It happened a few times that someone said to me that we would have to be careful when talking about S., for instance, since S. was commonly held to be such a person; S. would definitely know what we were talking about. People who wish to achieve this potential have to 'climb the *ngaape saar,*' which is the 'ladder' (*saar*) of particular, tree-dwelling spirits called *ngaaper*[12] (plural of *ngaape*). This ladder actually refers to the many vines that are scattered around in the forest. The tree-spirits are said to climb those vines in order to reach their houses (treetops). The leaves and barks of various vines are the major source for an extensively practiced herbal consumption. Men and women rely on different herbal substances. When humans (*memkor,* plural of *memok*) "climb this ladder," they consume herbs that enhance their physical, social, and perceptual capacities and skills.[13] Apart from this perceptual connection, "looking through bamboo" fundamentally marks the potential of sociability that a person may accumulate.

According to Bosmun sensibilities, a person should never claim by him- or herself to be able to "look through bamboo." Someone who does so is not taken seriously. It has to be an ascription by others who, by observing this person's behavior, come to recognize him or her as sociable. Very few and mostly old people reach that status. The key ideal is that one aims for sociability by exhibiting it in concrete action that is watched and assessed by others. From my living with the Bosmun of Daiden I can state with certainty that none of them would ever express pride in themselves; at least, not in the realm of everyday interactions. There are, of course, realms of expertise where a man or a woman might show proficiency, as in instructing novices during phases of male and female liminality, but it is highly unusual to boast. However, telling others that they were supportive in providing knowledge and in offering intellectual acumen is common. Accordingly, it would be appropriate for me to ascribe the trait of sociability and knowledgeability to those who helped me in breaking up the many walls that I often saw in the bamboo's interior, rather than taking personal credit for this.

Those who became part of my circle of consociates were mainly prompted by the fact that I agreed to my integration into the family of Nuŋgap and Samar. A "family" in the Bosmun social universe is not confined to its nuclear parts but extends far beyond into a vast sphere of extended kinship. Everyone in such a sphere has, in turn, his or her own set of relationships. I usually benefited from these alternative sets as well. Hence, many individuals (not all of whom are named here) fostered my understanding. I came to think of every single person as the center of a unique relational network. Below, I roughly describe my central encounters in 2004/05 and give a brief statement of what made those encounters unique for me. In introducing other key consociates, I also indicate how they relate to "my nuclear family" (by using standard kinship abbreviations). Readers may trace the relationships with the help of the kinship diagram (see figure 1.5), which accompanies chapter 1 and provides a schematic overview of the possibilities of being kin-related in Bosmun life.

In 2004, Nuŋgap and Samar were in their late fifties. In the beginning, Nuŋgap and I treated each other with politeness yet also with reservation, which steadily changed into mutual, cordial sympathy as we learned more of the other. With Samar, the woman who became my *maame* ('mother'), things were different. She accepted me with immediate spontaneity, with a balanced combination of warmth, calmness, and directness. If I made a cultural mistake, such as politely greeting her in the early morning hours and asking her where she was off to, she would wait only once or twice before telling me straightforwardly not to ask her. Then, she would explain to me that a woman who sets out in the morning to check the prawn traps she has put in the water the day before has to stay focused and must not be drawn into a conversation. Otherwise, the prawns will not go into the trap. In Samar's presence I felt least of all like an anthropologist, even though my encounters with her were among the most prolific for my enculturation and my anthropological investigation. The couple had three sons and three daughters. Two of the children were under twenty and three were over twenty; the eldest was over thirty years old and one son and one daughter were already married with their own children. The married son lived in a house nearby with his wife and a child. The married daughter lived in her husband's household in another part of Daiden. She and her husband came to visit their eldest of three children, who was living with Nuŋgap and Samar. Their other children also spent most of the time with Nuŋgap and Samar. That household was further complemented by Nuŋgap's younger, unmarried brother Kopri (see figure 0.3) and another classificatory brother of Nuŋgap, by two teenage daughters of a deceased brother of Nuŋgap, an adult son of one deceased sister of Nuŋgap, and three adult

Figure 0.3: Kopri and Nambindo.

sons of another deceased sister of Nuŋgap, one of whom had a wife and five children. Whenever visitors came to one of the members of this household or whenever its members went to visit others—regularly visiting one's own biological and classificatory kin is quite common—I took the opportunity to participate in these encounters. Due to the sympathy that this constellation of kin radiated toward me, I easily gained insights into the vibrant life of an actual Bosmun household. Later, I also delved into the lives of other households, but I did this via the relations that "my family" had within their span of extended kinship.

I consider it a good choice to have used the social position I was offered for three reasons. First of all, in a small-scale societal world like that of Daiden, everyone is linked to everyone else in some way or another. Therefore, it made no sense to concentrate "on isolated individuals, but on persons-in-interaction" (Wikan 1990: xxiii). Below, I return to this emically derived methodology.

Second, I felt people's urge to mark my social identity (see Hess [2009: 17] for a similar experience during fieldwork in Vanuatu). In Bosmun understandings, it is common to clearly know one's own and others' social commitments. This made it easier for all of us. Who, for instance, would take a break to sit down with me when I needed to revise specific data? Who would allow me to observe regular activities on a daily basis? Who would canoe the Ramu or old riverbeds with me? Who would lay down his or her work to walk with me to other places? I walked quite a lot but never alone. Since I was afraid of the forest-dwelling poisonous and nonpoisonous snakes, it comforted me to have a few people with me should something happen to me. Apart from that, walking with people through familiar places is a method of investigation, as Meinerzag (2006: 12) has shown for the Hinihon of the Adelbert Range in Papua New Guinea, where walking is the key "notion of being alive." At the Ramu River, canoeing has a similar connotation. Bosmun are highly mobile on ground and on water. Since canoeing was a novel traveling experience for me and the Ramu is inhabited by crocodiles, I was glad especially in the beginning to canoe with people who were particularly aware of my natural unsureness on this terrain. In due course I had to canoe with many different people, such as when traveling to Madang, which meant crossing the Ramu every time, and I always felt secure since everyone seemed to be concerned about me.

Third, since a central aim was to look at interpersonal dynamics, I thought it would be most instructive to concentrate on a concrete field of interpersonal relations. Thus, for example, I came upon what could be called a type of "mediated trust." Put in another way: each time I met "new relatives" in other Bosmun places, the reception was as if people already knew me. To my surprise, they were very well informed about several details of my life in Daiden and about my interactions with others. They knew everything that my core family knew of me, and they, too, embraced me with a sympathy that I already

knew from the others. I had not asked for such a preintroduction but it facilitated my work. It was as if the level of trust that I had achieved with my daily
conversation partners became automatically extended through what they told
my nonregular interlocutors who lived in other households and other places
respectively. I later observed that other social strangers similarly become attuned as long as a family member knows him or her and can define him or her
as a good-natured person. This I call "mediated trust."

Mbandu (see figure 0.4), a widow above the age of thirty and mother of
seven children (and the FBSSW of Nuŋgap and the MZD of Samar), was
the first person I considered a potential friend. She considered me a potential
new family member since, as she later revealed to me, she wanted to give me
a local personal name of her clan. She lived in the household next to Nuŋgap
and Samar's, but, for personal reasons, had to leave Daiden after two months,
and thus both of our expectations took another direction. Mbandu was among
the first to accompany me to other Bosmun places, and it is from her that I
learned to speak Tok Pisin well. She fervently did what I had asked of her:
she interrupted and corrected me whenever I made mistakes and thus my Tok
Pisin quickly improved. I also learned from her about the cultural rules of widowhood and how to cope with them from the perspective of a still young and
passionate woman who was struggling to overcome her fate. After she had left
Daiden, the frequency of our encounters ceased but the intensity of our talks
whenever we did meet did not.

Figure 0.4: Mbandu. Mbandu is carrying a son of hers on her shoulders in the typical
way children are carried in Daiden.

Kermban (see figure 0.5), the forty-year-old mother's brother of Mbandu's late husband, who was a FBSS of Nuŋgap, introduced me to the intricacies of the Bosmun local language. He showed great enthusiasm about saving the local language for future generations. Kermban had worked with the Bible Translators of the Summer Institute of Linguistics, who are well known in this and other parts of Papua New Guinea and who had started to study the Lower Ramu languages in 2002 (Harris & Harris 2002, 2004). Inspired by his experience with the Bible Translators, Kermban was inclined to work with me, too. After about nine months in Daiden, I could follow and comprehend conversations spoken in the local language, but I never reached the point of speaking it confidently, other than building simple sentences. This was not due to any unwillingness to communicate. People often confirmed that I am a *meri bilong toktok* ('woman who likes to chat'), which, in Bosmun understandings, is a sign that one is seeking sociable contact with others. The predominant usage of Tok Pisin these days made it an impossible enterprise for me to learn the Bosmun vernacular fluently because people themselves constantly switched into Tok Pisin. Verbal communication therefore predominantly took place in Tok Pisin, although I continued asking people for words, idioms, and meanings stemming from the local language. Kermban and I compiled a preliminary wordlist and distributed it in the Bosmun area in 2008 (A. von Poser & Saŋgam 2008; A. von Poser 2009). Whenever I returned to Daiden, I was able to easily evoke this vocabulary. Apart from the data relating to his local language, Kermban would also share his ideas with me about what Bosmun men of former, premissionary times were supposed to aim for during their lives. He is the youngest son of a highly renowned man who had died some years before and who had passed on to him his memories on lessons taught before proselytization changed the world order that had existed in the first half of the twentieth century.

Figure 0.5: Kermban. Kermban (also called Adam Saŋgam) looking at the dictionary that resulted from the meetings where I learned the basics of the Bosmun language. Yanzoŋ, his sister's son's son, shares our joy.

Kermban's sister Kaso (see figure 0.6), a woman in her sixties and married to a FBS of Nuŋgap as well as Ndombu (see figures 1.1, 3.3, and

4.1), Kaso's same-aged sister-in-law and Nuŋgap's FBD, belonged to a circle of elderly and middle-aged women who guided me through topics regarding Bosmun female agency, identity, youth, and maturity, and female material culture such as the production of net bags, bast skirts, and clay pots. In 2010, Ndombu was no longer part of our circle; she had died in 2008. The other women were my adoptive mother Samar, Ndoor (see figure 5.1), a former wife of Nuŋgap's MFFZSS, Nzoum, Nuŋgap's FFBSD, and Ndaat, Samar's FFZDD (see figure 0.7). From time to time, Tepe, a younger sister of Ndaat, Sete, Ndaat's BD, and Samndo, Ndat's ZD who was married to a younger brother of

Figure 0.6: Kaso.

Figure 0.7: "Jealous Women." Ndaat is playing a string-figure game that tells of two women who fight with one another because they are caught up in jealousy.

Nuŋgap, joined us. While walking or canoeing to other places, during which time I also learned a lot, my most frequent female companion was Nambindo, the FBDD of Nuŋgap and Kopri (see figure 0.3). Whatever I saw or heard while on my way to visit people, I recapitulated in this particular circle of women. Apart from the informal conversations that spontaneously took place whenever we saw each other, meeting those women became a regular matter in the period of 2004/05, and on my returns they were already prepared to sit down with me again. Depending on the topic chosen, we would come together once or twice a week. Sometimes we would also spend several days consecutively, and they appeared dedicated to conversing with me until I felt content with the outcome of our conversations.

Exploring issues of femaleness turned out to be one of the easier projects during my fieldwork. In Bosmun gender configurations, I failed to reach the status of a "gender-neutral ethnographer," and therefore the fact that I am female endured in my personal encounters with both men and women. Only once, for example, was I allowed to enter a men's house. This was when a new one was opened in Ndoŋon, another Bosmun place, in August 2005. Opening a men's house is a festive occasion during which male and female dancers enter the new building together. By shaking its posts through exaggerated dance, the stability of the construction is verified. After people had invited me to do so, I went with the dancers. Following my own ethics, I did not insist on people disclosing their male- or female-related (and secret) knowledge to me, since I felt uncomfortable putting pressure on people for the purpose of intellectual discourse. The only definite suggestion that I made to both men and women was that I would be looking forward to noting and recording everything that would help me make sense of social phenomena that were yet unintelligible to me. I remember one man expressing his pity by declaring that "if I were Peter or James or Marcus," he would have loved to give me a deeper insight into male concealments but "since I was Anita" and since people had decided to regard me as a *vunsi mes* ('a woman of their place'), as he would emphasize, this was not possible. Sometimes, the consequence of this taxonomy led me to moments of frustration because certain matters remained clouded and incoherent to me. On the bright side, it gave me experiential insight into how women feel when being excluded from male spheres and when excluding men from female spheres. On the whole, however, I felt honored; the more so as several men had declared in my presence that they were going to treat me like a *mbi*, a sister, which in Bosmun subjectivity is a woman's best social position. This is also encoded in a dance that I saw in 2005 that depicts a brother protecting his sister from her husband's assault (see figure 1.7).

Still, men provided me with important insights. My most regular male conversation partners were Nuŋgap and Kopri. Kopri was also my key male companion when moving about. As a former game hunter, he was also a *save fes* ('a well-known man') in more distant places beyond Bosmun terrain. Whenever we left familiar grounds, such as when walking to Kayan on the coast or to Giri further up the Ramu, people of the areas that we passed usually greeted him amiably. Nuŋgap and Kopri assisted me almost every day. Since both belonged to the generation of elders in Daiden, men from other households—from other families and other places—would commonly gather in Nuŋgap's *haus win* when communal matters had to be discussed (a *haus win* is a normal part of every household and serves as a 'resting platform' during the hottest daytime; it is stilted, roofed, and without walls so that breezes can easily come in). Thus, I was frequently able to win their visitors over for spontaneous as well as organized group discussions. Yaŋu (see figure 3.2), a man in his mid forties, equally supported my enterprise. This relation was facilitated mainly through his sister Ndaat who, as I said, was one of my closest female tutors. Yaŋu was one of the last men who had learned from the elders how to beat the local slit-drum (*mbiŋ*). The signals of a *garamut,* as people refer to the slit-drum in Tok Pisin, are a major means of communicating messages of various kinds. The slit-drum signals reach other places and announce socially relevant messages such as the death of a person, the seasonal arrival of eels, a fire outbreak, or that one is seeking another's assistance in sago making. In asking Yaŋu about the signals that were carried from time to time to and from Daiden, he also provided me with sociocultural meanings.

My paternal guides Nuŋgap and Kopri, as well as Yaŋu, instigated my connections in Ndoŋon, especially during the second half of my first stay at the Ramu. In Ndoŋon, I most frequently met with Pendame, a widower with two adult sons, and his brothers, as well as with Amok and her husband Ŋivi. Pendame was a classificatory FZDS of Kopri (Kopri had been fostered by another family than Nuŋgap and he therefore had somewhat different classificatory kin). Through his higher education and occupation, which had brought him to Europe, discussions with Pendame sometimes turned out to be different from those that I had with people who had not experienced life beyond the borders of Madang Province. With great passion for his ancestry and local customs, Pendame gave me an idea about his views on a life that combined modern with traditional elements. Amok, a woman probably in her mid seventies and a classificatory sister of Nuŋgap, made me aware of the intensity that the sharing of food can create in the realm of kin-relations where an exact bond of genealogical descent is no longer traceable.

When discussions turned to the deeper levels or secrecies of local knowledge, the men in general remained reluctant to elaborate, and everyone advised me to ask old Kose of Ndenekaam (see figure 0.8), who had been born prior to World War II and whom everyone considered "the last cultural expert." Whenever I went to see him and his family, he would also gather other men of his social network around him, such as Ŋgamndai and Ŋakne, to whom he had

Figure 0.8: Kose.

formally passed the custodianship of his clan-specific knowledge, called *yaam* (or *xaarak*, literally translating as 'to know / to understand'),[14] before personally abandoning it. As the village recorder of the Rom, Ŋgamndai also helped me to prepare a first census. On my second trip to the Ramu, I saw Kose again but was surprised to see how much he had aged since my last stay. In 2004/05, he had no longer been agile, but was still spirited. Sadly, Kose died shortly before Christmas 2006. He had been a FZS of my adoptive mother Samar, around seventy-five years of age when I first arrived, and the eldest man of the Rom clan-association into which I was socially integrated. Whenever we met, his affectionate reception made me feel immediately comfortable. He was a humble man of powerful authority. His second wife Ŋgiri, Ndaat's mother-in-law, equally welcomed me, and in 2008 she shared with me her last memories of him.

In relation to my ethnographic goals, however, there was a difficulty when meeting Kose. After a long history of proselytization, sometimes by different congregations in the same places, individuals or groups all over Papua New Guinea see themselves confronted with several "pathways to heaven" (Jebens 2005). This was also the case with Kose. During the last years of his life, he became convinced by a lately rising form of Pentecostalism that local cosmologies were evil and that if he were to talk about them he would bring damage to himself and to others. Catholic proselytization in the area has been more "moderate" compared to other regionally operating congregations such as Seventh-Day Adventism (see Josephides 1990). A woman who also favored the Pentecostal perspective told me that Kose's death had coincided with the building of a new men's house. The spirit that guarded this men's house was to be blamed, she concluded (the same spirit that had guarded Kose's life for almost all his years). Once Kose even showed me a flyer on Islam that someone had brought from town and asked me to tell him more about it. To my knowledge, Islamic ideas have not spread on the north coast up to now, but Pentecostal ideas have. At least one family in Ndenekaam promoted Pentecostalism as an alternative to Catholicism, which had become the key religious ideology in the region in the mid twentieth century. It took me a while to realize that it was not just because I was female that Kose would conceal certain issues (for he was reluctant to share all kinds of information) but because he had decided to fully condemn the spiritual worldview of his ancestors. Still, he continued to invite me to his home even as he noticed the nature of my exploration, which included an interest in ancestrally shaped visions of the world, and I kept visiting this lovely old man from time to time. The reception that he and his family gave me whenever I passed his household was endearing, and in these encounters I observed as much about Bosmun foodways as I did in my encounters with others. Another reason for not consulting Kose and others for their cultural expertise on clan-specific knowledge was that questions relating to this type of knowledge were leading me directly into the sphere of Bosmun political and economic contestation. I now turn to the methods I applied and how I adjusted them to people's responses. I also say more about contested knowledge and limiting conditions, and how I eventually chose the subject of this book.

Methods and Limits

I went to the field ready to apply the common methods taught in anthropological curricula, such as participatory observation in daily and non-daily activities, collecting linguistic information, genealogical inquiries, recording life stories and myths, and of course conducting interviews (mostly of a semi-structured and open-ended type) with individuals and in groups. My technical equipment was quite simple in comparison to the kind of technical devices that are available now. I relied on a cassette recorder and a film camera, and on my returns I upgraded my equipment by taking a digital camera with me. When spontaneous narrations unfolded, I decided not to disturb a speaker by quickly running away to get the recorder. I instead wrote down matters and asked people to reevoke the subject of a conversation at another occasion. Such recapitulations always took another direction when I taped them after the first dialogue unless I raised questions I was able to formulate on the basis of the information that I had gained in the earlier conversation. All data I observed I wrote down on paper, usually in the evenings or at nights, and often in the company of people who came to sit with me. I enjoyed this because, in between my reconsiderations of a day, we would chat and share betel nut and tobacco. I began transcribing recorded conversations and stories while still in Daiden, but due to the quantity I had to continue later, when I was back in Germany.

I also took text materials with me that I had found through archival searches done prior to my actual fieldwork. In preparation for the first visit to the Ramu, I had looked for earlier published data that would give me at least some preliminary facts about my potential fieldsite. The most detailed accounts I found were in the works of the German missionary and ethnographer Georg Höltker (1937a, 1937b, 1940, 1960, 1965a, 1966, 1969, 1975) and the British anthropologist Beatrice Blackwood (1950, 1951; see Knowles [2000] and Lutkehaus [1988] on Blackwood's anthropological work in general). Höltker and Blackwood were the first to live among Bosmun with the aim of studying their cultural life. Independently of each other, they each came for a short visit in 1937. Höltker stayed there from January to February and was accompanied by Father Much of the same congregation—the SVD congregation (Societas Verbi Divini / Society of the Divine Word)—which by then had established a certain degree of familiarity with the local population (Höltker 1937b: 965–966). Blackwood stayed from October to December. Neither Höltker's nor Blackwood's ethnographic enterprises were based on the intensive ethnographic fieldwork principles that I was able to enact due to my academic education several decades later. At their time, a firm methodology was still in the making; Malinowski's (1922) articulation of the appropriate empirical principles had been published only fifteen years before. Still, Höltker and Blackwood produced data of great value. Kose remembered both visitors. His stories about Blackwood were especially entertaining. He saw her when he was a young boy, and once she offered him something to eat. But since she was among the first white women he ever saw, he ran off in fear. This was his major experience with Blackwood and I shall never forget his chuckle. In Kose's presence, I felt something like a direct historical connection, which has now unfortunately been lost.

My aim was to discuss Höltker's and Blackwood's findings with the descendants of those people who had encountered my quasi-predecessors. I did not pretend ignorance of what Höltker, for example, wrote on Bosmun boyhood and male initiation practices (1975) or on the construction of secret cult-houses (1966). All his articles are stored in the library of the Divine Word University in Madang, with some of his material already translated into English (done himself in manuscript form). Bosmun can reach the town of Madang via a six-hour PMV ride (PMVs are Public Motor Vehicles that make up the regular transport system on Papua New Guinea roads). One Bosmun man who had gone through higher education told me that he knew of Höltker and what he had written on Bosmun women's fights (1969). On one of his next trips to town, he would go and visit the library again to check the other articles, he said to me. After all, "times are changing" and he was hoping that the following male and female generations would benefit from a higher education in the near future and thus gain access to alternative economic and intellectual worlds.

I used Höltker's texts in the following way: I never discussed his findings on manhood with women nor did I show them the pictures included in his materials that related to exclusively male topics. I also waited until later in conversations to bring up the topics he described. I first attempted to gain an idea about local and gender-dependent sensitivities. Only then did I suggest translating what Höltker had written in German. Prior to that, however, I would briefly describe the topic we were probably going to delve into so that the people who spoke with me could tell me whether they would want to discuss it with me or not. I would say, for instance, that I probably would have to say the names of certain spirits connected to secret spirit houses. Men's reactions were always that I could say them but only as I translated the material to them. In this way, I touched on facets of _yaam,_ that is, clan-specific knowledge. The best way to define this term and its ideational substrate is to say that it refers to a type of knowledge that can be used to gain political, economic, and magical power. To have _yaam_ is to have knowledge of certain myths and their secret aspects, such as the names of spirit entities, of secret ritual practices and magic spells, of melodies and chants, of the connections with the ancestors and thus of land rights. However, to have a lot of this knowledge is considered dangerous because it can cause envy in people who might subsequently react with an attack of death sorcery.

Let me give an example of the contested facet of _yaam._ Early on, I investigated the distribution of land and land rights. Initially, I wanted to explore whether Bosmun trace land ownership via the mythical pathways that traverse many social landscapes in Papua New Guinea and beyond (e.g., Rumsey & Weiner 2001). I wondered if local senses of place and belonging depended on stories of apical ancestors who, by traveling from place to place, created landscapes of physical distinctiveness and social meaning. One day, I sat with a man of a certain clan who made a drawing and put the names of all sections of land in it as well as the names of the land-owning clans. I did not keep my investigation secret, and thus two men from another clan came for a visit the following day. I showed them the drawing since its maker had told me to discuss it with the others. He was aware what I still had to learn: in the Bosmun area it is best to sit with at least two or three discussants and usually more. Only through their agreement may knowledge become valid. As we looked through the information that the drawing contained, the men were noticeably surprised that a man from another clan had given the "right picture" of the existing clan-land boundaries. They murmured: "_Em tru, em stret_" ('This is true, this is right') and reacted as if they had assumed the opposite. In this and in similar situations I realized that part of my work was becoming politicized. Moreover, at the time I arrived, people were involved in a land dispute with a neighboring, sociolinguistically different group. A twisted situation hence evolved for me: on the one hand, several people would not tell me about land ownership by the clans. On the other hand, the same people declared that I should definitely explore this issue since my report would help them to resolve the land dispute with the opponent group. In view of this, I started to think about shifting the angle of my study since I personally felt some stress about becoming involved in a land dispute. I did not eschew situations of conflict in general, nor did I close my eyes when verbal or physical fights occurred. Yet, telling me that once my book was finished, people would use it as proper evidence in political and legal debates with contesting groups, I became reluctant. I feared being unable to collect all the relevant data on which such a legal decision could be based, including data from neighboring groups and from all the current and future factions.

People's relationships to land are a part of my account and I trace a number of mythical pathways in the Bosmun landscape. I do not answer questions concerning rightful land boundaries but instead situate the study in a context in which land, or more precisely its outcome—food, is explored as a source for individual and collective identity. Over time, it became clear that I would focus on food and on emotional knowledge in interpersonal encounters, which is not concealed but shared and necessary to uphold sociality. Owing to the emerging nature of my investigations, people became more relaxed. Now, I could also better deal with the fact that people never knew the "full story" when talking to me. Whenever I recorded a mythical narrative, story tellers would add: *Mipela save hap hap tasol* ('We know it only partially'). Furthermore, mythical narratives were never recapitulated in exactly the same way. It turned out that "trying to find a single, authentic meaning of any myth is like looking for the end of a rainbow" (Lohmann 2008: 113). Variations always existed. Sometimes, details were omitted and sometimes they reemerged in different narrative contexts. Sometimes the sequence of events also became reversed.

This did not, however, conflict with my notion of myth or my methodological use of it. I see myth in the following way: first of all, myths "set horizons on behaviour" as A. Strathern and Stewart (2000: 68) tell of the myths and folk tales of the Highland Duna of Papua New Guinea. Myths are also "instruments through which dimensions of human actualities are enframed and grasped" as Kapferer (1997: 62) says in his study on Sri Lankan Sinhalese Buddhists. After all, I am convinced, as Tuzin (1997: 157) was, that "mythical knowledge must originate in experience of some kind." Everyday Bosmun life experience basically and essentially centers upon eating and not eating together and sharing and not sharing food with others. This is also at the center stage of all mythical narratives that I heard. Myth and actual life experience are linked in a continuous flow of mutual influence and counterprojection (Tuzin 1997: 158). Since foodways define Bosmun interpersonal sociality so notably, they are unequivocal in mythical narrative, whereas other aspects, such as the names of certain places and spirits that are connected to intellectual hegemonies and political legitimacies, are not. These aspects, however, are not at stake in my analysis. I should also note that elements in myth make sense to some people but not to other people, thus leading to different interpretations. In fact, "myth users can ignore or draw upon certain [...associations] in a variety of combinations for particular purposes" (Lohmann 2008: 124). My interpretations of Bosmun myths will, of course, always remain subject to discussion since they evolved at particular points in social time and social space.

People's decisions to reveal certain matters to me were also dependent on what the outside world (including the readers of my book) would think of certain local practices. Head-hunting and eating enemies' brains, for instance, were common practices in premissionary days. Missionaries believed them to have ceased by 1930/32 (Höltker 1975: 556). Although my conversation partners proudly spoke of their ancestors and of raids that served to keep intruders away, they usually explained to me that head-hunting was "cannibalistic." In using the English word "cannibalistic," which had been introduced by missionaries and colonial officers, they implied the judgment that head-hunting was wrong. As a matter of fact and current local perspective, head-hunting belongs to Bosmun past history. As it is past history, people see no reason to conceal it. In fact, it appears to me that classifying certain practices of the past as "cannibalistic" has historically emerged as a way to affirm one's belief in today's Christianity. Despite the fact that people now distance themselves from many practices of the past, these practices continue to fill individual and collective imaginations. It is as if stating what they are no more helps to sharpen what they are now. On many occasions, people wished to inform me about how customs used to be in the past. In December 2004, I wrote in my field notes: "Although many things are no longer observed, the past is very present through the medium of narration. As I participate in the mourning situation of [named person], people constantly come to me in order to explain to me how it used to be. I hardly get around to observing because there is constantly someone around me telling me how it used to be" (Field notes, 02.12.2004; my translation).[15]

I also came to realize that what is secret or public, male or female, right or wrong knowledge, changes over time and is a question of appropriate revelation at any particular time. Men would say about certain issues: *Ol meri i no save* ('Women do not know [that]'), and women would say: *Ol man i no save* ('Men do not know [that]'). Yet more than once, the versions I came upon in conversing with both sides turned out to be different. Once, I had an interview with men about a story that, as they said, "only men talk about." To my surprise, they began to recount the story after an elderly woman joined us. Later, I learned that due to her postmenopausal state she was not considered an excluded category of woman. Sitting amid the men, she spoke to them in a soft voice whenever they asked her for confirmation of certain details concerning the story. Knowing things does not mean that one can reveal them simply, and revealing things does not mean that it is knowledge that is considered true knowledge. Likewise, one has to keep in mind that what is classified as secret on one occasion can turn out to be public on another.

This brings me to the aspect of appropriate revelation, which also influenced my method of interviewing and conversing with people beyond the artificial atmosphere that automatically arises in the context of a prearranged interview. I soon became aware that it was best to adjust my research methods to the fact that being Bosmun is being relational. To invite an individual for a conversation was possible, and people did come to me or let me come to them. However, it almost always turned out to be the less productive (though personally never disappointing) way compared to delving into subjects with groups. Verbally construing realities in a relational mode also made it easier for me to follow people if they referred to their affines (their spouse's biological and classificatory parents and elder siblings) whose names they must not pronounce. Among consociates, I regularly heard someone requesting of the other one: *Yu kolim nem! Mi no inap kolim* ('You say the name! I must not say [it]'), which the person addressed immediately did since one usually has knowledge of the other's relatives.

My conversation partners seemed to enjoy speaking in multivoiced settings. I guess that such multiple speakership grounds in the local epistemological stance that treats reality as best understood through plural intersubjectivity, that is, the merging of as many subjective opinions, assessments, mutual affirmations, and corrections as possible. This was also imminent in political decision-making processes. A decision made by one alone had no power. It was treated as if it had never been uttered. On frequent occasions I saw that experiences of all kinds were told and retold among family members. In a repetitive (though not boring) style, each member narrated events anew, with his or her personal emphases and remarks, which in turn were taken up by the next narrator who continued to further entwine the story. Everyone was allowed to bring in personal views. Children were also allowed to take part in the continuous evoking of reality by means of overlapped commentary; yet only those who had begun to share food with others voluntarily (read: who had gained mental maturity from an emic point of view) were treated as serious conversation partners. Interruptions regularly occurred in Bosmun talk. This contrasts, for example, with the Yapese, who regard interrupting others as an act of devaluation (Throop 2011). Bosmun reactions to being interrupted while talking showed that overlapped speech was actually appreciated. Single speakers constantly encouraged others to overlap by providing them with what is called "conditional access to the turn" (Schegloff 2000: 5) in the literature on linguistic turn-taking. That is, by intentionally slowing down their voice or by searching for words, they invited others to take over or whisper add-ons. I think that this is well captured in the version of a story I have chosen to present in the appendix to this book as exemplary of how Bosmun story-construing operates. Even the elderly, people of high social recognition, usually allowed the younger ones to interrupt them. In the style of formal speech, Bosmun collaborative constructions of talk are produced "chordally" and not "serially" (Schegloff 2000: 6), that is, people most often speak simultaneously, not one after the other.[16]

Even when I recorded an individual's life story, people were most expressive when they were in the company of one or two conarrators. There is so much more information that people release in joint narration and conversation, and I was surprised to see how much they knew about each other and how much they let others know about themselves. The story that a woman gave me about her husband's sexual affair with another woman, for example, was coauthored by her four kinswomen and they knew exactly how the betrayed one had reacted and what she had done to win the husband back. She herself said that the others knew exactly how she had felt. Children also construed realities and stories relationally. I remember a group of male youngsters around the age of ten to twelve who frequently came to visit. On one of those visits, one of the boys wished to tell me a joke, the group said. They all sat down together and the boy began to tell the joke happily and swiftly but before making the point, he slowed down and stopped and looked at the others who immediately encouraged him to continue. He hesitated until another boy went on talking. Finally, the boy who had started the joke brought it to end by interrupting his conarrator.

Before describing the chapters to come, I would like to state how I tried to express my appreciation for people's support. I did not pay informants directly with money. When someone traveled with me to town or back, I paid for the food on the road and PMV fares. From time to time, I traveled to Madang and stayed a few days to call home, to restock what I personally needed in the field, and to make photocopies of my handwritten field notes (which were suffering from being exposed to the tremendous humidity in the Lower Ramu area). If I asked someone to stay in town until I was prepared to go back, I made sure that he or she had a place to stay with relatives living in town and I helped with the provision of food. In the beginning, I traveled with either Kermban or Nzu (see figure 1.6), a man above fifty and Nuŋap's MFBSDH, who, as the local magistrate of Daiden, had to travel to town regularly. Later, Yaroŋ (see figure 3.2), married to the eldest daughter of Nuŋap and Samar, accompanied me. It is common that a Bosmun woman does not travel or walk alone to places beyond the Bosmun area. Usually, a male relative accompanies her. If not, women travel in groups of female friends and kin. In keeping to this cultural code of Bosmun traveling, I not only learned about people's senses of social insideness and outsideness, but, like my adoptive family, I also felt comfortable in terms of personal security. At the end of my first stay in Daiden, I contributed a certain amount of money for communal purposes, and I bought rice and canned tuna for my farewell party. Whenever I had longer sessions with my conversation partners, I asked a "sister" to cook meals for us with ingredients that I provided. From time to time, I gave people small gifts such as salt, sugar, pencils, paper, bandages, batteries, and teabags from Germany. I had brought with me teabags of various sorts (and my mother kept sending more teabags while my fieldwork proceeded); they became temporarily famous (as did my mother), and whenever I returned people remembered them in particular. In appreciating people's help in the way described, I hope to have established a kind of reciprocity that they may accept.

The Chapters

In chapter 1, I sketch the ethnographic frame of Daiden in a general way. I place Bosmun in a historical context, and I provide details about the area and the languages that are spoken. I describe the physical environment in which Bosmun social action is embedded, and I outline the most elemental structures of relatedness.

Chapters 2, 3, and 4 address discussions about "moral," "emotional," and "embodied and emplaced" foodways. The separation into these themes should not be understood as a conceptual differentiation that Bosmun make (as I said, aspects of "person," "self," and "individual" are emically conflated), but rather as my attempt to structure the Bosmun material I was able to gather in an approachable way. I have also organized the chapters' beginnings in similar ways: they all start with local myths that feature ideals or failures of food-related behavior and empathetic responding, followed by analyses of actual interpersonal life.

In chapter 2, I introduce "moral foodways." I elaborate on the idea that the planting of sago palms (from which the staple diet, sago starch, is obtained) is an act that anchors people in a social grid of interpersonal dependencies and ties them to a piece of land. I advocate a notion of morality that is thoroughly tied to sago making; the term morality is meant to refer to the "rules for behaviour" and "anticipations of the consequences of keeping to, or breaking, these rules" (A. Strathern & Stewart 2007: xiii–xiv). In order to get a sense of Bosmun rules for behavior, I delineate socially appropriate ways of preparing meals, of offering food to others, and of talking about food-related activities, thereby showing that such activities are empathetic acts themselves.

In chapter 3, I focus on "emotional foodways." I turn to Bosmun life-cycle events and show how foodways are used to mark significant emotional moments in a person's life trajectory. I discuss interpersonal relationships: how they start, how they are maintained, how they are evaluated, and how they come to an end. The main themes touched are courtship and marriage, sexual reproduction and parental care, death and mourning. The central idea pursued in this chapter is that all the phases that emotionally challenge people are enacted in specific food-related ways.

In chapter 4, I explore "embodied and emplaced foodways." I pay attention to what makes a place familiar, what the prerequisite is for creating a social as well as an embodied sense of belonging from Bosmun points of view. This, in turn, facilitates an apt understanding of Bosmun configurations of malevolency, including sorcery. I conclude the chapter by stating that a person who displays benevolent empathy in his or her encounters with others largely avoids being accused of sorcery. Empathy, thus, is not only to be seen as a moral obligation but also as a strategy of protection.

The book ends with a conclusion in which I present a short summary of my findings and a perspective on how alternative visions about relatedness have recently begun to alter Bosmun sociality.

Notes

1. John has been given a local name—Toŋgri—and is regarded as a *vunsi mot*, 'a man who belongs to the place of Bosmun.' On behalf of the Catholic Church, John arrived in 1963 to work on development and education projects. He later joined the Australian administration and finally went into politics. In 2008, he was appointed Minister of Agriculture. At the time he was teaching in the coastal town of Bogia (opposite to offshore Manam Island) he met Sam Mbamak, a Bosmun boy, whose father was dying of cancer. Sam had to leave school in order to return home and John took pity on him. Finally, John adopted Sam and his siblings and is now married to a Bosmun woman.

2. See Carrithers, Collins & Lukes 1985; Csordas 1994b; Goodale 1995; Köpping, Welker & Wiehl 2002; Lambek & A. Strathern 1998; Morris 1994; Shweder & LeVine 1984; A. Strathern & Stewart 1998; M. Strathern 1988; White & Kirkpatrick 1985.

3. A benchmark study evidencing such distinctive configurations of embodied subjectivity is found in M. Rosaldo's (1980, 1984: 145–148) analysis of Philippine notions of the self. Another groundbreaking work is Lutz's ethnopsychological investigation among the inhabitants of Ifaluk in Micronesia: "On Ifaluk, as elsewhere, the body's structure and well-being are seen to be involved in an inseparable and systematic way with psychosocial well-being. What we might call 'the emotional mind' of Ifaluk ethnopsychology is solidly embedded in moral and social life, on the one hand, and in the physical body, on the other" (1985: 52).

4. I think of empathy as the (innate) ability that all humans share: we "think-feel" as Reddy (2001: 15) has described the way in which we perceptually frame our worlds. We do it in cognitively and emotionally blended ways. Reddy (2001: 15) approves of what Barnett and Ratner (1997: 303) have called "cogmotion" to refer to the merged nature of thinking and feeling. In contrast to rationalist philosophy grounded in Cartesianism, it is now being acknowledged that emotions are not simply inner bodily states detached from thought, intellect, or reason but are states that significantly co-influence human cognition (Ciompi 1997; Damasio 1994; Halpern 2001: 11, 67; Reddy 2001: 15).

5. There is also biological evidence for mutual affective intelligibility. Kirmayer (2008: 459), for instance, hints at the "built-in" interactional phenomenon of "sensorimotor synchrony," also known as the "chameleon effect," which automatically links us with others via unintentional imitations of others' attitudes, gestures, postures, or facial expressions. Neuroscientists have also exposed a "neural basis of intersubjectivity" (Gallese 2003) that exists in animal and human brains, a basis that attests to the premise that empathetic understanding is possible. So-called "mirror neurons" (e.g., Gal-

lese 2003; Rizzolatti & Arbib 1998; Stamenov & Gallese 2002) discharge in certain parts of the brain through the observations we make of others' actions, a neural activity that the brain would normally perform if we were to carry out those same actions ourselves (Gallese 2003: 174). The neurons of the observer implicitly, automatically, and unconsciously "mirror," copy, or simulate, the neural activity of the actual agent, allowing "the observer to use his / her own resources to penetrate the world of the other without the need of explicitly *theorizing* about it" (Gallese 2003: 174; original emphasis). As Fuchs (2008: 195–196) sums up the major findings of the current neuroscience trend, mirror neurons also discharge if the observer imagines or imitates an action. Furthermore, the neurons are only activated if the observer watches the actions of a living organism (not of a machine), and if they are goal- or object-related actions. According to Gallese (2003: 176–177), a mechanism similar to that which matches action observation and action execution seems to be at work; this could explain the assumed capacity of mutual emotional intelligibility. For a critique on the recent mirror neuron theory, see Hickok (2009).

6. In fact, Geertz himself proved his objections to be correct if, for example, one reads "Deep Play" (Geertz 1972) critically and follows some of his opponents, like Crapanzano (1986).

7. Empathy is substituted by projection whenever the knowledge that one has gained of the other overwhelms oneself (Hollan 2011: 203–204). Put yourself in the position of someone who listens to the misery of another one or put yourself in the position of someone who has suffered misery and listens to another's happiness. In both cases, one might feel overwhelmed at times. In order to cope with the emotional overflow, people start to project, that is, they imagine others in a way that does not necessarily match the others' true dispositions. Projection is thus only an intersubjective dialogue to a limited extent.

8. In his article *Grief and a Headhunter's Rage,* R. Rosaldo (1988) tells of his initial incomprehension of Ilongot head-hunting (in the Philippines) as a practice to cope with rage born out of grief for a deceased loved one. Only when his own wife dies in an accident does he come to understand people's rage in the face of death.

9. Other disciplines locate empathy in a similar way, especially in the healing or counseling professions (Gassner 2006; Halpern 2001; Katz 1963), where empathy is understood to play a crucial role in defining the relationship between caregivers and their patients. Elsewhere (A. von Poser 2011a), I have argued that the very idea of empathy as a means to intellectually manage emotions in an effort to approximate the perspective of another may well have led to scholarly preoccupation with empathy and methodology. As a result, attention has been drawn away from local expressions of empathy.

10. Different from sympathy or compassion, which are motivated by positive feelings, altruism, and the intention to care for others (see Buchheimer 1963: 63; Halpern 2001: 36; Katz 1963: 8–11), empathy also involves "gut-wrenching experiences" (Briggs 2008: 452). In gaining knowledge of another person, one may also exhibit an antisocial stance if he or she has decided (for whatever reasons) to "misuse" his or her knowledge. Divorced couples are a good example: during the time they lived together they might have gained knowledge of the other's weaknesses and might have helped the other to overcome them. After divorce, they might make use of this knowledge to hurt the other. Several authors corroborate that negative intentionality, manipulation,

and even cruelty or sadism are grounded in the empathetic approximations of others' states (e.g., Hollan 2011: 195; Kirmayer 2008: 461; Lohmann 2011: 107; Strauss 2004: 434). In *Ästhetik,* his book on the perception of art, Lipps (1903a: 139–140), too, pointed to the different facets of empathy: he talked of "accord" (calling it *Einklang*) as a form of "positive empathy" (*Positive Einfühlung*) and of "discord" (*Missklang*) as a form of "negative empathy" (*Negative Einfühlung*).

11. Other enriching and sometimes revising elaborations have followed. LiPuma (1998: 56), for instance, argued that everywhere in the world "individual and dividual modalities or aspects of personhood" coexist, and A. Strathern and Stewart (2000: 55–68) made a similar point when they proposed to address the person in the Mount Hagen area of Papua New Guinea as a "relational individual," following sociocentric benefits as much as egocentric benefits (see also A. Strathern & Stewart 2007: xiv–xv).

12. Male and female tree-spirits dwell in the forest in similar ways as humans dwell in their residential places. A *ngaape* is primarily perceived by its smell or the sounds it produces. However, people have a clear idea of what this tree-spirit looks like. If it becomes corporeal, it resembles the human body but with extraordinarily long fingers and toes. A *ngaape* is a spirit of two minds because it sometimes helps and sometimes hinders people. It has, for instance, a strong influence upon human spatial orientation, especially in the deep forest.

13. People consume herbs from childhood onward. There are prescribed amounts and durations of consumption. Magic is also involved. An incorrect usage of herbs, for instance, was always given as the explanation for why children are *bikhet* ('stubborn'). There was never any thought of there having been a pedagogic error.

14. The word *yaam* is also a male personal name. Bosmun have a system of avoiding the personal names of certain in-laws—one's spouse's biological and classificatory parents and elder siblings. If a speaker wants to use the word for 'to know / knowledge' but has an in-law whose name is Yaam, then he or she has to use the word *xaarak* instead. Many words in the Bosmun language have double or triple meaning, and often the word for a material object or a feature in the physical environment is also a male or female personal name.

15. I wrote my field notes in German:
    Obwohl vieles nicht mehr eingehalten wird, ist die Vergangenheit enorm präsent durch das Erzählen. Als ich an der Trauersituation von [namentlich genannter Person] teilnehme, kommen immer wieder Leute auf mich zu, um mir zu erklären wie es früher war. Ich komme kaum zum Beobachten, weil ständig jemand um mich herum ist, um mir zu erklären wie es früher war. (Feldnotizen, 02.12.2004)

16. Bosmun turn-taking may also be compared with what Feld has described as "lift-up-over-speaking" in the context of the Kaluli, which is:
    a good amount of interlocked, quickly alternating or overlapped speech. ... Like fire sticks laid in contact, the voices of Kaluli speakers ignite with a spark; they interlock, alternate, and overlap, densifying and filling any interactional space-time gaps. The Western normative concepts of individual speaker turns, floor rights, and turn-taking etiquette, notions rationalized in both speech act philosophy and conversational analysis, are absent from Kaluli conversation and narration. What might be heard as regular "interruption" is not that at all, but rather the collaborative and cocreative achievement of ... "lift-up-over speaking." ([1982] 1990: 251)

⤙ Chapter One ⤚
The Ethnographic Frame

In this chapter I introduce Bosmun starting from a historical perspective. This is the result of a particular concern that originally turned up during initial talks with people in Daiden. It is also in line with Kirsch's idea of exploring a particular people's historical encounters that move beyond the local level so as "to challenge representations of New Guinea that emphasize its isolation and difference rather than its historical connections to the rest of the world" (Kirsch 2006: 24). The first sections of this chapter seek to satisfy people's legitimate interest in the historical sources that relate to them in one way or another. I trace Bosmun history from past to present in written accounts and then briefly discuss their name and their language. I then proceed to a description of their actual location and how the residential structure has changed during the last seventy years.

The last sections of the chapter serve to segue into the following chapters. I sketch the physical setting with particular regard to the procurement of food and I outline the most elemental structures of relatedness in Daiden. In this context, I explain notions of moiety and clan and how the sharing of a platform is considered to be central for the cohesion of groups. I then briefly address how group leaders gain influence and how political decisions are made. Finally, I describe relevant kin terms as well as relationships of particular importance.

Historical Orientations

At different points in time, Bosmun encountered different people and representatives from nonlocal institutions who imposed their presence on them in different ways. Records have been made of such encounters and I have condensed what seem to me to be the most notable. These contacts brought sociocultural, religious, and economic rearrangements or alternative visions to be integrated into existing contours of life.

"Wandering Strangers" in the Ramu Basin

In terms of Western cartography, the meandering course of the Ramu was surveyed and mapped for the first time during the German colonial era, which lasted from 1884 to 1914, in northeast New Guinea. The first European to see the mouth of the Ramu was Otto Finsch of the "Neu-Guinea Compagnie" in 1885 (Anonymous 1885: 5; Finsch 1888: 297–298). The first to follow the Ramu on board a ship was Vice Admiral Freiherr von Schleinitz, who was on his way back from the Sepik River to Finschhafen with his steamer "Ottilie," in 1886. As the river had been encountered from aboard the steamer, the admiral decided that it should become known as Ottilie River (Anonymous 1887: 53–55). Ten years later the explorers Lauterbach, Kersting, and Tappenbeck set out from Astrolabe Bay in search of the headwaters of the Markham River. Eventually they found a river that was flowing northwest and not southeast. In the Bismarck Range it was named "Jagéi" and as they moved downstream they picked up another name—"Ramu" (Anonymous 1896: 41). No information is given as to where exactly they heard the name "Ramu" and what it might have meant. Since they had to abandon their voyage due to insufficient supplies, they could not establish whether this was the same course as the one explored by von Schleinitz. Thus, Tappenbeck led a second exploratory journey in 1898, this time ascending the Ottilie River. The result was the discovery that the Ottilie indeed joined the waters whose upper reaches already had been spotted (Anonymous 1897: 52–53, 1898: 51–59; Krieger 1899: 11, 118–119). Owing to the explorations of Tappenbeck and his colleagues, the name Ottilie, coined by von Schleinitz, never came into common usage (Hagen 1899: 16, 142; Höltker 1961: 286). More explorations followed, for instance, the Gogol–Ramu Expedition of 1913 (Braun 1916; Gehrmann 1916) and the Wattle Expedition of 1921 (Lord Moyne 1936; Lord Moyne & Haddon 1936: 269).

The first written accounts about Bosmun date from this period. Botanist Gehrmann (1916) of the Gogol–Ramu Expedition wrote some early comments about them, though he did not mention them by name. In October 1913 the prospectors took a two-day rest at a location that now forms the part of the residential area of the Bosmun group called Rom. Based on Gehrmann's (1916: 26) plotting of the campsite on a map and his diary notes, I conclude that his team came into contact with Bosmun. His description of the material culture and particularly of the environs matches both my own observations and what I learned through narrations:

24. October. Manam [a volcanic island] is frequently visible on the trip.... We pass many plantations, several villages, and a newly inhabited place. The people here already have very long dugout canoes.... The edge of the canoe is ornately carved. The people already wear the head decoration that is so characteristic of the coastal groups and the lower Sepik.... We see a lot of canoes, small coconut palms, and simple housings. The forest is not thickly wooded and has many grass clearings. ... At midday a strong wind blows.... Manam still towers over the treetops. Due to the wind, the Ramu has small waves; even whitecaps arise.... At twelve o'clock

we pitch a camp at a dry sago swamp. The locals seem to regularly rinse sago in this area.... In the afternoon, locals pass by, apparently establishing a new place, maybe at the location we passed today. Here, the Ramu has plenty of freshwater mussels (Anodonta sp.), and the porters are keen to gather them and to cook and eat them..... 25. October. Manam towers right in front of us. At night, one could see its firelight. Sago is rinsed throughout the whole day. People from neighboring villages visit us. They bring some coconuts. They are dressed with nice loincloth made of bark and red-dyed rotang belts. (Gehrmann 1916: 29; my translation)[1]

Another point that supports my conclusion is Gehrmann's remark about a newly emerging place. Gehrmann witnessed the onset of a larger residential shift brought about by various factors that I outline later. The emerging place he drew attention to was once a part of the customary hunting, garden, and sago grounds of the Rom. Over time, it turned into a permanent residential ground. More specifically, it was grassland surrounded by many sago palms and its given place name was Ndennden (literally meaning 'grassland area'). Today the name is pronounced as "Daiden," making it sound more Tok Pisin–like, as people explained to me. A fitting phrase that Rom repeatedly used in speaking about Daiden was, "we are living in the bush." As I was told, the first man who lived in this place was Tokne, the mother's father and father's father of some of my elder informants. Chronologically, this coincides with Gehrmann's observation. Moreover, the adjacent river section had and still has a plentitude of freshwater mussels compared to other sections, and the Rom are said to be their guardians since, according to a myth, it was a Rom woman who discovered them. Finally, Gehrmann's comment about the volcanic island of Manam is of interest. Manam is no longer directly visible from Daiden, per-haps because the location of Daiden has changed over time or the surrounding forest has grown since Gehrmann's time. It is, however, still possible to locate the volcano from Daiden by the smoke of its occasional eruptions.[2]

Colonial prospectors focused primarily on the upper part of the Ramu since it provided a convenient entrance into the Bismarck Range, which was sup-posed to hold gold deposits (Anonymous 1897: 52). The lower part, including its peoples, thus remained rather neglected by the administration (Lord Moyne 1936: 112). However, Catholic missionaries almost simultaneously began to spread in this area of New Guinea. Proselytization by the SVD (Societas Verbi Divini) in northeast New Guinea had started in 1896, and between 1900 and 1914 numerous mission stations were established along the north coast (Stef-fen 1995: 186, 190). In July 1926, Father Kirschbaum of SVD, who had set up the earliest mission station on the Sepik River in 1913, was among the first mes-sengers to pay visits to the Ramu (Höltker 1961: 287; Kirschbaum 1927: 202; Steffen 1995: 199). From the 1920s onward, local catechists were increasingly sent out from the coastal stations to the interiors of the Bogia District. The local catechists, too, helped to create more outstations (Steffen 1995: 200–212). In 1935, regular mission work started in the Bosmun area (Höltker 1937a: 1570). Around 1958/59, the Catholic Mission finally relocated its headquarters from the seacoast to the Mbur River (Howard 1957/58: 8; Kahler 1959/60: 3, 7), to the tributary that marks the heart of the Bosmun area. The mission station's move is also briefly described in the memoirs of Father Morin of SVD, edited by Father Fisher of SVD (1992: 51–52), who set out to missionize at the north coast of Papua New Guinea in 1944. In 2008, I brought the people of Daiden Father Morin's memoirs. Although they were originally published in Alexishafen near Madang, I had found the memoirs at the Anthropos Institute in Sankt Augustin, Germany. They were written in English and people were enthusiastic to read them; my house automatically became crowded every day (which, in turn, made me enthusiastic). My elder conversation partners remembered Father Morin well. Touched to see his picture on the cover of his published memoirs, they said, *Ah … gutpela pater bilong mipela ya, kela man ya!* ('Ah … our good Father, [who was] a bald headed man!').

Until the 1940s, most of the residential area of the Bosmun was located on the Mbur River, while the surroundings were primarily used for food-production purposes or as temporary dwelling sites. In 1936, a year before Blackwood's and Höltker's arrivals, another traveler came upon the residents of the Mbur. It was Lord Moyne, a collector of ethnographic objects by order of the British Museum. In his travelogue he stated: "[W]e stopped to speak to some natives at the entrance of a creek three miles long leading to a group of five villages known as Bosman or Bushmun. … The Bosman are a fierce tribe and apt to kill wandering strangers at sight. … This tribe have been inveterate head-hunters, and if the practice has now ceased it is merely due to fear of punishment by the government" (Lord Moyne 1936: 122–123). Fortunately, Lord Moyne and his traveling companions seemed not to have fallen into the category of "wandering strangers." They were able to continue their journey up the river after having purchased different objects like paddles, masks, and clay pots (Lord Moyne 1936: 123–124). According to Höltker (1975: 556) and Blackwood (1951: 266), it was Lord Moyne (1936) who introduced the Bosmun people into the literature. However, there is a colonial report from 1899 that not only refers to the "Buschmann" (Anonymous 1899: 565), but contains information that probably fits into a rather puzzling story I was told repeatedly about an unidentified white male who is believed to have lived several years with the Bosmun. The report purports:

From the mouth of the Ramu River in Kaiser Wilhelmsland, it is reported: In February of this year, the chiefs of the villages Buschmann [Bosmun], Margnitsch [Marangis], Borbor [Bodbod], and Kajan [Kayan] made the following report to the police station: In November of 1897, a completely naked and unarmed European came down the Ramu in a small river canoe and followed the beckoning of the Tamuls [probably a pejorative term for the local population] to land at their place, which is the village of Buschmann located about eight miles upstream. He was well taken care of; the Tamuls gave him food to eat and a loincloth to wear. He stayed about one month at Buschmann, and from there he left for Marg [Marangis] at Venus Point, guided by the Tamuls. Here, he stayed about two months (December 1897 and January 1898). Then, he walked further along the coast, in a southeasterly direction, and reached Barbor [Bodbod], where he immediately was shown the same level of hospitality as he had received in Margnitsch. The Tamuls had asked him to stay because they had been taught a lot by him; because of his white skin, they thought of him as a supernatural being, which is also apparent in the name they gave to him, "Barr," that is, the sun. He did not stay, but went past Kajan and came upon Bodian (a spot on a small island near the coast). There in Bodian, he seems to have suffered an unnatural or violent death in February of 1898. There is no evidence of his nationality since the Tamuls did not remember any word he might have used. It probably was an Australian gold digger who, following the course of the Ramu, fought his way through from British New Guinea. (Anonymous 1899: 565; my translation)[3]

The story I was given diverges at some points from the colonial report, and there certainly have been more "wandering strangers" in the Ramu River basin. But the narrative that lingers on in Bosmun collective memory is that of a white man who was kidnapped as a boy in a fight between Bosmun and an anonymous white ship's crew. As the Bosmun warriors fought back vigorously, the crew escaped hastily and did not realize that a boy had been taken. During the time of raids and active head-hunting, Bosmun regularly captured children or adults from enemy groups. The boy thus stayed. He is said to have been socialized by Bosmun until he attained manhood. He learned the local language and even went into the *dnene tomuŋ*, a structure (*tomuŋ*) built underground and covered with grass (*dnen*), where young males would learn to play secret flutes as part of their initiation. Höltker (1975: 567) provides a drawing of such a subterranean cavern that he saw in 1937 and he called "Flötenschule" ('flute school'). As initiation rites are no longer practiced in the way they were, these subterranean enclosures are no longer built. As an adult, the boy left the Bosmun area for unknown reasons. Whether he was the European-looking stranger who aroused attention in the years of 1897/98 remains uncertain. Evidence, at least for the presence of a white man and the Bosmun appreciation of him, may be traced in a photograph taken in 1937 by Höltker (1966). The photograph shows the interior of a *mirpi tomuŋ* ('spirit house') and Höltker states:

> The next to the last post ... shows at its base, below fringes and shells, a carved human figure whose facial shape does not resemble the otherwise prevailing artistic

style here. The Bosngun people [Bosmun] declared that it was meant to depict a particular white man (Englishman) who was known to the Bosngun as a trader and boy-recruiter and who somehow had gained their sympathy.... Was the depiction in the spirit house an attempt to captivate the magic power of the admired Englishman? (1966: 32; my translation)[4]

Höltker seems not to have read the colonial report, since otherwise he probably would have asked people about it. Whether it was true or not, depicting a favorable trader instead of a child stolen in a battle must have seemed less suspicious, especially when conveyed to someone representing the rising SVD Mission apparatus, which was spreading a dogma diametrically opposed to the practice of raids or head-hunting.

From the mid 1940s onward, Australian patrol officers commonly known as *kiap* began to pay systematic visits to the Lower Ramu and Hansa Bay area. Throughout the years leading up to Papua New Guinea's independence in 1975, their presence had become generally accepted. The Bosmun recollection of the time of colonial rule is a rather positive one. The establishment of an aid post, which started to operate at the Mbur around 1952 (Healy 1951/52: 9; Frawley 1953/54: 10) is remembered as a positive development, and, as people explained to me, it was the time when things on sale were cheaper and when "villages were tidy." Houses had to be placed in lines and bordered with flowers, and weathered ones had to be replaced immediately with new ones. Although today they are regarded as neglected, nobody really seemed to bother about weathered houses. Some negative feelings about the colonial period remain, however, because a patrol officer is said to have "borrowed" two stone objects that used to be of highest ancestral and ritual value. They were never returned and no one knows the officer's actual name, though it is said to have happened at the time of *Mista Siki* or *Mista Braun*. There are, in fact, reports made by two officers named Sheekey (1962) and Browne (1968/69).

Patrol reports about Bosmun do not only provide historical facts and dates. Some of the officers were also engaged in gathering ethnographic information (Browne 1968/69; Dyer 1952/53; Frawley 1953/54; M.A. Douglas 1970/71). That Bosmun have speculated about such inquiries is reflected in a report by the journalist McCarthy (1967), who paid a brief visit to the area in 1967, where he was told a creation myth. An extract of that creation myth appeared in the book *Legends of Papua New Guinea* (McCarthy & Pfund 1973) and in an account that McCarthy wrote for *Walkabout* magazine (1967).[5] McCarthy tells of his arrival: "The idea of a stranger just walking in and asking them [Bosmun] to explain some of their ancient beliefs must have sounded a bit remarkable, for the old chap turned and stared at me for more than a minute. The rest sat in silence" (1967: 20).

Patrol officers paid particular attention to the emergence of "cargo cult" movements, which centered upon the belief that European goods were delivered by ancestors or supernatural entities (e.g., Jebens 2004; Lawrence 1964; Worsley 1957). Having observed the arrangement of flowers in bottles on wooden tables in almost every Bosmun house, patrol officer Dyer (1952/53: 3) suggested that it was a "flower cult," especially because he had heard that flowers were believed to keep sicknesses away. A movement called the "Flower Cult" was indeed prominent in the Southern Madang District in those years (Lawrence 1964: 194). However, the patrol officer did not expect any disruptive consequences. Father Morin, too, writes about the "expectation of 'cargo'" (Fisher 1992: 41) for the year 1948; its "False Prophet" (Fisher 1992: 40), as Father Morin calls the leader, being a man called Kamndoŋ (subsequently written as Kaamndoŋ following my orthography of Bosmun words) from Ŋgoinmbaŋ. He convinced many people to discontinue any productive work, declared a taboo on all major foods, and told people to wait for cargo sent by the ancestors through the graves in the cemetery (Fisher 1992: 45–46). Kaamndoŋ's prophesy could be understood as a troubled response to the disturbances introduced to New Guinea through the colonization of lands and people's minds. Interestingly, the man had the same name as a local mythical protagonist who does not work, cook, or eat as humans do until he encounters Nzari, a major cultural heroine in Bosmun myth, who transforms him into a human / social being (see chapter 3). Father Morin tried to intervene but felt threatened and left for Kayan. A year later, Bosmun delegates visited him with huge gifts of food in order to apologize, which led the Father to remark: "Alleluia! The missionary has more joys and triumphs than troubles" (Fisher 1992: 47). Rumours of "cargo cult" activities continued to circulate as another report of 1970/71 indicates (M.A. Douglas 1970/71: 13–14), but there was no serious reason to intervene in any way.

Contrary to my expectations, patrol reports also show that some officers sought to give careful descriptions. A highly sensitive account referring to the topic of "cargo cult" activities illustrates this point:

> Any activities which may be considered aberrations from the norm of native behaviour can be traced to natural causes. These people were very upset by the war and have not been patrolled since the cessation of hostilities. There is no real evidence at all of cargo cult, or the often-accompanying subversive propaganda. Rather there is a friendly hospitality, a desire to co-operate, to improve villages and houses and to imitate many of our salutary customs. That these efforts are sometimes futile or frustrating, we are partially to blame. This is the over-all picture. Each smaller area has its own interesting facet and reaction to European culture encroachment. In areas that have lost their traditional customs (or have all but lost them), where a vague, daily, prayer recital is the only replacement for the once living and pregnant and traditional rituals and celebrations, we must expect unusual developments caused by this break with traditional thought and behaviour. (Cahill 1949/50: 4)

Apart from the patrollers' reports and those by early explorers, ethnographers, and missionaries, anthropological data on Bosmun life has been rather scarce. Bosmun are very briefly mentioned in a compilation by May and Tuckson (2000: 201–202) about the pottery-making industries of Papua New Guinea, and by Mennis (2006: 86, 270, 288) in *A Potted History of Madang*. Yet, the sources they rely on are the early works by Blackwood (1951) and Höltker (1965a). Moreover, linguistic investigations have been carried out, as in the works of Capell (1951/52: 135–138, 198–200, 1954: 21–22) or Z'graggen (1972), as well as some archaeological studies (Fairbairn & Swadling 2005; Swadling 1990, 1997; Swadling et al. 1988; Swadling & Hide 2005).

Finally, my ethnography may be added to the list of written accounts dealing with Bosmun. Of course, I also qualify as a "wandering stranger." This is what I was when I arrived, as Ndombu, my "father's sister," said to me when I had to leave. She also said that now that I had to go I had become one of them. This was during my farewell party, arranged as a big dancing feast (see figure 1.1). I was dancing with my "sisters" Koorop and Bambi when Ndombu approached us and told me that. She reinforced her words by spreading dry sago in front of our feet.

Figure 1.1: Throwing Sago. At my farewell party in 2005, Bambi (left) and Koorop (right) danced with me. Ndombu came and threw sago in front of our feet. The picture was taken by Taapi, a man living in Ndenekaam.

Seeking the Proper Name—The Predicament of Language Loss

According to the people who spoke with me, the group's actual term of self-reference is *Soŋenor*, although not one of the former visitors seems to have heard this name. It means "the people from Soŋe" and relates to their place of origin called Soŋevout. Soŋe is the proper name of a mythical protagonist, albeit not of the founding figure, and it is the name of a plateau (*vout*) where some important mythical events happened. The plateau is situated in the environs between the lower reaches of the Sepik and the Ramu Rivers. Although not secret, the name "Soŋenor" did not dominate in daily discourse when it came to articulating a collective self. It was "Bosmun" that mattered. People used "Bosmun" equally as a name for the area and the language and were well known by it in the wider region. Therefore, I too have chosen to use it. Its ultimate derivation, however, remains unclear. As can be seen from the quotes cited previously, the name used for the people living at the Mbur was spelled in various ways, but "Soŋenor" was not used. The name ranged from "Busch-mann" and "Bushmun" to "Bosman" and "Bosngun." As pronunciation is re-shaped continuously over time, such variation is not uncommon. What is peculiar, though, is an issue that I raise with regard to the often ambiguous efforts of classifying and denominating sociocultural or linguistic units. As Sillitoe points out: "The names given to these entities and now prominent in the anthropological literature are often contrived and sometimes comical in their derivation. Those who have christened these linguistic and cultural groups have often seized upon some frequently heard but unintelligible word to label them" (1998: 10; see also Keck 1994). Höltker (1965a: 8, 1975: 555–556) declared the only and correct name of the Mbur people to be "Bosngun." This term can also be found in the linguistic works of Capell (1951/52, 1954), although he does not say anything about its genesis. According to Höltker (1965a: 8) "Bosmun" and "Bosman" were only mispronunciations or rather simplified versions that had been introduced by white explorers, labor recruiters, and missionaries during the time of initial contact. Blackwood (1950, 1951) called them "Bosmun" only and did not comment further upon this subject.

Since I had read Höltker prior to my fieldwork, one of the first things I did was to ask about this name. I kept asking from time to time but was always offered the same explanation: the fact that Bosmun had been greatly feared and commanding head-hunters in the past must have motivated neighboring groups and other outsiders, like the missionaries, to label them as the "boss men." The way I tried to pronounce "Bosngun" did not make sense to any of my patient listeners, and it was only after seven months that by coincidence I heard M., an old woman, say "Mbosŋon." We had been sitting at the riverbank for hours waiting for a chance to cross the water. A relative of hers came to join us and they started talking while I was just relaxing and listening. Suddenly she mentioned a name, which did not exactly sound like what I had imagined from Höltker's spelling. But at least it sounded similar. Surprised, I begged her to repeat it again and again, which she kindly did. After I had practiced how to pronounce the name in the way M. had, a few other old people were indeed able to confirm my renewed questions, but not without stating that it was a term attributed to them from outside. Some assumed that it was a name that neighboring groups must have used in the past in order to refer to them, while others guessed that the term had been created solely by white colonialists or missionaries. I have adopted the first view, and I am convinced that Höltker must have picked up the name somewhere else. He had to pass through other peoples' territories to reach the Bosmun area and instead of investigating further on site he must have taken the first name for granted. Among my middle-aged and younger conversation partners the name "Mbosŋon" was completely unfamiliar. Language loss has certainly contributed to this state of affairs.

Unfortunately, most of the early linguistic inquiry done by SVD missionaries on local languages in the Ramu area was destroyed during World War II (Capell 1951/52: 130). However, subsequent investigations in terms of broader area language compilations followed (Capell 1951/52: 135–138, 198–200, 1954: 21–22; Z'graggen 1972). Laycock and Z'graggen (1975) classified the Bosmun language as belonging to a single large language group known as the "Sepik-Ramu-Phylum" (see Wurm 1982: 209–225). More recently, however, Foley (2005) argued for a reconsideration of their findings. Following his analysis, there are actually two different language families that have to be recognized for the area in question. On the one hand, there is the "Sepik family" and, on the other hand, there is the "Lower Sepik-Ramu family." The second includes the "Lower Ramu family" as one of its two major subgroups and is composed of nine languages, with Bosmun being one of them. The others are spoken by the people of Watam neighboring to the northwest, Kayan and Boroi to the northeast, Awar to the east, and finally Giri, Mikarew, Igom, and Tangu to the south and southeast (Foley 2005: 110, 112). My consociates referred to their local language as *mbiermba kaam* or *mbiermba niŋin*. *Kaam* is a term used to express linguistic demarcation (meaning 'sound') and spatial demarcation (meaning 'boundary'), while *niŋin* refers to the general ability to talk. *Mbiermba* is a type of vine that, according to a Bosmun myth, emerged during the time of world-creative acts. For this reason, I sometimes heard people also say *mbiermba kaama nda*, that is, 'we are the Mbiermba people.' Although they proudly spoke of their local language, considering it crucial for their sense of group identification, the current prevalence of Tok Pisin has led to its ongoing decline. Younger generations used the local vernacular only if they had to specify things for which there were no equivalent words in Tok Pisin. If there was a need to identify, for example, certain elements of the forest vegetation, they drew on the local language, which provides more lexical variety.

Blackwood (1951: 266) stated that during the time of her stay "[m]ost of the men and some of the women spoke Pidgin-English." Now, it is the first language to be learned and has undergone some vital alteration and expansion. In comparing elder with younger Tok Pisin speakers, the transformation of the language became obvious. Among the latter there was a progressive lexical growth (using more and more English words) and an enormous increase with regard to the speed of speech. To grasp the utterances of children and of adolescents was a real challenge for me in the beginning. They spoke a "regionalized" Tok Pisin that can be grouped under the rubric of a distinctly emerging Madang Pidgin.

Location—Past and Present

At the time of Höltker's and Blackwood's visits in 1937, Bosmun residential space was located on the north bank of the Mbur. There are four major residential units, which are simultaneously clan-associations: Rom, Maŋgai, Ŋgoinmbaŋ, and Ndoŋon. While the latter two still live at the Mbur, the people calling themselves Rom and Maŋgai have moved to different locations directly on the Ramu. Having made the previous forest grounds inhabitable, the Rom finally took up residence further down the river, but on its western bank. They enlarged Daiden and formed another place named Ndenekaam as well as a number of hamlets, some of which are located on the opposite side of the river. The Maŋgai completely shifted to their customary grounds located at the eastern riverbank near Bunapas Health Centre, a hospital originally established as an infant welfare clinic by the Church of Christ Mission in the 1960s (Browne 1968/69: 10; M.A. Douglas 1970/71: 5). Throughout the Bogia District this place is known as "Basecamp." It can be reached from coastal Bogia by car as long as the road is in good condition (during the rainy season this is hardly ever the case). During my stays at the Ramu, Basecamp was a major traffic point where local people gathered to sell betel nut to buyers coming mostly from the Highlands via Madang and the north coast.

Several events occurred at different points in time that need to be taken into account when considering why Bosmun residential order has changed. The most dramatic incident was undoubtedly World War II, which in 1942 turned Papua and the mandated territory of New Guinea into a theater of combat between Japanese invaders and Australian troops. During World War II, the local population had to face incredible devastation and dislocation (see Souter 1963: 238). The image of bombs dropping was among the most vigorously told memories of two old men whom I had asked to recount central childhood experiences. During the war, the Japanese established a base at Hansa Bay. The interior of the north coast was certainly of strategic use to them, and thus the whole area including residential places alongside the Ramu came under military attack. Bosmun, as the river's closest dwellers, took refuge with the neighboring Boroi. From there, many males were recruited to assist the armed forces at Hansa Bay. It was not until 1945 that these displaced persons were able to return home.

After the war, almost all Rom decided to move to their sago, garden, and hunting grounds closer to where Daiden is located. When they were at the Mbur, these grounds had been far off and always hard to reach. Although Bosmun are highly mobile people, a three-hour walk to and from their grounds can be very annoying. At that time, the relationship between the Rom and the other clan-associations was considered to be unstable because of a conflict whose origins dated back to the ancestors. Now, this dispute is said to have been settled. The conflict might be counted as a separate and thus second reason to relocate, as sooner or later it would have triggered some residential changes anyway. By relocating, the Rom were able to solve a problem that they otherwise would have been compelled to face on a daily basis. After I had experienced the lengthy and monotonous rainfalls of the wet season, which meant staying a considerable time in a house surrounded by high water, I asked some of my Rom consociates how they managed to endure the Ramu floods without losing their good humor. They answered that they appreciate the water, for during the days of conflict they had either to walk very long distances in order to fetch water or they had to fight for direct water access because they had to cross the areas of the other clan-associations. With a smile, they would add that the Ramu provides them with a richer yield of fish than they were ever able to bring in while at the smaller tributary.

A third factor in the residential reorganization was the extension of the Catholic Mission at the Mbur, both spatially and ideologically. The mission's headquarters were built on the ground formerly inhabited by Rom. A Rom hamlet at the back of the headquarters is still there, serving as a reminder that this was their ground. Apart from religious changes, the spread of Christianity also brought transformations in respect to demographics. In premissionary times, there had been strict practices to control sexual reproduction, an aspect to which I return in detail in chapter 3. On average, Bosmun women today bear six to ten children, as opposed to an average of four in the past. This has led to a rapid population growth of formerly unknown extent. Population estimates and censuses of the Bosmun region support this observation: missionary Höltker (1975: 555) estimated a population of 529 individuals in 1936/37; Z'graggen (1975: 44), who collected linguistic data of the wider Ramu region, determined 717 individuals in 1975; the Provincial Adminstration listed 1,226 individuals in 2000; and my own data indicate that by now Bosmun number about 1,500 people. Such an increase entails the necessity of creating more living space.

A fourth aspect that influenced people to move is the general struggle for economic progress in this region, which was prompted first by the German and later by the Australian colonial administration. Patrol reports from the area can help reconstruct these dynamics. The present-day road, for example, which connects Bogia with the Lower Ramu, was known as "Bosman road" (Calderwood 1970/71: 4; M.A. Douglas 1970/71: 6). It was the first direct connection that Bosmun had to the coast. The only way of transport before had been by ship. Since while I was still in the field no one told me who had built the road, I was astounded by the following account from 1968/69, which I later found in the National Archives in Port Moresby:

> The Bosman people ... have been over the past year or two working on a road which starts at Nubia plantation on the coast going inland to Sepen Village and coming out near the new airstrip at Bunapas.... They have been working on the road without any assistance or supervision and having walked along the road I have been impressed by the efforts of the Bosman people. The road itself travels along very flat country with hardly any hills to worry about. There are three rivers but they appear to be slow [sic] moving and can be easily bridged. However, this road may be subject to flooding during the wet season. Nevertheless it opens up another possible route to the Ramu River which may be well worth considering. (Browne 1968/69: 12)

At about the same time, the "New Bosman Camp" (Aisa 1971/72: 4; Browne 1968/69: 21) was set up near an old riverbed located at the eastern riverbanks. The camp's current name is Banis Kau ('cow fence') and it is maintained by some Ŋgoinmbaŋ people. Throughout the 1960s, economic activities in the Lower Ramu and Hansa Bay area were fostered by the Agricultural Department operating from the district's capital, Bogia. Agricultural field workers were sent out to assist the local population in several ways, mostly in building driers for copra production, which seemed the most profitable venture in this tropical lowland region (Browne 1968/69: 17; Sheekey 1962: 1). Economic development was occurring mainly in places situated to the east of the Ramu and extending all the way to the seacoast. As river-dwelling people, Bosmun are experienced canoeists and more than once I was with them as they carried incredible loads in their narrow canoes. Transporting large amounts of copra involves a considerable expenditure of time, which probably was reckoned economically inefficient. Another problem is that passage by vessel cannot be guaranteed at all times. The Ramu has strong currents and experiences frequent changes in water level. In order to participate in the new economic flow without having to overcome such natural obstacles, Bosmun developed other camps like Banis Kau.

In addition to external stimuli causing a few major relocations over time, the Ramu presents a challenge to people, in particular to those who are living right next to it. An expression that I often heard was: *Mipela save bihainim*

Ramu tasol ('We just follow the Ramu'). The Ramu keeps the people moving whenever it erodes the residential space, which happens little by little during every wet season. Heavy rainfalls lasting from about November to May ensure that a large part of the area regularly becomes inundated. Each year, the Ramu is expected to burst its banks with water levels varying up to four meters. In figure 1.2, I show a dwelling-house that once stood at a safe distance. I took the picture during the dry season when the water level was very low. The house was still used at that time, and people said to me that they would wait for the next wet season before relocating the entire household. I was impressed by how confident people were. A new dwelling-house at another place was, however, already under construction. Residential space is automatically rearranged, as was and is the case with Daiden. Most of its elder residents spent their childhood days "in the middle of the river," which is to say, on ground that existed before the Ramu swallowed it. Social memories are evoked whenever people look at the meanderings of the Ramu. Pointing to the river's midpoint, my conversation partners would say that most of *vunsi xur* ('the old place') was over there with only a small part left over. But even *vunsi ŋgaam,* the new and present ground representing Daiden, was threatened by the consuming waters of the Ramu. At the time of my third stay in Papua New Guinea in early 2008, much of my former home area no longer existed. During the previous wet season, huge water masses had eroded the riverbanks. Consequently, a considerable amount of ground was taken away again. People reasoned that if I were to return in the near future I would probably also say that "I once lived in the middle of the river."

Figure 1.2: Dwelling-House on Unsafe Ground.

Procuring Food at the Ramu

The tropical lowland that Bosmun inhabit is hot and extraordinarily humid. The local environment is first clearly distinguished by the Ramu, including its old and mainly horseshoe-shaped riverbeds as well as a number of smaller and bigger rivulets. The other dominating feature is the contiguous and indeed intriguing landscape, which alternates between medium rainforest zones, grasslands, hilly spots, and, above all, huge areas of sago swamps. River and swamp provide the staple diet all year round. A proper meal in Daiden consists of stirred sago (*erok*), which is topped by fish (generically called *ŋgu*) and vegetables (generically called *yimyɨt*). The processed starch of the sago palm affords carbohydrate and plays the major role in daily meals. After sweet potato, it is sago that ranks as New Guinea's second most important energy source (Townsend 2003: 4). Sago palms need to grow between twelve to fifteen years in order to accumulate enough starch, and they reach a maximum height of fifteen meters. To obtain sago, the whole trunk of the palm has to be cut down. Then, its bark must be removed so that its pith can be scraped out and shredded. Finally, the starch that is so elemental in the Bosmun cuisine has to be rinsed out of the shredded pith. Side delicacies associated with sago palms are mushrooms and sago grubs that emerge in the leftovers of the shredded and rinsed pith. In Bosmun labor division, the steps of felling the palm, removing the bark, and scraping the pith (see figure 1.3) are exclusively men's work, whereas women do the rinsing of the pith. Cutting down trees and palms is considered hard work and thus nothing for women, as men explained to me. This also applies to the clearing of potential garden grounds. Only men slash and burn. As we shall see in chapter 2, Bosmun draw upon a sociomythical

Figure 1.3: Scraping Sago Pith. Mbano (left) and Yaame (right) are scraping sago pith while Koorop, their sister, and Sindu, Yaame's wife (sitting left and right in the background), are waiting until the pith is shredded. Standing behind the men is Liklik Yombu.

explanation for why women do not work on the palm's trunk. The produce of a trunk segment of approximately three meters may feed a family of four to six adults plus four to six children for two to four weeks. To make sago flour from such a segment takes a nuclear family the whole day, sometimes two days. Despite the fact that there is a gender division with regard to the single working steps, men and women usually set out together and return together. While one part is working, the other part contributes with a relaxed presence, conversing, chatting, and joking. The processed starch of sago palms can be prepared in many different ways. One way is to mix the dry starch with, for example, squeezed coconut milk or banana and to place it onto a heated piece of a broken clay pot and roast it. A type of local sago bread is made in this way. People in Daiden favored _erok_, a pudding-like substance that results when sago starch is quickly stirred while hot water is added (see figure 1.4). From local culinary perspectives, fish or meats cannot be served without sago pudding. Sago is classified as the ultimate source for appeasing one's hunger. Fish or meats make a meal tasty, but never fully satisfying. It is sago that fills empty stomachs and that connects to Bosmun notions of life force and social as well as emotional stability.

Protein is, of course, also crucial to the Bosmun diet. The protein requirement is basically covered by the fauna of the Ramu, namely fish and, depending on the season, freshwater mussels, huge freshwater prawns (famous as "Ramu prawns" in Madang restaurants), and shrimps, or bigger and smaller

Figure 1.4: Sago Pudding.

types of eels. In the past, Bosmun men were highly skilled fishermen. While standing in the canoe, they would catch fish either with hooks or multi-pronged spears. This practice was abandoned with the introduction of fishing nets made of nylon, which are simply spread out on the water and checked twice a day: in the early morning hours, shortly after sunrise, and during the afternoon hours before the sun sets. Women still rely on their traditional tools for catching prawns and fish. One is a cone-shaped basket, usually placed at water spots where a lot of reeds grow. During the dry season, which lasts from May to October, a sandy beach forms alongside the main riverbanks where freshwater mussels, another Ramu delicacy, can be found. Women also dive for mussels in the water surrounding the sandy beach. Beyond the river offerings, the forest supplies people with game. From time to time, hunters return with wild pigs, fowl, bandicoots, or cassowaries. Pigs are very rarely kept. To honor a deceased relative, pigs are reared until they become mature. For other purposes, though, pigs are bought from neighboring groups.

In the past, Bosmun men used to trade sago or cooking pots, which were produced by women, for pigs and other commodities like sea salt and woven sleeping bags where people hid from mosquito attacks at night (Dyer 1952/53: 5, 7; Tiesler 1969: 73, 1970: 140–141, 170–171). Since they were the only group in the area with a pottery-making industry, taking the clay from a specific stream called Ndombo Aaok ('stream of the dead'), they had a unique position and were therefore referred to as "mother" by adjacent groups like the Kayan (A.T. von Poser 2008a). With the introduction of cheap aluminium pots and saucepans, the Bosmun economic position in this regard has begun to diminish, at least in the sphere of daily activities. In ritual contexts, however, Bosmun clay pots continue to be a requisite, and neighboring groups still order them. In her survey on pottery making in the Madang Province, Mennis (2006: 288) classified Bosmun pottery as "[g]one but not forgotten." Women below the age of forty told me that they no longer knew how to produce the pots and that they had lost interest in learning how to make them. Most of the women above the age of forty had learned pottery making in their youth but relied on the assistance of old women to refresh their skills.

To frame Bosmun food-getting practices in terms of well-known anthropological definitions is not unproblematic because the terms are too rigid to apply suitably to the subsistence arrangements in an estuarine environment like that of the Ramu. Bosmun subsistence activities are comparable to those of the Fly River populations on the south coast of New Guinea, and I follow Sillitoe in questioning the validity of prominent anthropological categories regarding food procurement:

> The subsistence arrangements in the Fly region confuse the standard anthropological categories of "hunter-gatherer," "cultivator" and so on, by which we continue

grossly to classify people. It is not only a question of determining at what point the management of plant resources moves these from the status of wild to farmed resources but also ... one of deciding how we are to categorise people who secure a proportion of their food needs from both gathering and cultivation. What proportion of their food supply do people need to cultivate to qualify as horticulturalists? ... [A]s is often the case with anthropological terms, the categories "hunter-gatherer," "cultivator" and so on, are too imprecise for meaningful debate in Melanesia. (1998: 25)

Instead of deciding how to categorize Bosmun subsistence on a percentage basis, I simply outline people's food-procuring modes including the ecological and social conditions that influence them. Men and women in Daiden regularly process sago and catch fish. Occasionally, men go on hunting trips. Women frequently gather all kinds of wild food plants, mushrooms, and edible grubs. People also practice "silviculture" (Obrist 1990: 455), that is, the planting of food-bearing trees such as coconut palms, which, apart from their planting, require additional human activity only insofar as the fruits have to be picked. Obrist (1990: 455–456) tends to classify silviculture as a separate category but concedes that it overlaps to some extent with the making of sago since some groups plant sago palms whereas others rely on wild ones. Bosmun practice both methods. They differentiate between *osnis* and *raarŋaosnis,* the former being swamps in which people themselves plant sago palms and the latter being swamps that are believed to be animated by a primordial creative force. The first category is guarded by single clans and families, the second by the clan-associations.

Finally, people also perform horticulture. They harvest produce like plantain and sweet banana, yam, taro, sweet potato, pumpkin, and watermelon. There are two distinct grounds on which to plant gardens. On the one hand, it is possible to garden in the forest. The clearing starts around September, planting is in October, and harvest is at the beginning of the dry season. Since I arrived at the time when Seres, my "brother," started his garden in the forest near Daiden, I could follow up the various working steps. In some way, Seres' garden, which lay on the path leading away from Daiden, became of special importance to me. When I went to other places, I always had to pass it. In seeing how the plants there began to take shape, the foreign Bosmun landscape, as it initially appeared to me, turned into a more familiar one. On my return from walking jaunts, I could hardly wait to see the garden as Kopri and Nambindo, my companions, would notice every time by commenting on my behavior and interpreting it as happy anticipation. Together we would laugh and call out "oh Daiden!" After all, it also meant a break after a long day of marching around. The second option for a place to set out a garden is along the Ramu banks. River gardens have to be planted around May and are ready to be harvested with the beginning of the wet season before the rising river runs over its banks. Bosmun engage in gardening in a very irregular way. There are always a number of gardens planted, though not by each family or during each alternating season. The description that suits Bosmun horticultural practices best would be to say that Bosmun are "purposive gardeners." People's purposes and motivations for making a garden are mainly social ones. If there are significant events planned for the future, like feasts for initiates or the deceased, the building of a new house or the settling of some sort of dispute, then gardens are planted. Otherwise, gardening is sporadic. There is also a practical or realistic reason for this. Gardening in floodplains is an unpredictable endeavor (van Helden 1998: 165; Yamada 1997: 8–9), and people's adaptations to their environment have proved horticulture here to be too insecure to provide constant food resources.

When I came back in early 2008, for instance, people told me that particularly heavy rains during the wet season of 2007/08 had enabled them to fish in areas that they had arranged as gardens. Although garden produce had been destroyed completely, new fishing grounds and an alternative source of food had emerged. People, in fact, had adopted a positive view of water despite its sometimes destructive force. After all, they know that the regular inundations caused by the nature of the Ramu keep the soil swampy and hence guarantee the growth of sago palms. As I was often told, it is the environment itself that not only allows but obliges people to be generous with regard to the sharing of food. The physical environment caringly nurtures humans; it is conceived of as being abundant in nourishing resources. Hence, humans should nurture each other likewise. Bosmun draw a parallel between their own habit of generosity and that of land and water, and consider their surroundings as a constant reminder of that duty. Moreover, people believe that nature's abundance will cease if they refuse to be generous in their daily relationships with others. This will be explained in chapter 2 when I turn to the myth that tells about the emergence of 'real sago' (*vees*). Prior to this, we need to ask what kinds of relationships exist in Daiden and how individuals connect to each other on different levels in the matrix of locally recognized kinship.

Sharing a Platform

The primary tenet of Bosmun social segmentation is a division into moieties, *raao* ('sun') and *karvi* ('moon'). According to the origin myth, the ancestors of both moieties drifted on rafts (*vaam*) across the sea until they arrived at a protruding and uninhabited plateau. One group landed by day, the other by moonlight and, therefore, one moiety is connected to the sun and the other to the moon. On both rafts were women and men, and they are said to have left a place called Imbando, which exists as a named location at the Lower Sepik

River (see map 0.1). This was at a time when the land on which people dwell today was completely covered by sea except for a single plateau. According to Bosmun ideas about primeval settlement, they were the first people to inhabit this island. I was indeed confused by this in the beginning. When describing their environment in myth, people sometimes would tell me of an island surrounded by the sea, and sometimes they would tell me of solid soil traversed by rivers and streams. This double image of a mythical space became understandable to me only as I learned of the different mythical paths left in the landscape by the ancestors. Following these mythical paths, it is partially possible to trace the gradual transformation of an existing seascape into a solid landscape.[6] As the ancestors stepped onto the soil, I was told, they erected platforms (*xonom*) as equivalents to the sea rafts. In myth, these sea rafts linger on as particularly distinguishing features, and Bosmun use the image of platforms as a metaphor for social fragmentation.

Each moiety consists of a pair of larger kin-groups. The kin-groups of the sun are the Rom and the Maŋgai. Those of the moon are the Ŋgoinmbaŋ and the Ndoŋon. These pairs are seen as having mother-child relationships and are called *maamapmooŋ* ('mother and daughter'). The Rom and Ŋgoinmbaŋ are regarded as mothers (*maame*), the Maŋgai and Ndoŋon as their daughters (*mooŋ*). The mother-daughter scheme is an allegory that does not explicitly refer to any specific female progenitors. Rather, in a general sense it is meant to signify the groups' close linkages and the sequential aspect of their descent. Bosmun kin-groups can be called clans or clan-associations (clusters that comprise a certain number of clans). Most of them trace their descent to one or more mythical ancestors, and in cases where this is not clearly known people say that memory must have become shallow. Nonetheless, a strong sense of unity prevails. The standard way to express the link between clan-associations of the same moiety is by saying that from time immemorial their members shared lands, swamps, waters, and, above all, food. The last aspect especially serves as a crucial hint to common ancestry. In my inquiries into the pattern of social organization, I soon realized that I just had to ask whose ancestral predecessors actually ate with whom. The image of sharing substances of a nourishing quality mirrors the onset of a vital relationship—the first and foremost of all relationships a human being automatically enters after birth when being nursed by the mother or someone capable of substituting for her in that role.

Every clan-association comprises a number of patrilineal clans. The clans vary in size and some of them split into additional subunits. The name of a clan-association is the same as the name of its major clan. The name Rom, for instance, refers to both the complete clan-association and a single clan within it. Generically, the clan-association but also the single clan is called *xonom*. Literally, the term *xonom* refers to a physical platform. As indicated above, the platforms serve as a terrestrial extension of the ancestral sea rafts. Each platform is a material expression for the cohesion of a group of people linked through the knowledge that their ancestors shared food. At different levels of connectedness, created by the layering into moieties, clan-associations, and clans, people will feel either more unity or more separation. The moieties and the clans they embrace have their own ancestral narratives, myths, and collective memories. There are particular songs, flute melodies, slit-drum beats, masks, carving patterns, and sets of personal names that constitute the intellectual and material properties of moieties and clans, while at the same time serving to differentiate them from other clans and moieties. Totemic relations based on shared consubstantiality between human and nonhuman beings exist. Bosmun identify as a group rather than individually with totemic entities and their corporeal or otherwise perceivable manifestations. This is unlike the Sepik cosmologies, for instance, where each person has a unique totemic link via personal names apart from the major clan totems (Silverman 2001: 28–29; Wassmann 1991, 2001). Bosmun personal names are nonetheless ancestrally related and belong to different clans. Again comparing to the Sepik, where clans possess paired chains of names that are passed on strictly between alternating generations (Silverman 2001: 28; Wassmann 1991: 222–247), Bosmun name-giving practices are more flexible. Whenever someone dies, his or her name is transferred to one of the newborn ascendants in one's clan.[7]

There are basically two types of *xonom*. The *nisnisi xonom* is the men's house. It serves the men as an enclosed (*nisnis*) podium used to discuss matters in a sphere secluded from women. The other is the *taana xonom*. It is a more exposed or open (*taan*) than the former and has a smaller, roofless construction. This type of platform is used for public announcements that concern both women and men. In the past, women were not allowed to set foot on these smaller platforms, although this did not mean that they were forbidden from listening to what was proclaimed from there. In fact, Bosmun men recognize the decisions made in the men's house as legitimate only once women are finally allowed to hear them. Once this has happened, decisions are said to be no longer negotiable. While it is still forbidden for women to enter the men's house, gender segregation by means of the "open platform" has been abandoned for the most part. I saw such a permanent open platform in Ndoŋon, which only men would step onto. Another one that I saw was for temporary purposes. It was during a feast that was the last in a chain of a complex, years-long, practice called *ndom taao,* which is part of the process of 'honoring' (*taao*) the 'spirit of a deceased' (*ndom*). The last part of this chain of events usually consists of the burning of the deceased's possessions, such as his or her cloth, eating spoons, or wooden plates. This formal procedure is likely to be performed when more than ten years have passed since the corporeal death of a person. A few days prior to the feast that I was able to witness, some young males erected a simple platform. When the feast was held, the platform was occupied by two male relatives who would distribute food to the participants. After that, the platform was abandoned for a while until it was finally removed.

As a rule, clans of the same association live in close proximity to one another and consider themselves to belong to a common residential aggregate called *vunis*. The term *vunis* refers to an occupied area bounded spatially as well as socially. However, parts of a *vunis* might be scattered throughout an inhabited landscape with rather tacit boundaries. What to an outsider might appear as different villages and different hamlets, in fact, constitutes a connected "clanscape" (Bender 1996: 323). Höltker (1975: 555), Blackwood (1951: 266), and Lord Moyne (1936: 122) mentioned five major villages, four of them bearing the names of the clan-associations and a fifth called Wemtak. Viamtak, as my conversation partners pronounced it, is actually a clan belonging to the Ŋgoinmbaŋ clan-association. Emically, a sociospatial connectedness is perceived regardless of any concrete distance that may make it look like a separate place. It took me some time to become versed with the unwritten borders in the Bosmun environment and not to wonder why two places a half-hour walk apart are seen as being tied, whereas the next one within about twenty minutes on foot is not.

There is a further aspect given in the accounts by Blackwood and Höltker that I consider in my description of *vunis*. Höltker (1947: 197, 1964: 37) reported that the Awar people at Hansa Bay were linguistically and culturally closest to Bosmun, and Blackwood defined the former as an "off-shoot" (1951: 266) of the latter. In fact, it was part of the common knowledge of both groups that the ancestors of present-day Awar belonged to Bosmun before they moved to their current coastal location at a point in time that is difficult to determine. Since then, the Awar language seems to have been influenced by the adjacent Austronesian-speaking population of Manam Island due to more direct contact (Levy 2005: 91). However, the older generations of both Bosmun and Awar were still able to understand each other in their specific vernacular, and single families still considered themselves as belonging to the same *vunis*. According to what I learned, the separation arose out of a conflict caused by an inappropriate distribution of food. Already in 1937, the split was said to have happened long before. Höltker (1966: 17) also noted that during his stay people were no longer able to remember the Awar's former place of residence. I was told a different story. The area where the Awar are supposed to have settled while at the Ramu is known, at least to Bosmun, as being located near a water channel called Ŋguornzen. Enclosed by the small hamlet of Nemnem, which used to be larger in the past, this channel is a frequently passed spot in the Bosmun spatial grid of daily movements. As I was told further, Ŋguornzen was the name given to the group that lived here, and the Awar were part of this group.[8] Since the channel and its surroundings are deeply associated with the Ndɨpɨr clan of the Rom association, the Awar probably once belonged to that clan. Another reason that supports this interpretation is the fact that Bosmun have a system of traditional delegates who are sent out to other places and groups if there is a need to convey messages, settle disputes, or fix dates for the trade of goods, or, these days, for sporting events. There are authorized *toupu motor* for distinct paths, men (*motor*) with the primary right to walk on a particular path (*toup*) in order to go and see a particular group of people. If such a delegate has to be sent to the Awar for any purpose, it will always be someone of the Ndɨpɨr clan.

The allotment of areas of responsibility to the clans is a central feature of Bosmun clanship. Three clans of an association are in charge of particular traits by which they are socially labeled: there are the 'warriors' (*yepsi xonom*), the 'mediators' (*ndɨara xonom*), and the 'beggars' (*rupaama xonom*). In the past, each group was meant to regulate life within and beyond the clan-association. The beggars are of particular interest. They were allowed to challenge given norms by behaving directly in opposition to them. They had the right to claim things from others by performing *rupaam*, which literally means 'to ask for food.' As we shall see, no one in Daiden should be forced to ask for food. The beggars created noticeable turbulence when asking for food, since in doing so they pointed to a lack of food-generosity and thus sociability. Those who were confronted were required to immediately fulfill the demands of the beggars, for otherwise they were put to death. Although today no one is put to death for this, members of the beggar group continue asking for food and thus reinforce the existing cultural code of "watching others and being watched."

Finding Consent

Beyond the triad of warriors, mediators, and beggars, members of a clan consider single males to be representatives of the collective and vest them with the responsibility of channeling sociopolitical dynamics, and thus also with power. Renowned persons are referred to as *kaakos* in the vernacular. Bosmun call them *bikman* ('big man') in Tok Pisin and the English term "chief" is in use as well. I had read about nearby Manam Island chieftaincy (Lutkehaus 1995: 26–30) and I knew about Kayan chieftainship (A.T. von Poser 2008a). Therefore, I looked for possible signs of a similar system in Bosmun political life, but did not find any such signs. Instead, I learned about the mythical path of a "despotic" figure leading from the Bosmun area to Manam Island. I refer again to this path in chapter 2. Bosmun do acknowledge sociopolitical authorities that direct the flow of life more than others, but their status is neither based on hierarchy nor based on an inherited right. Sons take over responsibilities from their fathers such as guarding certain spirits, songs, magical spells, or herbal recipes important for male purification rituals. Yet, it is not automatically guaranteed that a man will co-inherit sociopolitical power as such once he becomes a guardian of customary matters. In contrast to what has been written about the political rivalries of Sepik big men (Harrison 1990; Stanek 1983: 259–274; Wassmann 1991, 2001), Bosmun big men definitely appear to be more humble. At least, the way in which they communicate their ascribed role is of a different nature. They do not show off or push themselves to the fore. I was told that big men should never make themselves more important than others. They should be modest, and being a "know-it-all" is absolutely misplaced in Bosmun ideology. A significant point is that it is others who will state that a person is or has *kaakos*. This is similar to what I have described in the Introduction about the "people looking through bamboo." *Kaakos* is not so much a formal designation as an attitude grounded in personal qualities that are regarded as fitting into the Bosmun ideal of sociable humans. Its very recognition has to grow out of an affirming majority of the societal whole and never by means of self-proclaimed reputation. The power of individuals always comprises the powers of others standing behind those individuals.

This conforms to the way in which decisions are generally made. It is unusual to be obtrusive with personal opinions. Spontaneous choices and decisions made after one round of discussion are treated as deficient in validity, and no one will actually adhere to them. The appropriate form is as follows: participants make suggestions, which then circulate for a while until a consensus emerges. This might last for hours or days or might require several gatherings over a longer period of time. This decision-making procedure is basic in the Bosmun field of political and social affairs. It is called *koku taka xorpe*, 'to find consent' (literally, *koku* means 'one,' *taka* 'to put,' and *xorpe* 'consent'). People use the term *xorpe* also to refer to the 'gathering' itself. *Koku taka xorpe* implies two facets of action: in a first step, several standpoints have to be gathered. In a second step, they are discussed in a group, the ultimate aim being the achievement of the highest possible concord. Discord, if a solution is nowhere near, is expected to cause serious harm on the long run, ranging from poor garden harvest to personal illness or death. Shared subjectivities should lead to an opinion that will appear as proper in the eyes of the societal majority.

I once attended a land dispute between two opponents, members of the same clan-association, who both claimed the ground of a man who had left the area in question in order to live elsewhere long ago and who had subsequently died. His sons had been invited to come and take part in the settling of the dispute. About twenty other men, all of the same clan-association, were also present. One of the opponents had called for an administrative official from Bogia to come and decide the matter. The official asked both opponents and the sons of the previous occupant to explain the situation. No one actually remembered to whom the former owner had ceded the ground. Therefore, the official begged the sons, who made no attempt to claim the ground for themselves, to render a decision quickly. The brothers obviously felt uncomfortable, as did the surrounding crowd. This was all happening too fast and contrasted with the Bosmun method of talking matters over. Since the official had to leave to attend to other matters on his daily schedule, the brothers agreed to come to a decision and decided somewhat tensely within minutes. Afterward, I heard people talking, saying that actually nothing had yet been decided because several other men who definitely should have attended the gathering had not been there. For this reason, they decided, the issue was still subject to negotiation. In this and other cases I realized that the opinion of the majority always determined whether decisions were held valid and that a particular case could be rethought several times depending on exactly how majority was defined.

The idea of "consent finding" does not mean that there is no competition at all in Bosmun political life. There definitely is, and it is land disputes that make up the major source of dissonance. If a man illegally claims land, he does so by occupying it step by step. Others will not prevent him right away because ancestral lore has it that people should be allowed to use others' grounds for temporary purposes, which includes the setting out of gardens. If the claimant starts planting coconut or sago palms on that soil, his formerly accepted exploitation turns into misuse because Bosmun consider this an act of infringing on enduring ties and rights to the land. While a garden lasts a season, coconut and sago palms need to grow for about ten to fifteen years. Only then is a conflict likely to arise and people will begin to talk about organizing a *xorpe,* a 'gathering,' so as to avert further damage. The most effective competitive strategy is to be noncompetitive. How much influence a political actor may exert in a *xorpe* depends on the reputation he has gained as a food provider in daily social life. Bosmun foodways could be principally rephrased as a mode of "Fighting with Food," to borrow Young's (1971) well-known title of his food-centered study about the Kalauna people of Goodenough Island in southeast Papua New Guinea. However, to "fight with food" in Daiden is not manifested in the same way as among Kalauna. There, "the general motivation of participants in *abutu* [an institutionalised form of competitive food-exchange] is the desire of each party to shame the other by giving more food than can be simultaneously paid back" (Young 1971: 208). The practice of "food-giving-to-shame," as Young (1971: 207) describes Kalauna competitive food exchanges, occurs in Daiden only in the context of adultery and as an interaction between individual rivals who might outplay one another with the staging of feasts. Apart from that, political actors basically gain power by involving themselves and their families in the daily routine of food giving, which serves to create and strengthen harmony. Indirectly, of course, food exchange is used to build up a group of political followers.

Every adult male has the right to express himself politically in the men's house. Whether he will be listened to is dependent upon whether he already has contributed gifts of cooked food to the men's house. The display of food, in turn, depends on one's kin members' willingness to support one's political endeavors. Being crucial food procurers, women also have considerable influence. Prior to voicing one's ideas in the men's house, a speaker is likely to have aired these ideas in the shared cross-gender realm of the household. Thus, the scope of a man's relationships with male and female kin has to be taken into account to understand how he may behave in the political arena. This scope is indeed large, as will be seen in the next sections, and interpersonal linkages generally aid the idea of _xorpe,_ of finding consent and thus inhibiting trouble.

Personal Kin-Ties and Ideals of Mutual Affection

Matrilateral and patrilateral kin are equally important in Daiden. All known cognates have to be respected, but it is agnatic continuity that is regarded as making up a person's individual descent, called _niŋ koku_ ('a single bottom of a tree'). Men are said to be rooted in the soil whereas women are compared to flying foxes. Correspondingly, land is passed on from the father to the eldest of his sons, who is expected to redistribute parts of the inherited land righteously among himself and his younger brothers. It is also men who dig into the ground to erect platforms. Women move between these platforms, and they are said not to possess land since they can easily move as flying foxes do. But they do have certain rights of access to and use of particular land tracts, that is, primarily sago and coconut areas, which are either planted for them or given to them. In general, mothers hand over those rights only to their daughters and nobody else is allowed to benefit without permission. Interestingly, no one will reveal this in response to a question about the rules of land utilization. It is another matter when one actually traverses the land. On one of our walks, a male companion suddenly stopped and, while pointing to about ten almost full-grown sago palms, he started to explain to me (as I later noted from memory):

> K.: *Em ya, yu lukluk ya! Em mipela kamap long tais saksak bilong mama bilong mi nau!*
>
> A.: *Olsem wanem? Tais saksak bilong mama bilong yu? Ating, em bilong ol man, o?*
>
> K.: *Ya! Tasol saksak ya, em bilong mama bilong mi. Nogat man bai kam kisim.*

A.: *Olsem wanem?*

K.: *I no narapela bai kisim. Em mama bilong mi tasol.*

A.: *Na taim mama bilong yu i dai? Husait bai kisim?*

K.: *Em bai susa bilong mi. Mama bai givim go long susa bilong mi!*

A.: *I no yu o brata bilong yu?*

K.: *Nogat!*

A.: *Na husait givim tais saksak i go long mama bilong yu?*

K.: *Em mas mama bilong em.*

(K.: There, look at that! We now have arrived at the sago swamp area that belongs to my mother.

A.: How is that possible? Are you sure that this sago swamp belongs to your mother? I thought it belonged to men only.

K.: Yes! But this sago swamp is my mother's. No one else is going to claim it.

A.: How is that possible?

K.: No one else can claim it. It belongs to my mother.

A.: And what happens when your mother dies? Who will it go to?

K.: It will go to my sister. My mother will pass it on to my sister!

A.: Not to you or your brother?

K.: No!

A.: And who passed the sago swamp on to your mother?

K.: It must have been her mother.)

This, however, does not imply a constant passing-on via a female line as would be the case with a patrilineal legacy. Women might achieve such rights on a more individual basis. The same applies to men, apart from their fathers' bequests. According to customary law, a person can receive areas with coconut palms or sago palms as a gift of appreciation if he or she has provided some sort of social assistance, like caring for a sick relative or helping in burial procedures. Such areas might be replanted again and passed on to direct descendants, or they might be donated in the way already explained. But in a changing world, referred to as *taim bilong gridi pasin* ('time of greediness') by my consociates, this practice has started to be abandoned.

Patrilineal affiliation applies to all children except for the firstborn. The firstborn child is considered to be the first step in strengthening the bond between spouses because he or she serves as a sign of their sexual productivity and economic cooperation. A procreative and work-related efficiency enables spouses to behave properly within the given template of food-related practices. Each couple's first child is subject to the practice of *roosiŋgar.* That is, a firstborn is given back to the mother's parents so as to replace her. Bosmun do not apply a bridewealth system with large-scale transactions of wealth items like pigs, shells, and other objects representing some sort of affluence, as is the case in other parts of Papua New Guinea (Keck 2005: 35–47; Sillitoe 1998: 93–97). Instead, the firstborn child him- or herself becomes the gift to be bestowed upon the bride's patrilateral kin-group.

Bosmun prescriptions for marriage are neither exogamous nor endogamous with regard to moiety and clan. A man refers to his wife and to his wife's sisters (who are seen as a man's most suitable partners if his wife dies) as *mes* (generically: 'woman / female'). A woman refers to her husband and to her husband's brothers (most suitable partners if her husband dies) as *kaŋgat.* The only strict precept to be kept is that alliances between Ego and his or her second cousins (PPGCC)—or *seken kasen* as Bosmun call them in Tok Pisin—are not tolerated. The kinship diagram (see figure 1.5) shows all second cousins of Ego (the local terms are given later). This kin-relation outlines the realm of those people who are never to be considered conjugal partners. Ego's second cousins define the borders of one's recognized kindred. Only the children of Ego and his or her second cousins are allowed to intermarry. Ideally, brothers marry women who are sisters, or a man marries a woman whose brother will marry the man's sister.

Most of the men who spoke with me disliked the idea of letting their sisters and daughters find a groom outside their own sociocultural and spatial boundaries, although this is not forbidden. Men might find their women from outside, but letting sisters go and live too far away does not suit the special emphasis given to the relationship between opposite-sex siblings. As one father told me, he would allow his daughter to marry a non-Bosmun man because a man coming from outside would never be that jealous about the daughter's earlier male friends. A local husband definitely would be, since he certainly knew about the girl's *mian,* which is the period of pubescent moods and sexual awakening. The father would have to give this man some land in order to tie him down locally, preventing him from moving elsewhere and taking the daughter away. The father's life story showed that many of his sisters had died and, although he was not very old, only about fifty-five years, he seemed older than other men of the same age group. His intent to keep his daughter within reach was also linked to the wish to maintain his sons' social and emotional sources of stability. Indeed, Bosmun sisters and brothers share a special relationship. Lutkehaus (1995: 251) notes that cross-sex siblingship among Manam Islanders is "based upon complementarity opposition and the necessary affinity between male and female." This also applies to the Bosmun context of brother-sister relations. Brother and sister, *nduaŋ* and *mbi* as they call one another, ideally bear a relation marked by a deep certainty that they can trust

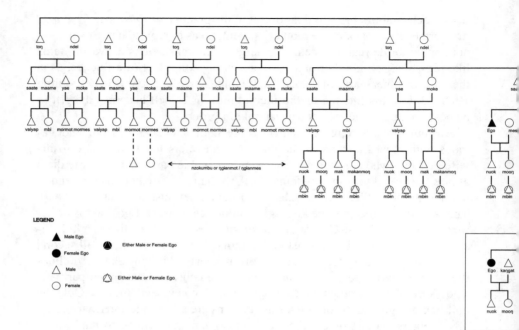

Figure 1.5: Kinship Diagram.

each other and always rely on one another. They protect and help each other in many respects, and as they assist each other during life, their children are expected to assist each other in the burial of the deceased parent. As a rule, the corpse of a man is buried by his sister's children whereas the corpse of a woman is buried by her brother's children. As a form of appreciation, the party who buried the corpse will eventually receive huge gifts of dry sago from the deceased's children (see figure 1.6).

The importance and intensity of the brother-sister pair is also encoded in Bosmun dance (see figure 1.7). The performance that I saw at one festivity in 2005 depicts a brother protecting his sister from her enraged husband. Siblings-in-law call each other *ndakanmot* (for males) and *ndakanmes* (for females). A brother will always have a close look at his sister's husband and a sister will do the same with her brother's wife. Ideally, spouses also engage in trustful and considerate relations. Yet, unlike spouses, brothers and sisters are said to never betray each other. They are matching parts of a dual harmony. Sibling rivalry does occur, but rather between same-sex siblings. There might be discord between brothers and sisters, but if this happens it is a serious conflict, as I once witnessed. A man wanted to marry a woman from another language group. His sister was opposed to it since both sides had been involved in a land dispute that went on for years. Whenever I saw the siblings meet by

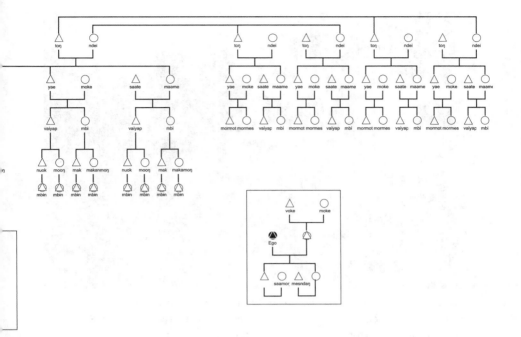

Figure 1.6: Preparing a Gift of Sago. Nzu (left) and members of his family prepare a gift of sago for kin who helped in a burial.

Figure 1.7: "A Brother Protects His Sister." Dance performance of a brother (performed by Yaasok in the middle) who protects his sister (performed by Sani) from her husband (performed by Mbobot), who wants to beat her.

chance, the sister would murmur repetitively: *Yu nogat graun, yu nogat tais saksak, yu nogat kaikai* ('You do not possess any ground, you do not possess any sago swamp, you have no food'). She insisted on rejecting the woman, and the conflict went on for months until the man finally yielded to his sister's counterarguments.

There are indeed many kin who have the right to a say in such matters. As the inventory of Bosmun kinship terminology indicates, the actual scope of who is to be counted as Ego's parents, children, and siblings exceeds the sphere of a nuclear family. When I thought about my adoption, I realized that suddenly there were several mothers and fathers and dozens of siblings to whom I was related. I had even become a classificatory mother to a lot of children. A brief outline provides the basic frame. Visually, my kinship diagram serves this purpose (see figure 1.5).

The term *maame* refers to Ego's biological mother and his or her classificatory mothers (MZ, MPGD, FBW, and FPGSW). Similarly, the term *saate* refers to Ego's biological father and his or her classificatory fathers (FB, FPGS, MZH, and MPGDH). Ego's parents' parents as well as the parents' parents' siblings and their partners are called *ndei* (for females) and *toŋ* (for males).

The term *yae* refers to Ego's mother's brother (MB), certain maternal cousins (MPGS), and paternal in-laws (FZH and FPGDH). The term *moke* refers to Ego's father's sister (FZ), certain paternal cousins (FPGD), and maternal in-laws (MBW and MPGSW). *Moke* is also used to refer to Ego's mother-in-law, whereas *voke* addresses Ego's father-in-law. The son-in-law is called *mesndaŋ,* the daughter-in-law *saamoŋ.* Ego refers to the partners of his or her classificatory children in the same way.

Ego's children are called *nuok* (S) and *mooŋ* (D). Male Ego uses *nuok* also to refer to specific nephews (BS, FGSS, and MGSS), and *mooŋ* to refer to specific nieces (BD, FGSD, and MGSD). Similarly, female Ego uses *nuok* to refer to a group of her nephews (ZS, MGDS, and FGDS), and *mooŋ* for a group of her nieces (ZD, MGDD, and FGDD). In both cases, the focus in Ego's generational level is on the same sex. Opposite-sex siblings and first cousins (osPGC) call each other's male children *mak* and female children *makanmoŋ.* Ego's biological and classificatory children's children are all called *mbin,* regardless of their sex.

Adoptions are common and traverse all the genealogies that I collected. Each couple has one or more adopted children formally referred to as *ŋgaŋgir.* Not only do couples have the right to adopt, but a single person is likewise allowed to care for a child. Usually, the adopted child belongs to the realm of the adoptive parents' biological or classificatory kin, so the biological parents normally do not refuse to accept a relative's wish to take one of their children. However, if they see over the years that their child is not being brought up properly, they have the right and duty to take him or her back. Adopted children should receive care equal to that of a couple's biological children. The term *ŋgaŋgir* is not a term of address. Adopted children are called either *nuok* ('son') or *mooŋ* ('daughter'). Two aspects are salient in the Bosmun scheme of adoption. First, there is no one-sided preference for either boys or girls. Instead, a couple seeks to balance the genders of its children by adopting a girl if there is only a son and vice versa. Each child should have an opposite-sex counterpart. Gender complementarity is significant with regard to the local mode of sago making. Prior to marriage, one's collaborators in sago making are usually one's opposite-sex siblings. Second, as the genealogies that I recorded show, it is frequently the case that a man adopts his sister's child. It might be the first-born child who has to return to the parents of the female spouse, but a man is likely to adopt more of his sister's children. Thus, a woman hands over a good number of her own biological offspring to her brothers and instead brings up her husband's sister's children. Yet, to take this as an underlying principle in Bosmun adoption would lead to an overgeneralization since there are other cases of adoption that are structured differently. For example, women do adopt their sisters' children and men take their brothers' children too.

However, a man's sister's child is his most beloved. This child is the one who carries the same *nimbit,* the same 'blood.' In order to illustrate this particular bond, I shall briefly describe the former Bosmun practice of challenging rivals before I structurally outline the field of one's siblings. This description is based on the particular account of one of my male interviewees and some of the issues touched on in this account were later checked for verification in conversations with other men and women. My interviewee explained that, by committing adultery, a woman would create a lifelong enmity between her husband and his rival. Similarly, a man could cause trouble by engaging in affairs, although his wife and her rival would meet in less formal ways than male rivals. They would meet in order to fight until one of them became tired of challenging the other or of being the target of the challenge herself. Men, however, had to meet on a more formal level of rivalry. An enmity between a man and his wife's lover was going to end only with an act of blood revenge, given that neither of the opponents was to lose their pride. The betrayed party had to challenge his rival in different ways so that suffering on both sides would be equalized. As a first step, the betrayed person would hold a feast. Holding a feast in the Bosmun manner is always linked to the display of ample food, which, as said earlier, requires great effort and the involvement of many helping hands. The challengee, attempting to defend his discredited pride, would have to beat the feast by holding a better one. Subsequently, there might be further steps of provocation, such as building a house or a canoe, which the adulterer would have to outdo. The biggest challenge, undoubtedly, was for the betrayed to kill his own sister's child. To sacrifice one's own sister's child sounded like a paradox to me, but it was explained to me that, in so doing, the betrayed would, in fact, deprive not only himself but above all his rival of his greatest treasure. For, the rival would have to emulate this deed. By sacrificing his sister's child, a man was believed to demonstrate the deepest respect toward her, for he himself was the one who was thought of as being most upset and wounded, having lost what was most valuable to him. After that, satisfaction was considered to have been obtained. The last such rival challenge, taught to be "immoral" by missionaries, is said to have happened during the lives of my informants' parents' parents.

Returning to the kinship diagram that accompanies my description, we see that female Ego calls her biological and classificatory brothers (B, FGS, and MGS) *nduaŋ*. Male Ego calls his biological and classificatory sisters (Z, FGD, and MGD) *mbi*. Same-sex biological and classificatory siblings call each other *vaiyap*. If there is a need to differentiate by age, Ego will call his or her elder same-sex sibling *vai,* the younger one *yap* (the term *vai* means also 'to hear / to listen'). *Vai* and *yap* can also be added as suffixes to the terms for opposite-sex siblings, if age difference is in question. A woman explained to me that, when asked about the sequence of giving birth to children, people choose a phrase that draws on practical experience. They usually say: "A. grabbed B.'s leg and B. grabbed C.'s leg and C. grabbed D.'s leg" and so forth. It is always the younger sibling who holds onto the leg of the older one. Proximity between biological siblings is recognized and expressed through the fact that they receive food from the same hearth, whereas classificatory siblings (PGC), first cousins as it were, receive food from other, though related, households. Emotionally, these classificatory siblings are almost as close as biological siblings. They stay strongly connected as long as their parents engage in constant exchanges of cooked food.

The terms *vaiyap* and *nduaŋ* / *mbi* are also used to refer to those second cousins of Ego who are the parents' same-sex cousins' children. Female Ego's *vaiyap* are FPGSD and MPGDD and her *nduaŋ* are FPGSS and MPGDS. Male Ego's *vaiyap* are FPGSS and MPGDS and his *mbi* are FPGSD and MP-GDD. The terms are the same as for closer kin, but it is through different social agency that genealogical proximity or distance is expressed. Regular, mutual food exchange that stands for emotional closeness marks relatives tied more closely in terms of genealogical linkage, whereas less frequent food exchange signifies the relationships with the linguistically identical yet genealogically more distant kin. To simplify matters, I refer to the *vaiyap* and *nduaŋ* / *mbi* kin constellation as "second cousins 1" in the following. Different social agency, including different social obligations, is also what differentiates "second cousins 1" from what I call "second cousins 2," who are Ego's parents' opposite-sex cousins' children (FPGDC and MPGSC). The local language term for this kin constellation is *mor* (*mormot* for males, *mormes* for females). Certain social expectations, rights, and duties connect Ego with his or her "second cousins 1" and "second cousins 2."

All second cousins are expected to show particular concern and respect for one another at all times. Apart from maintaining amiable ties in general, Ego is particularly obliged to take responsibility once a "second cousin 1" has died. Ego has the right to decide what will happen to the deceased's spouse, for example how the spouse should mourn or who or whether he or she should remarry at all after the end of the mourning period. A person should thus always attempt to be on good terms with his or her spouse's "second cousins 1" since one day these may wield considerable power over them—in positive or negative ways. They may "punish" a person by, for example, prolonging the bereaved's period of in-house mourning or they might be benign in shortening it. They will decide in the name of their deceased "second cousin 1."

A person should also be on good terms with his or her spouse's "second cousins 2." These take responsibility for one another in the following way: Ego has the right and the obligation to confront the spouses of his or her "second cousins 2" with jokes. These jokes are of a sort that normally would be regarded as offensive and disrespectful. I have decided to classify this relationship as a Bosmun variant of what is known as a "joking relationship" (Radcliffe-Brown 1940). According to Radcliffe-Brown, there are joking relationships of symmetrical and asymmetrical quality:

What is meant by the term "joking relationship" is a relation between two persons in which one is by custom permitted, and in some instances required, to tease or make fun of the other, who in turn is required to take no offence. It is important to distinguish two main varieties. In one the relation is symmetrical; each of the two persons teases or makes fun of the other. In the other variety the relation is asymmetrical; A jokes at the expense of B and B accepts the teasing good humouredly but without retaliating; or A teases B as much as he pleases and B in return teases A only a little. (1940: 195)

Bosmun engage in symmetrical joking relationships, although there is no immediate retaliation by the person teased. He or she has to tolerate the joking at first. Later, however, the person is expected to return disrespect of equal proportions. Thus, the roles of teaser and teased switch regularly. Moderate behavior and demonstration of shame usually define Ego's relations to close in-laws, whether to the spouse's parents, the spouse's siblings, or children's spouses. This is done in a reciprocal way. But with in-laws of more distant relatives it is reversed. They mutually engage in *ndombok,* which in general refers to the activity of playing and fooling around. They are allowed to deride one another in simple ways and likewise might present each other serious challenges. Assaults toward in-laws are pre-eminently verbal. Sometimes they are physical, but they are never really violent. To tease the spouse of a "second cousin 2" is a formalized way to either maintain or improve the social status of "second cousin 2." One time, a "second cousin 2" (MFBSD) of my adoptive father joined us while we had a conversation. As she sat down, she said to him: "I heard your wife ate too much fish and now she is likely to choke because of too many bones in her throat." Since I did not know about this kind of joking then, I jumped up in terror and wanted to run over to her. As they realized that I thought this was true, they started to laugh and cleared up my confusion by explaining that this was just a joke. Other similar instances have taught me that this was more than a joke. The woman's statement was an indirect critical reminder to my adoptive mother who, of course, would later be told what had been said about her. In pointing out the overconsumption of fish, she was giving advice to not become selfish. In another situation, I came to witness how two women, related in a joking relation, danced together during a feast. I had been informed that one of them was going to tease the other. Everyone knew except the victim. The peak in a series of tortures was obviously when the woman showered her victim with a huge amount of foul fish-muck. Those who circled immediately around the two particular dancers, including myself, could hardly stand the penetrating smell. The offended, however, took it with apparent tranquility—well knowing that her time of tit-for-tat would come. A third example shows how far the sphere of influence between "second cousins 2" extends. A man once took up one of his wife's relative's challenges. While building a canoe, the "second cousin 2" of his wife encouraged the man to build a canoe as well. For, if he could not build a canoe, the wife's "second cousin 2" remarked, how should he be able to erect a proper house for his wife and their children? In the end, the man started immediately to erect a new house for his wife. By means of a joke, the "second cousin 2" had been able to enhance the woman's social reputation. She in turn would find a similar way to appreciate her relative's support.

The last relationship to be discussed is the relationship between the children of the "second cousins 2." The children of all second cousins are allowed to intermarry. If the children of "second cousins 1" do not intermarry, which would renew the bond in yet a different way by turning them into spouses and thus into originators of a new family, the once existing kinship tie becomes completely "forgotten." This is different from what happens if the children of "second cousins 2" do not intermarry. Their relationship turns into a type of formalized friendship. Children of "second cousins 2" call each other either *nzokumbu* or *ngianmot* (for males) and *ngianmes* (for females) until their descendants, in turn, decide to intermarry. Only then does this particular relationship come to an end. Bosmun also use the Tok Pisin term *poro* ('friend') to denote people connected in this way. Therefore, I translate it as 'friend.' A 'friend' called *nzokumbu* always belongs to the same moiety (either to the same or the other clan-association). A 'friend' called *ngianmot* / *ngianmes* belongs to the opposite moiety. "Friends" are expected to encounter one another in respectful ways. They must not yell at each other, and they must not fight with each other. Most interestingly, "friends" are expected to share feeling states. In order to be able to empathize with the other, they should imitate the other's fortunes and misfortunes that might happen. If a "friend" suddenly has been caught in rain during a walk, the counterpart also has to get soaked with rain. If a "friend's" tools get broken, the other has to destroy his or her own tools too. Even if someone would break a leg, I was told, a "friend" would be bound to feel pain; although nobody would really expect him or her to break his or her leg, some sort of physical self-torture would be expected. Once, a man got drunk and tumbled over muddy ground while spectators gathered together and started to laugh. His "friend" had no choice. He had to emulate this deed and carry the burden of being laughed at by others although he had been sober. Another man told me that if his "friend" would beat his wife, he would have to beat his own wife and, of course, he would have to deal with the consequences. If a "friend" dies, I was told, it will be the counterpart who will join the widow or widower most often during the mourning period. A "friend" of the same sex as the widow or widower might also come and stay with her or him for the whole period of mourning. "Friends" who fail to respond in the ways described have to provide their counterparts with huge gifts of food. This type of relationship is indeed a critical ethical reminder: everyone should have an empathetic counterperson. It encodes an ideal of mutual affection and empathy that is at the core of Bosmun personhood.

Prospect

In my synopsis of the possible constellations of relatedness in Daiden, I have given some initial clues as to the role of food in marking social relationships. I noted that kin-ties in Daiden may be reckoned because people know their ancestors shared food. I relayed the story of a conflict grounded in the inappropriate distribution of food. I discussed the group of the beggars who, in "asking for food," cause awkward situations. I mentioned the case of the woman who insulted her brother by saying "You have no food!" and another case in which a woman was reminded "not to eat too much fish." In order to facilitate a thorough understanding of all this, I now turn to the deeper meanings of sago in the Bosmun universe. As noted above, people heavily rely on sago; it is the staple diet in this part of Papua New Guinea. Remarkably, though, no one is allowed to eat the sago extracted from the palms he or she plants him- or herself. Due to this law, complex food exchanges among kin have to be accomplished; we might call these "moral foodways."

Notes

1. The original source in German is:
   24. Oktober. Der Manam [Vulkaninsel] ist auf der Fahrt häufig sichtbar.... Wir fahren an vielen Pflanzungen, einigen Dörfern und an einem neu angelegten Platz vorbei. Hier haben die Leute schon sehr lange Einbäume.... Der Bootsrand ist reich geschnitzt. Auch tragen die Leute bereits den Kopfaufsatz, der für die Küstenstämme und den unteren Sepik eigentümlich ist.... Wir treffen viele Kanus an, kleine Kokospalmen und einfache Häuser. Der Wald ist schwach und weist viele Grasflecken auf.... Mittags setzt sehr starker Wind ein.... Der Manam steht noch über dem Walde. Von dem Winde ist der Ramu stark wellig, sogar schaumige Wellenköpfe erheben sich.... Um 12 Uhr machen wir Lager an einem trockenen Sagosumpf. Die Eingeborenen scheinen hier dauernd Sagowaschplätze zu unterhalten. ... Nachmittags treiben Eingeborene, die offenbar einen neuen Platz gründen, vielleicht zu dem heute berührten ziehen, im Kanu vorbei. Im Ramu gibt es hier viel Flußmuscheln (Anodonta sp.), die von den Trägern eifrig gesammelt, gekocht und gegessen werden.... 25.Oktober. Der Manam steht gerade vor uns. Nachts konnte man den Feuerschein wahrnehmen. Den ganzen Tag wird Sago gewaschen. Leute aus den umliegenden Dörfern besuchen uns. Sie bringen einige Kokosnüsse. Sie tragen gute Lendentücher aus Rindenstoff und rot gefärbte Rotanggürtel. (Gehrmann 1916: 29)
2. A tragic and devastating eruption occurred during my first visit in 2004/05. Manam volcano erupted several times and forced its population to take refuge in emergency camps along the mainland coast. In 2010, the island was still said to be uninhabited.

On our PMV rides from the Ramu to Madang and back, we would pass these camps. The camps were erected right in between former, quickly cleared-up coconut plantations. Eruptive activity reached the Bosmun area, too: ashes trickled down a couple of times about three to four weeks apart and covered every surface in Daiden and the surrounding environment.

3. The original source in German is:

Aus Kaiser Wilhelmsland, Mündung des Ramuflusses, wird berichtet: Im Februar d. Js. brachten die Häuptlinge der Dörfer Buschmann [Bosmun], Margnitsch [Marangis], Borbor [Bodbod] und Kajan [Kayan] der Polizeibehörde Folgendes zur Anzeige: Im November 1897 kam in einem kleinen Flußkanu ein völlig nackter, unbewaffneter Europäer den Ramu herabgefahren und landete auf Winken der Tamuls [eine wahrscheinlich pejorative Bezeichnung für die lokale Bevölkerung] des etwa acht Meilen stromauf am Ramu gelegenen Dorfes Buschmann bei diesem Ort. Er fand gute Aufnahme; die Tamuls gaben ihm zu essen und einen Schurz als Kleidung. Er blieb etwa einen Monat in Buschmann und wandte sich dann, von den Tamuls geleitet, nach dem Dorfe Marg [Marangis] auf der Venusspitze. Hier blieb er etwa zwei Monate (Dezember 1897 und Januar 1898). Sodann wanderte er an der Küste in südöstlicher Richtung weiter und kam nach Barbor [Bodbod], wo er gleich gute Aufnahme fand wie in Margnitsch. Die Tamuls hatten ihn gebeten, bei ihnen zu bleiben, da sie viel von ihm lernten; sie betrachteten ihn seiner weißen Haut wegen als etwas Uebernatürliches, was auch der Name, den sie ihm gegeben hatten, „Barr", d.h. die Sonne, andeutet. Er blieb aber nicht und wanderte weiter über Kajan nach Bodian (Platz auf einer kleinen Insel an der Küste). Dort in Bodian hat er, anscheinend auf gewaltsame Weise, im Februar 1898 den Tod gefunden. Ueber seine Nationalität konnte nichts festgestellt werden, da die Tamuls kein Wort, das er häufiger gebraucht hätte, behalten haben. Es scheint, als ob es ein australischer Goldsucher gewesen ist, der sich von Britisch Neu-Guinea, dem Laufe des Ramu folgend, nach hier durchgeschlagen hat. (Anonymous 1899: 565)

4. The original source in German is:

Der vorletzte Pfosten … zeigt auf dem unteren Teil unterhalb der Fransen und Muscheln eine eingeschnitzte menschliche Figur, deren Gesichtsbildung nicht in den gewohnten Rahmen des hier herrschenden Kunststiles passen will. Die Bosngun-Leute [Bosmun] erklärten dazu, das solle einen bestimmten Weißen (Engländer) darstellen, der als Händler und Boy-Anwerber den Bosngun bekannt und irgendwie sympathisch war. … Wollte man etwa die Zauberkraft dieses bewunderten Engländers durch die Darstellung ins Geisterhaus bannen? (Höltker 1966: 32)

5. *Walkabout* is a journal in which Australian patriotism was promoted for over forty years and in which writers "frequently depicted the dependent territories as possessions benefiting from benign colonial rule" (Quanchi 2003: 77).

6. Höltker, too, had problems understanding Bosmun myths with regard to their location in actual space. He wondered about another myth (Höltker 1966: 37–39), which tells about a voyage to and from Manam via the sea, making him doubt whether it was a Bosmun myth at all:

One is inclined to believe—of course, it is too early to prove it—that this Bosngun version is not meant to be at home here but rather at the coast or on Manam. Mostly, the traffic between the villages of the Bosngun is indeed along the Mbur River, but the canoes of the Bosngun have no outriggers. Thus, one may use them to travel the Mbur and Ramu downstream to the sea but not over the open sea to Manam (volcanic island). (Höltker 1966: 37; my translation)

The original source in German is:

Man möchte fast glauben—noch ist es zu früh, es beweisen zu wollen –, diese Bosngun-Version wäre gar nicht hier, sondern eher an der Küste oder auf Manam zu Hause. Zwar wählt der Verkehr zwischen den Bosngun-Dörfern unter sich meistens den Wasserweg auf dem Mbur-Fluß, aber die Kanu der Bosngun besitzen keine Ausleger. Man kann also auf ihnen wohl Mbur und Ramu abwärts rudern bis ans Meer, aber nicht auf die offene See hinaus bis nach Manam (Vulkaninsel). (Höltker 1966: 37)

Indeed, there is archaeological evidence to support several local myths prefiguring the existence of a seascape (Fairbairn & Swadling 2005; Swadling 1990, 1997; Swadling et al. 1988; Swadling & Hide 2005), making it possible to think that the myths' references to a seascape reflect actual geological history (see Barber & Barber 2004). Using radiocarbon dating techniques, archaeologists have shown that the entire region of the Sepik-Ramu Basin was once a large inland sea with only one plateau in between, which is the place where Bosmun have always lived. Archaeologists have called it the "Bosmun Plateau" (Swadling et al. 1988: 15). Due to distribution patterns of historic stone mortars and pestles found in excavations, the shore inhabitants of this inland sea must have "played a pivotal role for much of the early to mid-Holocene prehistory of Melanesia" (Swadling & Hide 2005: 289). The inland sea reached its greatest size about 6,500 to 7,500 years ago. Swadling et al. (1988: 14–15) have mapped both the Sepik-Ramu coastline as it was in existence 6,000 years ago along with today's coastline, thus matching what I had to imagine while listening to Bosmun mythical narratives.

7. Traditionally, a personal name was given to a single living person only. Due to the increasing population, families no longer have enough traditional names to go around. I was also given a local personal name. Yet, I learned that I was actually "Sapok junior," since another woman already possessed that name. With my arrival, she turned into "Sapok senior." To a certain extent, "junior" and "senior" are becoming add-ons to personal names in general.

8. When the Awar broke up and left, Bosmun renamed them Mianzen. Höltker refers to it as "Morzan" (1964: 37). The term's literal meaning remains unclear. Based on what I observed, Bosmun have a habit of applying vowels differently depending on context and speaker. Accordingly, it might be the case that *mian* comes from *muon (mbaŋ)* meaning 'other / opposite (side).' This in turn would be a hint to the dislocation that occurred in the more distant past.

⊰ Chapter Two ⊱
The Sago Spirit's Legacy and Bosmun Sociality

More than fifty years ago, the growing of rice was a major agricultural aim of the colonial administration in the Lower Ramu / Hansa Bay area. In 1957, a patrol officer stated: "The goal to aim for would be the gradual divorcing of the people away from the traditional staple of sago and replacing it with rice and other root grobs [sic] as it is obvious that the land will lend itself to this" (Johnston 1957). Except for one tiny rice-growing region, I never saw rice fields around Daiden or on my travels to and from the Bosmun area. The 1996 *Madang Resource Atlas* (Boskovic 1996) indicates that there is rice grown as a cash crop in the area but that this is further up the Ramu River beyond Bosmun country. I also never heard people talking much about the growing of rice. The patrol officer's proposed "divorcing" away from sago never took place.

As this and the following chapters illustrate, this kind of divorcing would have meant erasing an entire sociocultural cosmos. In this chapter in particular, I show how people in Daiden conceptualize sago palms and how the planting, procuring, and sharing of sago are constitutive of Bosmun relatedness across gender and age. In suggesting that Bosmun correlate the growth of sago palms with the growth of human bodies, the power of sharing sago in the creation of relationships and in the definition of well-being should become comprehensible. People's foodways are also constitutive of personal identities. People are known by others through their food-related behaviors and the unique social networks they individually build during their lives. Furthermore, I show how kin-ties are reaffirmed or severed. In this context, I introduce prevalent food-related idioms of moral content such as "the broken spoon," "the face covered by spoiled sago," and the habit of "eating in secret." Moreover, I show that certain questions should not be raised if one does not want to spoil a relationship. Finally, in paying closer attention to the regular shifting of food in Daiden, I argue that the taste of food in Bosmun cuisine is mainly to be understood in social terms.

A Sagoscape of Regret and Generosity

The first time I went to see how sago is processed, I caught sight of an action that certainly would have escaped my attention if I had listened only to

people's technical descriptions of how sago starch is obtained. I do not remember people bringing this action up by themselves in our early conversations; I heard about it only later, when I explicitly asked that interviewees
would go into detail about it. What I observed was only a small enactment,
but it directed me toward a narrative about the spirit of the sago palm called
veesenyeroŋ. Compared to other Bosmun myths, this story is lacking in length
and detail. Nonetheless, it is among the most important when it comes to
tracing their unique understanding of sociality. It tells about how this spirit
brought "real sago" to humans and how humans were taught about the moral
value of this food and about generosity.

While I lazed about with my adoptive sister, our sister-in-law, and a daughter of another sister of ours, enjoying a watermelon from which we put parts
aside for our brothers who were still engaged in their work, I saw the following: a second before the trunk of the palm fell, one of our brothers jumped
up, took his machete, and ran over to where the top of the palm came down.
There, he immediately lifted the machete and hit some of the top leaves. He
realized that I was looking at him in wonder and he explained to me: *Nogut
nyeroŋ bilong saksak bai ronowe!* ('This is just to prevent the sago spirit from
escaping!').

I had heard the term *nyeroŋ,* or *ndom* as people call it alternatively, in exploring present and ancestral notions about how humans are composed physically, mentally, and spiritually. *Nyeroŋ* is a non-solid or spiritual entity that
becomes visible only in the shadow of solid substances, including the shadow
of the human body. It is a life-generating force, which is necessary for both
human bodies and sago palms to exist and to develop properly. This largely
imperceptible yet sentient energy is not located within sago palms and human
bodies but connects to them from outside. Sago palms are enclosed by *nyeroŋ*
in the same way that human bodies are. *Nyeroŋ* could be imagined as a surrounding frame of energy or as a second invisible layer of skin, enclosing the
visible skin (*nit*). One of my interviewees explained it to me in the following
way: *Nyeroŋ … em save karamapim bodi bilong man kain olsem … trausis
wantaim singlis i save karamapim bodi. Dispela nyeroŋ i save karim dispela
bikpela bodi wokabaut.* ('The spiritual entity … it covers the human body like
… trousers and shirt do. This spiritual entity carries this big body around.')

I was also told that without *nyeroŋ,* the body remains a sick, lifeless, in-
sensible corpse. The body is called *vumbusak. Vumbu* literally means 'ill' (and
in a second sense 'the solid edge of something'), and *sak* means 'flesh.' If the
life-energy disappears, never to return, corporeal death will eventually occur.
A person's *nyeroŋ* never disappears into nothing. It leaves the body but stays
spiritually among the living, that is, among embodied persons. Once disembodied, it is called *ndom*.[1] A sago palm is said to need this energy, too. If the
sago's energy escapes prior to the scraping of the pith, its starch becomes ined-

ible. In hitting the palm's top, our brother built up a barrier to keep the trunk spiritually intact. Once the spirit is freed from its bottom, which happens when the trunk is cut down, it is able to—and tends to—escape. Thus, every time it has to be stopped. The sago spirit's attempts to flee are a constant reminder of how people originally received what Bosmun classify as 'real sago' (*vees*)—a process that relates to the story to which I turn now. Its message substantially permeates Bosmun life, as will become evident in my subsequent analysis.

Yesi's Gift and the People's Burden

At some point in mythical time and space, real sago emerged. Prior to that, people's diet relied on a starch food of lesser quality that originated from a different palm tree known as *neŋ*. The new palm type, which was to become genuine sago, grew on the ground in the yard of an old woman called Yesi. Thorns that occur on the leaf base of certain sago palm types had broken through the soil. Since Yesi did not know what they were, she hid them at first. When the palm had grown to considerable size, she asked Sani, her son, to cut it down to find out what the plant could be used for. When Sani was about to cut the log, a huge mass of sago starch suddenly poured out of it. It was the sago starch that people obtain now by scraping and rinsing the pith, a malleable substance ready to be stirred with hot water. When Yesi tasted it, she became aware that she had received an enormous gift. It was a gift offered by the spirit who guarded the unfamiliar shrub. Without any physical exertion, her house had become loaded with food. She was so delighted with the palm's generosity that she started to distribute seeds of the shrub among all the people she knew. She thought that everyone should benefit from the sago spirit's kindness. Everyone appreciated Yesi's offering, and due to her sharing the progeny of the shrub, huge sago swamp areas emerged.

However, these were not the swamps as they exist today, and people still did not know about the spirit's true nature. Another event had to follow:

People were not aware of why it was old Yesi who was first given the gift of starch, until the day a man called Nimbu cut down his palm with the assistance of his wife and their daughter. While helping her mother to collect the starch, the daughter stepped over the log inadvertently. She was menstruating but had no idea that she was about to offend the spirit by exposing her menstruation in the way she did. Noticing the girl's physical state, the sago spirit felt deeply humiliated and thus turned into a lizard so as to hide and flee. However, Nimbu and his family caught the lizard and finally consumed it. Once the lizard (the spirit's disguise) had been eaten, the paste-like substance that usually poured out of the sago trunk in abundance became entirely solidified. If people were to obtain the starch now, it would have to be under laborious conditions. They had to extract it by scraping and leaching the pith. Yesi's gift had turned into a burden, and henceforth people were to follow strict rules for how to treat sago palms. This was what Yesi was told when the spirit appeared in her dreams. She was also told that from now on the spirit was going to reproduce and manifest itself as wild sago (*mbu*) only, and if people wished to base their staple diet on the food-starch he had given them initially, men and women would have to plant it! The huge amounts of sago that people once had received generously were now only to be achieved through hard work and in a respectful way. People were allowed to continue to obtain starch from wild-growing sago. Wild sago, however, would always produce less starch than planted sago regardless of how hard people worked. Only planted sago areas would offer people ample starch, and in order to guarantee that generosity would continue, the spirit gave Yesi particular commands. Above all, the spirit commanded that no one, neither man nor woman, was permitted to eat the sago that was extracted from the palms one had planted with one's own hands. Nor was any material to be taken from self-planted palms to craft items for one's own use. If a person disobeyed this law, he or she would eventually become blind.

As we will see later, the spirit's reaction to the girl's unintended insult is significant in relation to Bosmun body and gender configurations, although it is not the only myth that highlights a masculine fear of menstrual blood. A number of narratives do so. What makes this story particularly important is that it tells how humans developed a sociomoral and emotional attitude toward sago and sago making. What the spirit in fact did, was to create a sagoscape of moral content—by turning his initial gift into a burden for humankind. The spirit's legacy is prevalent throughout the land. It is also inherent in people's reflections on life and interpersonal conduct.

In chapter 1, I mentioned that Bosmun differentiate between *osnis* and *raarŋaosnis,* human-made (planted) and spiritually empowered (wild-grow-ing) sago areas. In traversing the territories they call their own, Bosmun actu-ally traverse a symbolic space imbued with mythical meaning. Since, seen through a local lens, swamps encode one of the most fundamental morals, they conceptually may be called a "sagoscape." In the anthropological literature on "space" and "place," the idiom of "landscape" has come to denote the social, experiential, embodied, and political dimensions of people's perceptions of and engagements with their physical surroundings (Hirsch & O'Hanlon 1995).[2] For Melanesia, it has been shown that places connect to expressions of iden-tity and politics (Wassmann 1991, 2001), relatedness (Anderson 2011; Hess 2009; Leach 2003; Meinerzag 2006), gender (Stürzenhofecker 1998), myth, emotion, and memory (Feld [1982] 1990; Kahn 1990, 1996; Stewart & A. Strathern 2000). Therefore, when pondering over land in Pacific societies, "we are talking not simply about a material factor of production but about an ex-pression of sociality" (Stürzenhofecker 1998: 39). Interestingly, the Bosmun sagoscape may also be described as a "sentient landscape," a fitting phrase used by Poirier (2005: 11) to describe places in an Aboriginal world of the Australian Western Desert that "are perceived and experienced as sentient and intentional and endowed with consciousness." The swamps around Daiden are ascribed intentional agency. The food abundance they offer is seen as a benevolent stance that depends on how people respond to each other.

Areas of wild-growing sago remind people of the spirit's resentment and disappointment in response to what they did. Areas of planted sago mirror people's regret. The act of planting the sago shrub becomes a medium through which they demonstrate their attempts to reconcile with the spirit. The swamps tell about the gaining, the losing, and the regaining of food abundance. Moreover, they tell about *ndiar,* interpersonal generosity. Bosmun inextricably link food abundance to the sympathy they were offered by the sago spirit, and it is only by means of their social reproduction of this sympathy that humans are able to regenerate the initial gift of the spirit—swamps full of "real sago." Therefore, food abundance in Bosmun reflection is also deeply connected to interpersonal generosity, which culminates in the giving and sharing of food. When providing other people with "real sago," food scarcity cannot arise. Embedded in this sociosymbolic theory of food and place, the procurement of sago (and other foods) is more than just a certain type of subsistence activity that slowly evolved in this particular ecological locale. Likewise, the consumption of sago is not only a satisfaction of biological needs. Bosmun food ventures have to be reconfigured as playing a crucial role in the sociomoral sphere.

The logic of food abundance that Bosmun apply to sago palms is also applied to coconut palms (*viaraŋ*), betel nut palms (*mbook*), and a certain type of bamboo (*nzit*). Unlike garden produce, which is ready after six months, these plants need to grow for least six to eight years. People do not plant *viaraŋ, mbook,* and *nzit* for themselves, but for others. I was not given any further hints as to why people apply the notion of sago food abundance to those other shrubs. There is a myth, linked to a hero named Pares, about how the coconut palm came to spread. However, the myth does not give clues for why people were not allowed to consume coconut from the palms that they themselves planted. It could well be that the moral content offered by the story of Yesi and the sago spirit was extended to other parts of the Bosmun landscape. The grated and squeezed meat of coconuts provides people with fat and meals with flavor. Coconut husks are used as strainers for leaching sago pith. Betel nut, the fruit of the palm *Areca catechu* that causes slight intoxication, is chewed by everyone, at least today.[3] Besides clay pots, important cooking devices include tubes of the bamboo type *nzit;* filled with sago and leafy vegetables, for instance, and put directly into a fire, they are a valuable alternative in local food preparation. When reading further about Bosmun sago planting below, one should keep in mind that the same complexity applies to coconut and betel nut palms and to the bamboo type *nzit*. However, these plants are not as essential in nurturing the human body as are sago palms. Therefore, I focus on sago's significance for bodily and social well-being in Daiden.

Orientations for Sociality

When my conversation partners talked about sago and sago production, they did so with what seemed to me unusual reverence. Like other sago-eating people of New Guinea (Townsend 1982: 17), Bosmun feel a deep loyalty toward their staple. People even stated: *Saksak em mirakol kaikai bilong mipela!* ('Sago is our miracle food'). By no means did I hear people complaining about sago, as people are known to do in other parts of Papua New Guinea. Tuzin writes about the Ilahita Arapesh of the interior Sepik region: "[B]etween approximately February and May … is a time during which sago is so much the daily fare that by April people are complaining about the monotony of the diet and yearning for the yam harvest to begin" (1992: 104). The Maisin of Collingwood Bay even think of sago as a "famine food" (Barker 2008: 48). In Bosmun considerations of food, sago pudding suggests continuity and stability but never monotony, and sago could never be a sign of food crises like all other foods could be. My personal perplexity faded as I learned of the myth that was the subject of the preceding section. Going out to the swamps is considered an important, if not the most highly valued, event in the rituality of everyday life. It enables people to produce, eat, and share sago. Producing, eating, and sharing sago substantially binds people together and enables them to reckon kin-relations.

One could say that procuring sago is a rather strenuous type of labor and that swamps are "miserable places to tramp around" (Townsend 2003: 4), especially during the wet season when myriads of mosquitoes participate (during the dry season, there are fewer mosquitoes but never none). I was amazed to see Bosmun attitudes toward work in such an environment. People usually set off to procure food at ease and in a good mood and they would return in the same way. People looked upon sago making as a life-affirming and physically and sociopsychically balancing activity that creates positive feeling states and makes people *xuop* ('happy' / 'contented'). This is also reflected in the term used to refer to the activity of sago making. The term *ve* denotes the entire procedure of extracting the palm's starch, as well as the act of dancing. In coparticipating in those activities several times and listening to people's utterances in conversations on either food procurement or dancing at traditional festive occasions (and the dance parties that are popular among the youth), I gained the impression that people think of both activities as equally enjoyable.

When people met acquaintances on their way to a sago swamp, they often said: *Mipela go wok saksak nau!* ('We are setting off to produce sago now!').

By means of casual utterances, they constantly located themselves in social time and space when coming across familiar people. This was different when meeting strangers. In this case, people passed by undemonstratively. However, meeting a complete stranger in familiar lands does not often occur. When meeting kin on the trail, people state, frequently of their own accord, where they are coming from or where they are going to, or they may ask others the same in anticipation of a frank response. Many times I was assured that people liked being asked because it indicates wishing to be connected to others, an attitude that defines a person as amiable. This type of casual interrogating also suited my anthropological endeavor. Although people did not necessarily go into much detail, they at least generally and clearly informed me about the course they had chosen. This was particularly so when people embarked on a sago venture. They commonly commented on their undertaking with a beaming glance and anticipatory tone of voice. To emphasize that someone is on his or her way to a swamp is considered the peak of Bosmun male and female adult life: one should become an industrious sago laborer and a constant food provider. Emically, this is the key to involving oneself within the template of morally approved action. To make sago is to have one's own subjective and interpersonal universe in order. To think of sago is to think of one's place, of one's health and vitality, and, most crucially, of one's ability to consociate with others.

Planting Palms—Making Kin

Following the sago spirit's legacy, Bosmun sago ventures are meant to create interpersonal dependencies and a certain harmony between individuals. The core implication of the myth is that every person should seek at least a minimal level of interpersonal equality. This equilibrium is necessary to have people with whom to exchange sago sources on a regular basis. Whereas one may eat one's own garden produce and hunted meat, one must not eat the sago one has planted oneself. Of course, everyone might process sago growing wild in the swamps, but people actually access those areas rather for more exceptional purposes. It might be for feasts or communal trade with other groups—at times when particularly huge amounts of sago, exceeding a single family's sago supply, are in need. During *toupmbi ŋgimŋginir* (the time from approximately November to February), when "paths are muddy and areas hardly accessible," people may also be forced to move to the spiritually empowered swamps, if easy to reach, in order to secure the dietary subsistence their families need. Apart from that, people prefer to process sago in planted areas. It is in these swamps that the network of Bosmun interdependencies comes to light, and assuming those networks are in balance, it is here that people will find food abundance.

WHAT SAGO PALM STANDS TELL

In Bosmun sago cultivation, only a first palm is actually planted. Further plants will then spread by themselves, given that the space around the mother is continuously cleared. Sago palms reproduce themselves vegetatively with suckers automatically emerging around the lower part of the trunk. Thus, continuous reproduction is possible in principle. Guarding the growth and spread of a first plant and its progeny is a long-term endeavor. Surrounding trees have to be cut down and leaves covering the soil around the trunks have to be gathered and burned regularly. Such an area makes up a person's constantly growing sago palm stand. A huge sago palm stand might come to an end depending on how closely it is bordered by other people's sago areas and what kind of relations are reckoned between the owners or users of neighboring sago palm stands. A border (*kaam*) between sago palm stands has no fence as gardens have. Any natural feature in a swamp on which the bordering parties agree, such as another plant growing in between or a small stream running through the area, can serve as a spatial marker. An extension is likely to be negotiated if the bordering parties are close relatives. If not, swampy grounds suitable for the planting of sago have to be found elsewhere.

Who exactly will plant and / or donate a palm to whom and at what time depends on how many sago palms a person or a family currently has and who planted those palms for them. When a child is born, a relative will plant a sago sucker that is thought of as growing in the same way as the newborn. Both men and women are allowed to plant for same- and cross-sex children. However, a man's sago area will be passed on to a son and a woman's to a daughter. No one should suffer from not having his or her own sago area. This is understandable since without sago one cannot reach full social recognition in Daiden. There is no social act in Bosmun life that does not include some sort of food-related activity.

Connecting a newborn to the world starts with the ascribing of a sago palm to him or her. Usually, it is the father or the mother who will put roots into the earth as a sign for the new life, but any other (paternal or maternal) relative who intends to offer particular care for the child in question is welcome to plant a sago palm. In cases where a couple still holds a copious sago palm area and can foresee that there will be enough palms for each of its children, it is not really necessary to plant a new shrub for every newborn. Nevertheless, every child must be assured of a number of palms for his or her future life. This is also mirrored in the customary gesture that indicates one's wish to adopt a child. Immediately after birth, a person may send to the birth-house a container that serves as a cradle and is made of the flower sheath of a certain palm. It is the same type of container, though smaller, that is used to store foods, especially processed sago paste. As I had the enormous luck to be present when a young woman gave birth to twins (a girl and a boy), I was able to watch sago-connecting practices at the early stages of being-in-the-world, such as the bedding of a baby in a container normally used for food storage. If the mother agrees, the baby will be bedded in the container that has been handed in from outside. If not, a baby is placed in a similar container. Bedding a baby in that cradle is not only practical and soothing, but symbolic. It connects a new life to already existing lives in which food matters significantly in a social sense.

Planting palms strengthens kin-ties and expresses and affirms intra- and intergenerational kin-relations. Even if the apical ancestor is no longer traceable, familial ties between two or more persons or kin-groups are believed to exist as long as people remember that food-based links existed in the past between those persons or groups. In the present, those links to the past are either (individually or collectively) reinforced or neglected. The following example is but one that shows the dynamics of making kin in Daiden: I once asked a middle-aged man about his relation to an old woman who had been born in Ndoŋon but who, through marriage, had come to live in Daiden. I had seen that both were quite fond of each other and therefore I assumed a kin-relation, although the genealogical information I had gathered povided no hints. In fact, neither of them knew their exact genealogical relation, but the point of reference for their connection was that the old woman and the man's mother had assisted each other with food because their parental generations had assisted each other with food. Therefore, the man felt obliged to that woman but—and this is interesting—not to her children. He and the old woman considered there to be no real need to maintain the relation for the future. Her children were adults with their own children in a stable, long-standing network of safety, and they were not particularly eager to carry on the connection either. As I explored further, no one actually felt uncomfortable about this since, in any case, the connection could be reinforced at a later point in time. Currently, however, re-creating this relationship was not deemed necessary.

Newly planted sago spots mirror the more recent and accurately traceable kin-relations of palm planters and palm receivers and of those people who regularly procure food together. Sago stands that were laid out in earlier times and that now harbor a plentitude of palms echo the increasing vagueness of past genealogies. Whether it is gardens, such as among the Maisin, or sago swamps, "[l]and ... forms a central element in a person's genealogical identity" (Barker 2008: 52); even when it comes to marking the shallowness of genealogical memories. It is common to call a sago area that was started three, four, or even more generations ago one's own without knowing who the actual initiator was. I frequently heard statements such as "my father took the stand over from his father who took it over from his father and maybe it was his father who started it but it could have been someone else as well." What is crucial is that there definitely was some social or "civilizing act" (Tuzin

1992: 108): there was someone who did the planting and who thereby reinforced interpersonal relatedness. Bosmun maintain claims over sago stands
through actual labor or through the efforts put in by Ego's paternal or maternal
relatives of first or second ascending generations. This type of sago tenure is
comparable, for example, to the tenure system of the Auwju of West Papua. In
summarizing the study of Vriens and Boelaars (1973), Townsend (1982: 14)
states for the Auwju that "[r]ights to cultivated sago are established by labor
(or the labor of one's ancestors) and are always divided among the heirs and
held individually."

Every adult in Daiden holds an individual sago area. With one's own sago,
a person steps into a world of relatedness. My consociates emphasized their
connections to others frequently and in doing so gave rise to feelings of comfort for themselves and others. It seemed to me that, from Bosmun perspectives, the oddest way to live is to be disconnected. Goodale (1995: 73) wrote
about the New Britain Kaulong in Papua New Guinea "that one can have
peace only by living alone." This, I suppose, is not thinkable in Bosmun considerations of what gives peace to a person. The way people substantially relate to one another is discussed in the next section.

RECEIVERS, PLANTERS, DONATORS, MEDIATORS
One of the most fundamental relations a person is going to enter is the relation
between a palm planter and a palm receiver. This relation may begin once a
child is considered to be strong enough to live (this is deemed to be so when
mother and infant leave the birth-house); but the child may also receive palms
later. To start a new palm stand guarantees that both sides—planter and receiver—will benefit. A planter has to be repaid with gifts of food. A receiver
is presented with a whole palm in the end.

If, for example, my father's brother planted a palm for me, I (as female Ego)
would be supposed to show my appreciation for this act by giving food to him.
This would begin once I embarked on the journey toward young adulthood.
From time to time, I would send food gifts to my palm planter or, if we were
residents of the same household, I would be keen to prepare meals for him regularly. If it were my brother who received a palm from our father's brother, his
wife or his sisters—probably including myself—would do the cooking, since
this is primarily done by females. My brother, in turn, would reciprocate our
assistance by helping if one of us were in need. In fact, everyone else indirectly involved in fostering a primary relation between planter and receiver
would gain some recognition. What also needs to be taken into consideration
is that neither I nor my brother could give food that stems from the palm that
my father's brother himself planted for me (or for my brother) to my father's
brother. While we could eat sago from the entire developing stand, it would
remain taboo for him. Thus, every time I would think of providing food for the

person who planted sago for me I would have to exchange my own processed starch with the starch produced from someone else's palm. Therefore, I would constantly seek to balance and widen relations in my social surrounding. One may process sago for oneself and the members of one's household, but if it was one's parent who planted the palm, one has to attend to one's exchange partners regularly so as to provide the parent with food regularly. Imagine the scope inherent in the fact that one neither eats the food nor takes any materials from one's self-planted sago palms (and coconut palms, betel nut palms, and the type of bamboo mentioned above). One may not even use the bast tissue of self-planted coconut palms of which sieves (regular tools!) are made to rinse sago starch out of the pith.

Apart from being a planter and receiver, a person is also likely to become a palm donator and mediator. A palm donator relies on the assistance of a mediator. A mediator helps a donator who wants to cultivate a sago palm stand for shared use. A mediator need not belong to the closest realm of relatives and is only asked to give particular assistance on occasion. If a potential donator fears that he or she is probably going to face a sago shortage in the future, he or she may ask a third person—a mediator—to do the planting. Thus, a palm donator bypasses the actual taboo of not being allowed to eat or take materials from the palm that he or she presented to somebody. Donator and receiver will then share a stand. Figure 2.1 shows the different food-based relations that every person comes to enact as receiver, planter, donator, and mediator. The Bosmun network of food-dealing agents is complex and everyone creates his

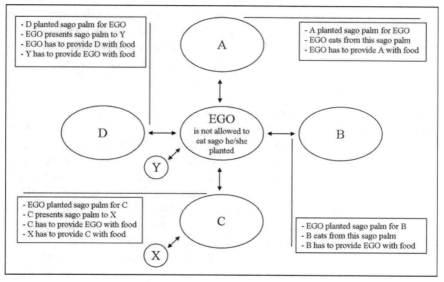

Figure 2.1: Planting Palms—Keeping Kin.

or her path of individual uniqueness in this relational world. There is no single path that will exactly resemble another path, and one must consider a number of persons who all enact a different food-related agency.

Sago palms do not only provide food. The leaves are used for sewing thatch shingles, for weaving baskets, and for making torches. The leafstalks are used in building structures for the rinsing of the pith, and as hods or burning material for firing clay pots. Fibers taken from the leaves' midribs are used for the making of bast-skirts and other forms of decoration. Sago palms fill people's material world to the same extent as they fill their stomachs. A person needs to have a good supply of sago palms to consistently live a materially sufficient and socially empowered and spirited life that depends on assisting others and being assisted by others. Therefore, people sometimes also donate palms to others with the intention that they themselves may take benefit from the emerging stand should it become necessary.

One could wonder why a person does not ask another person to plant only for him or her. It is uncommon in Bosmun understandings to let a mediator plant exclusively for one's own purposes. The reason is that feelings of comfort do not manifest largely because one has enough sago but because one received the sago via good and trusted relations, because someone else showed concern for one. This is similar to ideas of the Ilahita Arapesh, where "the planting of sago is a solely altruistic act performed for one's descendants" (Tuzin 1992: 108). A mediator is appreciated differently from a palm donator. He or she will be given a special gift of garden produce only once or be allocated space in a newly arranged garden that may be used for only one season. The actual palm receiver has no obligations with regard to this planter but does have obligations with regard to the donator, who will take responsibility for the palm's further spread. It is the donator alone who must reciprocate the mediator's act. This is done by means of some sort of garden activity.

GARDENS VERSUS SAGO PALMS

Gardens are not as prominent in the Bosmun physical and social environment as are sago swamps. In my understanding, gardens do have social importance, but swamps dominate over gardens in the production of social meaning inasmuch as they visibly dominate the landscape. Modes of sociality deeply tied to gardens and gardening have been explored elsewhere in Papua New Guinea (Barker 2008: 51–52; Leach 2003; Meinerzag 2006). In her analysis of Hinihon notions on person and place, Meinerzag (2006: 103–139), for example, shows that the Hinihon people transform villages—to be seen as a product of colonial history in this particular local context—into "empty villages" because they prefer to dwell in gardens, which are seen to be the result of social relations. Bosmun gardens are the result of certain social relations, too, but it is the practice of sago planting that creates lasting social networks and inter-personal dependencies.

Consider that a garden is linguistically encoded as *reŋepak*. This literally means 'several plots' or 'something that is divided' (*reŋ* is 'plot,' -*pak* is 'more than one or two'). As I was told, a garden would not thrive without the holder's willingness to create and maintain social balance with others. The same logic applies here as with the swamps. The best way to show such willingness is by sharing the garden with others. A garden holder, either male or female, never occupies all the plots in a garden. As a rule, a holder should allocate a number of plots to others. Every garden I saw had such plots that were separated by trunks lined up on the ground. My "brother" Seres, for instance, shared parts of his garden with six relatives who belonged to the realms of both his maternal and paternal family (see figure 2.2). Should any one of his tenants clear ground for a garden in the future, then he would, of course, have the right to get a plot, unless the tenant had already done him another favor. Once both sides in a garden project have benefited, the mutual commitment has been satisfied.

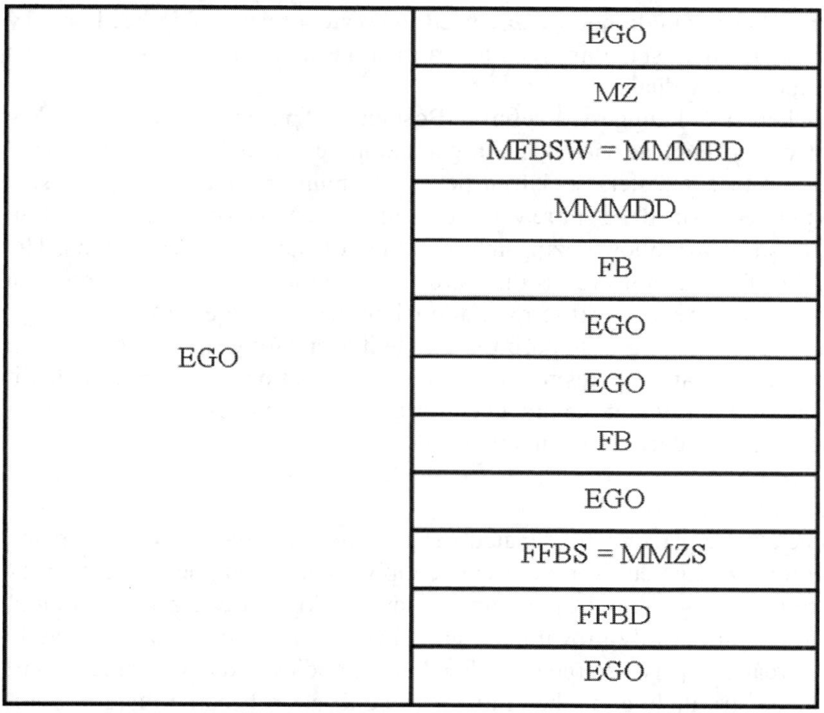

EGO	
	EGO
	MZ
	MFBSW = MMMBD
	MMMDD
	FB
	EGO
	EGO
	FB
	EGO
	FFBS = MMZS
	FFBD
	EGO

Figure 2.2: Seres' Garden in 2004/05. The work in gardens serves to create short-term mutual obligations with maternal as well as paternal relatives.

A garden also shows a person's more general attempts to be generous. Put differently, a garden is a medium to transact generosity without directing it toward someone in particular. Having to walk past Seres' garden every time I went beyond Daiden, I became aware of this. I once came back with a group of people and they stopped at the garden since they saw new banana shoots lying outside the garden fence alongside the path we had been following parallel to the garden. Everyone in the group either took several of the shoots or attached a knotted leaf to them, and we continued walking. They explained that banana shoots put outside the fence are free to be carried away and that this is the common way to deal with new banana shoots that emerge around a banana tree. Would they need to tell the garden holder that they had taken the shoots? The group answered that this was not necessary. There were five of us in the group: two were related to the holder in terms of close kin, one was very distant kin, and one had no kin-relation with the holder. Still, everyone was allowed to take shoots. If they had not, others would probably have taken the shoots. Those who wish to create or reinforce their relationship will tell the holder of the garden that they have taken the opportunity of acquiring the shoots. Those who do not see any need to create a relationship need not say anything. In contrast to this scenario, transactions involving sago always focus on specific individuals.

In chapter 1, I suggested defining Bosmun as "purposive gardeners." My intent was to indicate that Bosmun gardening very much depends on social drive and that it fosters social purposes. Bosmun are thus also "purposive sago planters," since the entire venture seems to be based on social motivation or altruism if we follow Tuzin's interpretation of Ilahita Arapesh affairs. The central difference, however, is that gardening / garden food serves immediate purposes and creates short-term relational processes whereas sago planting / sago food serves long-term purposes and builds enduring rights and duties. If we take a look at how Bosmun correlate palms and persons conceptually, it makes sense to say that the practice of sago planting is designed to foster attachment and enduring trust in others.

PALMS AND PERSONS

Appreciating a person who donated a sago palm for one's future is a lifelong imperative. A sago cultivator does not simply plant a palm; he or she contributes to the rising strength of a human body. Looking after a sago palm until it matures into a fully grown palm and blossoms requires at least twelve to fifteen years. This is also the age when human bodies (male and female) start to change strikingly and when minds are believed to become mature. Symbolically, the palm's maximum height correlates with the maximum size of a human body (see Schindlbeck [1980: 556] for a similar correlation made by the Middle Sepik Sawos between sago palms and human beings). As I investigated the growth, the quality, and the care of palms, trees, and plants, a man gave the following equation that others affirmed: *Gro bilong saksak em olsem gro bilong man. Tupela em wankain tasol … saksak mipela i no inap lusim.* ('A sago palm grows in the same way as does a human being. The two are of one kind … we cannot give up sago.')

Ethnographers of the Sepik region have reported that sago palms are considered to be one's own children (Schuster & Schuster 1974: 7; Tuzin 1992: 108). It is difficult to determine whether such a belief was held in the past in Daiden when one takes into account more than eighty years of regional Christian proselytization and incoming notions of Western science taught in schools nationwide. Interviewees never said that they conceived of sago palms as their children, but they did speak warmly and passionately of them. As I show in chapter 3, sago is also anchored in local ideas of procreation. At least, sago palms and human bodies are thought to be similar in their substantial and spiritual composition. Both are wrapped by *nyeroŋ,* the non-solid spiritual entity that animates them. There is also a myth in which a major male protagonist turns sago palms into human bodies to fight against an enemy party. Whenever recounting the myth, people insisted that this had really happened. In any case, sago palms are people's indissoluble partners because they hold the food that human bodies need to fully develop—physically and socially.

When a sago palm changes form, notably by developing flowers (which it does only once), the human body also changes form. The more children's bodies develop the distinctive physical signs of maleness and femaleness respectively, the more parents motivate them to actively participate in the gender-specific tasks of food production. Children participate in sago ventures from an early age by simply following their parents or other family members, and they then playfully imitate them; girls play at the rinsing spot and boys imitate male activities with sticks that are shaped like sago scrapers. From the age of ten onward, youngsters enter the adult world of social rights and obligations by proving themselves as attentive sago producers. It is commonly held that, through the making and sharing of sago, they gradually reach social and emotional maturity and reduce what is called *rorer* in the local vernacular. The term *rorer* has three meanings. First, it refers to the mental constitution of the child, which is thought to yield irresponsible behavior. Second, the term is used to describe an adult who suddenly behaves crazily / unsociably / egocentrically. Third, it denotes the state of being in a sound and deep sleep during which the spiritual entity (*nyeroŋ*) that is believed to animate humans can temporarily leave the body. To be *rorer* basically means to behave in opposition to the ideal of *ramkandiar.* I refer to it as "insanity" / "social immaturity" / "unsociability." A person described as *rorer* does not cherish relationships through assessing others and allowing others to assess her or him. It is noteworthy that *rorer* is connected to an emic "theory of mind" (A. von Poser &

Ubl forthcoming). "Theory of mind" research is concerned with determining the age at which children develop the competence to attribute mental states to others, a skill that enables them to anticipate and / or influence others' intentions, beliefs, or desires. According to findings in Western developmental psychology (e.g., Sodian et al. 2003), children are said to acquire this ability around the age of four. According to local understandings, children begin to lose *rorer* only as they voluntarily share food with others and actively take part in sago making. Only then are they believed to have acquired the ability to share the perspective of another.

The person who plants sago for a child thus helps in guiding the child to socially acknowledged maturity. In processing the first palm, a youngster takes over the responsibility for his or her personal fortune and becomes able to gain social power. With increasing food-related activities, a person's voice and status strengthen. I witnessed this on frequent occasions such as in the following case: A young man married a woman no one in his family really liked. As a sign of disagreement, his classificatory sister (MeBD) destroyed several tools (including a sago scraper) newly made for him by their uncle (the man's MyB / the sister's FyB). The uncle, who was over fifty years old, worried about the destruction of the tools because he had received gifts of food from his nephew (ZS) as a reward for his effort. However, the food-based relation the uncle had with his niece (BD) was stronger than the one with his nephew. Being aware of her authority in that particular case, the young niece yelled overtly: *Mi wok long redim kaikai bilong man ya! Mi yet mi lukautim em long kaikai! Mi save go wok saksak na mi yet mi wok long tingim em olgeta taim!* ('It is me who prepares food for this man! It is me who cares for him with food! I am the one who makes sago and I am the one who always takes care of him!')

No one, including the uncle who had planted a sago palm for his niece during her infancy, considered the young woman's statement disrespectful. The people I asked about it said it was a justified claim. In a reverse situation, I was told that the uncle of course could raise his voice in the same way. Bosmun statements of power were indeed frequently made in relation to whether one had maintained a palm stand and / or whether one had procured and cooked food for others.

In engaging in all kinds of food-related activities, a person individuates him- or herself, and others are aware of the individuated self because socialized agents should carefully watch each other. This individuated self can be glossed by the local term *sim*. On the one hand, *sim* linguistically refers to a 'chain of hills.' On the other hand, *sim* refers to that which ultimately makes one different from all others. One might enact similar *sim* as did one's father or mother. A common phrase that I often heard was, *Em bihainim saate sim* ('He / she follows his / her father's way') or *em bihainim maame sim* ('he / she follows his / her mother's way'). One's *sim* might be similar to that of others but will never be the same. *Sim*—the personal contours of one's being—sharpen with increasing age and as one starts to create personal networks of interdependencies apart from the ones received automatically by birth. Others' personal networks are always taken into account when pondering their states. Similar to Barker's (2008: 54) observation in Maisin culture, where "people pay close attention to exchanges," Bosmun carefully track what kinds of food one has given, or has been given by, whom, at what time, in what context, and for what reasons. They track it both in everyday life and in the context of feasting. They also track who was supposed to have given, but did not give, food to others. Cases in the following section illustrate how foodways are used to either reaffirm or sever kin-ties.

Reaffirming or Severing Kin-Ties

To make Bosmun communal feasts and events of personal significance successful, it is necessary that such occasions do not pass without people eating a lot. Figure 2.3 shows the girl Namtaaxe at a feast following the phase of her social seclusion, which girls have to enter at menarche (*mbuki*). Menarche is linked to the onset of female procreativity. Once it starts, a girl is no longer a *moptiŋ* (a 'baby crayfish' that has not laid eggs yet). Menarche is a vital episode in a chain of other life-cycle events and the first step toward female maturity. The girl turns into a female being (*mes*) with distinct powers and

Figure 2.3: Feeding Namtaaxe.

obligations. Therefore, a girl has to be isolated from the public until she gains female skills relating to material culture and social knowledge about how to properly deal with her new physiological state. The girl's movements and actions should be confined to a defined space in the parental house. According to ancestral lore, a girl had to remain in seclusion for years. Namtaaxe stayed in isolation approximately a month because today girls have to go to school (there is a primary and a secondary school in Ndoŋon; they teach up to grade eight).[4] Namtaaxe received about thirty plates of food that were brought by relatives to mark and support her step into female adulthood.[5] Spectators commented on who exactly brought food to Namtaaxe and, even more important, who was still expected to arrive. To appreciate the food-gifts, the girl was fed a bit of each portion by one of her classificatory father's sisters before she was allowed to eat with her own hands again. Then, the food plates were distributed among the attending crowd. During menstruation and after childbirth, women must not touch food with their hands. Instead, they are fed by their kinswomen. Lifting a taboo is called *suruvok*. Interestingly, Bosmun ascribe a particular gesture and a particular sound to the moment when they perform a *suruvok*. One takes a bit of food into one's hand, circles the head with it and, while doing so, one makes a smacking sound. In doing that, one's *nyeroŋ*, or spiritual wrapping, is reinforced. In bringing food to a girl at such an occasion, relatives strengthen her spiritually. Through paying attention to the many food plates that surrounded the new "young woman," her individual set of kin-connections became apparent. Moreover, the plates that had arrived were not just a reminder of existing kin-ties but a reaffirmation of them. Bosmun food contributions in the context of feasting allow for positive and negative creativity in regard to kinship. Relatives who were expected to support the girl but who intentionally did not come were likely to jeopardize the continuity of the existing kin-relation. Certain foodways unite, certain foodways disunite.

Although there are socially prescribed norms for dealing with others that entail certain role behaviors, individual expressions of both affection and aversion are accepted as natural and I came upon them quite often. Most of my conversation partners were impulsive and outspoken, and everyone was known by his or her *sim* or personal contours. The vital point is that those natural expressions were usually made in relation to a person's individual foodways and by assessing one's own reactions to them. I gained the impression that thinking about others in Daiden *is* thinking about their foodways. Whom in particular to associate with was most often linked to what opinion one had of the other as a food-dealing agent. In this context, people clearly differentiated between what was expected of a person and how he or she actually met those expectations. Brother and sister, for instance, should be on good terms because they stem from the same parentage and because ideally they are meant to trust and mutually support one another. However, if one of them fails to signal trust, the other is likely to respond in kind. The way such lack of trust is articulated becomes obvious in the following statement by one of my elder female interviewees. She spoke to me about the relationships she had with her brother (B) and with her classificatory brother (FBS) and why she favored the latter:

Man ya em brata tru tru bilong mi tasol em i no save tingim mi long kaikai. Em ...
em i no brata tru tru bilong mi olsem narapela ya ... tasol em save tingim mi long
kaikai olgeta taim na em kamap olsem brata tru tru bilong mi. Olsem na, mi no bisi
long narapela. Mi save wari long dispela man tasol.

('That man is my real brother but he never cared about me as regards food. This one
... he is not my real brother like the other one ... but he always provides me with
food and he became a real brother. Therefore, I am not concerned about the other.
I just care about this man.')

People commonly articulated whom they liked in particular by means of foodways. In assessing her brothers, the woman added that she ate more regularly with her classificatory brother, as if to tell me that this was another crucial factor for calling this man a 'real brother.' In the Introduction I referred to Battaglia (1990: 56), who points to the emotional facet of giving gestures (including the giving of food). Interestingly, Battaglia also hints at the importance that these gestures have for social relationships beyond given expectations, stating that they "contribute quite unsystematically to a form of giving that is potentially the undoing of systems of descent and alliance, since it tends to foster exceptions to social rules according to a logic of emotional analogy" (Battaglia 1990: 56).

Two other examples show how foodways articulate fondness beyond social rules. A man marked his darling among the daughters of a classificatory sister by telling me that he ate sago balls only if they were made from the hands of this daughter of his sister. He added that he never ate them prepared by someone else. Another man told me that he no longer ate a specific type of fish because his first granddaughter almost choked on the bone of this fish when she was five years old. Ever since, the girl had refused to eat that fish. Feeling pity for her, the man said, was the reason why he had stopped eating this fish. Consociates usually know of one's foodways and the meanings they bear.

Except for periods of famine, people in Daiden are never really in fear of starvation since there are always others who will help with the provision of food. This is even the case when one becomes the subject of indictments. I observed two cases where a person was exiled. One was when a man was accused of being a sorcerer. The other was when a widow started to engage in a new relationship with a man although her time of formalized mourning had not yet ended. Both had to leave their places of residence at different points in time in 2005 and neither was back by 2010. The man had been forced to leave behind his wife and their children; the woman had left her affinal relatives. In both cases, I felt worried about their hardships, but whenever I met one of them in other households where they had found shelter, a feeling of persecution was not predominant. I realized that the refuge that they were given was in familiar places where interpersonal dependencies had been established in the past by shared sago labor and shared food consumption. Nevertheless, their individual situations were not easy. The man had been sheltered in at least four different places since 2005 and was still hoping to return home where his wife and children were waiting. The woman remained in one place and it was clear that she would not return. Her consanguineal relatives would not send her back. Although they harbored her, which she deserved due to her efforts in the past, she felt ostracized by her family. In 2010, she told me that not one of her male relatives was willing to help her in the making of sago:

> *Mi kamap olsem man ... nogat brata husait i laik helpim mi. Em ... mi dispela kain meri ya ... mi mekim rong. Mi ken wokim dispela wok, em i no hevipela samting. Mi gat strong lo katim saksak. Tasol ... i no luk gutpela. Ol pikinini tu... ol i les lo helpim mi.*

('I have become like a man ... [I] have no brother who wants to help me. It is ... I am this kind of woman ... I made [this] mistake. I can do this work, it is not difficult. I am strong enough to cut the sago palm. But ... it does not look good. The children, too ... they do not want to help me.')

When telling me that she had to do "men's work," she appeared sad and frustrated. Although she physically felt strong enough to do this kind of work, she suffered from doing this work alone in the swamps. I now turn to the sociosymbolic description of swamps.

Swamps—Not a Place for Dispute

Going out to the swamps is an important social event. It is always a group and a male-female matter. Husbands and wives or brothers and sisters set out together. Such core teams are usually followed by a bunch of children. A couple's company is made up of its own offspring but the spouses' younger siblings are frequently welcome to join, too. If one becomes sick or is otherwise occupied, siblings or other kin can spontaneously be called to assist. If they live further away, slit-drums are used to convey the message. As for many occasions, there is a particular slit-drum rhythm to call a person to come and help in the making of sago. In following people to their swamps, I learned about their unique sense of gender complementarity and that particular place.

SAGO MAKING AND GENDER COMPLEMENTARITY

Bosmun men and women take part equally in sago making. Since sago making is such a central part of everyday life, the sexes frequently fuse socially because they share the space of the swamps. This is different from what Stürzenhofecker writes of gender and space among the Duna: "[B]oth sexes use the landscape around them as a venue for sociality. ... During the daytime, men and women move through separate spaces; only occasionally do their pathways cross" (1998: 148). Couples and opposite-sex siblings in Daiden frequently walk the same path or canoe the river (and old riverbeds) together, not only to visit the swamps for work but to visit relatives in other places. Most of the time, men and women share spaces. It is more during the festive ceremonial contexts that gender segregation becomes prevalent. Although ceremonial contexts are no less important, they are the rarer instances of sociality.

From several conversations with people and from everyday observations of male-female encounters, I gained the impression that both sexes think favorably of the other. I never heard men saying that women's part required less physical exertion. Nor did I hear women speaking negatively about men's efforts in the swamps. The making of sago not only necessitates but encourages gender complementarity and mutual respect. Of course, there is gender segregation in Bosmun life; even in post-proselytization times. Consider the girl's fortuitous act of humiliation against the sago spirit in the myth depicted at the outset of this chapter. As the spirit became aware of the girl's menstrual blood, his male gender became evident. The spirit had purposely revealed himself to aged Yesi because her menstrual flow had stopped long before. She had lost what Bosmun men consider a highly dangerous essence that would have been a risk to the masculinity of the spirit. Consequently, women were banned from working at the palm stem. Nevertheless, they were not entirely banned from sago making. Rinsing the pith became their domain.

It could be theorized that women extract the starch from the pith as a form of "punishment" because it was a female who caused the solidification of the sago paste within the stem. There is, however, also a countertheory: female bodies have given evidence of their inner power (wombs) to transform fluids (men's semen) into solid substances (babies) by means of childbearing, which, in the myth of Nzari, is regarded as a milestone (see chapter 3). Women are also the ancestrally legitimated producers and possessors of clay pots. They knead the clay and transform it into a stable and functional form. In traditional cooking-tool technology, clay pots were the only device with which to produce sago pudding—the very substance said to remove feelings of hunger and make human bodies grow. Therefore, women leach the sago pith, and they also engage in planting practices. However, as people emphasized, it was preferable for senior women such as old Yesi to do the planting. It is also using materials of the sago palms that female hands have planted that men's houses, for instance, can be thatched. A person is not allowed to enter a building whose thatch materials have been provided from his or her own palms. In theory, to guarantee that all Bosmun men may enter all the men's houses in the Bosmun area, thatch materials have to be taken from palms planted by the hands of mothers, daughters, sisters or wives. In view of that, Bosmun sago swamps are places where gender affairs are kept in balance.

In chapter 1, I wrote that women move between platforms whereas men erect them. Likewise, women basically create social ties whereas men protect and contest them. In that, women and men depend inextricably on one another. Linked to the gendered labor of sago making is also an "ethic of care" (Strauss 2004: 435), according to which couples should share the empathetic efforts of assessing kin. Empathy in Bosmun subjectivity is not just rendered as an (inter)subjective process, but as a collective moral obligation. Asking whether empathy is gendered, Strauss (2004: 435–436) argues that women in the United States seem to have greater empathetic concern or, as it were, a greater "ethic of care" than men but that such sex differences and ascriptions vary across cultures. Apart from the subjective assessments that individuals make and the emotional reactions, which are certainly influenced by their personal biographies (Hollan 2011: 196), empathy in Daiden is ideally to be fulfilled jointly by brothers and sisters or husbands and wives. Marriage is not only meant to bring together the opposite sexes for the purpose of sexual reproduction. My interviewees frequently emphasized that opposite-sex pairs are supposed to assess together how kin might feel, if necessary, to undo each partner's possible mistakes, as a husband's social mistake is always a wife's mistake and vice versa. Husband and wife should compel each other to watch others carefully. In chapter 4, I present parts of an interview with a woman who tells of her disappointment with her husband with regard to this matter. While still unmarried, one's navigations in the social world should be balanced by one's opposite-sex siblings. An unmarried man, for example, who receives a plate of food from kin other than his sisters will ask his sisters to prepare a meal that he can send back. If this man does not have many sisters or if there are other reasons why they cannot assist him, he might respond later (even years later), when married, to gifts of food that he once received. Members of couples, like opposite-sex siblings, should scold each other if they see that the other fails to reciprocate in the way expected in encounters with kin.

PLACES OF TRUST AND "BROKEN SPOONS"
Sago swamps are, above all, not the appropriate place for dispute, but rather for mutual reassurance. It could be said that residential areas are the proper place for episodes of articulated anger or fights. This is where the men's houses and the platforms that accompany the houses for cooking and sleeping are.

This is usually where many people meet. I witnessed several outbursts, either between two opponents or two opposing parties, and they always occurred in public and no one took care to conceal them. From Bosmun perspectives, verbal or physical conflicts are incidents that are witnessed by third parties and thus occur in a public space. Conflicts should not be hidden from the view of others. As I will show at the end of chapter 4, this practice serves a serious purpose. If two opponents come together, they will have in mind those who belong to their relational fields and who might involuntarily become involved because they are related. Accordingly, in moments of dispute, others are very much expected to be present. If it really comes to a fight, opponents might count on the support of both close and extended kin. This is not the case when out in the swamps. Swamps are the places of closest kin and consequently fewer people. If there is a place to dispute, it should be a space where a lot of people who may make up one's shield gather. They may judge whether it is an appropriate moment to fight or not. During one escalation I heard a woman repeatedly shout: *No ken paitim man ya! Em i no kaikai gut!,* which means 'Do not beat the man!' He did not eat well!' Notably, this saying did not imply that physically harming another is an immoral act, but that the man was not prepared to fight.

Due to the sago spirit's legacy, sago abundance is sustained in those swamps whose holders engage in morally approved behavior. Being a 'good' or 'sociable person'—a *moto* / *mese yaaoŋ* (*yaaoŋ* meaning 'good')—is linked to persuading others of one's own food-generosity. As noted earlier, it is inappropriate to try and make an impression with self-proclaimed generosity. One's attempts to be generous are always qualified by how others will perceive them (to self-proclaim one's concrete efforts, however, will not be judged as inappropriate). Food-generosity keeps a person's relational field alive and extends it. This is significant since interpersonal discord is believed to spoil the whole processing of a palm and the sago starch's quality. In order to avoid what could be called a social expiration date, all the steps of processing and preparing sago need to be done with a certain amount of concord.

A sago-making venture should come about in an atmosphere of good moods and without haste. Thus, men take their time to build a small sitting platform from the bark that was stripped off the palm. They scrape the pith only while seated (see figure 1.3). It was explained to me that the habit of being seated while pounding the pith into shreds indicates people's willingness to invest time in this work, whereas standing would be to precipitate and think of other, more important matters. Women rinse the pith diligently but not in a hurry, and if they do not finish in one day, they will take the remaining pith home and rinse it the next day. In any case, sago makers should never be without company. Such company was always present when I accompanied a group or when I passed a sago site while on my way to another destination. I also observed that others came to entertain women who had to rinse the remaining pith near the household.

Ideally, bad temper / anger / aggression (_poŋ_) must not occur between people who belong to the same sago-processing party. There is no one else more responsible for one another's well-being than the consociates of a sago-making group. I gained the impression that shared foodways are the ultimate means to create affection, mutual trust, and reliance. If discord emerged, the regularity of those shared foodways was likely to be interrupted. In 2008, a woman told me that she had a quarrel going on with her brother. As I had extracted "meanings" from the foodways that I had observed in 2004/05 and 2006, I asked her whether she was assisting him with food at the moment. Her immediate answer (and what I expected she would tell me) was: _Nogat ya! Mi no tingim em long kaikai nau! Mi no salim kaikai i go long em. Mi wok long straik ya!_ ('Of course not! I do not give food to him at the moment! I do not send food to him. I am on strike!')

This meant that she would neither accompany her brother to the sago swamps if he needed help from her, nor cook for him. I also asked how long she intended to neglect him this way. She reckoned that it would not be too long because her anger was not that huge. At that point, however, her refusal had already lasted a few months. When feelings of anger arise, the constellation of a regular food-procuring team is changed. The offended person will deliberately accompany a different sago party and must be replaced by another person until he or she decides to return.

Such refusals were quite common and usually everyone in the familiar social surrounding was informed about them. Food-related refusals were openly talked about and commented on with either worry or amusement, depending on the quality of a conflict. Some refusals were resolved after a short period. If this was the case, people knew those short-term refusals were meant to indicate minor complaints. Some that I knew of had already lasted a few years and some had become a lifelong matter. Such was the case between two men who had entered an affinal kin-relation based on an exchange marriage. Brother and sister of one family had married sister and brother of another family. As in-laws, the men were supposed to be in a relation of mutual assistance and respect, but then one sister died and her brother accused the husband of being responsible for her death. This had happened about ten years ago. Ever since, the in-laws had disregarded one another intentionally and everyone related to them knew that their relation was veiled by shame originating from a previous dispute.

Factually and metaphorically, shame or a lasting dispute is referred to as _xaam mbitit_, which literally denotes an 'eating spoon' (_xaam_)[6] that 'broke' (_mbitit_). Bosmun spoons are crescent shaped and are made of either coconut shell or nautilus shell. Several personal histories that I heard included stories of conflicts that were adjunct to food-connected expressions. 'Spoons had broken' many times for different minor or major reasons. This is not to say that Bosmun life trajectories were full of conflicts per se. I just emphasize that if people mentioned moments of interpersonal tension they would always talk of damaged foodways in some way or another. Since the relational scope of a person in Daiden was wide enough, his or her trouble was often soothed by other relatives. This was done by relocating the person to a swamp of positively inclined relations. Consider the following example: M. came into conflict with his mother's brother, N., who had fostered him since M.'s mother had died. M. in fact grew up with N. When I arrived, the young man was part of his mother's brother's nuclear family. Everyone appreciated him. He had gained recognition in the way a Bosmun male normally does. By now, he was an industrious sago processor. Then, M. fell out with N., and N.'s children refused M.'s assistance in the making of sago since they took their father's side. M. had to seek comfort with another relative of his paternal kin. G., the paternal relative, took M. into his household and showed him the swamps of his paternal family. On a pathway an hour away from Daiden, I met the two of them by chance. G. said to me that he was about to show M. a swamp that was waiting for him. He added that he was only now telling M. of the swamp in question. G. had concluded that M. needed support in the face of the current situation.

Two aspects become apparent here. The first is that a person should not work in a swamp that could become the scenario of misdirected relations. To avoid the possibility of such a scenario, people in danger of such a situation withdraw from their regular sago-making team and temporarily or permanently join another team. Through marriage, partners build new sago-making teams. They leave their former sago-making groups, which were made up of either biological or classificatory parents or siblings. From the teenage years onward, a sago producer actively weaves a network of long-term relations. He or she first looks after parental and collateral kin. Later, when the parents may have died, siblings become his or her continuing anchor. The network becomes extended with marriage as one also looks after affinal kin and finally after one's own children. An array of long-term relations is thus continuously in the making, and there will be always others to go to in situations of trouble. M. temporarily left his maternal family and found comfort at the side of his paternal family.

The second aspect, which confused me more than once, is that an adult might have certain sago-use or land rights without necessarily knowing about those rights until others rather arbitrarily reveal them to him or her. It is quite common that a network of safety is created in the way we heard of in the above case. M. was approximately thirty years of age. Up until then, he had been part of a stable network from which he was suddenly dismissed. So, G.

felt it was time to give M. an alternative sense of belonging that would soothe him. It was not the case that M. was prevented from being able to produce sago. He too had lent sago grounds to his foster family, grounds that he had received from still another relationship. As I quickly became aware, people have strong claims to their grounds, and thus I expected another reaction by M., despite the fact that I knew he was in possession of some other grounds. But the situation played out differently. M. did not accuse G. of not telling him about his rights over paternal grounds. This was what I had imagined. Instead, he responded appreciatively. Once one knows about one's own rights, these rights will be defended naturally. However, if rights are revealed late but with good-natured intention, I was told, there is no distrust of a person's intentions. Rather, one will assess how the other arrived at the decision. G. had thought that M. had been brought up in his maternal family with care. Thus, there had not yet been a need to inform him of what he held for him. M. was aware of G.'s assessment.

A particular attitude becomes evident here. Bosmun foster the idea of mutual trust and ever-growing bonds among food-dealing agents. To approach people with food opens their hearts. People, in principal, want to begin relations with others. If they see that some food or a swamp in which to produce food is offered or returned to them, this marks the onset of possible trustful connections. In 2008, M. and N. were on good terms again. Since M. had lived almost all his life contentedly in N.'s household, he returned. Everyone was happy. However, M.'s identity had taken on a new shape. He now lived with the actualized relationship G. had offered him. His individual field of relatedness had widened. Moreover, N.'s family was now also aware of M.'s shifted social status.

Let me provide a final example that underscores the fact that sago swamps are the mirror of lived morality and that negative outbursts, signs of immorality, should not be staged here. Two elderly men had been contesting ownership of a sago palm stand. They were normally on good terms and had both subsisted on that stand. From time to time, however, they would argue about who was the rightful owner, and lately they were arguing more frequently since the time had come to pass it on to the next generation. I witnessed one such dispute and learned that both men's children (some of them already adult men and women) were indeed tired of their fathers' ongoing quarrel. The mechanism of Bosmun multirelatedness finally brought the quarrel to an end. The men's children had strengthened their own personal relations among themselves, and none of them was keen to participate in this quarrel. Besides, the whole dispute appeared pointless because there was no space left for the palm stand to extend further. If there had been space, people were convinced, the younger generations would have gone on by means of shared usage since there was no need to spoil the existence of good relations. The eldest son of one of the men cut down the last mature palm including its suckers in order to prevent the passing on of disharmony that had already manifested itself in that swamp in the transition from the previous to the present generation. This act finished the quarrel. It also ended the shame that the younger generations had felt about their fathers' social transgressions. Both, in fact, had shown a facet of what Bosmun idiomatically call "murky faces." I will now explore Bosmun habits of sharing and eating food. Vital to those habits is that they are exercised with "shiny, smiling faces."

Foodways of "Murky" and "Smiling Faces"

Up until now, I have been illustrating cases of interpersonal encounters in which particular foodways were performed as the result of disputes. However, a reverse connection also exists. There are certain foodways that definitely cause insult. Grave interpersonal discord indicates that someone has become a *ngumu mbakmbak*, 'a face (*ngum*) that is covered with spoiled sago (*mbakmbak*).' This is the common idiom for a selfish, stingy, greedy, and lazy person. *Mbakmbak* has different meanings. First, it is a color term that refers to all nuances of green, blue, brown, and black. It basically denotes darker colors inherent, for example, to certain types of leaves or waters. Second, it refers to a stage in the material quality of processed sago. Once a certain amount of sago starch has been processed and stored in a container, it stays tasty and edible until a whitish layer called *mbakmbak* forms on its surface. Although it is apparently light-colored, this layer is said to turn sago into a "dark" substance and make the starch taste rancid. The layer can be removed once, but then a food preparer will think about producing new starch for further consumption. Third, the term *mbakmbak* relates to negative / unsociable intentionality in the realm of social behavior. It refers to 'murky faces,' faces that do not laugh and that are the result of bad-tempered minds and self-centeredness. Ideally, people should encounter each other with 'shiny and smiling faces' as did Nguarkavien, a female mythical figure who is considered the epitome of a person who enacts *tip yaaon*, 'sociable behavior.' She was a generous girl who suffered from parental neglect. To end her suffering, she turned into the 'bird of paradise' (*nguarkavien*) and flew away.

In Bosmun understandings, self-centeredness culminates when someone 'eats in secret' (*ngunguru aam*), which is another prevalent local idiom. It is used to reproach others who are too self-sufficient and tend to neglect their food responsibilities toward kin. There is a definite repertoire of food-sharing and eating habits, which I explore below. I start with the description of a specific situation that I observed during my first stay in Daiden. It can be seen as an emblematic situation since it shows how deeply benevolent foodways are ingrained already in children's actions.

A Lesson by Chance—Children Play "Cooking"

Sago swamps and the hearth sites of households, where meals are prepared, are the most important spots where Bosmun children become socialized. Children learn about the food-related "virtue of giving" (Barker 2008: 54) by observing what their parental and other-kin tutors do. Adults do not sit down explicitly to teach their children good behavior. Rather, they watch their children and comment on what they see. If they see that a child behaves selfishly, they interfere directly and make clear that this is not good. A child holding on to a mango, for instance, while other children stand around and watch, is told to share it. If the child is still obstinate, which most children are from a Bosmun adult perspective, the adult tutor simply takes the mango away, cuts it into pieces, returns a piece to the child and divides the remaining pieces among the others. The lesson is an embodied act without much said. I saw this many times with children younger than about six. Older children shared food and told the younger ones to do the same.

If I learned something about how Bosmun parents (and their nuclear and extended kin-members) bring up their children, it was mostly through my observations of how Liklik Yombu, the daughter of one of my "sisters," grew socially (see figure 1.3). Calling Yombu *liklik* ('tiny') fits in with how she was perceived and described by others. During my first stay in Daiden, she was said to be eight years old but looked tinier and more fragile than her companions of the same age. Her mother's father tenderly spoke of her as *liklik bebi rat taim em i bon* ('she was a tiny baby rat when she was born'). She was self-confident and assertive and became my most intimate narrator among my younger guides. Being with her quite frequently, I became aware of how the idea of sharing becomes increasingly incorporated in children's actions. Once, for instance, Yombu became seriously ill with malaria, and many of us felt depressed seeing this formerly lively child now lying down, weak and totally exhausted. After a while, her father's sister offered to care for her because the parents had to look after their remaining children. After about two months, Yombu eventually recovered. The following days, her parents and her mother's parents and siblings prepared Yombu to perform a display of food for her father's sister as a symbol of gratitude. Sago was produced and fish was dried, and whenever I came to see what was going on, everyone said busily: *Yombu bai karim kaikai i go long anti bilong em* ('Yombu will bring her father's sister a gift of food'). The girl, too, was prepared. More than once, she said to me with a proud voice: *mi bai karim kaikai i go long anti bilong mi* ('I will bring my father's sister a gift of food').

The following description tells how Bosmun children playfully learn how to create and appreciate social relatedness. They imitate the foodways their adult fellows use in expressing and strengthening relations. They copy what they see daily at the firesides of households. The house in which I lived was usually surrounded by children's busy gab—children running around and shouting, singing and laughing, quarreling with each other, and getting on together. One day, there was nothing of the "noise" I had come to expect. Instead, I saw several of our children sitting under a stilted house next to mine. The scene was unusually quiet compared to what I normally saw and heard. I was curious about it and went across to the children. To my surprise, I came upon a "cooking scene" played by Yombu and Nzenzema, her "second cousin 2" (MFZSD) of about the same age. They were surrounded by other playmates such as Nzenzema's brother Mbono who cautiously watched the girls' peaceful play. Yombu and Nzenzema "cooked sago and greens." The girls had stirred "sago" (mud) with hot (cold) water in "clay pots" (coconut shells) and were about to pour it on "wooden plates" (mussel shells). The "hearth" (a grid made of sticks) on which the "clay pot" had stood was still in use. The "greens" (ordinary leaves) meant to supplement the "sago" were boiling in a "bamboo tube" (can). Figure 2.4 shows Nzenzema with her brother Mbono in the background holding their youngest sister.

Ideas on human universals came into my mind as I suddenly fell back into memories of my own childhood. I had played similar cooking games with my Serbian friends in my mother's home country during the holidays, and I had also played them at my father's place in Germany, where I grew up. These ideas intermingled with ideas about the conundrum of cultural variation as I paid closer attention to how the girls distributed the "food" they had "cooked." There were more "plates" than actually needed, at least with regard to those who attended the scene, and it was evident that some "plates" were intended to be sent away. Yombu and Nzenzema playfully enacted what they knew from the realm of female activities whereas Mbono, Nzenzema's brother, imitated male manners. Cooking is mainly women's work, but while women prepare meals, one can fairly regularly observe brothers, fathers, husbands, or sons sitting next to them, watching them and entertaining them in relaxed moods. Mbono imitated what adults explained to me as *ramka vaas*.

Figure 2.4: "Sharing Sago." Nzenzema is distributing the "sago" (mud) in "wooden plates" (mussel shells).

This literally means 'to watch (*vaas*) something with one's eyes (*ramak*).' In a transferred sense, it means 'gazing at and thus appreciating food.' In the Introduction, I mentioned that the term *vaas* means 'to see / watch' and 'to think-feel into others.' By mindfully looking at a meal that is currently being prepared or that is offered to one, one shows appreciation for the person who prepared or offered it. This habit is but one within the spectrum of Bosmun food habits.

HABITS OF PREPARING AND SERVING FOOD

To have food and to have a fire (*suak*) in one's hearth (*serap*) with which to prepare a proper meal is as essential to the question of what makes people in Daiden feel comfortable as sago making itself is. What I saw in Yombu's game mirrored what I saw in regular adult social action. A lot of time is devoted to cooking, not only for specific social or ritual events but also for daily consumption. Food should never be prepared in a hurry, nor should it be served too hot. In times past, meals would be served in beautifully carved wooden bowls, which can still be seen although they are being replaced more and more with enamel dishes. The impression I gained from the households that surrounded my house in Daiden and from those that I visited is that a Bosmun cooking spot is a stress-free zone. Women take enough time to stir sago and to boil fish and leafy vegetables, and no one should hassle them while they prepare the meal. Hastiness in food preparation may cause distrust or jealousy (*ŋanzi,* a term also used to denote 'envy').

This idea relates back to a myth that tells of a group of women, among them Masimbo, and a spirit-man named Mbanmbandoŋor. Every time the women went to catch fish at a lake, they would immediately prepare the biggest part of their yield for the spirit-man who lived in the lake, and after his consumption each of them would have sexual intercourse with him. Afterward, the women would carry back the leftovers and quickly cook them for their husbands, who became curious about the insufficient yield and their wives' unusual hastiness. The myth ends as the husbands discover their wives' liaison with the spirit-man and expel them by sending them away on rafts.[7]

A meal has to be prepared thoughtfully. Ideally, it should be given to those one does not want to hurt. Cooking and serving a meal is ostensibly a slow-going activity through which people demonstrate relational harmony and order. If a meal is cooked in a good mood and with a smile, and if it arrives lukewarm, then there is no reason to be suspicious of another's behavior. Meals in Bosmun cuisine are never to be served hot. This would be a sign that the cook was in hurry, and being in a hurry while preparing food indicates in Daiden that someone is trying to conceal something. A cook is usually given ample time to prepare the meal for the whole household. There is almost always someone who looks after the children or fulfills other household tasks while the cook works.

Whether or not an individual has cooked a dish with the required pleasure is in fact quite easy to discern. While there are times during strong sea winds when food is prepared on hearths within the walled sleeping house, for the most part Bosmun cooking is a public performance. It happens outside or on a roofed cooking platform that has no walls, where everyone can see the activities engaged in by the cooks. Once, I saw an interesting construction that in my view underscores that cooking is an activity to be seen by others. A group of adolescent girls were sitting on a platform, which they had built in the branches of a tree (see figure 2.5). They were clearly visible but as I paid closer attention I realized that the group was actually cooking up in the tree.

Figure 2.5: Girls Cooking in a Tree.

The tree stood near a well-frequented road and the girls' attitude seemed to say "Look at us! We are cooking!" People who passed would stop and chat with them, and it was an atmosphere that spread a joyful mood on both sides. Those who watched and those who were watched responded positively to one another, especially as the adolescent girls were starting to become attentive sago makers and cookers.

At least three large meals are served every day. During the night, when a woman rests, her cooking devices should rest too. Traditionally, men were not allowed to bother women to start a fire again. If they were hungry, they would cook for themselves. Only in the context of festive occasions that start with sunset and end with sunrise do women cook during the night for the dancers and singers (see figure 3.3). Whether in a secular or a ritual context, plates should be filled with the same amount of food. This was what Yombu and her consociates had done. Disregarding this obligation can cause trouble, as I saw one afternoon when a plate of food came flying out of a neighboring kitchen-house accompanied by some scolding. A daughter had filled plates with food, but the one she gave to her mother contained a smaller amount of food. The mother instantly felt upset and threw the plate at the daughter, who was on her way to bring another plate of food to kin living in another household. The mother scolded, saying that she had brought up her daughter and that she had fed her. How did she dare to give her that plate! To be presented a full plate of food does not mean that one has to eat it up completely. Once satisfied, one may leave the plate for another who still wants to eat. However, to predetermine that one will consume less than others and to consequently put less food on a plate is considered a disrespectful act. According to the mother, this was what the daughter had done. The daughter had shown her mother what should not be shown, a "murky face."

"DON'T EAT IN SECRET!"
The scene of the group of adolescent girls cooking up in a tree that I described in the last section was appreciated by everyone who saw it or heard of it. The girls had cooked in an open space, and everyone would interpret this as a sign that they would not "eat in secret." They cooked the meal in public, and they would share and eat the meal in public. To consume food in a hidden spot is an absolute social faux pas. Except for times of social liminality or illness, people do not eat inside their walled houses. The mother who scolded her daughter reminded her not to fall prey to this bad attitude. Another form of *nguŋguru aam,* of 'eating in secret,' would be to send for another to come home to eat. It is even worse to do this while he or she is in the presence of others. To "eat in secret," hidden from the views of others, is seen as exactly the same as someone calling another person to the hearth because the meal is waiting there. Not once did I hear or see that anyone said to someone else "come home, your

meal is ready!" People tend to be home at times when meals are prepared, but to say that a meal is waiting at home is interpreted as signaling a person's refusal to be generous. If a family member is currently away, one anticipates there are others who will take care of him or her in terms of food. If someone is out but still near, the right action is to carry the plate of food to where the other is. The act of carrying food to someone is an important part of caring.

Moreover, it is mainly a female performance of pride and self-confidence. Most often, women walk around with plates of food, but sometimes children carry them too. Men may also carry plates of food from one household to another, but will carry them in their hands whereas women carry them on their heads. To carry a plate is not regarded as a sign of oppression but as a sign of female independence and power, especially regarding the creation of sociable ties with others. Bosmun women gain influence by means of their gender-specific foodways, which also makes them highly attractive to men. The women I saw walking around with plates on their heads did so in a leisurely manner and with good humor. The bearing of Bosmun women when carrying plates of food often reminded me of models walking on a catwalk. Women moved their arms and legs more slowly and with a certain swing that was absent when they walked around without food. Being critical food procurers, they receive credit and hence can exercise control in certain social and political spheres. Referring to the status of women, I should also mention that the posts of spirit houses (which have not been built since the 1970s) were decorated with female figures carrying plates on their heads. I was told that it was common to paint such figures on the front and middle standing posts of a spirit house. Although spirit houses were taboo for women to enter, this nevertheless demonstrates a positive conception of female agency. Whenever I heard Bosmun men talking about women preparing food, there was always an admiring tone in their voices. Whereas women in other parts of Papua New Guinea must not "dress or act in ways that suggest a sense of entitlement to the symbols of public prestige" (Wardlow 2006: 56), Bosmun women are encouraged to acquire the symbols of public prestige. In local understandings, this also adds to their male partners' reputations.

If a plate receiver is surrounded by others, he or she is automatically given the opportunity to continue the generosity by offering those around him or her the meal that has just arrived. I discussed this topic with a man whom I witnessed having a dispute with his future wife after she had tried to call him away from some acquaintances in order to eat. The woman was from a neighboring area and thus he scolded her by saying that the women of his place would never do this. I asked him if it was true that he would probably have to go hungry from time to time if she shared his meal with the others. He replied that being hungry in this particular situation was not an issue, even though there are cases in which a wife's neglect of her husband in providing food can cause shame / dispute or "spoons to break." What did matter from his point of view was that people would recognize him and his female partner as having the trait of *ramkandiar*. This trait is externalized most explicitly through food-generosity, which for the most part happens on a nonverbal level of expression.

"Don't Ask! Watch Carefully!"

Since having food defines Bosmun well-being to an enormous extent, people should always keep an eye on what happens at a household's fireplace and whether it is currently being used. If it is not, there will be reason to worry about the members of the household. Those who are inclined to worry (usually one's kin) will see themselves as in demand for providing help. What is crucial though for the unique understanding of Bosmun empathy is that food-related utterances such as the following are never to be posed: "Are you hungry?" "Is there enough food for you?" "Do you wish to eat more?" or "Shall I give you some food?" Such direct interrogation concerning food hurts people's feelings and deeply upsets or insults them (*noi*). A person is comforted when he or she is shown that another attempts to assess his or her state. A conventional question that is allowed and that helps the asker speculate about a person's "food-state" without having to directly address the issue is: "Where have you been and where are you coming from?" Depending on where and with whom a person has been, one may assess whether he or she has received some food. Once, I arrived in a hamlet at night after a long day out, and the teenage daughter of the household's head asked me two or three times whether I really wanted to eat something. Her father scolded her and said: "Do not ask her!' Just bring her something!" Obviously, he felt ashamed. When I asked people to describe *ramkandiar* to me, I was always given information about food-related attempts at positive empathy such as the following: *Yu no ken askim em! Yu yet yu skelim sindaun bilong em! Em i gat kaikai o em i nogat kaikai? Plet pot i stap? Ples faia i on? Ples pulap long kaikai? Yu yet yu mas lukluk na skelim. Nogat? Kisim plet kaikai karim i go!* ('You must not ask him / her! You yourself must assess his / her state of being! Does he / she have food or not? Are there dishes and pots around? Is the fireside in use? Does a place have enough food? You yourself must watch and assess it. There is nothing? Take a plate of food and carry it [to him / her]!')

As the statement shows, states of feeling are linked to whether one has food. There was indeed a lot of food-talk going on in Daiden. People examined in detail who ate what with whom, who cooked what type of food, and who went out with whom to get food; people also reiterated what kind or amount of food was obtained when and where. These were common topics that almost always occurred in Bosmun discourse across gender, age, and household. However, as I was repeatedly told, to openly ask another whether he or she is hungry or whether he or she wants to have a plate refilled with food is highly upsetting. Instead, one should apply a strategy that can be defined as empathetic, based in particular on careful observation rather than on direct interrogation. Associational linkages in Bosmun imagination emerge primarily from observed information. This empathetic mode is the Bosmun ideal of human conduct and their conduit to interpersonal stability. Remember that a person who does not follow the sago spirit's legacy is going to become blind. The word *vaas* ('to see / watch' and 'to think-feel into others') is linked to two further words already mentioned in the Introduction—*yaam* and *xaarak*, which both translate as 'to know / understand.' These verbs can be used separately or together. The three verbs *vaas*, *yaam*, and *xaarak* are also used serially in speech. We see this in the quote of another man with whom I frequently chatted in a mix of English and Tok Pisin. Often, the man would also utter sentences in the vernacular to underpin what seemed important to him (and would immediately translate for me): "The overall thing for us here is based on observation. *Pasin bilong ai i stap. Mot-a ramakniŋ vaaska xaarka yaam ma mongora!*" ('Our way is to observe. You must use your eyes and watch over [others] and thus you will know / understand [them]!')

The phrase *pasin bilong ai* was commonly used as the Tok Pisin equivalent of the term *ramkandiar*. In Bosmun understandings, observation is morally good and should serve to create an atmosphere of mutual concern between individuals. This notion implies also a distinct facet of Bosmun personhood. People 'disclose' (*taana tak*) themselves or make themselves transparent to an extent that in other life-worlds could be seen as an overexposure of personal privacy or intimacy. Assessing the feelings of others is a sociocultural imperative, and *vaas* and *taana tak* are the paramount social directives that are encouraged from an early age. These directives make Bosmun empathetic processes possible and help individuals to create substance by which they may be understood by others and with which they may assess others' dispositions. It is unlike what Throop (2011) tells about Yapese strategies of concealment that are said to be worth striving for. In Bosmun moral theory, these strategies are regarded as nonvirtuous. Whereas Yapese have to gaze off in different directions when talking to one another, Bosmun cause affront by doing so. Instead, people seek eye contact and usually try to turn their bodies to face others more directly. To show one's back to someone is—in Bosmun body language—to indicate social or emotional trouble. Nevertheless, Bosmun think of eyes in a way similar to how the Yapese think of them. Eyes are the "crucial expressive site for discerning another's true feelings and thoughts" (Throop 2011: 128). Since kin in Daiden openly seek to empathize with others, gazing into one another's eyes is essential.

Ndiar as such—generosity channeled through specific palm-planting and food-sharing practices—was instigated by the deeds of the sago spirit. But *ramkandiar*—'watching others and being watched'—is based upon another myth that tells of a male ancestor called Ramakniŋ. Later, I delve into the argument that Bosmun empathy is an emplaced phenomenon. We will see that this emplaced sense of empathy is also connected to the story of Ramakniŋ. The word *ramakniŋ*[8] literally means 'a pair of eyes.' Ramakniŋ is an ambiguous figure. On the one hand, he is the Bosmun epitome of an egocentric tyrant. People most often described his nature in this light. He is seen as diametrically opposed to what defines an amiable, good-natured person. On the other hand, he is commonly believed to have prompted Bosmun food-related empathy—although he is not the one who promoted the virtue of reciprocity, but rather the mandate to "watch others carefully." The myth is short but quintessential, and it localizes a mythical path from the Bosmun area to Manam Island, or Moinamba as it is called in the Bosmun vernacular.

A Chief's Path Leading off to Manam

Ramakniŋ and his family belonged to the Somnzen clan [of the Rom clan-association]. The world was in order until Ramakniŋ started to behave like a "chief." He claimed special attention and care should be offered to him without reciprocating it. At all times, he would sit on his open platform, holding his spear, observing and scolding everyone, and expect his family to serve him food. He would even request to be carried off to relieve himself, to be cleaned after urinating and defecating, and to be carried back to his platform. However, he did not state explicitly that he wanted food to eat. He would simply remain sitting on his platform, watching passers-by and awaiting their reaction. Since people felt obliged to care for him, they did so for a while. There had been no precedent of a character comparable to Ramakniŋ. No one knew of the attitudes of such selfishness that Ramakniŋ had imposed on them. Finally, his family became annoyed with him, took away his spear and expelled him. Ramakniŋ set out alone by canoe and arrived on Manam Island.

Bosmun do not follow the principles of chieftainship and hierarchical relations. They think of chieftaincy as a type of hereditary leadership based on what they know from nearby Manam Island. In fact, in their theory of how societal structures inside and outside their local universe came into being, it was Ramakniŋ who brought chieftaincy to Manam.[9] Ramakniŋ's major emblem is a spear decorated with cassowary feathers. In her ethnography on Manam, Lutkehaus (1995: 280) writes that a supernatural being instigated Manam hereditary leadership, called "*tanepoa*," by leaving either lime or cassowary feathers behind. In defining "*tanepoa*ship," Lutkehaus (1995: 294; original emphasis) also underpins that generosity is central to the enactment of Manam chieftainship. From a Bosmun perspective, Ramakniŋ's manners do not correlate with generosity and benevolence. Precisely because of the lack of those traits, he was sent away. Yet, I was told that although he was a terrible character, he "watched others," and thus opened the way to a new mode of interpersonal, empathetic communication. Ramakniŋ's descendants transformed his intentionality that, due to his overt selfishness, had a rather negative connotation into positive intentionality. Ever since, members of the Somnzen clan must not leave any leftovers of sago lying around. They must collect every tiny piece of sago that they see. The logic that Bosmun connect to this tradition is that it is a reminder to use one's eyes carefully and in ways that do no harm to anyone.

When someone said to me that he or she had watched another person doing something, it was common that he or she would add a comment about what the observed situation actually meant. A father, for instance, told me incidentally that one of his daughters had stopped eating sago pudding a few days ago. To intentionally stop eating a specific food is a particular means of emotional communication. Equally important is the fact that the father automatically added a comment that showed that he was assessing his daughter emotionally: [Em] *banisim em yet long kaikai* erok. *Tasol em i no autim wari bilong em yet. Ating, bihain em bai autim. Mas i gat sampela kain wari stap wantaim em.* ('[She] has deliberately stopped eating sago pudding. But she has not revealed her worry yet. I think she is going to tell [us] about it later. There must be some kind of worry [that distracts her].')

Ramkandiar is, first of all, to use one's eyes (*ramak*) to watch others carefully and to accrue knowledge about them. Secondly, it is to use the accrued knowledge to respond to others, ideally in kind ways (which is to exercise *ndiar*). No one could actually remember someone being born blind or having become blind during the prime of life, and thus the answers I was given on whether blind people could have *ramkandiar* or not remained purely speculative. People assumed that even blind people must be able to internalize and externalize this trait as long as they were capable of sensing others' physical and emotional dispositions. A blind person would have to carefully listen to what a third party stated about the person he or she was concerned about and would thus gain insight. Blind or not, whether to take for granted the information one receives from a third agent depends on what relation one has with this third agent. This again is an example that shows how the mechanism and the force of multirelatedness turn up within the regulation of Bosmun ideational matters. If amiable foodways have defined a relationship so far, one will tend to turn the version of reality told by a third party into one's own. Thus, constantly, relational-based views of reality emerge. As said, positive foodways are a mechanism to instigate feelings of trust. I do not wish to make naive statements such as that once a Bosmun receives a plate of food he or she is immediately convinced of the other's reliance and good-naturedness. I rather have in mind the enduring relations made between people through years of hard work and constant reciprocities. As people would imagine, blind people can also create such ties. Nevertheless, seeing, and watching in particular, is the source of the prime ability to create connections with others. It is the perceptual mode that enables people to respond to one another most cogently. Old people, of course, might suffer from loss of sight. However, with increasing age they also gradually divorce themselves from the most vibrant and life-affirming activities in life.

The Shifting of Plates and a Social Taste of Food

As I have described, the processed starch of sago palms has to be exchanged regularly among households. People also deliver plates of cooked food on a regular basis. The number of plates cooked in a household depends not only on how many members a household obviously has, but also on the members' relationships with others. Related people who live nearby should be included at least once a day in the provision of meals. While gathering data on food exchange, I saw myself forced to reformulate my notion of what counts as a household's social boundary. The idea that everyone who cooks for a household is automatically a part of it in terms of residential belonging, as one could expect according to habits of cooking (and the articulation of identities linked to it) found in other societal settings around the globe, is not strictly the case in Daiden. Plates from elsewhere, from spatially separated but socially connected households, are expected to arrive more or less constantly.

Earlier, I explained the huge matrix of what a person in Daiden theoretically regards as his or her kin-relations. From time to time, everyone included in such a matrix has to be looked after with a plate of food, assuming one wants to sustain the relationship. As I paid closer attention to this habit and started to follow the plate bearers, I discerned kin-relations more easily than I would have by using the common methods of collecting genealogies. The complexity of Bosmun kin-ties was overwhelming, and I more than once had doubts about my own capacity to think in such complex ways. But by following people directly when they carried plates or sent others to carry them, I started to memorize the relations of extended kin since I could trace the faces behind those relations in social space. This applied at least to those relations among the living generations that I encountered.

Anderson takes up the concept of pathways in her study on the Wogeo Islanders in the Schouten archipelago of Papua New Guinea, where "[p]aths … are not only metaphors of people's lives as movement in time. Paths are also concretisations of relations between people belonging to different places: relations that through time have been maintained by people who previously belonged to these places, or more recent relations that people have found it worth while or necessary to maintain" (2003: 51). This holds true for the paths Bosmun plate bearers move along daily. I also realized that the regularity and the frequency of the food shifts express either genealogical proximity or distance.

Apart from that, there was no strict pattern for whom in particular to provide with food. Bosmun moral theory states that everyone should offer and be offered generosity. What became apparent, however, was that by sending food to others, individuals were given space to emphasize their individual connections with others and to articulate amity for specific kin. A woman, for instance, who was especially fond of two of her five brothers, sent food to those two brothers more regularly than to the remaining three.

On another occasion, I heard the following statement in an encounter between two women: *Ah ... mi tok mi bai karim kaikai i kam long yu. Tasol nogat, mi no kam long yu.* ('Ah ... I said [to myself] that I would come to you and bring you some food. But no, I did not come.') Such a statement might be used to indicate an interpersonal problem. On the one hand, it sounds like a confession of guilt. Someone became "murky," forgot to send food to the other and now wants to reconcile by hinting at his or her own failure, thereby making him- or herself vulnerable in the hope that the other will forgive. On the other hand, this statement might also be interpreted as an affront. Someone felt neglected and now wants to remind the other of his or her failure by pretending to be a "murky face" him- or herself. In both cases, the statement has empathetic content.

The sharing of food is a constant screening and reassessing of one's kin-connections. Whenever sago pudding is stirred, a number of plates will definitely be delivered to others. Theoretically, men and women should send food to their biological and classificatory same-sex and opposite-sex siblings, to their biological and classificatory parents, to their biological and classificatory father's sisters and mother's brothers, and to their in-laws. Take for instance the household I stayed closest to: at least once a day, the male household head would send plates of cooked food to two of his cousins (FBS and FBeD), to another cousin's son (FByDS), and to his sister (eZ) and her son (eZS), and one plate would be carried to another nephew (yZS) and his wife. The male head's parental kin and all his other sisters (Z) had died. If they had still been alive, plates would have been carried to them. One brother (B) lived within the same household and was thus automatically encompassed in the daily provision of food. Another brother (B) of the male head, however, lived in another place an hour away. The female household head's closest kin (B's, Z's, and M) also lived in another place half an hour away. They received plates of cooked food only approximately once a week. If they were staying nearby, I was told, they would also receive plates on a daily basis.

One can meet plate bearers on walkabouts to other places fairly regularly. Plates are also regularly shifted between extended kin, but not as frequently as between close kin who live nearby. Approximately once a month, the male household head would also send plates to his MFBS's children, and the female head would do the same with her extended kin. All those relations that a household's couple keeps are usually reaffirmed. Not only do plates leave a household each day but each day plates from other households arrive. Such quotidian shifts of food are a recurring societal phenomenon to be found in many parts of Papua New Guinea. I either saw such shifts while on my way with Bosmun to visit other places or I heard and read about them. Similar food shifting routines occur in the neighboring places of Kayan (A.T. von Poser 2008a) and Giri (Herbst n.d.), and in more distant ones such as in Gapun (Kulick 1992: 27), on Wogeo Island (Anderson 2003: 58–59), or in Collingwood Bay (Barker 2008: 53). Such food shifting does not serve the principle of "basic necessity," as Barker explains regarding Maisin food practices:

> Maisin households produce exactly the same foods, with some variation in quantity depending on household composition and the skills of individual gardeners, fishermen, and hunters. ... Most of the time, there is no practical requirement that compels people to share beyond their own household. Yet, each day, villagers give produce, betelnut, tobacco, and other gifts to their kin and neighbours. Most evenings ... young children can be seen bearing small plates or pots of cooked food from house to house. (2008: 53)

Theoretically, Barker (2008: 53–60) frames the phenomenon of food shifting among the Maisin by drawing upon Sahlins's (1972) notion of "generalized generosity," which is upheld and externalized interpersonally by a regular exchange of material goods such as food, the physical efforts of hard work, and immaterial goods such as mutual guidance and advice. The core aspect of this type of generosity is that it is not exercised with calculation or immediate equalization. To immediately make a return gift as a response to the gift that one has just received is to spoil the social goodwill that was, in fact, offered with the gift (Barker 2008: 55). This matches the Bosmun food-shifting routine. Earlier, I stated that Bosmun constantly keep their minds on their consociates' foodways. This is not just a sign of a calculating social strategy. As I have asserted, it is also the general, existing method to maintain and grasp a person's individuality. Getting a sense of someone by exploring his or her individual foodways is even done with people who do not belong to one's own social circle and with whom one does not engage in the exchange of food. Also, whenever I was asked to narrate my experiences of meeting people in places other than Bosmun, my conversation partners' questions always led me to reflect in detail upon foodways particular to those places. Tracing others' foodways does not serve calculative purposes alone. It is a marked mode to make sense of the social world and those one encounters in this world.

Tuzin (2001: 76) also paid attention to such "like-for-like exchanges" among the Ilahita Arapesh. He merged his findings with theories stemming from French sociology and anthropology (Tuzin 2001: 28, 75–77). When sago is exchanged for sago and yam for yam, Tuzin says, then Durkheim's ([1893] 1933) idea, originally formulated in 1893, of the "solidarity ... termed *mechanical*" as opposed to "[o]rganic solidarity" (Tuzin 2001: 75) becomes relevant. The latter occurs among industrialized peoples where individuals as (social) organs constitute a whole (social) body. They are not self-sufficient units and therefore need to exchange things of and for basic necessity. Contrary to this, Ilahita Arapesh and Bosmun families rely on subsistence strategies that allow for almost absolute economic independence. They are self-sufficient units in terms of food and shelter, and thus a mechanical solidarity is prevalent in which the exchange of things is not really necessary except when theorized as a "mechanism for promoting interdependency *for its own sake*" (Tuzin 2001: 76; original emphasis). Following Mauss's ([1925] 1966) ideas on the gift as a socially motivated transaction, Tuzin concludes with a categorical differentiation between commodities and gifts. Things exchanged in societies based on organic solidarity are mere, impersonalized commodities, whereas things exchanged in societies such as Ilahita Arapesh—and I may add Bosmun—have moral content (Tuzin 2001: 77).

In Bosmun life, the shifting of plates of food is morally and emotionally charged, and is linked to local empathetic processes. This becomes clear if we look at how it is performed. By and large, the shifting of food is a nonverbal routine, as is the way of assessing another's state of being. We have heard of certain questions that are never to be posed in local food-related discourse. Similarly, one will not arrive with a food plate in another household and say: "Look at the meal that I have cooked for you!" On the way, a plate bearer might inform passers-by whom the food is meant for; but in the presence of the actual receiver, the plate is put down without making any further explicit reference to one's own intention. Likewise, the recipient will not say: "Thank you for that food!" He or she will briefly gaze at the plate appreciatively and that is all. Many times I had the chance to watch plate bearers arriving as I sat with informants. In these contexts, I never saw any attempts made to state publicly one's own act of generosity in the presence of someone toward whom it was directed. A food bearer just puts down a plate and if the household residents are busy, he or she will simply leave after a few minutes without saying anything about his or her reason for coming. Those who live in this household will still have taken notice of him or her, and will respond at some point later in time by returning a plate. This can be the same or the next day for close kin who live nearby. If it is a plate that came from extended kin, there is no need to return the gift immediately. All members of a household may eat off a plate that comes from elsewhere (unless it is food from a self-planted palm), but usually they know for whom a particular plate is meant by taking notice of who brought the plate. Thus, it is left for the intended recipient, who may redistribute it again.

When returning a plate of food, the former recipient need not ensure that it contain the same amount of food or the same category of food. If it is to contain food that fills up empty stomachs and creates lasting relations, it is sago pudding topped by fish, prawns, or mussels and leafy vegetables (the latter cooked in coconut milk). If it is garden produce, the key food to create short-term relational processes, it is plantain, yam, or taro topped by fish, prawns, or mussels and leafy vegetables cooked in coconut milk. Though plates within a household should be filled equally, a return gift does not need to be so. As people often said to me, one should give what he or she is able to give. If one has to feed a big family or currently has to collect larger amounts of food for a festive event, a designated plate receiver will not require the same amount back. Most vital is the lasting quality of reciprocity, not the exact matching of the quantity of food that is reciprocated.

Bosmun food-shifting also provides insight into the constitution of "taste." There is no generic Bosmun term for "taste," nor could I detect a particularly multilayered terminology to grasp the possible spectrum of different tastes in Bosmun cuisine. Although sago seasoned with locally produced salt and coconut cream is indeed tasty, there generally is no huge taste variation in view of the relatively uniform food offerings in the Bosmun environment. However, a Bosmun constitution of taste must be seen in the light of the premise of social relatedness. Food that tastes good will be described as *peskete,* food that does not taste good is described as *ŋaamŋaam,* and food that causes the teeth pain is called *ndair mbimbit* (*ndair* are 'teeth,' *mbimbit* also denotes the 'wrinkles in the forehead'). The last idiom embraces food tastes that are too sweet (caused, for instance, by too much sugar) or too sour and too bitter (caused, for instance, by the juice of lemons). Nonetheless, food that causes the teeth to hurt might be classified as *peskete,* as something that tastes good. In a similar way, food that is cooked in the way it is cooked in every other household might be classified as *ŋaamŋaam,* as something that does not taste good. Bosmun taste, ultimately, is a "social taste." People assess what kind of person has prepared an actual meal and thus unique, person-centered appreciations of such meals emerge. I was told that regardless of whether a sago pudding appears to have the right consistency or not (which depends on the right mixture of starch and water), a person who does not show a "murky face"—a sociable person—cannot produce something that does not taste good. Whether someone will be seen as having a "murky" or "shiny face," in turn, is subject to one's assessments of him or her as a food-dealing agent in long-term relations.

Prospect

In this chapter, I have focused on the making and unmaking of kin in Daiden through a set of recognized foodways said to be moral and immoral. As we have seen, one of the major social habits of consumption is that one should not "eat in secret." From all the food-related incidents that I saw, I chose to tell of the girls who cooked on the branches of a tree to provide an example of how social and mental maturity is acknowledged and articulated from Bosmun perspectives. I wanted to bring forward the idea that the habit of eating in public symbolically encapsulates the local value of transparent personhood, which should facilitate the careful watching and assessing of others. In the following chapter, we hear of Nzari, the mythical heroine, who decides to approach a man whom she considers unmarried because she does not see a woman carrying food to him while she is observing him. To keep the daily shifting of food plates visible to the eyes of as many as possible is in fact to keep relatedness true. Think of the man who got upset because his partner called him home to eat. Through a Bosmun lens, this reads as the undoing of a relationship; only a few months later, the man decided he was not going to marry the woman and they split up. Due to several other occurrences in the story of Nzari, foodways in Daiden also entail emotional meanings, as should become clear in the following analysis of Bosmun life-cycle events.

Notes

1. According to Christian teachings today, the "soul" of a deceased departs to a final destination called "heaven," and corpses must be buried in the ground of a communal cemetery. This is the answer I was given when I asked directly about the fate of a disembodied spirit and about mortuary practices. Yet, in contextualized situations I heard other explanations. The spirit of a deceased person (*ndom*) does not really depart to a faraway place, but rather dwells in close vicinity to the living—namely, in the direction of where the sun sets. Many of my interlocutors still believed that the spirits of the deceased continue to be present among the living and that they can encroach on their lives. At feasts, for instance, dancing groups must always enter the ceremonial ground of a residential space from the west. There is no other path to take. As I was told, the living cannot make successful enterprises of customary performances without the support of the deceased. In beginning a dance performance, the spirits of the dead are formally invited, from the direction in which the sun sets, to accompany the living. I also learned in a contextualized situation that in premissionary days corpses were buried beneath the dwelling-house of the deceased with their heads facing west. I became aware of this as I listened to several people accusing a man of being responsible for the ever-changing watercourse of the Ramu. People said that the man had made a mistake. In the early 1990s, he had buried his father in the ancestral way, not in the modern graveyard but under the father's dwelling-house. This house, however,

stood too close to the banks of the Ramu, and therefore the crocodile spirits of the Ramu kept changing the watercourse so as to reach the decomposing corpse that they smelled.

2. See also Bamford 1998; Bender 1993; Ellen & Fukui 1996; Feld & Basso 1996; Fox 1997a; Ingold 2000; Rumsey & Weiner 2001; Tilley 1994; Ucko & Layton 1999; Wassmann & Stockhaus 2007.

3. In the past, betel nut was chewed only on particular social and ritual occasions. Now, even children start to chew betel nut from an early age. However, most parents take care that their children do not mix the betel nut with lime (produced from burned mussel shells) and pepper vine. The combination increases intoxication but has to be chewed carefully since too much lime burns the oral cavity.

4. I talked to several middle-aged mothers and fathers, all of whom said that due to compulsory schooling, today their daughters stay in seclusion for no more than a month. This attitude of fitting once sophisticated practices into a newly emerging social and economic fabric was described as *sotkat* ('shortcut') to me, and it was applied within several domains of ancestral conventions.

5. Boys no longer seem to be benefiting from such publicly exhibited reaffirmation, since almost all rituals in boyhood that led into male adulthood have been abandoned. Bosmun males receive a similar kind of reaffirmation only much later when they start to erect their own dwelling-houses (which every young man should have accomplished prior to marriage). In order to have his house roofed, a man depends on the helping hands of others since, as I stated earlier, one is not allowed to enter a house roofed with sago leaves from his own palms. Therefore, food appeals have to be made during the whole day when a house is roofed. Roofing a house is mostly a one-day enterprise, and the men who do the roofing (the future house owner himself only builds the substructure) have to be given proper meals up to five times a day, as I counted at one such occasion. This can only be successfully accomplished if the future house owner moves within a social circle of good relations to help with the provision of food.

6. The term *xaam* refers (1) to the eating spoon, (2) to a type of tree, and (3) to a male personal name. Another word for 'eating spoon' is *mbaak* with its plural form *mbair*. If I have an in-law who is called Xaam, I must call him Mbaak, and if I want to refer to the eating spoon I must use the second option. The same would apply in the reverse case if my in-law's name were Mbaak. Then, I would have to address him (or the eating spoon) with Xaam.

7. No one ever clearly confirmed to me that these were of the rafts that created a mythical track to the protruding island when the Bosmun area was still surrounded by the sea. However, some of my informants identified the place from where Masimbo and her female fellows were expelled as Imbando, a mythical (and actually existing) place in the vicinity of the Lower Sepik.

8. *Ramak* is the singular form for 'eye.' *Niŋ* refers to 'a pair.' In the Bosmun language, the plural form linguistically starts with three. Thus, 'eyes' in general (not confined to 'two eyes') are referred to as *rimsi*.

9. To denote a Manam 'chief' or a 'leader' in general, Bosmun apply the same term that they apply to their own type of sociopolitical leadership—*kaakos*. However, when they speak of *kaakos* within their own area, they do not refer to a leader empowered by inherited rights but to a leader who gains authority and affirmation through individual talents.

⊰ Chapter Three ⊱

Nzari's Journey and the Enactment of Life-Cycle Events

Like other Bosmun myths, the story of Nzari is a narrative of positive and negative foodways. Mythical ancestors also engaged in malevolent foodways. The world did not come into existence by sociomythical virtue alone but also by sociomythical mistakes. Interestingly, stories that tell of the mistakes of cultural idols do not simply create "paradoxes in mythology" (Lohmann 2008: 116), but invite the people who have become familiar with these stories over time to form their own opinions about them. Referring to a particular Asabano story character who is said to have brought death, decay, and witchcraft to humankind, Lohmann states: "The very strangeness of mythical beings' actions, it would seem, is part of the appeal of myths. It makes them memorable … and it makes them appealing subjects for contemplation, speculation, and interpretation. Myth users can think about why the characters acted as they did, and what this says about the human order that they established in their myth's charter" (2008: 116). The story of Ramakniŋ presented in the last chapter is such an example. Though he was known as a tyrant, his descendants traced back to him the precept of "watching others." To fully grasp Bosmun motivations in interpersonal flows, I believe, the story of Nzari has to be taken into consideration. Here, the motif of assessing others via food-related behavior occurs as part of lived agency.

With Nzari in mind, I discuss how moments of interpersonal intimacy are communicated in Daiden through another set of recognized foodways. I provide more information on the associational context underlying empathetic processes in Daiden. What does it mean for a man and a woman not related in terms of recognized kinship to share bananas or sago? What do clay pots and conjugal consumption taboos tell us about procreation? What do relatives mean when they hinder a young couple from jointly making sago? What kinds of foodways exist to express parental care, discontent with another person, or the loss of a beloved individual? How are people commemorated? What emotional values do objects such as sago scrapers and eating spoons have? In answering these questions, I introduce more food-related idioms and explanations. Toward the end of the chapter, when I talk about food taboos with regard to collective and individual mourning, I claim once more that kin in Daiden is made rather than given.

Nzari's Pathway

Nzari is the most powerful female character in Bosmun myth and one of the heroic figures who was adored in premissionary times. She is a *raaraŋ*, a 'supernatural entity,' and more specifically, she is a *ŋgaape*, one of the very first tree-spirits that existed. Nzari's mythical path traverses the landscapes of several sociolinguistic groups along the north coast and offshore as well as the Lower Sepik-Ramu inland area.[1] According to the Bosmun worldview, Nzari is the patroness of womanhood. She gave women the markers of female identity that are universally considered respected and powerful insignia: fire, clay pots, and cooking skills, as well as knowledge about childbirth. The fact that Bosmun men hold women in high esteem is attributable to Nzari. Although she is primarily regarded as being responsible for female affairs, her story is an epic of human sentiment in general. It is recounted by both women and men and is not confined to a single clan. Details vary according to the narrators but, on the whole, Nzari concerned everyone. The myth is as much a story about positive empathy as it is about empathetic failure. It tells about human joy, love, and sexuality, male-female harmony and union, interpersonal kindness, respect, and sympathy, about trust and mistrust, loss, abandonment, and rejection.

Beyond narration, I came across Nzari's figure in various ways similar to the ways in which I came upon other mythical figures. Bosmun mythical knowledge is scattered. I saw Nzari on a carved image—as an abstract female body with straddled legs decorating old, battered paddles traditionally used by women (see figure 3.1). In the string-figure games that are popular with women and children, Nzari's representation also turned up. Whenever I saw that particular string-figure game being performed, it was accompanied by excited laughter, since that specific string body overtly imitates sexual intercourse. String-figure games in Daiden are personified or objectified and while shaping a string, women tell succinct tales (see figure 0.7). In this way, they teach children, especially girls, lessons. Nzari seemed to be all-pervading. A betel nut that was reddish inside, for instance, was to be chewed by women; due to the red color that bears connotations of female blood, it was called "Nzari's betel nut." Out in the forest and in the vicinity of nearly every household stood a tree called *roombuŋ*, whose leaves are important in local healing practices. This tree also relates to Nzari's deeds.

Walking through land with people or canoeing the Ramu and its rivulets gave me access to their cosmological view because the whole environment was created by ancestral potency at a time before human beings existed as they do today. Many times when I passed a *roombuŋ* tree people would point to it and remind me that this was Nzari's tree. Bosmun mythical narratives, including that of Nzari, are frequently framed as journeys from place to place and might be called "topogenies," a term suggested by Fox (1997b: 8) to refer to place-anchored song and storytelling on Roti in Indonesia.[2] Bosmun performances of place-related sung recitals (*saane*) can take up to fifteen hours, starting with sunset and ending with sunrise. A glimpse of Nzari's tale occurs in a huge recital called Mbunset, a mourning chant that refers to several culture-instigating protagonists, comprising forty-five verses that individual chanters may repeat at will. Nzari's home, where she set off from, is located in the hinterland of the Mbur tributary—at a place called Yaeŋ, which is a spot of little use, with nothing to offer except clear water and floating grass. According to Bosmun collective ancestral memory it is here where Nzari once lived in the hole of the tree *roombuŋ* together with her mother, a python. Yaeŋ is believed to be the place where the ocean and the first island came into existence, and afterward certain lands and rivulets, and the Ramu. Yaeŋ is believed to be an unusual spot since it does not share the typical characteristics of the remaining environs that are predominantly distinguished by mud-

Figure 3.1: Female Paddle Showing Nzari.

colored waters and swamps full of sago palms. Nzari took part in creating the physical world but she was not the only one to shape it entirely; several mythical agents contributed. Sometimes their actions overlapped. I was told that the island already existed when Nzari entered the mythical stage. The formation of the Mbur tributary, though, is ascribed to her and / or Saane, another protagonist whose (male) identity merged with Nzari's (female) identity in some versions, whereas in other versions their identities were strictly separated. During Nzari's time, the sea was believed to have started at the mouth of the Mbur at a place still localizable called Ndaametap.[3] At that place, Nzari is said to have found a sago palm stem. She used it to paddle out to the infinite sea where she finally formed the island of Manam.[4]

Narrators basically recounted four central episodes with regard to Nzari's endeavors; these episodes were sometimes complemented by other minor ones. With the exception of one episode in which Nzari appears as an old woman, she usually appears as an independent young woman of exceptional beauty who is open to men's desires to get involved with her. It is, in fact, Nzari who approaches men first. Since she is in possession of extraordinary powers (*ndoor*) to instigate love / longing (*soŋgae*), her approaches are always successful. Nzari's story usually starts with how she comes upon a man called Soŋe. The story presented below is based on the original verbatim account that I received from M., K., and Ŋ. in October 2004 (see Appendix).

Soŋe: Connecting and Disconnecting Foodways

Soŋe was among the first males to attract Nzari's attention and vice versa, and thus she decided to follow him. She noticed Soŋe as he was building a canoe in the forest near where she lived with her mother, a python. She watched him stealthily and since she saw that no woman accompanied him regularly to his working place or looked after him by at least carrying food to him, Nzari reasoned that Soŋe was not married. To prove this, she secretly placed various gifts at a spot Soŋe would walk by, casting a spell so that he would find the gifts. The first gift was betel nut, the second a ripe banana. Each time, Soŋe was excited about the gifts and started to speculate about his hidden benefactor. The third time, Nzari placed a coconut shell filled with a small portion of stirred sago and hid herself where she could see him. Again Soŋe felt elated, as did Nzari in seeing his reaction. Finally, she resolved to reveal herself. This time, she prepared a huge portion of stirred sago that she would carry in a food-storing container. She dressed up, took a new betel nut to chew, and walked toward him. Her scent, which preceded her actual appearance, exerted a pull on Soŋe and as she came into sight, he became enraptured by her; never before had he seen such a woman! Nzari hurriedly told him that he should quickly eat the meal she had brought so that his wife would not jump to false conclusions if she saw the two of them in this situation. Soŋe replied that he was unmarried and in turn warned her to be cautious should her husband arrive and see the two of them together. Nzari, too, said that she had no spouse, and thus they became partners.

Nzari and Soŋe lived in the forest until she became pregnant. She then followed him to his home. They lived in harmony, and she gave birth to a son called Mbobot. Nzari stayed in a birth-house until Mbobot started to crawl. Then it was time for the couple to resume their cooperative work of sago making. Nzari called her snake-mother to come and look after her son while she was away with Soŋe. She bedded her child together with her mother in a large clay pot, but told no one that the python was her mother. Nzari, however, had a premonition and told her mother to send a sign should they become threatened. Eventually, the python was discovered and put to death by Soŋe's relatives, who did not know that it was Nzari's mother. While rinsing sago out in the swamps, Nzari saw ashes falling down and covering her breast, and thus she felt that her mother was dead. Instead of telling Soŋe the truth, she pretended that her breast must be sensitive because her son was longing for milk, and that they would have to go back. Upon their return, Soŋe's relatives were already cutting up the snake in order to cook it. Despair befell Nzari, but she hid her tears by pretending that smoke from a fire had got into her eyes. She was disappointed that Soŋe did not recognize her misery, but she did not reveal the truth. After the relatives had finished their meal, Nzari secretly took the bones of the snake, decorated them, and buried them.

The next day, Soŋe went out to burn a grass field. He asked Nzari to cook banana for him for when he returned. In her pain and now full of desire for revenge, she cut Mbobot, the child, into pieces, mixed him with the banana, and cooked it. A relative of Soŋe heard the child's cries, but Nzari said that she was decorating the child (piercing the child's earlobes and nasal septum in order to decorate those body parts) and that that had made the child cry. Then she took all the belongings that she had brought into existence, like female bodies bear babies—fire, plates, clay pots, dogs, and fowl—and stored them inside her body by swallowing them. Then she left, first destroying every canoe except her own so that no one could come after her.

Soŋe returned home in anticipation of the meal. He wondered where Nzari was but soon started to eat the meal she had left for him. While he was eating, he realized that something else was in the meal of cooked banana. He was about to consume his own child. (In some versions he does so.) At that moment, he became aware that he had done Nzari a great wrong, although he did not know what exactly it was. He ran after her but could not reach her. All the canoes were broken. Nzari was already out on the water but still close enough to tell him about the snake's real nature and the agony that his family had brought upon her. She yelled that it had been her mother who had fed her and not her husband! Soŋe tried to apologize, but according to Nzari, it was too late. She embarked on her next journey.

In the mourning chant Mbunset, there are two verses (called *simando*) that are dedicated especially to the tragedy of the man Soŋe. I discovered this as I recorded and translated the chant in August 2005.

Simando-oo simando simando simando simando simando simando simando
simando simando
Yeyak ma simanda-e simaranda

Sokve ma simanda-e simando
Mbobot ma simanda-e simaranda
Soŋe ma simanda-e simando
Simando-oo simando simando simando simando simando simando simando
simando simando
Yeyak ma simanda-e simaranda
Sokve ma simanda-e simando
Mbobot ma simanda-e simaranda
Nzari ma simanda-e simando

aa-a Moinamba ma simandaro-o-o-o
aa-a Sokve tok ma ŋgoris-oo
aa-a Tei tok ma tei tei
aa-a Sokveeitok veeitook

Simando is a word used to express lament in song. When investigating what people associated with these verses, I received more information about the fate of Soŋe, who created his own path of torment. Carrying Mbobot in his arms, he cried and followed Nzari who had left for Moinamba (Manam). The information that the father cries while carrying his dead child is not linguistically encoded in the chant but was given to me as an addition (chant novices are informed of this addition by their tutors only in the chant-learning process). Yeyak is the place where Soŋe comes to halt and listens to the call of the bird Sokve (*Sokve tok ma ŋgoris*[5] means 'Sokve is also a bird') and who becomes his scout (*tei*). Like other Bosmun bird names, Sokve's name has an onomato-poetic derivation. Many of my conversation partners were excellent imitators of bird voices. Sokve's call is *sokveeitook veeitook,* and the bird cries out that Soŋe will never again see Nzari. She is on her way to meet another man.

Kaamndoŋ: Lessons on Fire and the Human Repast

Nzari headed for another landing place, on ground that had mangroves (today, there are no mangroves in the Bosmun area). There, she discovered Kaamndoŋ, a partially male being, sitting on the branches of a Calophyllum tree (*simbir*). Nzari hid herself in another tree to watch the strange being. From his tree seat, Kaamndoŋ waited for fish to appear on the water surface, fish that he would catch by hand. Then, he would dry the fish in the sun and consume them. Kaamndoŋ had no fire. Because of this, Nzari doubted that he was human, and started to mock him by throwing stones at him. Finally, Kaamndoŋ saw her shadow in the waters and urged her to come down. As she climbed down, he instantly wanted to embrace her, but Nzari realized that he had no genitals at all and hence held him off. His body odor, too, was disgusting, and she thought that this was due to the fact that he ate raw fish. Nzari said to herself: "This man does not prepare food in the way human beings do." Kaamndoŋ, in fact, had no knowledge of fire and its use in cooking. As Nzari started to talk about fire and what she would use it for, Kaamndoŋ became anxious. Since Nzari inevitably felt attracted to men, she wished to engage in sexual relations with Kaamndoŋ. Since she was a powerful woman, she reshaped him according to her desires and revealed her bodily powers to him. First, she pierced his body at the spot where (in humans) the anus is. Kaamndoŋ instantly felt relieved because now he was able to fart and defecate. His anxiety settled, and he sat next to her on a platform that she had told him to build. Then, Nzari intentionally threw down a lime spatula and asked him to pick it up. As he looked for the spatula beneath the platform and was about to get up again, Nzari quickly crawled to a gap in the platform, put her legs astride, and let fire pour out of her vagina (*kan*). Seeing that, Kaamndoŋ again became fearful, but Nzari reassured him by instructing him how to handle fire and make a hearth on which she could put a clay pot that also had come out of her vaginal orifice.

To renew Kaamndoŋ and give him a human scent, Nzari boiled the leaves of her tree *roombuŋ*. With this water, she washed him. Then, she took the longish umbel of a breadfruit tree (*kaonzo nduan*) and a pair of inedible fruits of round shape (*yimbin*), stuck them onto his body, and thus Kaamndoŋ received male genitals (*eis*). Then the time came for the final lesson. Nzari took Kaamndoŋ to the swamps. Here they produced sago, ate together, and had sexual intercourse. Kaamndoŋ was delighted as Nzari told him that what they had just done was what makes humans human. However, she also made clear to him that this was meant to be a highly intimate matter between a man and a woman. Nzari's she-dog, who had followed the couple, had witnessed the scene by chance and told them that she had seen it. Nzari feared that the dog would gossip. To keep their intimacy untouched, Nzari cut the dog's tongue short (ever since, dogs have been believed to be unable to speak like humans). After showing Kaamndoŋ how to eat properly and have sexual intercourse, she gave him spears, a paddle, and a canoe, and he became a fisherman. They complemented each other in labor and conjugal life.

One day, Nzari became annoyed by two fish that splashed her while she was fetching water. The fish were Mindu and Ŋgoirpak, two malevolent female beings who could take on human shape. They taunted Kaamndoŋ by stealing one of his spears, and he wanted to chase them. Nzari felt that the fish were going to do harm to her and Kaamndoŋ. She begged him to stay but he did not listen to his wife's objections. He wanted to retrieve the spear he had received from Nzari. Mindu and Ŋgoirpak incarcerated Kaamndoŋ at a place far away from Nzari's home and abused him. They did not allow him to leave the house and they constantly kept him sexually stimulated, which deprived him of all his energy (it is commonly believed that women's substances are dangerous to men). He attempted to escape since he knew that Nzari was waiting for him. "She was right," he thought. Kaamndoŋ convinced Mindu and Ŋgoirpak that they should have game to consume, and that he should go out to hunt it. Out in the forest, he met a male *ŋgaape* (a tree-spirit).

Since these women were known to harass everyone, the spirit assisted Kaamndoŋ in escaping. He made a paddle and canoe, spears, and other weapons for him. Kaamndoŋ, in turn, would provide the tree-spirit with pig meat. On the night of his escape, Kaamndoŋ took a banana that resembled his penis in size, and placed it between the women who believed that they were still holding onto his body. Kaamndoŋ tied up the sleeping basket (a traditional version of a mosquito net) with the women inside, locked the door, ran to his canoe, and set out. The women tried to chase him, but Kaamndoŋ repulsed them with his weapons. Finally, he returned home. Nzari was still there but ready to leave him. Kaamndoŋ had ignored her warnings. She was just waiting for him for a last argument.

The following account that tells about the end of this episode is taken from a narrative that I received from a group of women in mid 2005. It is presented in the original language to emphasize the force of food in emotionally challenging encounters. K., a woman in the circle of my female narrators, in particular, talks about how Nzari hurts Kaamndoŋ by pointing to what he needed to be given by her in order to become human. K. forcefully enacted the tension between Nzari and Kaamndoŋ by raising her voice in different ways and with different levels of intensity. Thus, it is also due to this woman's individual, passionate performance that I vividly remember her words, which I present here:

Nzari ... daunim olgeta samting bilong em! Daunim haus bilong em, daunim plet pot bilong em, daunim dok mama bilong em, olgeta samting. Daunim pinis, em go sidaun wet i stap. ... Nzari lukim [Kaamndoŋ] na tok: "Longtaim yet mi sidaun!" ... Kaamndoŋ kam tasol [na tok]: "... Mi kam! Nzari! Nzari! Mi kam! Yu stap we? Nzari! Mi kam!" ... Nzari sanap lukluk long em i stap. Em haitim em yet i stap. [Kaamndoŋ] toktok olsem i go. Em krai. ... [Nzari] go daun tasol kisim kanu, em go sanap autsait. ... Taim [Kaamndoŋ] toktok raun pinis long hap bilong tupela, kam autsait, em lukim Nzari sanap namel long wara. [Em tok:] "... Em ya! Tupela meri ya, tupela kisim mi go na ... tupela meri nogut i kisim mi go na bagarapim mi. Yu kam! Yu meri bilong mi ya! Yu gutpela meri bilong mi ya! Yu kam!" [Nzari tok:] "Ah? Kaamndoŋ mbaang! Kaamndoŋ mbaang! Yu no save kaikaim kaikai long faia! Yu no save kaikaim kaikai long pot! Yu save kaikai fis i no tan long em wantaim grile yu daunim i go daun! Maus bilong yu i sting! Insait long bel bilong yu i sting! Snek pulap long bel bilong yu! Yu stap. Mi go nau." ... [Kaamndoŋ krai:] "Yaka-aa ŋgom mese! Yaka-aa Nzari! Yu kambek!" Nzari tanim lukluk long em pinis—em pul! Pulim!

(Nzari ... swallowed all her belongings! She swallowed her house, she swallowed her plates and her clay pots, she swallowed her she-dog, everything. Having swallowed everything, she sat down to wait. ... Nzari caught sight of [Kaamndoŋ] and said to herself: "I have been sitting here a very long time already!" … [Finally] Kaamndoŋ arrived [and said:] "… I am back! Nzari! Nzari! I am back! Where are you? Nzari! I am back!" … Nzari stood up and watched him. She did so from a hidden spot. [Kaamndoŋ] continued calling after her. He cried. … [Nzari] went down, took a canoe, and went out [on the water]. … After having looked for her all over their place, [Kaamndoŋ] went further out and saw Nzari in the middle of the water. [He said:] "… Look! Those two women, they took me with them and … those evil women took me and spoiled me. Come back! You are my wife! You are my good wife! Come back!" [Nzari said:] "Ah? Kaamndoŋ! I cared for you! Kaamndoŋ! I cared for you! You did not eat food cooked on fire! You did not eat food cooked in a clay pot! All you ate was raw fish, and you even gulped down its scabies! Your mouth stinks! Your belly stinks! Your belly is full of worms! Stay! I am off!" … [Kaamndoŋ cried out:] "Ooh my wife!" Ooh Nzari! Come back!" Nzari gazed back at him for a last time—then, she headed off and away!)

In this version, Nzari swallows all her belongings, including the fire, and stores them within her womb (*nis*).[6] On other occasions, I was told that she left a fire with Kaamndoŋ as a constant reminder of what he had gained and lost. After this episode, Nzari turns into a matured woman, a mother figure, and she encounters a people who have no knowledge of female maturity or of what women of a high age look like because the women of this group have no knowledge of normal childbirth. In fact, Nzari comes upon a primordial form of the Caesarean section.

Women: Nzari's Present to the Men
Nzari came upon people who were surprised and disgusted by her appearance. Nzari had turned into an old, matured woman. Those people had never seen such a woman and thus had no sympathy for her. Nzari was marked by features of old age. She was almost blind, she was no longer agile, and her dress looked neglected. Only one young girl felt pity for Nzari, and although everyone else kept away from her, the girl helped the old woman to step out of her wrecked canoe. In the distance, Nzari heard other people crying and said to herself that someone must have died. The girl told her that a child was to be born and that the child's mother was soon to die because they would have to cut open her belly in order to deliver the child. Nzari wondered as the girl continued by telling her that in this place the fathers always survived their daughters, the brothers their sisters, and that the children were raised without their mothers. Nzari realized that these people lacked the knowledge of how female bodies could deliver babies without having to die. Nzari decided to teach them the knowledge of childbirth. However, she would reveal this knowledge only to women. Nzari told the girl to bring her the tree that had grown in her wrecked canoe. As on any other journey, the *roombuŋ* tree was with her. Nzari continued pretending that she was old and frail; she trembled and could not climb

the ladder that led to the house of the mother-to-be. The girl helped her again. The weeping party did not want the disgusting creature to enter one of their houses, and therefore Nzari started to radiate her magical authority by casting spells. She was embarrassed to see that the soon-to-be mother was still in the house where she normally lived with her husband. In order to spread her magic, Nzari demanded a space secluded from men. She chased the men out of the house and changed it into a *miriri tomuŋ* (a birth-house). Then, she took leaves from her tree, and as she was chanting a spell she rubbed the belly and back of the pregnant woman. In doing so, she pointed to the orifice from where babies were meant to emerge. Eventually, the mother delivered her child without having to die. The child's father longed for his newborn and was prepared to bemoan his dead wife. He, too, was seized with anger because the old woman had denied him access, but then Nzari told him that his wife was still alive. The man became overjoyed and began to think of the old woman in a different light. Nzari stayed for a while and enjoyed the kindness that she was now offered. Then, she set out again.

On her last station before reaching Manam, Nzari again turned into an old woman before she changed back into a young beauty. Thus, she once more makes humans sensitive toward maturity and old age.

Sentiment for the Aged

Nzari encountered two brothers. The elder brother reacted in the same way that the group Nzari had met before had. He was disgusted by her old age and neglected appearance. Her canoe was broken, her bast-skirt dirty, and her net bag shabby, and he wanted to chase her away. The younger brother felt ashamed in view of the elder brother's manners, and invited her to come with him. The elder brother was furious about this but the younger insisted and gave the old woman shelter in his part of the house that he shared with his brother. Since the younger brother worked hard, he asked the old woman to cook for him. With delight the younger brother accepted everything that she cooked, whereas the elder refused it and said: "I do not want to eat food made from those poor hands." The younger brother was very kind. He even helped the old woman to prepare food. He assisted in pouring the water into the clay pot as she stirred the sago and he collected firewood. Nzari began to become seriously attached to her young partner and thought about revealing her real identity to him and, of course, to the elder brother who should know whom he had mistreated. Rejuvenated, Nzari placed a plate of food on her head and started to walk over to where the brothers were working. The elder brother saw her first and was overwhelmed by her beauty. He immediately announced his intention to marry her but the younger one opposed. He realized that it was Nzari. He had been the one who had shown sentiment for the old woman first. He had not mocked her because of her senescence. The brothers started to fight, and the quarrel culminated as both pulled on Nzari while she was still balancing the food plate on her head. Finally, they tore her into halves and killed her. At least, she made the brothers believe that they had killed her. Due to her magical powers, she did not die; instead, she left for Manam.

My interviewees told me that they had no knowledge of Nzari's further fate on Manam. All they knew was that Nzari lives on the island.

Marking Significant Steps of the Life Cycle

In the coming sections, I trace Nzari's ideational heritage in people's verbal and enacted expressions of feelings that are connected to elemental phases in a person's life trajectory—courting, marriage, sexuality, procreation and childbirth, attachment to children and other kin, detachment, death, and mourning.

Courtship and Marriage—Sharing Bananas and Sharing Sago

The way in which Nzari and Soŋe (her partner in the first episode) intimately connect and disconnect is marked by how Nzari offers Soŋe food and how he responds to her offer. In this episode, foodways turn out to be an empathetic method: in placing food for him and watching his reactions, Nzari appraises Soŋe. Since there is no one else who cares for him with food and since Soŋe is happily surprised as he finds the gifts, Nzari ascertains that he is free. In order to prove what she already assumes, she utters a food-related phrase that is the common idiomatic expression in local myth to describe the onset of a male-female partnership. In all narratives that tell of how a man and a woman start to engage, the phrase "eat the meal quickly so that your partner will not see us!" is uttered. As I was told, this phrase might also occur in dialogues of flirtation between courting couples who might secretly offer food to one another. After Soŋe has eaten Nzari's meal, they become both sexual partners and collaborators in the procurement of sago. In marking the borders of kin-relations, Bosmun consider who eats sago with whom. When it comes to the marking of intimacy between a man and a woman, the same code applies.

I never heard the phrase of articulated courting that I found in Bosmun myth being uttered openly between courting couples. Courting is not as public as are other manifestations of interpersonal affection, such as disputes. Nonetheless, I had the opportunity to observe that Bosmun flirtation is food-related, too. Several times I heard food-related compliments such as the one that a young man made as he saw a young woman walking by. Actually, the young man was talking to me, but the woman passed by and caught the man's attention so that he followed her with his eyes, called out her name and declared with a grin (so that she heard it): *Em meri bilong painim abus ya!* ('This is a woman who is skilled at hunting!'). The woman pretended not to notice, but I could see that she walked off with a slight smile.

Courtship between young unmarried adults is allowed. They should have time to assess their future partners and should give their parental kin the opportunity to assess their choice. Two people in courtship are referred to as *ŋaspakmot* ('boyfriend') and *ŋaspakmes* ('girlfriend'). Interestingly, *ŋaspak* literally translates as 'a few bananas.' When assessing the man Soŋe, Nzari made a gift of ripe banana before she decided to share sago with him. As we have seen, banana and garden foods in general do not have the weight that sago has in creating long-term relations. Thus, the sharing of bananas is a sign of interest that does not necessarily lead to a binding relationship. Courting couples do not (or should not yet) share sago. Only married couples do this. This is explicitly manifested when a new marriage is announced in Daiden. There are two ways to get married. People marry due to prearrangements made by their families, or lovers run off together. In the latter case, a man elopes with his wife-to-be at night, with the help of his "messengers" who—prior to the "theft"—must have asked the wife-to-be for her permission. Such a 'messenger' is called *ndaaremot* or *ndaaremes* (*ndaare* also refers to a type of rat). After the elopement, the lovers stay in a camp in the forest, where they are self-reliant. They may also find shelter with more spatially distant relatives who approve of the relationship. If the parents are willing to affirm their children's partner choice, a couple may return home, which is usually to the male spouse's parental household. Remember that Nzari stayed in the forest with Soŋe before she decided on virilocality.

Isolation from the nuclear family can take up to a year if the parents are hesitant to accept their daugther's or son's chosen partner in marriage. In April 2008 I talked to a young woman who had just recently returned with her partner from their time in exile, which had started in May 2007. What she told me about the consequences of her self-decided marriage is comparable to what I heard from other elopers. As a sign of disapproval, her father and mother had burned down their unwanted son-in-law's newly built house. They had also cut down all his betel nut palms. Despite this, the couple had held strongly together, forcing the parents to give in eventually. Disapproving of a marriage that has not been prearranged by the parental generation seems to be a habitual response. The father who destroyed his son-in-law's house and betel nut palms was, in fact, the son of a couple whose relationship once also had been disapproved. To first disapprove and then give in was frequently the pattern of parents in dealing with self-decided marriages. I think that such disapproval (even if it results in a house being set on fire) is a formalized mechanism indicating a daughter's parents' determination to protect her against potential mistreatment by her husband and making him aware that he must expect interference by his affinal relatives.

To approve the onset of a conjugal relationship, a couple and their parents gather for a meal. At this gathering, the bride will officially prepare the first meal for the groom—a plate of stirred sago. This is the first step that ties a couple in a formal way. It is referred to as *mbairim raaŋ*, meaning that the newlyweds replace (*raaŋ*) their former eating spoons (*mbair*) with new ones. However, prior to eating and thus approving of the relationship, the bride's mother has to fulfill a specific task according to customary practice. She will give the new couple advice by explicitly railing against them. The bride's mother's performance is especially serious if the conjugal relationship was not based on prearrangements. Everyone is allowed to listen to this formalized mode of open critique. More than once did I see a mother going to a household with exaggerated motions, yelling at her daughter and son-in-law that they must not show "murky faces." Since with marriage a woman usually leaves her consanguine kin and moves to the house of her husband, it was common that a mother demanded that her son-in-law allow his wife to visit her natal family. Mothers also took the opportunity to remind their sons-in-law of their future wives' pasts, of both their good sides and "mistakes" that these may have made prior to marriage.[7] This was done to protect daughters from unfounded jealousy by their husbands. As I said, courtship is allowed, and thus spouses usually know about the other's former engagements; this can sometimes cause trouble. Apart from individual feelings, jealousy is a part of the expected role behavior among spouses. I was told that the fact that one's partner is admired by others fosters one's reputation because one's care is said to make the partner admirable. *Ol narapela, ol mas grisim meri bilong yu! Olsem na—yu man!* ('The others, they have to flirt with your wife! This makes you a man!') a man uttered in this context. Women also made such statements about their husbands. A woman can be proud if other women try to approach her partner. However, this is all these other women are allowed to do. If a woman thinks of another woman as a serious rival, she will challenge her by proposing that they fight.[8] Whenever women fight with clubs, I was told, magic is involved. The more powerful the magic the more likely is the holder of a club to win the fight. Those who win are said to have "danced like a fowl" (one of the animals that Nzari had brought with her).

Jealousy seems also to be tied to a particular phase in life—when a couple is at the prime of procreation and joint sago production. A woman made this clear to me when she stated how her feeling of jealousy toward a woman who had been the former girlfriend of her husband suddenly came to an end after more than twenty years. Like many other rivalries, this one was well known in Daiden. Lately, however, one could see the two women sitting together in harmony at communal meetings such as church service or *mama grup* ('mothers' group') gatherings. My interviewee explained her loss of jealousy by correlating it to the fact that she no longer gave birth to children. Since she was no longer procreative with her husband, she no longer felt the threat of losing him. Thus, she said: *Bifo, mi save jeles nogut tru. Tasol taim mi karim las bon pikinini bilong mi pinis, belhat bilong mi em pinis. Mi lus ting long meri ya.* ('I used to be extremely jealous. At the time I gave birth to my last child, however, my anger ceased. I do not think about that woman anymore.')

To temper what could become serious outbursts of jealousy, even culminating in violent physical acts, mothers raise their voices toward young couples. In one instance, I heard a mother yelling at her son-in-law: *Maski dispela pikinini meri bilong mi i gat pikinini stap. Yu bai no inap daunim em! Taim yu stat lukluk long em nau, longtaim pinis yu save long stori bilong em!* ('It does not matter that this daughter of mine already has a child. Do not dare to reproach her [because of that]! When you showed interest in her you already knew about her past!')

Should the man indeed become angry because of events in his wife's premarital life, she could easily divorce him without being judged badly by anyone. Divorce remains a lifelong option for both partners, and relatives do not hesitate to encourage it if they see that one of the spouses is suffering from the partnership. Spouses do not have to "dismiss" their partners' affairs as is, for example, expected by Murik wives (Barlow 1995: 107). A precedent was set by Nzari, allowing a spouse to leave their partner if he or she feels bound in misfortune.

In general, prearranged marriages are held to be more stable. In these cases, many kin have pondered whether a man and a woman should become a couple. In the next section, I present parts of an interview that I conducted with K. and S., a couple whose marriage had been prearranged. I took the interview in June 2005, and it tells of how K. was tricked into bringing food to S., her future husband.

A Prearranged Marriage in Retrospect

K. and S. had married more than forty years ago, and they still were a contented couple with five adult children. At the time of World War II, S. was a youngster of approximately thirteen years. K. was born shortly after the war and thus more than fifteen years younger than S. I asked them when and how they became a couple, and K. started by telling me the year of their marriage:

K.: *Sikstifaif!* [She laughs].

A.: *Sikstifaif?*

K.: *Em kam long lif, em polis! … Em kam long lif nau na ol papa na mama … olsem …*

S.: *Ol i laikim mi bai mi maritim em nau. … Ol lain bilong meri ol i laikim mi. Orait, na ol i kam toktok wantaim ol i … olsem …*

K.: ... *ol lain bilong em* ...

S.: ... *toktok wantaim ol papamama bilong mi, ol kandere bilong mi, na mi yet mi no save olsem, mi join pos polis long nainti fiftifaif me wan.* ... *Olsem* ... *mi man bilong harim ol tok bilong ol mamapapa na i save bihainim ol papa* ... *na i save go long wok. Olsem* ... *ol i tok long wanem samting* ... *olsem* ... *go antap long kokonas mi go antap* ... *o ol bikman ol i stap long hausboi na ol i kaikai na ol i tok olsem:* "*Ey! Kisim ol plet i go long haus!*" *Mi mas karim i go! Mi man bilong harim tok bilong ol bikman. I go go go na ol i lukim pasin bilong mi i gutpela.* ... *Wanem wok long komiuniti i kamap* ... *long wok long rot o long katim ples kiap—bipo—mi mas wok wantaim ol* ... *na sampela yangpela i save les na mi* ... *nogat, mi no save les. Orait, i go go go nau na ol toktok:* "*Disela man ya, man bilong wok, gutpela pasin bilong em*" ...

K.: *Ol skelim pasin bilong mi tu!*

S.: *Ol skelim pasin bilong meri ya nau. Ol tok:* "*Em tu, em gutpela meri. Gutpela pasin bilong em.*" *Orait, em nau ol mamapapa bilong em wantaim ol kandere bilong em ol i kam toktok wantaim ol kandere bilong mi nau* ... *Ol lain bilong mi tok:* "*Mipela i laikim olsem pikinini bilong yupela* ... *bai maritim pikinini bilong mipela.*" *Orait ol i tok:* "*Oh! Laik bilong tupela! Yumi i no save long tingting bilong man na tingting bilong meri na* ... *bai yumi mekim wanem?*" *Orait, ol i makim tasol na i stap. Ol i no toksave long meri ya. Na mama bilong em* ... *mi no save* ... *ating em i bin tokim em pinis na mi, mi nogat. Mi, mama bilong mi* ... *i no tokim mi, ol rait tasol:* "*Ol i makim wanpela meri long ples i stap.*" *Mi stap long Mosbi.*

K.: *Mi yet mi no save. Ol i no bin toksave long mi.* ...

S.: *Wanpela man i rait nau* ...: "*Ol i makim wanpela meri bilong yu na i stap long ples!*" *Na mi tok:* "*Ey! Mi no save nau! Mi no save long disela meri ya!*" [S. smirks] *Mi rit i go go go na mi lukim nem bilong meri ya* ... *na mi tok:* "*Aaah,*" *mi holim leta olsem* [he acts as if holding a piece of paper and looking at it carefully]. ... *Pas bilong papa bilong em i go kamap* ... *i tok piksa long mi:* "*Wanem ol pipia laplap i stap long skin bilong yu, taim yu laik kam long ples, rausim disela deti samting i stap na yu kam nating!* ... *Yu gat meri long ples i stap!*" ... *Mi lap tok:* "*Ey! Papa i makim wanpela meri bilong mi na* ..." *Orait, taim mi kam, mi no save toktok wantaim em, nogat ya. Wanpela hausboi i stap* ... *mi sindaun wantaim papa bilong* [named person] ...

K.: [calls the man's personal name]

S.: *Em tumbuna bilong mi.* ... *Orait, ol toktok pinis. Orait, mama bilong em i tanim wanpela saksak* ...

K.: *Anti bilong mi, meri bilong* [named person], *anti bilong mi.*

S.: *Ol* ... *em tanim wanpela saksak pinis na tokim em:* "*Yu kisim disela saksak na go givim disela tumbuna bilong yu.*" *Giaman long* ... *na bai tumbuna givim long mi! Bai kamautim nem bilong mi na bai mitupela marit! Orait, em nau* ... *putim saksak olsem, putim saksak olsem na i kam* [S. imitates K., putting a plate on her head] *na mi givim baksait sidaun i stap. Taim em kam, em kolim nem bilong tumbuna bilong em. Yu kolim!* [S. forgets his name and asks K. to call it]

K.: [calls his name]

S.: *Em tok: "Ey! Saksak bilong yu ya!" Em tok: "Aahh! I no ken givim long mi! Yu givim long man bilong yu!" Naaa ...* [he pauses] *em nau, em i pulim saksak i kam antap tok ... na mi yaaa ... mi sem nogut tru! Meri ya ...*

K.: *Mi ronowe go hait!*

S.: *Em i mekim olsem ...*

K.: *Mi no save!*

S.: *Em i no save. Em sikrapim het bilong em na em i krai wantaim na go.*

K.: *Mi no save mi bai marit* [she smiles].

S.: *Na mi yaaaa ... skin bilong mi indai pinis! Mi nogat toktok, mi sidaun olsem i stap* [bends his head down]. *... Mi kirap tasol, karim beg bilong mi, mi go ... slip long bet bilong mi krai i stap. Mi wari nau. I stap nau na ...* [named person] *singautim mi: "S. oh! Yu mekim wanem?" Em tok long susa bilong mi yet, tok: "Meri bilong mi i no meri bilong yu! Olgeta taim mi save krosim em long kaikai, askim em. Em nau yu marit nau!" Em nau.*

(K.: 1965! [She laughs].

A.: 1965?

K.: He came on leave, he was a police man! ... He came on leave and our fathers and mothers ... like ...

S.: They wanted me to marry her. ... The family of my wife was fond of me. Alright, and they came to talk with ... like ...

K.: ... with his family ...

S.: ... to talk with my parents, my mother's brothers, and I myself had no idea of that; I was with the police I had joined on the first of May 1955. ... It was like ... I was a man who would listen to what the elders would tell me and I would follow my fathers ... and I used to work. It was like ... I would do what they wanted me to do ... such as ... climbing a coconut palm ... or if the elder men were in the men's house, eating and telling me: "Ey! Take the plates and carry them off!" I would be the one to do that! I was a man who would listen to what the elders said. Some time went by and they realized that I had a good character. ... Whatever work came up in the community ... such as road building or clearing the patrol officer's place—[this was] before—I would work with them ... and some young people would not ... no, I was not lazy.[9] Alright, some time went by and they realized: "This is a man who knows how to work, he has a good character." ...

K.: They would also assess my character!

S.: Now, they would assess her character! They said: "She is also a woman of good traits. A good character she has." Alright, so her parents and her mother's brothers came to talk with my mother's brothers.... My family said: "We want your child ... to marry our child." Thus, they said: "Oh! It is up to the two of them! We do not know his thoughts and her thoughts and ... what shall we do?" Alright, they just agreed and left it that way. They did not tell her though. And her mother ... I do not know ... I think she told her but in my case, no, my mother ... did not tell me anything, they [his family] just wrote me: "At home, they [the families of both] have marked a wife for you." I was in Port Moresby [at that time].

K.: I also did not know. They did not tell me anything ...

S.: Now, a man wrote to me ...: "At home, they have found a woman for you!" And I said [to myself]: "Ey! What shall I do! I do not know that woman!" [S. smirks]. I read and read and I read the name of that woman ... and I said [to myself]: "Aaah," I was holding the letter this way [he acts as if holding a piece of paper and looking at it carefully].... Her father [also] sent me a letter ... in which he said metaphorically: "Whatever old cloth covers your skin, when you want to come home, throw this rubbish away and come without anything! ... At home, you have a wife!" ... I laughed and said [to myself]: "Ey! My father has marked a wife for me and ..." Alright, when I came [home] I would not talk to her, nothing of that. There was a men's house ... and there I sat with the father of [named person] ...

K.: [calls the man's personal name]

S.: He was a [classificatory] grandfather of mine.... Alright, they [the families of both] already had talked [about their plan]. Alright, her mother stirred a portion of sago ...

K.: She was my aunt [a classificatory father's sister], the wife of [named person], she was my aunt.

S.: They ... she stirred a portion of sago and told her [K.]: "Take this sago and carry it to this uncle of yours" [S. refers to K.'s uncle as grandfather, since the man was also his grandfather]. That was a trick ... because the grandfather would give it to me! He would call my name and [thus] we would be [looked at as] a married couple! Alright, okay ... she put the sago like that, put it like that [S. imitates K. putting a plate on her head] and she arrived, and I was sitting with my back to her. When she arrived, she called the name of her uncle. You call it! [S. forgot his name and asks K. to call it]

K.: [calls his name]

S.: He said [to me]: "Ey! Here is your sago!" He said [to K.]: "Aahh! Do not give it to me! Give it to your husband!" And so ... [he pauses] okay, he lifted the sago and said [that] ... and I ... I felt deeply ashamed! She ...

K.: I ran away and hid myself!

S.: She did so ...

K.: I had no idea!

S.: She had no idea. She would scrape her head [a gesture to express one's surprise], and with tears [of shame] in her eyes she would walk off.

K.: I had no idea that I was going to marry [she smiles].

S.: And I myself ... my skin was dead! I had nothing to say, I just sat down like that [bends his head down]. ... I rose to my feet, took my bag, went ... to sleep and cry in my bed. I worried now. Thus I remained until ... [named person; a man married to an elder sister of S. and thus allowed to call S.'s name] called me: "S. oh! What are you doing?" He said [something] to me about my own sister, saying: "My wife is not your wife! I always scold her with regard to food, [I have to] ask her [for food]. But you are married now!" This is the way it was.)

If a determined couple follows the prearrangements made by their parental generations as was the case with K. and S., they will engage in further food-related exchange. A bride will start to cook for her groom and he will eat that food. Finally, they will go out and jointly produce sago. Below, I say more about this aspect, but first it is necessary to explore the food-related talk in K. and S.'s account. The way K. and S. fell victim to their relatives' trick was described in regard to the food donation, and it caused feelings of shame or timidity in both of them since the message was clearly uttered and confirmed by the fact that a transmission of food was involved. From this account and other life stories that I collected it is possible to conclude that being ashamed in this particular situation is the expected response. Likewise, it might be theorized that once a new couple starts to apply food-productive skills together, feelings of shame will gradually reduce and intimacy will increase.

A plate bearer must not emphasize that he or she has brought a plate of food to someone. However, K. said to her relative "here is your sago." In this case, it was obvious that she would do so. She was a young woman who carried a plate of food to the men's house where her elder relative was sitting and chatting with a young nonrelative of hers. If a young woman puts down a plate for a male who is not related to her in terms of kinship, this is likely to be regarded as a sign of fondness for that man. This interpretation rests upon how Nzari usually approached men. Interestingly, in telling S. that the plate K. had brought was meant for him, the relative made an empathetic suggestion based on food-related behavior.

Finally, what the man married to the sister of S. said to him with regard to food is also of interest. He said that he saw himself forced to regularly scold his wife, S.'s sister, due to a food scarcity that obviously existed because S. was still unmarried and thus still relied on food gifts from his sister that, in fact, were meant for her husband and their offspring. The man had "to ask for food!" A person in Daiden, however, should never be compelled to ask for food. S. was given two lessons: first, an adult should be married, and second, regular food exchange should define a couple's interactions. These food-based conjugal interactions were apparently disturbed because the sister had to care for her brother who by now was at a marriageable age.

OF SAGO AND CLAY POTS, OF HUMANNESS AND PROCREATION

In the story of Nzari, fire, hearths, and cooking pots are defined as emblems of civilized humankind. They are necessary to transform raw food into cooked food and subsequently unsocial into social human beings. In the process of transforming Kaamndoŋ, her second partner, into a fully social human being, Nzari completes his body by providing him with male genitals and an anus. In this, the myth contains a vital feature common to many Melanesian myths. Kahn (1986: 151–153) reminds us that Melanesian forms of sociality are frequently started as physical bodies receive orifices and digestive tracts. She declares for the Wamira of Milne Bay Province: "The possession of a mouth is a common sign of a civilized being" (Kahn 1986: 151–152). The same applies to the orifice that Kaamndoŋ is given and to his genitals, which, according to Nzari, are equally significant for becoming social or human. After reshaping Kaamndoŋ's body according to her ideas, Nzari goes on to define a further human requisite—the precept of sexual intercourse between male and female, which she relates to the joint making of sago. She shows him how to produce sago and becomes his sexual tutor.

Sexual union and procreation between conjugal partners officially start as they embark on their first joint sago venture. As I already said, the first step to affirm a conjugal bond is when a couple starts eating together. The first joint sago venture of a young couple is the second formalized and food-based step to strengthen the union. The outcome of shared food procurement and shared sexuality is a couple's offspring. The first child is the last marriage-affirming step. Even if this firstborn is returned to the mother's parents, as custom calls for, the event is deemed to bind a couple together in a serious way. The couple has given evidence of its joint productivity. Although newly wed partners are expected to take on the joint production of sago right from the start, they will be mocked by elder relatives who used to be the primary food providers for either the male or the female spouse and who because of that have the right to mock. This type of mockery suggests a profound linkage between sago making and procreation. When the couple wants to go to a sago swamp, relatives will call out (relating to the female spouse): *Yu no ken hariap long karim pikinini. Em i no taim yet!* ('You should wait with delivering a child. This is not yet the right time!'), or (relating to the male spouse): *Yu no ken hariap long givim bel long meri ya!* ('You should not hasten to impregnate your wife!'). Among the

Kaluli, linkages between sago making, sexuality, and marriage also exist, but here sago and marriage seem to have a rather negative connotation. At least, one gets this impression from reading Schieffelin's account about the male Kaluli spouse: "The newlywed sits by the cooking fire eating sago and greens while his buddies cut up a tasty marsupial" (1976: 69). Game, too, is important to the Bosmun diet, but I was told that all foods except for sago pudding belong to a category called *kaikai long laik* ('food that is nice to eat' [but that does not satisfy]) in Tok Pisin. Sago is considered the ultimate source of life and marriage the ultimate constellation to procure sago. Therefore, from Bosmun perspectives, marriage is not disadvantageous but gainful. Discouraging new partners from jointly visiting the swamps serves to remind them that they should always control their *mian*,[10] their 'sexual desires.' I shall give more details about the existing linkage between sago making and sexual reproduction before I turn to the reasons why sexuality is a matter to be controlled.

In Daiden, parallels are drawn between masculinity, or more specifically, male semen, and sago. A first hint at this correlation was given in the story of the sago spirit in chapter 2. Another hint can be seen in relation to the name of an important cultural hero. His name is the secret name exclusively used by men to refer to what is openly called *mbikit* ('male semen'). This hero turned into a very important *mirip*, a 'spirit mask.'[11] He gave sago to an old woman and asked her to stir and mix it with a certain type of wood. Eventually, he covered his face with the resulting sago substance and thus a transformation took place. The hero's facial lineaments changed so tremendously that the first spirit mask came into existence (see Meiser n.d.: 96; Z'graggen 1996: 47).

It is noteworthy that the hero needed the assistance of a woman who stirred the sago in a clay pot. Bosmun clay pots are, in fact, seen as objects of transformative force. In the episode that tells of Nzari's relationship with Soŋe, we heard that the sleeping place of their son Mbobot was the clay pot in which Nzari also stirred sago. From Bosmun views, there is a correlation between clay pots and wombs, on the one hand, and between fire and blood / vaginal fluids, on the other. The clay pot originated from Nzari's womb. It actually emerged in the world as an extension of her body. Fire, too, poured out of her. This correlation is expressed in two significant ways. First of all, Nzari's body is incorporated within Bosmun household architecture. The hole in the platform on top of which Nzari sat with straddled legs to reveal fire to Kaamndoŋ resembles the hearth construction found in every Bosmun kitchen. A Bosmun hearth rests upon a smaller, earth-covered platform, which is set within a square-shaped opening in the kitchen floor. This floor opening holds the fireside where cooking pots are placed. Women are the guardians of this fireside. They extinguish it at night and light it in the morning.

A second important expression for the correlation of pots and wombs is that prior to its use as a cooking device, the newly made clay pot has to be washed with herbal water. The herbs used come from Nzari's tree *roombuŋ*. The women who showed me the entire process of pottery making explained that a clay pot is not going to produce good sago if it has not been washed with *roombuŋ* leaves. In a similar way, *roombuŋ* herbs are used when a woman delivers. In order to facilitate childbirth, the belly and back of the pregnant body have to be washed and rubbed with the leaves of this tree while a wise midewife casts a particular magic spell, the spell Nzari taught the women who belonged to the group that practiced the Caesarian section. The use of *roombuŋ* leaves to facilitate childbirth explains why there are so many trees of this type around residential places. The correlation of wombs and pots can also be found elsewhere, such as in Amazonian notions of gender and pro-creation. McCallum states that among the Cashinahua "[c]ooking food ... is analogous to making babies. Similarly, pots are analogous to wombs" (2001: 52). This applies also to Bosmun considerations of procreation and body con-figurations. By pouring sago into the clay pot, a husband's semen is sym-bolically put in a wife's womb. Within the womb (clay pot), the semen (sago paste) becomes transformed into and materializes as the mother's milk (sago pudding) with which an infant is fed (for similar accounts on such substantial connections, see Godelier [1986: 57], Stasch [2009: 148], and Tietjen [1985: 128]). Apart from a link between pots and wombs, there is a strong association between sago pudding and mother's milk. There is the common saying: *erokot maame miri mimiŋ,* which translates as 'sago pudding is the liquid (*mimiŋ*)[12] of a mother's breast (*mir*).' When used as a verb, *mir* also denotes 'to deliver.' Mother's milk provides the same energy as sago. People perceived as physi-cally weak are said to have lacked nurturance through mother's milk or sago in early infancy. Since, apart from mother's milk, sago is considered the most elemental food to feed a child, primary caretakers start very early to accustom their babies to eating sago. This is comparable with food-socializing practices among the Western Province Gogodala (Dundon 2005: 31) as well as among the Murik, where "[l]earning to like this 'social' food ... is considered essen-tial to becoming 'Murik'" (Lipset 1997: 58).

It sometimes appeared to me as if it were not the female body that people considered the baby's ultimate feeding source, but the sago that a woman con-sumed during pregnancy and after delivery. During my third stay in Papua New Guinea, while teaching in Madang, I had the chance to more thoroughly grasp Bosmun senses of being in town. Among the food-related statements that people made when articulating their longing for home was one of a preg-nant woman who had to stay in town for personal reasons. With what appeared to me to be a slight tone of melancholy, she said: *Mi laik go long ples. Mi mas kaikai planti saksak. Mi les long taun. Mi mas kaikai erok!* ('I want to go home. I have to eat a lot of sago. I do not like the town. I must eat sago pud-ding!') Another woman who joined our conversation immediately added: *Em gat bel*! ('She is pregnant!'). It was as if this woman reinforced the obvious fact of a causal connection between pregnancy, child growth and sago. I saw that women ate a lot of sago during pregnancy and after delivery. Mothers, sisters, and female affines alternately provided huge plates of sago pudding for the new mother.

Conception in Bosmun procreative theory is said to result when male semen and female vaginal fluids (including female blood) merge within a woman's womb. These liquids are said to both equally contribute to the body parts and substances of a fetus. Serial intercourse is considered necessary in order to successfully impregnate a woman. Moreover, women engage in sago making until their bellies reach considerable size. The embryo is believed to grow and acquire strength only if it was harbored in a hard-working, food-productive body. Thus, mothers-to-be engage as long as possible in the tasks that they normally fulfill when not pregnant.

Nzari's approval of sexual intercourse, called *eisi mimɨk* (literally: *eis* 'penis,' *mimɨk* 'to enclose'), was ubiquitous in people's utterances. These utterances did not match the negative connotation that lies in the Tok Pisin words used to refer to sexual intercourse. *Pasin nongut* literally means 'bad behavior.' *Pamuk pasin,* another Tok Pisin idiom, means 'a whore's behavior.' These idioms, which Bosmun speakers also generally filed under the phrase *tok sem* ('sinful speech'), were probably used the first time by early missionaries when there was need to talk of sexual matters. My impression was that customary Bosmun attitudes toward sexual agency mirror what Hogbin ([1970] 1996: 89) declared for the Wogeo people: "Coitus is neither shameful nor immoral—it is simply dangerous." As I see it, the myth of Nzari underscores the importance of men in the life of women and vice versa.

Although sexuality is a social principle, promiscuity was not prompted as an ideal to be sought after. Even if Nzari was a character who always ended up leaving her partners and finding new ones, her ideal was to be with a single partner—as long as he respected her. I see a plea for monogamy (or, at least, serial monogamy) prevailing in the narration of Nzari's life. Both the scene where Nzari met the pair of brothers and the scene where Kaamndoŋ met the fish women indeed render polygamy a troublesome enterprise. People should remarry after a partner has died. No one is disregarded for not wanting to be alone. However, most of the marriages during which a case of adultery had occurred ended in divorce. N., an old woman, told me of her former husband's adultery and how she reacted to his suggestion to let another woman participate in their marriage. Interestingly, in defining herself in that situation, N. used a food-related image—a box of canned tuna: *Em faul nabaut wantaim narapela meri ya ... na ... olsem na mi tok: "Mi no wanpela tinpis bai yu putim insait long katen wantaim ol narapela tinpis!" Na olsem na, mi lusim em pinis. Mi no sa wari moa long em. Hau mi stap ... em mi stap.* ('He fooled around with another woman … and … thus I said [to him]: "I am not a tin of tuna that you can put in a box with other canned tuna!" And thus, I divorced him. I stopped worrying about him. Ever since … I have been living this way.')

I frequently heard such self-assured statements by women. After I came to know about Nzari, I stopped wondering why this was. In a way, her fortune reads as a powerful counterstory to the one of the sago spirit, in which men basically play the advantageous role. The sago spirit brought an imbalance by ousting women from the sago palm trunk, but Nzari's possession of fire and the clay pot as well as her ability to swallow things through her mouth and deliver them through her vaginal orifice counterbalanced this act. Principally due to Nzari's innovations, Bosmun men appreciate the presence of women. After all, Nzari took away men's former grief over the loss of their sisters, wives, and daughters. It is also notable that, although men as husbands understand that they can be attracted by women other than their own wife, men as fathers and brothers are keen to interfere if they see that their daughters or sisters are treated like "a tin among other tins," to paraphrase N.'s words. I knew of two men who had polygamous relationships. They were considered to be difficult by basically everybody. The wives did not live in the same household. A Bosmun woman does not share her hearth with another except for her kinswomen. Höltker (1969: 72) also tells of a man who had two wives, the one living in one place, the other in another place, and how he witnessed a fight between them. The questions that create difficulties are: Where should a man involved with two women sleep or eat? Whom should he take to the swamps? In the cases I knew of, the women who wooed the men's favor had more or less regular fights with one another because of such questions. The men were considered lazy, and people reckoned that this was due to sexual overactivity. In what comes next, I discuss ambivalence in the attitude toward sexuality and how it is materially mirrored by the two entrances of the Bosmun dwelling-house.

A Conjugal Consumption Taboo and Two Entrances into a House
Sexual reproduction is regarded as crucial, but Kaamndoŋ's fate is also a story of male sexual abuse. This is told in the scene where Kaamndoŋ meets the fish women. They abuse him by keeping him sexually aroused and thus drain his entire vigor and self-control. This, however, is not what Nzari intends. It was she who warned him not to follow the women. In the myth's third episode, Nzari places unmistakable limits on sexuality. Firstly, she builds the birth-house, a private female abode, from which she expels all men and commands women to remain secluded from men (and sexually abstinent) until their children make their first attempts to crawl. Sexual abstinence is formally marked by a constraint with regard to the shared consumption of spouses. Idiomatically, Bosmun denote this consumption taboo as *paar mbitit* (literally: 'a broken hand'), which refers to female hands that do not cook.

Indeed, a woman's "hand breaks" frequently; each time she menstruates or gives birth to a child, she must not partake in the making of sago, nor may she hold the stick (*nanmakae*) used to stir sago. She must not cook for her husband who, for the time being, relies on food prepared by his (biological or classificatory) sisters and mothers. If a husband does not have many female kin, he prepares food for himself, which no one considers discreditable. But even if he has female kin, he should not excessively burden those who have to look after their own children. The woman cooks only for herself and her prepubescent children. If she has adolescent children, they will care for themselves. She also must not cook for other adults. Everyone knows that as long as a wife is not cooking for her husband the two of them should also avoid having any bodily contact. The moment of restored sexual contact after a birth comes when the couple's new child begins to express him- or herself with increasing bodily motion and facial expressions. This is the sign that the child is strong enough to survive. The most definite sign is when a baby starts to crawl.[13]

At this point, partners must ritually mark their union, again underscoring the connection between sago production and sexual intimacy. The wife has to rinse a small quantity of sago pith. While rinsing the pith, the wife takes the watery starch to wash her body. In so doing, I was told, a woman seeks contact with the sago spirit, who—because of his own masculinity—is always with men but only temporarily with women since women have dangerous fluids that the spirit must evade. Once a woman has washed herself in this way, the spirit is said to come closer again. A woman then takes a wreath made of various barks, leaves, and vines and slips through it headfirst. This wreath is thought to contain some energy of the sago spirit. By going through this ring, a woman recomposes her own *nyeron*[14] and returns to fully socially active life as the sago-making collaborator of her husband. The second ritual marking also connects to food-related action. Husband and wife hold onto a sago stirrer jointly and prepare a portion of sago pudding, which they eat together. From then on, they are free to resume sexual intercourse, and the husband may again eat food prepared with the hands of his wife.

Nzari gives a second clarification concerning male-female sexuality. Spouses should come to a reproductive close once their own children start to reproduce. When she encounters the group that cut women's bellies, Nzari appears as a wise, senior midwife. Her physical strength has ceased, but the wisdom she has achieved provides her with another form of strength and recognition. Thus, she is able to give full attention to the pregnant woman. At the birth that I attended there were two women present specifically to comfort the expectant mother, and I counted another eight women (excluding myself) who surrounded that triad. Expecting a child is no lonesome endeavor in Daiden. It should ensue in an atmosphere of female consociates, preferably of elder women who no longer need to look after their own small children. The role of

Nzari as an old and wise midwife is the major symbolic source of this idea. Women who become pregnant while their own daughters are pregnant are said to bring shame to their families. As younger and less experienced women, the daughters should receive consoling attention from their mothers.[15]

As parents leave sago making to their children, they formally enter another phase of life—the phase of wisdom and increasing asexuality. However, they only achieve this stage after having gone through the stage of productive and reproductive activity. Sago making and sexual reproduction are the primary practices guaranteeing societal perpetuation. People are nevertheless conscious of the importance of keeping sexual contact to a minimum, as coitus per se is deemed to have a "dangerous" aspect, as I suggested above when quoting Hogbin's statement on Wogeo sexuality. Above, I noted that sexual reproduction becomes a moral problem for women as they grow older. Sexual activity also poses a constant threat to men's bodily maintenance. This is based on Bosmun notions of the female body and its fluids. People attribute ambivalent powers to female bodily (and especially vaginal) liquids and odors, and it is due to these powers that male bodies are in constant tension between gaining and losing their vitality. This is common thinking found throughout Papua New Guinea (e.g., Godelier 1986: 58–63; Hogbin [1970] 1996: 95; Keesing 1982: 7, 9; Meigs 1984). Women, too, try to avoid contact with other women's intimate substances, although they do not fear what men have to fear; they may simply become temporarily weary. Rather, what women fear is that they may transmit to men other women's substances with which they may have become contaminated. Therefore, a new mother and her midwife must not touch anything until they have ritually cleansed their bodies. The female body is a paradox to Bosmun men because it charms and potentially also harms them. The scent (*eŋ*) of a woman is said to bewilder men and to instigate liking and longing. Smelling a body is, more generally, an important sensual experience in Daiden. In the past, anointing one's body with fragrances made from the leaves and oils of various local plants was an established part of tuning one's body for adulthood. Male and female bodies thus became more attractive. Remember Soŋe's enchantment as he smelled the body of Nzari. Now, traditional body care is done less frequently but not less forcefully. Standing amid a crowd of Bosmun dancers was an overwhelming olfactory experience. I always enjoyed it, except on the occasion where a woman ritually poured foul fish over another woman.

During menses and childbirth, the female body is said to evaporate fluids that are normally enclosed. This is an unsafe time for men since female scents become even more powerful. People never told me that a woman's scent during such phases has an unpleasant smell, as is the case elsewhere in Papua New Guinea (e.g., Meigs 1984: 32). On the contrary, the smell is thought to be attractive. Direct contact, however, has a debilitating influence on male bodies and minds. Respiratory illness, an increasing frailty of bones, rapid senescence, and inattentiveness are said to result from sexual overactivity or other activities that involve contamination with female vaginal secretions. Therefore, men do _rerak_ in order to maintain physical and spiritual vivacity. Literally, this term means 'to reconstitute' / 'to transform' / 'to change [into something better].' A snake that sheds its skin does _rerak_ as well. As boys become older they learn how to _rerak_.[16] To treat the body with herbs by either consuming herbal juices or rubbing the skin (especially one's joints) with leaves or herbal waters is a type of _rerak_. Immediately after the birth of his child, a father has to _rerak_ over a period of three days, during which he has to consume, to rub onto his skin, and to inhale the smoke of burned, herbal substances. This is done with the assistance of male and female relatives. A sister stirs sago mixed with herbal water that the man must eat. Brothers or mother's brothers help to rub the man's skin and light the fire in which to burn the herbal substances for inhalation.

Another, more private, practice is penile incision.[17] Höltker (1975) gives a brief portrayal in his article on Bosmun boyhood and male initiation. I discussed his descriptions with Bosmun men who told me that penile incision was still practiced by some men. Höltker was told that penile incision was regarded as necessary to remove the female blood that every human body contained by way of conception and birth. The blood had to be collected in a leaf and was reabsorbed by consuming it (Höltker 1975: 558–559). According to Bosmun theories of the body, blood changes into a strength-providing substance once it becomes disembodied and reincorporated.

In creating joy in men's hearts, Nzari empowered the women so much that another male cultural hero, called Siandam, had to balance out her emotional accomplishments by introducing a third type of _rerak_. The mythical path of the warrior Siandam is the Ramu River. In Bosmun mythical time-space, the Ramu came into existence later than the island surrounded by the sea, giving evidence that Siandam's deeds chronologically follow those of Nzari. Siandam brought to the Bosmun area warfare, pain as a revealing experience in initiation, and "ritual prostitution," as Lipset (1997: 178) calls the practice in the Murik case. There, the man Sendam is the instigator, and the narrative that the Murik have of him (Lipset 1997: 192–195) is quite similar to that of the Bosmun warrior figure. Murik wives had to engage in ritualized extramarital sexual intercourse, since this was thought to lessen their husbands' jealousy and sexual addiction, states said to prevent a man from turning into a real warrior (Lipset 1997: 178). Today, this type of _rerak_ is no longer considered desirable for the life scheme people have; this change has been in the making since Christianity grew to be powerful in this area. After all, people are no longer warriors. My interviewees felt rather uncomfortable when talking about this kind of ritualized sexuality.[18]

The male body is no paradox to women. Men are believed to influence women's states of longing by secretly transmitting fluids such as saliva or semen to them.[19] Yet, these fluids do not really impair a woman's physical vivacity. In contrast, via the intermingling of male semen and female blood, male fluids partake in a very significant transformation of the female body by instigating pregnancy and subsequently childbirth. With childbirth, women are said to reduce their menstrual flow steadily, which in turn also minimizes the dangerous potential of their bodies. This transformation is an acknowledged part of the lives of women and men. It creates not only new lives, but also "mothers" who are needed to assist men when condensed male strength is required and where young female bodies would naturally interfere. In premissionary days, certain ritual arrangements relied highly on "mothers." Boys had to undergo painful torments during initiation. If a mother knew that her son was among the novices, she would go and wash in the river. This was said to ease the son's pain. Initiation was ultimately meant to disconnect the corporeal bond between mother and son, yet in the process of initiation this bond was not fully broken. Mask dancers or warriors set for a raid would only eat from the hands of old, postmenopausal women, and although several of these practices have been altered or abandoned, the role of "mothers" is still essential. Take soccer, for example, a ritual of today's times. I heard from a coach that prior to and during competitions the players are advised to eat only what a *lapun mama* ('old mother') has prepared for them. If they ate from younger women's hands, they would lose the game. When men engage in sexual acts with women, they assist in transforming them from menstruating into non-menstruating women. In doing so, men of the present bring up "mothers" for their future male generations as did their forefathers for them. Prior to Nzari's arrival, people had no sentiment for the aged. Matured women did not exist, only young ones who irrevocably passed away when giving birth to a new life. I got the impression that Nzari's appearance as a savior of life was still powerfully reverberating in people's lives.

The traditional dwelling-house—a critical part of Bosmun household architecture—mirrors local gender configurations.[20] In transforming it into the first birth-house, Nzari created a marked female domain within the dwelling-house. Its structure captures both male-female complementarity and male-female ambivalence, the latter of which is recognized with reference to the fact that sexual union leads to bodily weakness, at least in males. The outside design of the dwelling-house expresses the ambivalent side of a male-female relationship. It has two separate entrances, one at the front and one at the back of the house. One entrance is used by men, the other by women. Both entrances lead into a gendered yet connected space within the house. Husbands are expected to sleep on one side, wives on the other. However, there is no wall, no solid obstacle inside, and thus a house's inside scheme—as opposed to the outside scheme—provides ideational and actual space for the merging of male and female.

As I was told, this inside space is where partners should meet for reproductive purposes. The story of Nzari shows that sexual reproduction is as crucial as food procurement, but not as public. This is conveyed when Nzari punishes her dog because she fears that the dog, who saw her with Kaamndoŋ, will gossip. I was also told that too many spirits dwell in the forest who may feel offended if partners have sexual intercourse at the spot where the spirits live, and that they would therefore bring *ropuk* to the partners. *Ropuk* refers to human mental or bodily disorders caused by the spirits out of revenge. A young man who wants to signify his entrance into adulthood builds his own house (usually close to his parents' house). When ready to marry, he will ask a woman to share this house with him. Once they start to procreate, the man will have to provide his wife with another temporary abode, the birth-house.

Parental Sentiment Channeled through Foodways

I now turn to the way in which parents emotionally attach to their children. Food is again the medium for exhibiting attachment, but motherly attachment is immediate and direct whereas fatherly attachment is indirect, at least during the early years of infanthood. As the primary biological caretaker, the mother nurses her child and thus creates a direct and tangible relationship. Her body produces the milk that is said to have the quality of sago pudding. Since sago is connected to semen, a mother also stores fatherly substance in her body, accumulated through the joint procurement of food and through coitus. The father's substance is thus transferred to the child via the motherly body. The first indirect but food-based contact between a father and his child is thus established. The mother feeds her child with milk and later with sago, which female kin bring to her for as long as she has "broken hands." The father procures sago with the assistance of biological or classificatory sisters and mothers if these individuals are not too old. In doing so, he starts to care for his child even if he has not seen him or her yet. Through the mother's receiving sago from female kin while in seclusion, a couple's anchorage in the social world becomes either reaffirmed or contested. If a couple had shown "murky faces," they would receive less social and emotional support. If they have been generous, the woman would know that she could rely on positive empathy and material responsiveness from her female visitors. Equally, her husband would receive assistance. At the same time, the couple's child will become rooted in their relational network. Let us take a closer look at how mother and father should respond to their infant. This is necessary in order to grasp the Bosmun dimensions of direct and indirect caretaking more thoroughly.

MOTHERS "GAZE"; FATHERS "IGNORE"

According to the myth of Nzari, mother and infant are substantially connected through a particular kind of "bodily empathy" (Lohmann 2011). The mother knows that her son is longing for her because of the sensation that she feels in her breasts. As Lohmann points out, empathetic assessments may also be "experienced as sympathetic clues on one's own body, discovered through the senses rather than mentation" and may be "used as a means of long-distance 'perception' of the state of other people" (2011: 105). As he shows in the context of the Asabano, someone who sweats without physical exertion takes this as a sign that another person is soon to arrive. A kind of bodily inter-subjectivity is assumed to exist with one's consociates. As an Asabano says, "[w]e know this is true because people walking are hot, so you are hot too" (Lohmann 2011: 105). Although Lohmann (2011: 106) makes clear that this is a rather "shallow" variant of empathy in that it provides only superficial information about another's states, it is nonetheless intriguing to see what kind of ideationally pervasive and embodied ways enable people to relate to others. In chapter 4, I return to another dimension of Bosmun bodily empathy by describing how human bodies bear the signs of one's physical exertion and therefore become points of reference when assessing others empathetically.

Due to Nzari, the sensual fostering of empathy in infants is gendered. In chasing men out of the house in which women deliver, sensual practices such as "skin- and gaze-ship" (Mageo 2011) are considered exclusively women's work. Mageo explores skin- and gaze-ship between infants and caretakers in Samoa as well as the impact these sensual practices entail for the development of trust and empathy. Skin- and gaze-ship are "contact" and "distancing practices" that lead to the development of either "secure" or "insecure attachment" and to either fostering or "undermining trust" in others. Psychologically, the attachment quality that the infant caretaker exhibits leaves imprints on the infant's later empathetic behavior. Both contact and distancing practices are significant for "shaping empathy," since too much attachment can misalign the boundaries of self and other and too little attachment will limit one's trust in others (Mageo 2011: 71–72). In comparing Western with Samoan mothers, Mageo writes that, "[u]nlike the Western mother who holds her child in a face-to-face position, when a Samoan mother or others held the baby, they turned it towards the family group or to the road where villagers passed" (Mageo 2011: 74).

In Daiden, mothers should permanently keep a visual focus on the child. In "watching him or her carefully," the mother is the first person to perform *ram-kandiar* toward the child. In that, she begins to introduce the child into a social universe that puts a strong emphasis on interpersonal attentiveness. Moreover, the mother's intense gaze is held to be essential for the infant's health. Only as he or she starts to crawl is he or she literally put into relational space and sensual touch with others. A mother who fails to gaze intensely at her infant is said to cause him or her illness or even death. However, whether to hold her responsible if the child gets ill or dies depends on her social repute. I knew a mother who had lost a child shortly after birth. Since many people considered her a generous woman, no one held her responsible. Instead, the death was interpreted as the result of a sorcery attack instigated by the family of a man whom the woman had rejected prior to her marriage to the actual father of her children.

Whenever I looked into the shared lives of adults and infants, I saw that both women and men were compassionate with their offspring. Children were protected and embraced with sympathy by basically everyone. Yet, unlike with the Murik, where "men and women are touched by a nostalgia for the bliss of infantile satiation at the mother's breast and gaze longingly at a baby nursing itself to sleep" (Lipset 1997: 58), a similar display of affection in Daiden is a privilege of women and children. According to ancestral lore, men have to "ignore" their own children (and small children in general) until they grow to the age of approximately five. This is a considerable period of time. To "ignore" one's child means to avoid any bodily or eye contact. Holding one's infant in one's arms or caressing it should be no part of the primary attachment experience of Bosmun fathers. However, no one frames such ignoring as a symbol of immorality or neglect. It is seen as natural and significant that a father creates attachment by procuring food for his infant and for the mother. Fatherly concern and longing are channeled in this way for several years. Silverman states about the father-son relationship among the Eastern Iatmul in Papua New Guinea: "When a boy reaches the age of about five or six, he begins to have increasingly limited contact with his father. Any further trace of paternal intimacy is abhorrent" (2001: 72). In Daiden, the chronology of the intense and less intense moments in the relationship between father and child (boy or girl) looks different. Unlike with the Iatmul, in Daiden this relationship is marked by limited contact from the very onset (with the child's birth); only later is it replaced with direct sensual care.

The reason for such sensual detachment is that a small child is thought to absorb the strength of male adults and, in particular, the strength of the father. Sensual avoidance was strictly adhered to by the warriors of premissionary times. Although they were no longer warriors, several men in Daiden told me that they still heed this obligation of avoidance. Physical vivacity is essential for survival in their subsistence world. A man has to avoid coming into contact with his own children's urine (*ŋgiambar*), feces (*yuxur*), and saliva (*sombit*)—fluids that are believed to have a debilitating influence on men similar to that of women's fluids. To avoid a child's saliva means also that the father does not eat off the plate or spoon belonging to his child. In order to grow, a child needs to gather strength from both mother and father. The motherly body does not suffer from providing that strength through direct sensual care, since the infant's body is still seen to be a substantial part of it. The body of the father, however, loses its vigor, not only after his wife's delivery but already during procreation.

When male interviewees considered the process of aging in my presence, they would often refer to their sensual contacts with infants. A senior but not yet really old man felt that he had aged too rapidly. He explained this fact by relating it to his emotional response to his children. It was because "he had loved his children too much!" He had lived his whole life sensually too close to them. I also observed that he had his grandchildren around him all the time, holding them tenderly and carrying them around or lulling them to sleep. Although men should "ignore" their babies and small children on the whole so as to retain their strength, they are not prohibited by ancestral lore from feeling love or sorrow for them. Sorrow / grief / anguish is referred to as *outut* (the term *outut* is also used to indicate strong physical pain). The expression of a father's grief (*ye*, literally: 'to cry') for his deceased baby is also imparted in the chant Mbunset, according to which Nzari's first partner Soɲe carries the dead body of his son Mbobot. The verse features exclusively a father's grief.

The moment when fatherly ignoring turns into unreserved care is fixed and articulated in a way that renders the male body as a corporeal indicator of social time and interpersonal relations: the child has to reach a physical height equal to the height of the father's hip. As long as the child is shorter than this, their relationship is seen as somewhat fragile. As the child crosses this line, the relationship becomes stronger. Direct sensual contact is now permitted, and a father might express his concern more openly. Normally, he now produces toys and items of social value for the child. Bosmun children are encouraged to *ngaaŋgo*, to 'imitate' and 'practice' what they see in the adult world, and parental tutors provide them with toys with which they playfully gain an understanding of what matters socially and interpersonally in this world. A girl is likely to receive tiny decorative things, ropes to play string-figure games or wooden plates that the father has carved. Most of the older women I met were still in possession of wooden plates that they had received as young girls by their fathers. Whenever I was shown the plates, women would comment: *Papa bilong mi i wokim plet. Em hanmak bilong em i stap long em* ('My father produced this plate. He left his traces on it'). Höltker (1965a: 22) mentions another form of 'playful education' ("Spielerziehung"), which only elder informants remembered. With the help of their parents, children crafted small figurines made of the same clay as cooking pots. In kneading and burning the clay, they playfully acquired the knowledge of how to produce clay pots. One of my elder female informants, for example, remembered how her father had brought her bast to produce a tiny skirt and other materials for decorating the figurine's body.

A son will be given sticks that are shaped like sago scrapers. Later, a real sago scraper (as well as other tools for canoe or house building) will follow. Also, small hourglass drums are made for children's hands so that small boys can actively participate in adult dance performances, thereby playfully adopting male adult roles (see figure 3.2). A Bosmun father actively participates in vesting his children with the most significant material markers of Bosmun identity; these are also moral and emotional markers. Above all, he personally comes closer to his children. He might freely caress them, watch them, and talk to them. As we shall see in the next section, the emotional bond between parents and their children becomes stronger as a child starts to actively reciprocate via food procurement the previously one-sided parental care.

It would be wrong to conclude that Bosmun fathers have no sentiment for their tiny infants because they neither touch nor gaze at them. The fact to be argued once more is that sentiment is channeled by a father's foodways. By regularly providing their children with food, Bosmun men emotionally reconfigure and escape the limitations imposed upon the father-child relationship by the imperative of sensual detachment. I asked fathers how far they would go in "ignoring" an infant. Would they let a baby hurt itself, for example, when

Figure 3.2: Learning to Dance. Yaroŋ guides Kaake, his son, and Kɨmɨn, his wife's brother's son, in a dance performance. The boys also receive advice from Kɨmɨn's mother's mother's brother Yaŋu, standing to the right.

they saw that he or she was about to fall down from a stilted platform? All of them said that they would of course intervene. When the fire broke out in 2004 (described in the Introduction), a baby was sleeping in one of the buildings that was eventually destroyed, and it was a man who courageously rescued her.

Another misleading conclusion would be to say that nostalgia as described above for the Murik is entirely absent in the hearts of Bosmun fathers. There is, however, a difference. Bosmun men do know of feelings that arise in view of a newborn, but in a more general sense. Male images of babies being nursed by their mothers mainly derive from memories grounded in a man's own child-hood experience. Boys up to the age of five are allowed to enter birth-houses, where they can see their own mothers or other women handling the newborns. Boys themselves frequently carry babies around (see figure 2.4, which shows the boy Mbono in close sensual contact with his small sister). Since children are believed to be born *rorer*, meaning they lack full soundness of mind, boys may stay sensually close to maternal bodies until they begin to change physi-cally and thus also mentally. Boys and girls gain the particularities of male and female gender only later and in a processual way. As children they stay somehow neutral (see Lutkehaus & Roscoe [1995] for a more general discus-sion on Melanesian models of how and when gender is achieved). What boys experience in a birth-house at an early age, women assured me, will be quickly forgotten when they grow older. But as long as the boys are still young they are very well informed, as I observed. Once, while inquiring into the geneal-ogy of a particular family, I asked a father how many children he had. In tell-ing me the number of his children, he did not mention his lastborn. He still had not seen his latest child (who had just recently been delivered) and thus did not include him. A group of boys and girls around the age of four to six surrounded us, and in a chorus they shouted: *Meri bilong yu i karim pinis ya!* (Your wife has already delivered!').

THE BIRTH-HOUSE—ACCEPTING OR REJECTING FOOD

To erect a birth-house is another significant way for a man to express his fa-therly concern. Every woman should have her own private abode. Kinswomen who will deliver around the same time may share such an abode. However, in erecting the birth-house for his wife, a man takes the chance to reassert his conjugal relationship and claim a connection to the newborn. The first birth-house that a father builds should be located near the household of his parents-in-law, since a firstborn has to return to his wife's family. I saw such birth-houses in the vicinity of almost every household. The knowledge of how to build such a house stems from Nzari. It is smaller than a usual dwelling-house but walled, roofed, and stilted, and with a gap in the floor. Unlike in the dwelling-house, the ground space between the stilts of the birth-house is fenced, and instead of the hearth, the gap in the floor of the birth-house has a ladder that leads down into the fenced area. Here, a woman is supposed to deliver the child on the ground and bury the umbilical cord in the soil. During my stays in Daiden, birth-houses were still being built, as were men's houses—the male and solidly expressed counterpart to the female retreats. Women also see it in this light. An elderly woman proudly expressed: *Haus karim ya ... em haus tambaran bilong mipela ol meri. Ol man bai no inap lukim.* ('The birth-house ... is the spirit house of we women. The men are not allowed to see [what happens inside].')[21]

However, today the new attitude of *sotkat* ('shortcut') directs and transforms the customary practices of the past. A new mother today remains in seclusion no longer than a few weeks before she returns to the dwelling-house that she shares with her husband. In 2008, I talked to a young mother who was not willing to spend time in a birth-house after the delivery of her third child. She said with sincerity: *Mi les long dispela kastam. Mi bai no inap kalabus olsem. Dispela samting ya em samting bilong ol tumbuna long bifo.* ('I am tired of this custom. I will not incarcerate myself this way. This is a practice of the ancestors of previous times.') With regard to the birth-house, this woman was the first who uttered such a cultural critique to me. It remains to be seen whether the physical structure of the birth-house—as part of Bosmun social architecture—will prevail in the future; any changes in this tradition, of course, have also to be taken into account in the structural design of the dwelling-house.

In her demand for a birth-house, Nzari created the basis for a formalized and solidly expressed appreciation of motherhood and female power. In search of a life that navigates toward modernity, young women especially (although not all of them) are gradually ceasing to copy the ancestral images of womanhood and power that were still ingrained in the verbal and lived deeds of the middle-aged and elderly women whom I had the chance to talk to. Not one of them considered the birth-house to be *kalabus* ('imprisonment'); it was seen rather as a key vehicle for the right to recognition—for their children and for themselves. Likewise, the women described menstruation (which is also tied to restriction of movement) as their personal *taim bilong malolo* ('a time of relaxation').[22] Apart from this evaluation, women of course know that their bodily fluids might harm others and thus prefer to stay semi-secluded during menses so as to prevent becoming the subject of accusation when illnesses break out somewhere in the social vicinity. The consequences of abandoning customary practices like seclusion in a birth-house were predominant in people's reflections on their lives. The fact that demography has changed tremendously is even formally recognized in a song. By chance I heard the following verse sung by a young woman while she was sitting near my house. It was sung to such a beautiful melody that I immediately asked her to repeat and translate it. The verse includes another critique:

Ndoŋono Ndoŋono Ndoŋono
Rome Rome Rome
Mirire soŋgae
Mbaaŋa ŋaase—aa aa

[Women of the place / group] Ndoŋon Ndoŋon Ndoŋon
[Women of the place / group] Rom Rom Rom
[You women] like to deliver [children]
[But you are] too lazy to care for [them]—aa aa

The singer said that this was just a *kompos singsing* of recent origin and not *raarŋa ma taka*, not what 'an ancestral creator-being had established.' This *kompos singsing* was a 'verse' that a man had recently 'composed' as a symbol of resentment. It encoded his personal assessment of what was increasingly happening these days: the women of this place were so occupied with giving birth to children that no time was left to properly care for all of them. I was further informed that this verse had become an integral part of a conventional chant and that incorporating such new compositions into older chants was not uncommon. Although the verse was of recent origin, the young woman added that it should be performed at traditional feasting events. Its content corresponds to a rather negative side of today's reality and the women of this place should take its message seriously. The young woman sang this piece after she had heard of the new pregnancy of another woman who was already a mother to several children.

As I have underscored, a father creates primary attachment to his child by erecting a birth-house. This also shows concern for the woman he has married. In 2005, I observed people scolding a man because he was hesitant to provide his wife with a private abode despite the fact that the signs of her pregnancy were already clearly notable. He did finally build it, but soon after the birth his wife left him and went to stay with her parents. She also took her child with her. The man's relatives had no objections to the wife's leaving because in their eyes, too, he had failed to act as a "good husband." After all, he had been too lazy to build his wife and their child a proper place of comfort, and this sooner or later would have had further consequences. If he were too lazy to build a birth-house, he would also turn out to be an idle food procurer. These objections were too serious, and therefore the marriage had broken. The woman in this case was of the same age as the woman mentioned above who felt confined when she imagined herself staying in a birth-house temporarily. She did, however, demand a proper birth-house in which to harbor her newborn.

In order to begin the final part of this chapter, in which I explore Bosmun ideas on the prime of life, aging, and death, it makes sense to end this part with a brief conclusion on the cultural perception of newborns. People in Daiden thought of newborns in a way that is comparable to perceptions elsewhere in Papua New Guinea. Yupno consider a newborn to be "an incomplete human being" (Keck 2005: 119). Maisin deem the infant to be "not yet socially human" (Barker 2008: 76), and a Baining baby is a "natural creature who is not automatically considered a … *social entity*" (Fajans 1985: 372; original emphasis). In view of the high infant mortality rate in the Pacific (Crocombe 2001: 658) and in rural areas of Papua New Guinea more specifically (Rannells 2001: 58), this perception indeed reads as an appropriate psychological adaptation to the threat of losing one's offspring. The death of children seems thus to become more bearable. In Daiden, however, this psychological adaptation is also permeated by sociocultural explanations. Although the birth-house is the place where new life starts, this life is yet fragile and lacks social recognition. Let us take into account that Nzari takes her son's life after she has decided to leave Soŋe. We might say that in killing Mbobot Nzari rejects not only the product of her sexual contact with Soŋe and their joint food labor, but the very affirmation of their relationship. She divorces her husband by returning the "food" they once produced together.

If a woman is discontent or angry with her husband, she will indicate her state by placing a food plate filled with water onto a high shelf hanging in the house. She will tell him to go inside and take his meal, an utterance she would not normally make. Since she deliberately has filled the plate to the brim, the water is likely to splash over him. In this case, a husband should realize that he is behaving wrongly on the empathetic "two-way-street" (Halpern 2001: 41) and should rethink his attitudes. He has been given a message that should remind him of Nzari. His wife has signaled that there is a problem to be solved and should he refuse to attune to her, she will go on to disconnect herself by no longer sharing food with him. Figuratively, she basically does what Nzari once did.

Another significant aspect to be emphasized is that Nzari prefers her mother to the child because of a difference in attachment to each. When leaving Soŋe, she exclaims that it was her mother who nurtured her and not Soŋe. In that, she also hints at the child's incomplete social status. Mbobot received food without reciprocating it. Nzari had just begun to feed the child, whereas she had been nurtured by her mother until she had developed into an adult and thus a reciprocator herself. Here the story's message is that the endurance and mutuality of foodways is absolutely vital to finally establish emotional attachment.

This message, I believe, was deeply anchored in the thoughts of my consociates in Daiden. From what people told me about children who had died at a young age, I gained the impression that the loss of a baby or a preadolescent child was accepted more easily than the loss of a child who had already established him- or herself as a self-determined agent in the web of social, food-reciprocating relations. The idea that infants are socially not considered full humans is also evident in the fact that—prior to the coming of the missionaries—women in a birth-house could decide whether a newborn would stay alive or not. Through the lens of local food symbolism, this also means that women could decide to accept or reject the "sago" they had procured with their partners. Due to Nzari, infanticide was not considered unethical. It was an option at times of crisis—when famine arose due to environmental disasters, during wars, when a couple already had enough children and no one was available to adopt the baby, or during interpersonal disputes including discord between conjugal partners. Finally, the burial of an infant gives a hint about its state. If an adult dies, his or her funeral becomes a communal and ceremonial matter. If an infant dies, it is buried only by the mother and her close kinswomen in a less formal way.

Although it is culturally accepted that a father does not mourn his young child's death, individual variation has to be taken into account. Let me give the short example of the death of an infant in 2008. A baby less than six months of age died (shortly before her death, a huge flood had brought illnesses such as diarrhea and infections, and there was social trouble in the sphere of the parents' extended kin). The baby's mother's brother said that there was no reason to mourn the deceased since she was just an infant, and a few other people related to the parents reacted similarly. But the baby's father was so stricken that he decided to stay in isolation, at least for a couple of months, together with his wife. No one misjudged the man for doing so, yet no one paid particular attention to his grief. As Hollan (2011: 196) states for the Toraja, empathetic responsiveness depends also on the "differences in people's life experiences." The man's parents had died when he was still a child, and other relatives took over responsibility for him. In hindsight, however, the man talked about it as hardship because in his eyes it was not true care that he had received. Therefore, his particular life experience deeply affected the way he dealt with his own children; they should not encounter the same hardship and his deceased newborn should not just receive a casual farewell.

Despite the factor of individual variation, there was nonetheless a rather collective consent about when it is most inappropriate to die. To this I move now.

The Wind That Brings Sadness

Kiniri xaame is a gently blowing wind that begins every year around May or June and ceases around September. It starts at the beginning of the dry season when people feel particularly elated because the enduring rains of the wet season have come to an end. Having reached their climax during those heavy rains, the symptoms of malarial disease now fade. Wounds of any sort heal better since humidity in the area diminishes slightly. Many roads and short-

cuts throughout the forest that have been blocked for months become passable
again. Everyone moves around more freely and more frequently. From May
onward, the regular diet of sago and fish becomes supplemented by prawns and
mussels. Apart from sago making and fishing, women now dive in the Ramu
in search of mussels. Men start to build new canoes, or they mend old ones.
The arrival of the dry season is also the time to start with the construction of a
new dwelling-house or with a new garden. It is the time to be extraordinarily
busy. The end of the rainy season is a moment of general euphoria (*ŋgusuŋgu*)
for young and old, and I often heard people expressing their excitement in a
food-related way: *Em taim bilong kindam* [or *kina*] *nau*! ('now we have the
time of the prawns [or mussels]!').

For those people, however, who have recently lost a beloved partner or other
close relative, *kiniri xaame* becomes a wind of commemoration and sadness.
Its literal translation is 'the wind of sadness / numbness.' *Xaame* is the generic
term for 'wind.' *Kinir* refers to the feeling of sorrow and emotional distress. It
also refers to bodily numbness, and thus feelings of sorrow become corpore-
ally configured. Once this wind emerges, a bereaved person is thought to fall
into this state of physico-psychic sentiment because the partner or relative is
now missing in the moment of once-shared euphoria, a state said to arise when
people feel full of activity and have unimpeded access to the sago-abundant
swamps. Food and food-linked objects or activities are highly prominent in
framing the commemoration of beloved individuals, just as this wind is.

I heard about the wind that brings sadness to people's hearts—and bellies,
as we shall see—when I participated in a funeral and in the ritual demarcation
of a new widow at the end of 2004. Although I had arrived just a few months
before, the widow allowed me to spend the night (following the burial) with
her and her female consanguineal and affinal kin. We numbered about thirty
women and I hardly slept at all that night. I reevoked what I had observed over
the course of the day and listened to what the women were willing to tell me in
such a situation. Except for the widow, who should avoid talking, the women
may speak softly to one another throughout the whole night.

The death of a Bosmun adult is a collectively recognized event. Burying
the corpse is accomplished by men and women together. Men dig a hole and
erect a roofed structure above the hole, whereas women cover the corpse with
earth once it has been laid to rest. In consideration of the death, all fireplaces,
cooking pots, and plates have to be put to rest for a minimum of three days and
three nights. Only empty stomachs can match what people feel when they lose
a beloved person. Therefore, no one in the vicinity may cook, procure food, or
eat. Nor may people go to their gardens or swamps. The smell of the deceased
person is said to stick to the living and is believed to destroy the soil's produce.
At the funeral that I attended in 2004, the men jointly gathered in a men's house
and the women gathered in the households surrounding the household where

death had occurred. The closest relatives stay with the widow and the widower respectively. Gathering in a crowd is said to protect the living from assaults by the deceased's spirit, who is now disembodied and therefore troubled and aggressive. Once a *nyeron* detaches from a body and turns into a *ndom,* a disembodied spiritual entity, it is thought to radiate the power of blindness until the unanimated corpse is put in the ground and covered. Hence, everyone who attends a funeral is temporarily in danger of losing their eyesight. The loss of sight, in turn, hinders people in their enactment of *ramkandiar.* The deceased's spirit attempts to deprive the living of what he or she has been deprived of—a life that centered upon "watching others and being watched." Prior to my leaving the cemetery, a woman stopped me and quickly tied a leaf in a knot right in front of my eyes. I was surprised, but she explained with a soothing tone that although I had seen the dead corpse, nothing could happen to me since in tying the knot in front of my eyes she had made sure that I was protected. She then went on to tie further knots in front of other people's eyes.

With the death of a spouse, a now-widowed person is formally stopped from participating in the usual events of life. Bosmun mourning is a long-lasting in-house affair for both widow and widower. In the past it lasted for several seasonal changes. People reasoned that it is only through experiencing intense ephemeral disconnectedness from everything that asserts life that one is finally freed from sorrow. When I arrived in Daiden, I met another widow who already had spent one year in seclusion. The seclusion would have continued for another long period of time had she not revolted, finally leaving her virilocal household and returning to her parental kin. Always open to the questions I asked (as sensitively as possible), she explained that she had no longer been able to stand what she thought to be unjustified hardship imposed on her by her late husband's relatives. How long one has to stay in isolation is decided by the deceased spouse's "second cousins 1." Since, in this case, the spouse's relatives must have had an aversion to her, they were not yet willing to end her phase of seclusion. The widow protested that she was still in her prime, and considering the fact that she had been left alone with six children she should have been given the chance by now to provide food for her family. The husband's "second cousins 1" remained reluctant to dispense her from seclusion since, in their opinion, the widow had failed to respond as a proper sociable partner. Not all affinal relations end in quarrel after the partner has died. The woman who became a widow in 2004 stayed in seclusion only a month because her affinal relatives were particularly fond of her. Although rumors had spread that she had fallen in love with a man who must have caused her husband's death through the use of sorcery, she was commonly accepted as a food-generous person. After all, her children were adults whom she had brought up, and they were supportive of her. Thus, she was allowed to quickly take up her normal life again.

Kosir, as the custom that a bereaved partner must submit to is called, might indeed turn into a demanding state in an individual's life. *Kosir* prescribes a life that, in fact, is an anti-life. To laugh and converse vibrantly, behavioral traits normally considered to make a person likeable, or to groom oneself in the usual way by bathing frequently in the river or oiling the skin and hair, are taboo while practicing *kosir.* Hair must not be cut. Men must not shave. Widow and widower are banned from all major activities and must not leave the house (except for short visits to the forest to relieve themselves and to bathe in the river). They should not be seen by others except by relatives who assist them in seclusion. Above all, widow and widower are stopped from procuring and touching food. They have to be fed as babies and old people are fed. In *Celebrations of Death,* Metcalf and Huntington ([1979] 1991: 44–48) recall Radcliffe-Brown's (1964) report on mourning Andaman Islanders, who are said to temporarily belong to the realm of the deceased and therefore need to be isolated. This has relevance for the conceptualization of Bosmun widowhood. In-house mourning indeed becomes a quasi-death. Once the partner has gone, the bereaved must temporarily abstain from life, too.

This prohibition is marked officially in plain sight of all the mourners who have come to see the funeral. The day after the burial, the bereaved is ritually washed and has his or her working tools and eating spoons taken away. Taking these objects away is an obligation to be fulfilled by the deceased's "second cousins 1." Apart from eating spoons, widows hand over tools such as the stick for stirring sago or clay pounders (pottery tools used to smooth wet clay). Widowers have to give away sago scrapers, axes, and knives. Before finally entering the temporary abode of seclusion, the widow or widower will share a last meal with the deceased. The meal contains the food that the deceased's last repast consisted of. I also saw a plate of food that was symbolically offered to the spirit of the deceased. This food was consumed by the deceased's "second cousins 1." The last plate of food indicates that a conjugal bond is coming to an end, as is the kin-tie between the deceased and his or her "second cousins 1." This implies that the children of the deceased and his or her "second cousins 1" are no longer configured as being kin and thus may now intermarry.

In-house mourning becomes a time to reflect upon the quality of one's own food-based relationships because the quality of those relationships becomes particularly relevant. The intensity of suffering in seclusion depends highly on the positive or negative intentionality of one's close and extended relatives. If a person has had good relations, he or she is likely to be cared for with the greatest attention. If not, he or she will probably suffer from noticeable neglect. This is similar to what I stated about interpersonal assistance when a woman gives birth. A mourner in seclusion is exposed to moments of unequal dependency during which he or she is disadvantaged. Such unequal dependency will be balanced once the helping relatives face similar situations. The time to balance out the offered care, however, is not clearly determinable, since the time when one becomes a widow or widower is not predictable. Apart from that, one cannot expect help and concern if one has not proven to be a caring and reciprocating person. It is due to a person's previous sociable deeds, rather than future promises of caregiving, that others will look after this person at critical moments in life. It is soothing to know that one can look back at one's own good relations, and one generally is eager to sustain good relations prior to situations of crisis.

"The Wrong Time to Die"

Like other events that shake or reassure present states of reality, death is a phenomenon that was reflected upon intensely and openly in Daiden. In the case of the man who had passed away in 2004, I witnessed a tremendous collective expression of grief. In incessant lament, family members kept surrounding the laid-out body of the deceased until people from other places eventually arrived to bid personal farewells. Extroverted weeping is primarily a female duty. Among the men, only the male "second cousins 2" of the deceased are allowed to lament openly. Motherly and sisterly lament is lyrically and individually encoded and recalls the deceased's merits, his or her biographical peculiarities, his or her fortunes and misfortunes. I noticed that the particular expression of grief that I witnessed was mixed with considerable anger that culminated in food-related lament. Several times, I heard people murmuring agitatedly: *Em i no taim yet long em bai dai. Em i no pikinini nating. Em i no lapun nongut tru. Man ya wok long wokabaut yet na em karim stik bilong paitim saksak wantaim em.* ('It was not the right time for him to die. He was not a mere child. He was not extremely old. This man was still walking around and he carried a sago scraper with him.')

"To walk around with a sago scraper" is another Bosmun idiom that relates to foodways and to a certain period in a person's life. It refers to the age when a man is still an active food provider—no longer a helpless, dependent child and not yet senile. Following this reasoning, it was not understandable that the man had passed away. Men and women are at the prime of life as long as they produce sago. I remember a man beyond the age of seventy whom no one called an old fellow. He was still an industrious sago maker and was therefore regarded as a young and energetic man. As active food providers, people are entrenched in unique webs of vivid relationships. In their forties and early fifties, people usually have a lot of living consociates of the same generation, but this is not the case from sixty onward. Estimates produced by the World Health Organization (WHO) for 2012 indicate that the recent life expectancy in Papua New Guinea is sixty-two years for males and sixty-five years for females (World Health Statistics 2012). Once people reach an advanced age, the relational field naturally becomes thinner. Same-aged consociates die and with them the remembrance of their food-related connections. With increasing age, a food provider turns into what he or she already was in infanthood—a food receiver. Only then, I was told, are people expected to die.

In Bosmun understandings, sago making is what embeds people in life. Since infants and old people do not engage in the making of sago, they remain potentially closer to death. Another example illustrates this. I was surprised to realize that a mother and a daughter spoke of the same man, although the mother frequently talked of him as "the husband who had died" whereas the daughter talked of him as "the father who currently lived elsewhere." In order to clarify this, I asked the mother once more and she again referred to him as dead (*ninkut*). However, this time she added with a complaining tone that she alone had to care for her family because her husband had stopped visiting the swamps and that she had to ask her siblings and children to assist her. She was twenty years younger and felt a vitality that her husband no longer exhibited. From a biomedical view, the man clearly showed the signs of senescence. He could hardly walk and was frequently confused or *rorer*, as people defined his state, a state that one also has at birth. I then listened to how others defined old age, and in collecting similar assessments I eventually discerned that once a person retires from the making of sago, he or she formally admits to getting old. Death at this age then becomes foreseeable and somehow acceptable. This is not to say that the death of an old person is not tragic. The cultural perception of old people is different from that of infants despite the fact that both are food receivers and dependent on the goodwill of others. If we are to follow Fajans (1985) and her analysis of Baining personhood, we may conclude that both infants and old people in Daiden are considered less social than people who are industrious food reciprocators. Bosmun food-based social existence bears a lot of resemblance to Baining sociality, where "[t]he whole life cycle is perceived in terms of the social and cultural values of food giving / food taking, production / reproduction, and reciprocity" (Fajans 1985: 373). I argue, however, that no signs of sociability remain from an infant; the sentiment created is insufficient to situate the infant in the food-based cosmos of Daiden. It is only once they grow physically that children grow socially and emotionally. They are therefore not equal to old people in social terms. On the contrary, old people have had the chance to leave their imprints of sociability in the lives of others and are hence commemorated with intensity. As parents, they fed their children until they became adults. This gives them the right to take food without reciprocating it once they become old.

The difference between infants and old people is also noticeable in the collective response if one of them dies. Children are buried by women only and without much formal attention. If an old person dies, the case is different. It takes several years to collectively forget the name of a deceased. Only when pigs that have been raised through the feeding of sago pudding are consumed, can the 'honoring of a deceased' (*ndom taao*) come to an end (see figure 3.3). However, the time to emotionally cope with the loss of an old person is said to pass more quickly. Bereaved relatives are calmed by the idea that a person of an old age must have had a multitude of good relationships, supposing that he

Figure 3.3: Group of Plate Bearers. Ndombu is leading a group of plate bearers in the early morning hours to the ceremonial ground where singers and dancers are waiting for their last meal before the feast comes to an end.

or she pursued the ideal of generosity. The last step of *ndom taao* is performed only for people of high social standing. As I saw in different mourning situations, grief for an old person was not mixed with anger as it was when the man died "who was still carrying a sago scraper in his hands." As long as one is producing sago, one's life force is considered unbroken. The man in question had not retired from his work, he had not fallen back into the state of *rorer,* he was still a vital reciprocator. People were particularly upset in view of the man's death because theoretically he had been at the peak of his generosity. The man had been taken by death at the wrong time.

Sad Bellies
Empty stomachs are the appropriate and immediate collective response to the occurrence of death. Everyone who has heard of the death should abstain from food for at least three days and nights. In this way, the social collective offers sympathy for the kin of the deceased. Individual sadness is also expressed through food-related enactments. For years, the next of kin usually refuse to consume the kind of food that was part of the deceased's last meal. If the last meal was sago, which is considered the only nutritional source that really fills empty stomachs, then the suffering of a bereaved turns into an experiential state of permanent hunger. Concerning the perception of hunger among the Baining, which is similar to the perception of hunger in Daiden, Fajans (1997: 119) states: "It might seem that hunger should be classed as a physical state and not as an emotion or sentiment, but I would argue that for the Baining it is both." If someone dies in Daiden, not all kin have to abstain from the kind of food that was the deceased's last. It is common sense that only those who have felt a particular fondness for the deceased will do so. Basically, every adult was currently under one taboo or another in respect of a deceased. All seniors who spoke with me could look back at several food taboos they had imposed on themselves during their lives. It was explained to me many times: "I do not eat this because [a specific person] has died." Every food taboo that I heard of in this context was connected to a deceased to whom my interviewees connected specific emotional memories. If someone did not eat a particular kind of food, the reason behind it was either social discontent or emotional torment. Rarely did people say that they refused a certain kind of food because they could not digest it or because they did not like its taste.

Again, an association can be made with the Baining context, where people impose food taboos onto themselves after bereavement (Fajans 1997: 141). Ideationally though, these food taboos serve a different end from those in Daiden. According to Fajans (1997: 146), Baining consider such taboos as "an appropriate means of symbolically severing the social ties that have connected the living with the dead." Bosmun instead consider food taboos that relate to a relative's death a means of strengthening the social ties even after corporeal death. They are meant to keep remembrance alive. Moreover, Fajans states that Baining do not necessarily know why someone has assumed a food taboo. She tells of a wife and a daughter, for instance, who did not know the reason why the husband and father refused to eat pig (Fajans 1997: 125–126). To my knowledge, people in Daiden were informed about their kin's reasons for choosing food taboos. I assume that such differences are grounded in the different local concepts of the person. First, Baining take a stance of "not speculating on others' subjective attitudes [which] is common in many non-Western societies" (Fajans 1997: 122). As I learned, speculating on others' sociophysical and emotional states is a moral duty in Daiden. Second, old Baining people gradually "desocialize" as they enter the phase in which their productivity declines and they no longer maintain their self-sufficiency (Fajans 1997: 100, 110–111). In addition, "[t]he products of a person's labor should 'die together with their owner'" (Fajans 1997: 140). In Daiden and in neighboring areas (e.g., A.T. von Poser [2008b] on Kayan notions on social death), corporeal death does not mean that a person instantly dies in a social sense. As noted, pigs have to be grown to considerable size. Only then may the "honoring of a deceased" come to an end. Also, long after his or her death a person's labor is remembered by the descendants who grew sociophysically and emotionally through this person's provisions of sago.

How long to commemorate a beloved or respected person is generally one's own decision and depends on how old and how close the deceased was. Some people tabooed a certain kind of food for one or two years, whereas others had not eaten a certain food for decades. In 2008, I talked to an older woman who was preparing herself for *suruvok,* the 'lifting of a food taboo' that she had imposed on herself after a son of hers had died in adolescence. I was impressed when she told me that she would soon be going to eat rice again—after twenty-six years of refusing it. The boy had died in 1982, as she remembered, and rice had been part of his last repast. Only now was she emotionally prepared to end her mourning. Her individual fate certainly influenced her long-lasting refusal of rice. She had given birth to two girls and two boys. The first boy had died in infancy, the second in adolescence. A couple should bring up both a boy and a girl since a brother needs a sister and vice versa. The woman felt sad and guilty because her daughters had no brothers other than an adoptive brother. She had refused to adopt more children since she feared attacks of sorcery, which, as she believed, had already come upon her sons. Only when her younger daughter also gave birth to a boy in 2008 (the elder had delivered a boy in 2006), did the woman feel that, in view of her growing grandsons, she had been freed from her sorrow. The way she ended her personal mourning was marked in a food-based way. She asked a male relative to hunt a pig for her; she distributed the pig, together with rice—the food that had reminded her of her suffering for so long—among her kin.

Even if a food taboo is finally lifted, people still may hold onto food-related objects to commemorate a deceased. When I asked a very old man to tell me about his first wife, who had died more than twenty years ago, he told a grand-child to go and bring him an eating spoon (made of coconut shell). While telling me about their marriage, he held the spoon in his hands and looked at it from time to time. As our conversation ended, he handed the spoon over to me and said that this had been his first wife's spoon. During the last step of *ndom taao,* when the spirit of a deceased is honored for the last time in a col-lective ritual context, all the belongings of the departed are burned. Or so I had thought. Everyone in the man's household, including his second wife, knew of the spoon and everyone respected it as a symbol of remembrance. Another food-related memory thus may prevail even if one again starts to consume the food that was tabooed.

In chapter 1, I introduced the relationship between the children of "second cousins 2," who refer to each other as *nzokumbu* or *poro* ('friend' in Tok Pisin) and who ideally share feeling states. I had difficulties in tracing this rela-tionship genealogically. It marks the very end of the vast sphere of extended kinship in Daiden. However, people's shared foodways in commemorating a deceased again helped me to comprehend Bosmun kin-ties. Individuals I pre-viously had not imagined as relatives revealed their relationship to me rather casually by saying that they were sharing a food taboo since a common rela-tive had passed away. People related as *nzokumbu* jointly abstain from a certain kind of food, and they only lift it once every one of them agrees. According to Bosmun theories of feeling, moments of joy become intensified when shared. Likewise, moments of suffering become easier to contend with. Moreover, the sharing of a food taboo is not only a collective response to losing a kin member, but a reinforcement of the links that one still has with the living in a wide network of relations.

Let me conclude this chapter with another example that illustrates the power of a relational mode of living in regard to decision-making processes and the shared quality of feeling states. Relatives might encourage each other to lift a food taboo if they think that sufficient emotional effort has been put into the mourning process. A man told me that he had been on good terms with his parents-in-law. He had treated them according to what he had learned from his father. The man said: *Papa bilong mi em givim skultoktok long mi. Em tok: "Mono vokep mokem eimi puru seraŋdam."* ('My father gave me ad-vice. He said: "You have to look after your parents-in-law in the same way that you look after the yam sprouts [in your garden]."') I suggested that due to this good relationship he certainly had imposed upon himself a food taboo when his father-in-law had died. He said "no," although, of course, he could have done so. Everyone, above all his wife and his mother-in-law, had said to him that a taboo was not necessary because he had always been a caring son-in-law. He had followed his father's advice as every man should, and others had recognized his potential of *ndiar,* of being a good person. In the relational assessment of the son-in-law's proper reaction, one has to take into account that it was an affinal relation and not a consanguineal one. Social closeness has an influence upon the way food taboos are applied. Affinal kin-relations are marked mainly by mutual respect and less by emotional familiarity. Referring back to chapter 2, in which I talked about the social evaluation of gardens and swamps, the idiom using the image of "yam sprouts in the garden" to mark an affinal relation mirrors the intrinsic social distance, which is theoretically absent in consanguineal relations that are sustained via care and trust mediated through sago labor out in the swamps.

Prospect

I hope to have shown in this chapter that one needs to pay close attention to food-related enactments and expressions in order to understand Bosmun feeling states and definitions of self and other. Take, for instance, the woman who used the image of "canned tuna" to describe what she would have become had she accepted her husband's proposal to have another woman join their partnership. Take the man who kept his first wife's spoon as a memory of her long after she had died. Take the mother who refused to eat the kind of food her adolescent son had eaten prior to his death. These were but some examples that illustrate how important the relation to food is when making sense of personal emotional worlds. I also hope to have conveyed the idea that, in order to achieve an understanding of other people's states, contemplating their foodways is indispensable. In the following chapter, I examine Bosmun notions of placial belonging, social distance, and social boundaries. Again, food-related explanations are involved. The last example in this chapter, in which the metaphor of garden food served to display one's attitudes toward affinal relatives, gave an initial clue as to the expression of social distance. In what comes next, I finally ask how people in Daiden conceive of strangers, that is, of persons beyond the borders of recognized kinship. To answer this question I have to turn to local perceptions of familiar and unfamiliar places and to the embodied and emplaced dimensions of foodways in Daiden.

Notes

1. Outside the Bosmun area, Nzari is also known as Jari (Hogbin [1970] 1996: 34–35; Lipset 1997: 168; A.T. von Poser 2008a), Zaria (Lutkehaus 1995), or Daria (Höltker 1965b; Z'graggen 1992, 1996: 49–71). She even became famous on a national level when her story was staged by the Raun Raun Theatre (Murphy 1998).
2. Rumsey and Weiner (2001) refer to this narrative style, which is a unique mode to organize and memorize knowledge, as "emplaced myth." It is a prevalent feature

throughout Papua New Guinea (e.g., Harrison 1990; Hirsch 1995b; Jorgensen 1998; Kahn 1990; 1996; Kaniku 1975; Schwab 1970; Stewart & A. Strathern 2000, 2001; Wagner 1996; Wassmann 1991, 2001; Weiner 1991).

3. The entrance to the Mbur tributary has indeed a distinct feature. Due to its black riverine sediment, the Mbur clearly contrasts with the rather muddy-colored surface of the Ramu and is thus also frequently referred to as *blekwara* ('black water'). People usually canoe next to the banks of the Ramu so as to avoid the strong currents in the middle, which are hard to navigate. When approaching the Mbur by canoeing the Ramu on its western side, one is suddenly in black water. It indicates a small waterway yet to come. From further away, this particularity might easily be overlooked.

4. Yaeŋ and Manam, Nzari's point of departure and her final destination, are inextricably connected in Bosmun place theory. Each time Manam erupted in 2004/05, I was told that the waters of Yaeŋ foamed accordingly. People reckoned that Nzari must have left Manam for unknown reasons. Some even thought Nzari had returned to Yaeŋ. In 2008 when Manam was still active I heard more speculation: the volcano continued to be active as a sign of punishment by God, because in the meantime the islanders of Manam had abandoned God and returned to premissionary beliefs.

5. Since I was told that it was a single bird who had guided Soŋe on his path, I wondered why the bird was referred to in the plural form of the generic term for bird (*ŋgoris*) and not in the singular (*ŋguarak*). The answer I was given mirrors the dynamics inherent in any sociocultural reproduction. The man in charge of transmitting the chant to following generations reckoned that the person who had taught him must have changed the singular into a plural form because *ŋguarak* was also the name of a male person. If this person were an in-law of the chanter and were therefore obliged to avoid his name, the latter must have modified the word so as to avoid breaking a taboo.

6. On the one hand, the term *nis* generally refers to the 'inside' of human and other organic bodies like trees, for example, and to the 'inside' of constructed, nonorganic bodies such as houses, canoes, or masks. On the other hand, *nis* refers to the locus inside the female body where a new life forms. *Nis tak* means 'to become pregnant' (literally: 'to put [something] in a womb'). There is also a bird's call that goes *nis-nisnisnisnis*. This bird's call is said to convey the message that a woman has become pregnant before the woman herself actually announces it. If people expect a young married woman to become pregnant soon, they will pay more attention to this bird's call. Once a family knows that a female member is pregnant, the children belonging to that family are allowed to run around and imitate this call. Several times I heard children onomatopoetically intonating the bird's call. People outside that family who hear those children will instantly guess that someone must be pregnant.

7. Premarital affairs are not uncommon and sometimes result in the birth of a child. He or she normally does not suffer from his or her status since he or she is mostly adopted by a married sister or brother of the mother and thus becomes integrated into the comforting scheme of a mother-father pair.

8. Women's fights have been described by Höltker (1969). Based on his observations in 1937, he wrote that Bosmun women use specific clubs roughly two meters long. Fathers make them for daughters, but daughters can also inherit them from their mothers. These clubs are believed to be empowered by female magic, and thus the older a club, the more powerful it is. Kinswomen accompany the rivals and are expected to interfere to prevent severe injuries. Men and children also watch such fights (Höltker

1969: 71–72). Höltker's report is similar to what I was told and to what I observed as two sisters met for a fight because of an unequal distribution of food. Early in the morning, I heard a woman's yell and came out of my house as did my neighbors. The woman had come by canoe from a nearby hamlet where she lived, carrying with her a huge club to challenge her sister. The sister had been informed and thus she, too, was holding a club in her hands. As I saw, there is more gesticulation and verbal assault than direct club-fighting. Every time one of the women shouted or uttered incriminations she would wave her club in the direction of the other, who would try to ward off the strike with her own club. It was as if both raised their clubs so as to underpin their words with the sound of the colliding clubs. Neither got hurt and after half an hour the challenger retreated.

9. I already stated that individuals should not proclaim their own merits. It is via reflection by others that one will achieve the status of being socially accredited and amiable. In the interview with K. and S., S. said to me that he used to be a "man who liked to work." This self-declaration, however, was made without the slightest sign of arrogance and it was uttered by a man of over seventy years of age. Put differently, at this age he had provided ample evidence that he was a sociable agent. He had brought up a huge family with children and grandchildren. He would not have succeeded in this with a *ngumu mbakmbak,* a 'murky face.'

10. The reproductive potential of human bodies is recognized with the distinct signs of puberty that come forward in two ways: first, with the visibly transforming signs of the body and second, with *mian*—the awakening of a specific previously unknown interest in the opposite sex and mutual allurement. The onset of sexual desires does not, however, mean that one may fulfil them immediately. In premissionary times and during the early days of Christian conversion, boys and girls had to enter long-lasting phases of seclusion once these signs became noticeable.

11. In the past, beautifully carved spirit masks were used in dance performances during festive occasions. Today, some are still kept, but most of the old ones have already been sold to traders like "R.," who was a frequent visitor to the Lower Ramu during my stays in Daiden. He bought various carvings for little money to resell them at high prices to rich customers outside of Papua New Guinea (as I found out later when searching the internet). In the beginning, I had problems with the fact that people sold their material culture to "R."; especially as "R." was looking only for old carvings. Moreover, his method of negotiating increased my dislike of him, as he asked the sellers with such persistence to price down their items until they finally gave in. In the very beginning, I tried to convince people not to sell their carvings, but I quickly realized that I had to revise my own "traditionalistic" point of view. I became aware of how hard people struggle these days to earn the money needed to send their children to school. School fees for primary and secondary schools range between 50 and 150 Kina and the fees for the high school are incredibly high, up to 1,500 Kina per year; these amounts can hardly be acquired in a rural Papua New Guinean subsistence economy.

12. The term *mimin* also refers to the substance of human brains. In terms of its somewhat milky color and sticky quality, brain substance, mother's milk, and sago pudding indeed bear resemblances. In head-hunting times, enemy brains were ritually consumed since people believed that the brain contained a person's mental and physical strength, which could be absorbed by eating it.

13. In the past, a child at this stage was invested with particular ornaments. A child's ears and nasal septum were pierced. Rings and shell necklaces were put on. Girls' hair was mixed with red clay and the bodies of both boys and girls painted with particular dyes and oils. Today, ritual decoration of infants is almost nonexistent because people try to sell traditional adornments to traders. Moreover, to have a pierced nasal septum is seen as inconsistent with present life. Of the people I met, only those over fifty had pierced nose septa. Those of a younger age considered it "out of fashion."

14. As I said in chapter 2, *nyeroŋ* connects to the body from the outside. This also became clear to me as a specialist on magic told me how he had helped a little boy to recover from a severe illness. The boy's *nyeroŋ* had been stolen by a bush spirit. Ŋ., the specialist, knew which spirit it was, and he also knew how to convince the spirit to release the boy's *nyeroŋ* again. He offered food to the spirit and thus gained power over the spirit. Ŋ. captured the *nyeroŋ* in a ring made of vines, brought it back, and imposed it on the boy's body—from his head to his feet. After "spiritually dressing up" again, the boy finally recovered.

15. To avoid shame, women were allowed to fall back on local herbal substances known to cause abortion or infertility. Owing to Christian influences, traditional modes of regulating population growth, including abortion, are now being stigmatized as primitive and sinful. This, however, does not mean that abortion is no longer practiced. I also know of a case in which a woman consumed battery acid (which is also used to dye bast-skirts today) in an attempt to induce abortion. If the attempt to abort fails, a senior woman will not leave the house during pregnancy, so as to avoid being seen by others. I met such a mother and, although she was still at a reproductive age, at least from a biomedical point of view (approximately thirty-seven years old), she felt ashamed because her daughter had just recently delivered.

16. In the past, Bosmun boys had to undergo harsh tortures both in a physical and in a psychic sense. Höltker (1975) provides an account based on firsthand knowledge of Bosmun initiation in 1937. It basically matches what S., one of my eldest informants, told me about his experiences during initiation. He also showed me scars on his back and legs. S. was a youngster of approximately thirteen years of age and among the last who, as a child, had worn traditional loincloth prior to the introduction of Western clothing styles that people prefer now (see Colchester's [2003] volume *Clothing the Pacific* about the social implications of Western dress codes imposed onto Pacific peoples).

17. Hogbin's ([1970] 1996) ethnography *The Island of Menstruating Men*, first published in 1970, on the Wogeo people is probably the most famous New Guinea example in this regard (but see also Lipset 1997: 160–161; Tuzin 1980: 66–72; A.T. von Poser 2008a: 132).

18. People felt differently, however, when telling me about extramarital sexual acts as a peace-making strategy. It was common that a reconcilement between two opponents was made formal through an exchange of their wives until each gave birth to a child. The wives then returned to their husbands who would take care of each other's children.

19. Bosmun engage in the practice of love magic (*ndoor*), which always involves the transmitting of body essences in some way. A spell needs to be accompanied by delivery of bodily essences to be effective, and objects or foods that are offered to the person whose attention one wants to attract must have been in contact with those essences.

Love magic is not only used to attract a new devotee, but also to diminish one's own partner's possible interest in extramarital affairs. Since one's saliva can cause another person to become dependent on him- or herself, "French kissing" is dangerous, if not culturally inappropriate. As girls told me, boys try to spit into their mouths in order to convince the girls to become involved with them. Today, youngsters increasingly imitate "movie kisses," the most beloved movie in recent years being *Titanic* with Leonardo DiCaprio and Kate Winslet. Movies are shown in local cinemas (areas fenced with sago leaf thatch) whenever a working generator is at hand.

20. The last dwelling-house said to be traditional as regards both its construction and its material aspects I saw in 2004/05. By 2006, the Ramu had taken away the ground on which it had been built. Bosmun house design has changed and is still being altered. Most houses still have two entrances, but new houses have rooms inside. Linguistically, there is only one word to refer to the inside of a house—*nis* (which as I stated earlier also denotes 'womb'). There is no word for "room" in the local vernacular since in the past there were no "rooms" that would subdivide the *nis* of a house. Moreover, a house's walls are made differently today. Traditionally, front and back were closed by horizontally arranged bark laths (see figure 0.1) and the sides by sago leaves. Today, bamboo is used. When asked why they prefer bamboo to the former style, people said they had seen it in other north coast places and liked it. No one said that using bark for house construction was a more arduous task than using bamboo. To have "rooms" inside a house is equally a projection of alternative house designs that people have come to know through experience with the outside world.

21. Men are neither allowed to enter birth-houses nor want to, since it would pose a major threat to their vitality. This does not mean, however, that men do not know what happens inside a birth-house. The men I talked to were quite informed about child delivery, and the story of Nzari is recounted by both men and women. Men seem not to forget what they saw in childhood, after all.

22. This description fitted my observed impressions. A menstruating woman can be idle the whole day without having to fear gossip about her being lazy; she can chat with passers-by or simply hang around with younger children while the other members of a household go about their work as usual.

⇥ Chapter Four ⇤
Ropor's Belly and Emplaced Empathy

In this chapter, I undertake a discussion of embodied and emplaced food-ways. Again, I have chosen a myth in which to set my material. It is the story of the man Ropor and it tells about the human belly as the locus of life and volition (see Lohmann 2003). Ropor's belly becomes violated and, although the violation happens unintentionally, it serves as a lesson for what happens when someone becomes the victim of death sorcery. My conversation partners believed that death sorcery, the worst form of malevolent empathy, causes the loss of the intestines. After recounting the deeds of Ropor, I investigate Bosmun notions of familiar and unfamiliar places. In so doing I describe local configurations of social insideness and outsideness. Going beyond the moral and emotional functions of foodways discussed in the preceding chapters, I now elaborate on embodied foodways as the third crucial dimension for what renders a place in Daiden familiar and suggest that empathy becomes em-placed: benevolent empathy is anchored in places where people relate through common foodways, whereas malevolent empathy is anchored in places where people do not relate on the basis of such foodways. I discuss local ideas about places of trade and raids, which, in the past, made up the outside world, as well as the more recent outside world of the town. This is followed by a discussion of socially ambivalent places within Daiden, in which I look at places that are held to be inhabited by various kinds of spirit entities. In this context, I also talk about the reason given to me for the outbreak of fire that I saw in 2004. Finally, I pay attention to the meaning people ascribe to the households they do not belong to. I argue that the less people know about the foodways in other places, the more ambivalent these places and their inhabitants appear to them. It is in such places that suspects of sorcery are mostly expected to live. The chapter ends with the proposal that *ramkandiar*, 'watching others and being watched,' is a conscious collective strategy of avoiding what people fear most—the development of antipathy that may culminate in the exercise of sorcery attacks. In perpetuating the ideal of sociable relationships as based on the exchange of benevolent foodways, life is thought to be kept intact and free from ill will. Due to this model of causality, kin are usually able to fend off the suspicions of nonkin.

The Story of Ropor

Ropor is the cultural hero who gave ideational shape in particular to Bosmun manhood. Ever since he emerged on the stage of sociomythical action, men have had to seek a certain distance from women. Ropor built the first men's house, thus creating a counterdomain to women's birth-houses. Thanks to Ropor, men began to gather in these houses and began to conduct initiations in the *ndene tomuŋ,* the secret subterranean cavern where novices learned how to play the secret flutes (*mirpi nzit*) and started to dress as men—with bark belts around their bellies. As we shall see, Ropor had to bandage his belly because he became badly injured by his wives. The story presented below is what I have summarized from several accounts given to me on various occasions by different narrators. Some of these accounts were taped, some not. Spontaneous narration easily enfolded, for example, when I asked "could you tell me what a *toupu mot* is?" and the answer was: "Ropor was a *toupu mot*!" (As stated in chapter 1, *toupu motor* were the delegates who were authorized to walk freely to neighboring areas in order to arrange exchange relations). The following account is therefore to be seen as a composition derived from partial glimpses that I acquired at different moments during my stays in Daiden.

Betrayals and Violent Foodways

Ropor was married to the women Yaŋnde and Taŋgru. One of them was the mother of his son. Nevertheless, Ropor fell in love with a female tree-spirit named Semenbo. Semenbo approached him secretly with food, first with the gift of a banana, then with a gift of sago (in the same way that Nzari approached men), while he was building a canoe in the forest. Ropor realized that Semenbo was not just attractive but a *ndiara mes* (a 'food-generous woman'), and thus he developed a deep fondness for her. Ropor frequently went to the coast (to a place located near Marangis) to trade clay pots for sea salt. Whenever he returned, he stopped at Semenbo's place and left most of the traded salt with her. To his wives, he would bring back just a small amount of salt, whereas when meeting Semenbo he would always bring a lot of salt. The wives sensed a betrayal and asked the son to follow his father to find out about the obvious shortage of salt. They cast a spell so that the boy could hide in the canoe of his father. As they arrived at Semenbo's place, the boy saw the father's betrayal and revealed himself. Knowing that the son would tell his wives about his secret, Ropor became nervous, but Semenbo told the boy to stay and she gave him sago and fish to eat. Food-generosity was one of Semenbo's characteristics. The boy ate, but out of loyalty to his mother and the second wife of his father, he furtively hid the fish bones in his hair so that he could take them with him as proof of what he had discovered. When the boy and his father came home, the boy told his mother to comb his hair, knowing that her fingers would catch in the bones. When this happened, the wives became convinced that Ropor had betrayed them. The boy told them what he had seen and where Semenbo lived. The next day, Yaŋnde and Taŋgru went to visit her. They secretly watched how Ropor offered salt to Semenbo and the women became enraged. As Ropor left, the women came into sight, pretending that they were visitors with good intentions. Being a generous woman, Semenbo instantly placed a clay pot onto the hearth in order to stir sago. The women made Semenbo believe that they wanted to assist her in removing the pot from the fire, but then shoved her into the hot water, where she died a painful death.

When Ropor returned to Semenbo's place, he found her dead body tied to the middle post of her house. Ropor had no doubt that Yaŋnde and Taŋgru had killed Semenbo. His anger grew, but he eventually returned home and acted as if nothing had happened. However, he was prepared to avenge Semenbo. He put her decaying body into the water and told the women to catch fish there. Ropor watched them as they were pulling nets through the water. Finally, they caught the remains of Semenbo's body and screamed. At this moment, Ropor speared them to death.

After having killed his wives, Ropor prepared a meal for his son. He stirred a portion of sago and mixed it with plenty of fish. He did not cover the sago with fish (which is the usual way to serve sago and fish), but tucked the fish into the pudding so that it could not be seen. Then he told his son to eat. He poured the food into the boy's mouth and told him that he had to eat everything up because the mothers would be away for a long time. The boy struggled, but his father continued pushing food into his mouth. In the end, the boy choked to death on the fish bones. Ropor took his son's body and threw it into the water, whereupon the boy became a fish.[1] Once this was done, Ropor took his belongings and set out on the water in a hollowed palm stem (of a pandanus type locally called *suooŋgor*).

Ropor's Death and the Hills of Lament

Ropor came upon the sisters Nziŋgam and Piatam, who found the hollowed palm stem in shallow water near their canoe base. Although it was unusually heavy, the stem looked like proper firewood and thus the elder sister said that they should carry it home. They did not see Ropor hiding in the stem. Whenever Nziŋgam and Piatam stirred sago, Ropor came out of the stem secretly and stole a piece of their meal. The sisters realized that some food was always missing and planned to find out why. The elder sister was to go to the banks, bathe, and play flutes (prior to Ropor, the women used to play the flutes). This was what they usually did after cooking and prior to eating. The younger sister was to hide in the house and watch what happened. As Ropor appeared, she instantly fell in love with him. He was a powerful and attractive man. She told the elder sister what had happened and she, too, felt attracted to him when she saw him. The sisters started to fight, but Ropor convinced both of them to marry him.

Nziŋgam and Piatam were supposed to marry the brothers Katembaŋ and Ndoŋembaŋ once they became women (after menarche). However, once they had met Ropor, the sisters asked their brothers Manzena and Ripuk to tell Katembaŋ and Ndoŋembaŋ that they were not going to marry them. The brothers, too, were fond of Ropor and did what the sisters had asked them. They considered him a good man. He even took care of the sisters when they went into seclusion at menarche (today, this care is done by women). When the sisters had finished their seclusion, they married Ropor. Although they lived happily together, Ropor thought that, as women have their kitchen-house, men should also have their own space, and he therefore began to build what was to become the first men's house.

Katembaŋ and Ndoŋembaŋ began to plot their revenge. They pretended that they were willing to assist Ropor in building the men's house. One day, Ropor wanted to eat breadfruit and climbed a tree. The brothers cast a spell and the tree grew higher and higher so that Ropor could not come down. Flying foxes flew by and helped him, however. They cut their wings and a huge vine (*kaambon*) emerged from the blood that dripped down. Ropor used the vine to come down (in some versions, Ropor cuts into his own finger and the vine emerges from his own blood). Then, he went to make sago and the brothers accompanied him. The brothers cut the palm so that the falling stem would strike Ropor dead, but he was too nimble and got out of the way. Finally they tried to strike him dead with a huge post while he was constructing the house. Again, they failed. Ropor became weary of the brothers' attacks. He told Nziŋgam and Piatam to store plenty of food within the house and gave rise to a terrific storm so that the brothers could not leave their house to find food. As the hunger became unbearable, they left the house and died in the storm.

From then on, Ropor lived in harmony with Nziŋgam and Piatam and their brothers Manzena and Ripuk. Ropor was a man with magical powers (*sae*). Every time he went to work in the forest, he removed his intestines (*moŋ*) from his body and hung them onto a tree. In this state, he was able to work as effectively and long as he wished to and never became hungry. In order to keep his secret concealed, he told his wives to play the flutes every time they brought him food. Whenever Ropor heard the melody, he quickly swallowed his intestines and recomposed his belly. After a while, Nziŋgam and Piatam became tired of carrying the food and the flutes. One day, they approached Ropor without advance notice and saw the intestines hanging at the tree. Ropor pretended that these were animal intestines. He ate the sago that the sisters had brought, but it came out again through his anus. Ropor pretended to be sick. After Nziŋgam and Piatam had left, he tried to put his intestines back but it was too painful. He put the intestines into water to make them soft but the pain persisted and he had to bandage his belly. Ropor was disappointed. The sisters had disregarded what he had asked them to do and therefore he decided to end his life. He told the sisters to help him hunt a bandicoot. He said that they should go to a particular grassland area where he would join them. Ropor turned into the bandicoot. When Nziŋgam and Piatam saw the bandicoot, they killed it. Since Ropor did not join them, the sisters went home to cut and wash the meat. While doing so, they found a chain that Ropor had worn in the animal body and thus discovered that they had killed him.

Full of guilt, Nziŋgam and Pɨatam left the place where they had lived with Ropor (located between Daiden and Ndoŋon) and went toward the place Mboŋgeŋgat (alongside the Mbur River). Each time they looked back and lamented, a hill rose in the landscape. Manzena and Ripuk, the brothers, followed them. At one of those hills (called Siŋ), the sisters passed the flutes to their brothers and told them that from now on the flutes should be played and seen by men only. They also passed all the knowledge that Ropor had given them to the brothers. Then, the sisters left their home area for Yin (Sanai, located in the hinterland of the Mbur), where they turned into stones. Ropor himself turned into a *mɨrɨp* (a major flute-spirit).

Ropor's story is significant in three ways. First, the story gives clues concerning the value of food sharing in Bosmun subjectivity. Although Semenbo is the reason for Ropor's cheating on his wives, she is considered the archetype of the food-generous woman. Semenbo even welcomes strangers, the wives of Ropor, to come and eat with her. In hearing how people spoke of her, I gained the impression that Ropor naturally had to fall for her because she exhibited the kind of morality claimed to be particular to Daiden. Everyone felt pity for Semenbo, and nobody was worried about the wives. Second, the story shows that secrecy causes problems. Ropor kept his relationship with Semenbo secret and she died. He also kept his magical hanging bowels secret and this was his undoing in the end. Third, and important for the discussion in this chapter, the story of Ropor indicates that foodways can have a thoroughly violent aspect. Ideally, foodways should be used in life-affirming ways, but they also bear the potential to destroy life. The last meal that Nzari offered Soŋe already hinted at a more central feature of the myth of Ropor.

Throughout the myth, the protagonists apply foodways that bring death to others—Semenbo meets her death by being pushed into a cooking pot, Yaŋnde and Taŋgru meet their death as they are catching fish, the son who had his share in Semenbo's killing chokes on the sago pudding that his father forces him to swallow, and Katembaŋ and Ndoŋembaŋ meet their death when they are driven by hunger into a fatal storm. Finally, Ropor, who has the secret about his belly, turns into game and lets Nziŋgam and Pɨatam hunt and kill him. In the end, all those who used foodways to violate life are gone. Even Nziŋgam and Pɨatam decide to abandon their home area because they killed their beloved husband. They disobeyed his order by carrying food to him without making themselves noticeable. As I have made clear more than once, carrying food is a public performance in Daiden. One does not walk around secretively with food! All the protagonists in the myth of Ropor who either had negative intentions or were drawn into situations that ended badly became dislocated or relocated beyond Bosmun country. This recalls the fate of the despotic figure of Ramakniŋ. In expelling him, the local core ideal of *ramkandɨar,* which was a prominent theme in all the myths that I heard in

Daiden, became emplaced. Frequently, my conversation partners described *ramkandiar* as *vunsindiar,* as the ideal of this place (*vunsi-* stems from *vunis,* 'place').

Ples na hapsait—Bosmun Configurations of Social Landscapes

When I asked people what they thought about life outside their home area or when I listened to conversations in which speakers discussed the subject casually, the following questions always guided subjective and intersubjective assessments. First, does the place in question nurture its inhabitants as sufficiently as the local environment does? Second, which types of food are obtainable in different areas? Third, what do people do in order to procure food? Finally, how much time do people spend on the preparation of meals? Answers to these kinds of questions help in understanding how people in Daiden configure places socially. What makes a place appear good or poor? How does a place create a sense of belonging? What kinds of people live here and elsewhere?

First of all, a general distinction has to be made between two social realms or frames of reference in which Bosmun inside-outside constellations come to the fore: the intragroup realm concerning social dynamics within the group of people who share a collective sense of "being Bosmun," and the intergroup realm concerning social dynamics between this "Bosmun group" and other groups. In the local, day-to-day life of intragroup relationships, senses of "insideness" and "outsideness" prevail most significantly in the demarcation between kin and nonkin. The place of kin, with its platforms, households, and hearths, is where one's dispositions are being assessed by others and where one feels entitled to assess others. It is the place where one is given food without having to ask for it, and, as we see below, where one shares regular embodied practices with others that are connected to the making of sago. Outsideness on the intragroup level is defined through the image of households where one does not sit down to eat and where one does not share the bodily activities of joint food procurement. This is where one does not have or no longer sees a need to reckon kin-relations (if such relations existed). In Tok Pisin, people frequently framed inside and outside, familiarity and unfamiliarity, with the phrase *ples na hapsait* ('[our] place and the other side'). According to my interpretation, it is both a spatial and a social description. It may be the place just "on the other side" (of the river, for instance), but it may also be the space where one has no position as a food-dealing agent. The borders of familiar and unfamiliar places are nonetheless flexible. They become expanded or reduced. A new marriage can bring different households together; a dispute can separate previously connected households.

The other type of inside-outside configuration is with adjacent groups, with close or distant neighbors who were commonly distinguished by sociolinguistic "otherness." This is what I refer to as the intergroup realm. People of other areas speak other languages, and from a local viewpoint it is believed that they also rely on other premises in managing their lives socially, in particular with regard to interpersonal encounters. *Ramkandiar,* I was frequently told, must be unique to Bosmun. Traditionally, inside-outside configurations existed with some groups via trade relations and with other groups via inimical relations. Later, the local boundaries of known worlds widened. With colonialism, post-colonialism, and the developing independent nation of Papua New Guinea beginning in 1975, a further outside world came into social sight—the urban space where other "Papua New Guineans," local nationals and expatriates, meet or live.

A striking indicator in socially constructing self and other is, of course, language, as Kulick declares for the Gapun living in between the Lower Sepik and Lower Ramu region: "It is now generally agreed that New Guinea communities have purposely fostered linguistic diversity because they have seen language as a highly salient marker of group identity.... In other words, New Guinea villagers have traditionally seized upon the boundary-marking dimension of language, and they have cultivated linguistic differences as a way of 'exaggerating' themselves ... in relation to their neighbors and trading partners" (1992: 2). However, in addition to language as a boundary marker in the definition of self and other, the people who spoke with me drew upon two further markers: they perceived of themselves and others as relying on different forms of sociality and embodiment. People often articulated these differences to me by using food-based images, and frequently in a stereotypical way. A group living further up the Ramu (in a similar ecological setting), for instance, was perceived as giving primary dietary value to *aibiga / kuit,* a type of plant with edible leaves, which is a common supplement in Bosmun cuisine. Even though this other group also heavily relies on sago and fish, they were referred to as the *kuvi* people (*kuvi* being the plural term of *kuit*) because they consumed these staples in proportions different from the Bosmun. Several of my informants stated that at least one meal per day in their area may consist simply of these leaves, which led them to conclude: *Namba wan kaikai bilong ol em i aibiga tasol. Kaikai bilong mipela em i no aibiga! Em saksak stret wantaim fis tasol.* ('The food they prefer consists just of [the leaves of] this plant. Our diet is not centered on this plant! It is just sago pudding with fish.')

I interpret such statements as social assessments of other places and groups and as demarcations drawn between collective self and other. Based on what has been said in this book about the deeper meanings of sago, I also claim that in assuming that another group relies mainly on food other than sago, Bosmun also assume the existence of a different way of life there.

I now explore Bosmun embodied experience and its importance for creating a sense of social and placial belonging. Investigating how Bosmun physically experience and incorporate place is, I believe, also fundamental to an understanding of their sense of the outside world.

Embodying Place and Encoding Time, Age, and Gender

Several scholars (e.g., Csordas 1990; Eves 1998; Ingold 2000; Lyon and Barbalet 1994; A. Strathern 1996; Telban 1998) have drawn upon the *Phenomenology of Perception* proposed by Merleau-Ponty ([1945] 1962) and his claim for the body as the world-constituting agent. Telban, for instance, writes about movement and action among the Ambonwari of East Sepik Province in Papua New Guinea, that "[t]he way of sitting, the way of cooking, the way of eating, the way of arguing, or even the manner in which adolescent girls walk ..., or gestures of support ..., or techniques of fighting ..., are all embodied habits acquired and recognized by those who share the same 'way of the village.' ... The 'lived body' ... manifests itself through the way acts are performed" (1998: 62). Csordas declares "embodiment" to be an anthropological paradigm when stating that "the body is not an *object* to be studied in relation to culture, but is to be considered as the *subject* of culture, or in other words as the existential ground of culture" (1990: 5),[2] and Lyon and Barbalet underline that "[i]n a significant social sense the body ... is not simply the body we have but the body we are" (1994: 56). Most compelling in the discussion of embodiment is the plea for a "collapsing of dualities" (Csordas 1990: 8) in the Cartesian sense of mind and body, culture and biology, or cognition and emotion as we know them. According to Csordas (1990: 36–37), an opposition between body and mind does not hold true on the level of perception but only as we make use of our capacity to reflect upon and objectify the worlds in and around us.[3] In favoring "embodiment" as a paradigm to dissolve the duality, Ingold (2000: 170–171) warns us, however, not to forget that what is called "embodiment" or "embodied mind" might equally be called "enmindment" or "enminded body." If we do not adhere to such an interchangeability of terms, we cannot really convey that "[b]ody and mind, after all, are not two separate things but two ways of describing the same thing—or better, the same process—namely the environmentally situated activity of the human organism-person" (Ingold 2000: 171).[4] Ingold's claim to include the "environment" (2000: 18–20, 171)—to be understood as subjective, relative, and never complete and thus not simply "nature"—is of particular interest. In further elaborating Bateson's (1972) "ecology of mind" (and putting it in relation to Merleau-Ponty's work), Ingold ultimately suggests an "ecology of life" (2000: 19, 171). He uses Bateson's formula "organism plus environment," but offers a different interpretation: there are not two separate entities linked via a "plus" in a still dichotomous scheme, but a "whole-organism-in-its-environment" that must be thought of as "one indivisible totality" (Ingold 2000: 19).

Against this theoretical backdrop, I now turn to aspects of Bosmun embodiment. Apart from subjectively knowing their environment, I realized that people had a shared sense of placial embodiment or a "same way of the village." This shared sense is essential when attempting to comprehend what constitutes a place as familiar, safe, and trusted in Daiden. It was with and through bodies—one may also say that it was "as bodies"—that Bosmun made sense of a large part of their universe. Above all, placial incorporation is achieved through the consumption of local foods and of sago in particular. However, it is not just the consumption of sago but its preparation that instigates people's symbolic and sensual merging with place. Sago is said to taste best when it is stirred in clay pots that local women have produced. Sago bread, too, is said to have a special flavor and a special nurturing quality when roasted on the broken piece of a heated clay pot. When prepared in a frying pan, it leaves people hungry, I was told. In my opinion, such statements yield the perspective that the local soil is immanent to Bosmun consumption per se, not only in a symbolic but in a very substantial sense. Incorporating place by "consuming its soil" is also a prevalent feature that is revealed when one asks what kind of water people prefer to drink.

To explain this, I evoke one of my travels to the Ramu in 2008. It was during this journey that a fellow traveler reminded me of what I had heard and seen more than once during earlier visits to Daiden. Frequently, my travels with people to and from their homes helped me adjust my perspective. We arrived at the Ramu as usual—around midnight and after a six-hour drive on the north coast road. The regular PMV[5] to the Bosmun region normally drops passengers alongside the eastern riverbanks, and often in grasslands that were described to me as *snek kantri* ('snake country') when I arrived for the first time. Here, one is likely to spend the night or wait at least several hours until a relative arrives with a canoe to pick one up. My Bosmun consociates were the most patient, relaxed, and good-humored travelers that I have ever met. No matter how long we traveled on the road and no matter that one or two hours by canoe still lay ahead of us, my companions always felt euphoric whenever we set out again on familiar water. Canoeing the Ramu is a familiar kinetic skill, and thus I often felt that, after a phase in town, place became gradually reincorporated with every stroke. This time, I traveled with a group of two men and four women, and we were lucky to find a vacant canoe docked at the banks. One is allowed to use such a canoe if one has figured out who the owner is. This is what my traveling party did before we embarked (the next day, the canoe has to be brought back and the owner must be informed). I got the impression that leaving the town behind is basically a moment of rejoicing for everyone, and I remember what a woman belonging to our group uttered once we were out on water. She was sitting in front of me, and she eagerly began to drink water from the Ramu, shoveling it with her hands. After she had quenched her thirst, she contently exclaimed: *Ah! Wara bilong mipela, graun bilong mipela! Dispela wara ya … em gutpela wara, em swit nongut tru, em graun i stap insait! Graun ya em swit nongut tru! Mi save laik dring dispela wara tasol, em graun i stap insait. Wara long taun … em kol wara nating ya!* ('Ah! Our water, our ground! This water … is good water, it is very tasty, [because] it contains the ground! The ground is so tasty! I want to drink just this water, [because] it contains the ground. The water in town … is nothing but just cool water!')

Hearing this, I asked the others in the canoe about the quality of water, and they affirmed the woman's assessments of town and home water. The strong currents of the Ramu keep its stream constantly stirred and thus muddy. A crucial way to incorporate one's place is by drinking this water enriched with mud, and people also use it for the rinsing of sago pith and for cooking. The Ramu is also where people usually go to bathe (though not to relieve themselves, which is usually done in the forest). Although Ramu water is very muddy, it is said to be good and clean because it is not stagnant but runs into the open sea. I remember talking to a man who had recently come back from a visit to a neighboring group. Aside from the different food habits he had observed there, he said the water had been awful, "just rock water." While drinking *ston wara* ('water that runs over rocks') as he would call it, he longed for the Ramu with its different water quality.

I was also told that bathing in the Ramu, up to three times a day or more, rejuvenates people's bodies. Secluded widows and widowers who have to experience a quasi-death are likely to be scolded if they bathe too often in the river. Living in a household that was located very close to the riverbanks, I was able to make out how often people came to the river in order to take a bath. *Yu go waswas ya!* ('Go and take a bath!'), I was regularly told when I said that I was tired after a long conversation or after a long walk. To go and take a bath in the river was a very common recommendation people gave each other. Children are also bathed in the Ramu from early infanthood on. This way, another crucial aspect of Bosmun identity becomes embodied right from the beginning of life. After all, catching fish, the most regular way of obtaining a protein source in Daiden, is linked to a constant bodily immersion into water. I frequently saw people standing in water when, for instance, cleaning fish (see figure 4.1). We may say that the Ramu reshapes human bodies in the same way that it reshapes the adjacent ground by eroding and releasing it again. Ground that was once solid becomes flooded and muddy and finally turns into a swamp—the perfect place for sago palms to grow and new food sources to emerge. We may also say that, in an ontological sense, river, swamps, and human bodies form a substantial unity.

Figure 4.1: Cleaning Fish. Ndombu and members of her family have been standing in the water of an old riverbed since the morning.

Let me give a further impression of the particularities of Bosmun embodied experience that I observed while we traveled to and from Madang. Interestingly, sensual and haptic practices involved in people's foodways "on the road" resembled local sociality. The habit of giving food without directly asking the other whether he or she wants it is also practiced among familiar cotravelers in the small space on the back of PMV trucks, but even with the people one does not necessarily know well, most of my companions turned out to be "notorious food sharers." Food sharing on PMV rides was a highly haptic experience, showing that "[t]ouch is a powerful vehicle in the interactions between human beings" (Finnegan 2005: 18). Hands touched other hands, hands gave and hands received—without saying a word. Locked too much in a non-Bosmun frame of thought as I was at first, I attempted to do well by the person who traveled with me. However, everything that I gave to my cotraveler was immediately redistributed among those sitting around us. In the beginning, this troubled me since I thought that he or she always remained hungry while traveling with me. A PMV does not necessarily stop in places where one can buy food, and usually we would reach the Ramu or Madang at midnight. As I became more and more aware of the power that the sharing of food has in Daiden, I relaxed. Eventually, I also ended up putting food in other people's hands and receiving from them without verbal communication.

When people described bodily well-being to me, they often spoke of a *vumbu rumbus,* which can be translated as 'a complete body.' It means to be healthy, agile, of shiny skin, and of muscled physique. In explaining *rumbus* to me, a man said that I should think of the full moon. When the moon becomes full, it is called *rumbus.* A body is *rumbus* once it reaches maximal physical strength. This strength begins to accumulate when young people start to produce sago. The local environment shapes Bosmun bodies significantly and invests them with a particular sense of social and corporeal identity. The ultimate place that shapes a *vumbu rumbus* is the sago swamp. It is noteworthy in this context to say that, instead of viewing tiredness as the result of too much physical exertion in the swamps, people presented a reverse causality to me. The feeling of exhaustion arises if one is not working hard, if one does not engage in regular movement and physical actions. Constant industriousness cannot cause people to become tired and sleepy. It is through the merging with place on various experiential levels that Bosmun bodies feel well.

Bosmun senses of place also project onto people's skin. Landscapes provide people with unique "skinscapes" (Howes 2005). In defining the term, Howes explains: "In many societies the skin of the earth is thought to be replicated in the skins of the individuals who live on it. Just as the landscape may resemble a body, the body may seem like a landscape, with its own hills and valleys and rivers" (2005: 33). In addition to fostering social recognition and emotional stability, sago making notably marks people's bodies with "readable" signs. Bosmun hands and feet bear the signs of sago making in a collectively shared way. I regularly heard someone utter: *Nil saksak i sutim lek bilong mi* ('the thorns of the sago palm have pierced my feet') or *nil saksak i sutim han bilong mi* ('the thorns of the sago palm have pierced my hands'). Sago thorns were among the most important placial icons in Daiden, playing a significant role in the placial transformation of bodies. From a biomedical point of view, wounds stemming from this experience are indeed unpleasant. They become inflamed easily and are sometimes so painful that people have to restrict the movements that normally define their daily rhythms; yet, apparently no one complained. This may have to do with the fact that such wounds give evidence of one's food-based agency. To return with scratches, cuts, or pricks was part of Bosmun sensory routine, and it was also a recurring topic in verbal discourse. To belong to this place, it seems, is to share an actual embodied sense of it, including wounds that originate from people's industriousness in the swamps.

Everyone I talked to in Daiden had an idea of how it felt to be pierced by sago thorns. People also distinguished the different sensations of such wounds during the dry or the wet season. This leads to another aspect of Bosmun placial embodiment. Bosmun bodies also echo time, gender, and age. Sago is procured throughout the year. However, wounds resulting from sago labor are worse during the time of heavy rains because the high humidity slows down the formation of scars. Likewise, moving to and from the swamps is sensually different during the dry and the wet seasons. During the wet season, people more or less waded through the grounds, and the rain kept their bodies constantly wet. Since food has to be procured regularly, rain drops trickling down the body are particular markers of seasonal time. The dry season is also ingrained in local sensual perception; wounds heal more quickly and movement becomes less restricted.

Gender, too, is encoded in the embodied acquisition of the world. A Bosmun "sense of sago," a phrase coined by Dundon (2005) to refer to sensual experiences of sago among the Gogodala of Papua New Guinea's Western Province, is indeed gendered. Women bear the signs of sago making primarily on their outer hand surfaces. When they rinse the pith they do so by squeezing it with the backs of their hands, which are therefore covered with patches of hard skin. Callouses on female hands are an essential marker of female identity. In 2008, I had the opportunity to reciprocate at least a bit of what I had received from my "sister" (and our family) in terms of accommodation. She and her husband came to stay with me in Madang in what rural Papua New Guineans would call a typical *haus bilong waitman* (a 'white man's house'). My husband Alexis and I lived on the campus of Divine Word University. We had a small two-room flat including a kitchen and bathroom. There was no need to walk long distances to fetch water or collect firewood and there were no mosquitoes once the door was shut. It was a typical house in town. Frequently, my "sister" compared the town food that I offered her with local food and the way it was obtained. I had the impression that a local "sense of sago" deeply pervaded her comments about her being away from home. During one of our conversations, she showed me her hands, took mine, ran them over hers, and said proudly: *Ol han bilong mipela ... ol lain i save wok saksak ... ol han ya ... ol i luk kain olsem!* ('The hands of us ... of us sago making people ... these hands ... they look like this!')

Both women and men gain strong musculature and corporeal agility through sago labor. However, this labor leaves different imprints on male bodies. Men bear the signs of sago making primarily on their inner hand surfaces, since their hands embrace the sago tool when pounding the pith. Moreover, men usually "bathe" in sago pith while scraping the palm-stem. Their hard-working, perspiring bodies become covered by the substance that they shred. When a palm-stem is finished, men almost sit amid the pith. Men's sensual memories linked to the making of sago are thus different from those of women.

Finally, the sensual experience of place also differs according to age. Children in Daiden sensually comprehend place in ways different from the ways in which adults and elderly people do. Although their hands and feet may experience sago thorns from an early age as they follow their parents to the swamps, their bodily sense of place is not yet entirely culturally developed. Once they become sago producers, they are expected to develop this sense. Old people, on the other hand, have experientially left behind what is considered the prime cultural achievement within the Bosmun sensual apparatus—the "complete body" of the industrious sago laborer. With old age, people know what their bodily sense of place was when they were at the prime of life.

Keeping in mind the type of embodiment that informs a Bosmun sense of placial identity, I now follow different paths leading into outside worlds—beyond Bosmun terrain. I trace the paths that were established by trade and warfare. In discussing trade and raids, I partly rely on Bosmun passed-down memories and imaginations of the past; former modes of trade have been altered due to sociohistoric and economic upheavals and raids have been abandoned. Yet, images of the past were frequently construed by speakers in different contexts and thus have value in serving my aim of detecting Bosmun notions of emplaced empathy.

Traditional Outside Worlds

Hollan and Throop allude to a critical aspect concerning empathetic processes by pointing out that these "do not unfold in a political or moral vacuum. Rather, they are encouraged and amplified in some contexts and discouraged and suppressed in others. For example, all societies everywhere attempt to prohibit empathy in at least some contexts to pursue other highly valued goals, such as training soldiers or hunters" (2008: 393). From what I was told about traditional inside-outside configurations, I eventually discerned that benevolent empathy (as the basis for mutual amity and hospitality) was encouraged in situations of trade, whereas malevolent empathy or the suppression of empathy (as the basis for acts of violence) was pursued in situations of warfare and head-hunting. Certain empathetic stances were cultivated as compulsory for certain encounters in certain places.

PATHS OF TRADE

Traditionally, Bosmun participated in a complex trade network extending over the New Guinea's north coast region (Tiesler 1969, 1970). This trade network linked several groups in socioeconomic ways. Bosmun gave clay pots to Watam, Marangis, Boroi, and Kayan (all located in the coastal direction) and received sea salt, woven sleeping bags, or bark belts. Shell decorations, masks, and dances, as well as paint, were mutually traded with Giri and Sanai. Children were also exchanged between all the participating groups in this trade system (Höltker 1962: 93–94; Tiesler 1970: 170–171). This served the purpose of mutual language acquisition necessary for the successful communication between trading partners. This trade network no longer exists in the way it did. New modes of trade have emerged. One is the trade called *maket long wara* ('market on water'). From time to time, boats whose owners sell nylon fishing nets and other items from town arrive at the riverbanks of Daiden. The other type of trade has brought changes with regard to traditional gender roles. Today, women sell fish on the market of Bogia, whereas traditionally they did not leave their home territory (as said in chapter 1, the preferred marriage was group-endogamous). Traditionally, the outside world was traversed by men only. Women did play a significant role in the trade system as producers of some of the items but not as traders.

I saw that people still engaged in trades with neighboring groups for ritual purposes and that they still relied on their traditional "delegates." The distinct paths linking the groups were even followed when people organized regional sports games. The system of delegates is of particular significance when theorizing about Bosmun inside-outside configurations. Delegates had the right to walk freely to other groups—even during times of conflict—without having to fear an ambush. This kind of privilege was usually transferred from fathers to sons. Ropor was such a delegate. Each clan-association had their delegates. If Rom were in need of sea salt from the coast, they sent a particular man to negotiate. If all clan-associations were in need of sea salt, four delegates (one on behalf of each association) set out together to mark a date for an exchange meeting. Each outside group, in turn, had delegates who were allowed to enter Bosmun terrain safely. A man wanting to trade an item without relying on mediation through a delegate was likely to be killed not only by the other, but by his own group.

Notably, strangers may cross Bosmun territory if they do not sneak about. Once, we came upon a man who was a total stranger to the walking party that I was a part of. After we had silently gone past the man, a companion said that we must have encountered a *ŋgaape*, a tree-spirit. I had learned that tree-spirits are imagined to have extraordinarily long fingers and toes. Yet, when we met the stranger my companion did not comment on the man's physical appearance. What made the man a potential spirit was that he was not localizable in any of my companions' known social spheres. A complete stranger, someone who does not fit into any such category, may be considered a spirit. Later, when I asked once more about the encounter with the "tree-spirit," people reasoned differently: the man was probably a delegate, on his way to an exchange enterprise. Whether he was a tree-spirit or a delegate, my companions concluded that there was no need to become suspicious.

Interestingly, delegates were also called *ndiara motor*, men who epitomize *ndiar*, the ideal of food-generosity. The paths connecting Bosmun and their traditional trading partners were paths of sociability, positive resonance, and formalized mutual trust and respect. After all, trades were sealed by sitting down together and sharing a meal. On both sides of these partnerships, the participants were expected to encounter one another benevolently. Even if disputes broke out between some members of both groups, the law was upheld that a delegate from a different sociolinguistic group was never to be attacked while on a path to his partner. If feelings ran high, a delegate carried the leaves of a particular type of ginger (*veŋ*) to remind of the frayed tempers that could be associated with his right to physical integrity. It seems that being a delegate required a good mixture of courage and composure. In a way, the paths of delegates and the places of trade lie in between what is familiar and unfamiliar. They were considered risk-free zones, but remained only partially familiar. Delegates arrived, sat down, negotiated, ate, and left. From Bosmun perspectives, places are peculiar if they cannot provide people with the appropriate sense of familiarity. I have argued that this sense of familiarity comes into being through particular social and embodied practices. In figure 4.2, I have schematically summarized what I see as the central ideational configurations that are applied in Daiden to make sense of inside and outside, familiar and unfamiliar.

PATHS OF RAIDS

Apart from the paths of trade, the forefathers of present-day Bosmun went on raiding expeditions, reaching places as far as Misingi / Kwanga, approximately where the Middle Ramu region starts. This is a distance of more than fifty kilometers, which was conquered by both walking and canoeing for days

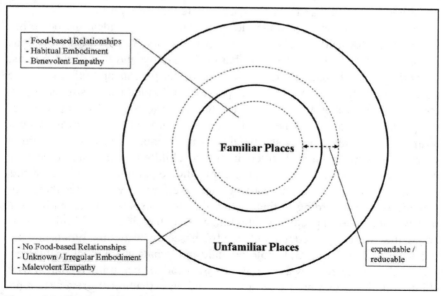

Figure 4.2: Emplaced Foodways.

on end. Bosmun warriors defended their ground not only by repelling invading foreigners, but by actively attacking their enemies' positions. During raids, when the warriors entered foreign grounds, the ideal of caring for others became diametrically reversed. They suppressed what was cherished in everyday social, localized life. The warriors attacked from an ambush and returned with many head trophies. Enemies were those with whom sociable relations did not exist as based on food exchange or trade. Enemy territory therefore gave space to a different form of male embodiment, that of physical combat and violence. I refer to this as irregular embodiment.

I have suggested that in Daiden both the positive and negative potentials inherent in empathy become emplaced. The myth of Ropor is a story that configures home as a place devoid of unsociable agency. During raids, it was common to capture children and young adults. These were either sold to trading partners or adopted. Although initially a captive, called *tum*, the child or adult was later treated with care and commitment equal to that given those born into the community. Like any other person, he or she was able to gain esteem and a proper place in the local social universe. Without any discomfort, elder interviewees pointed to the fact that one of their ancestors had been such a captive. They did not reflect upon this subject with embarrassment or pity. Instead, they explained how a *tum* had found his or her social entry into this place. The head-hunting party did not worry about the fate of captives who were traded to other groups, I was told. Yet, if a captive remained, he or she had to be given food, was expected to forget the fate of having been torn from his or her former life, and was to be assimilated into the group.

Walking on the paths of trade, delegates amplified the ideal of sociability that directed local life. Walking on the paths of war required a tremendous empathetic shift on two sides—on that of the captive and that of the raiders. A captive probably had to witness how his or her parents and other kin were executed in battle and how his or her place of childhood was destroyed. Next, the captive was taken to a place where he or she would find the opposite of the previous situation—benevolent attitudes exhibited via foodways whose ultimate significance he or she would learn, of course, only in the coming years. As my conversation partners imagined, children taken in a raid became integrated in food-related ways, including the social and embodied aspects of placial incorporation. The warriors, too, were required to alter their empathetic stance according to their actual location in social space. While on a raid, warriors were expected to fight, kill, and catch their enemies' children. At home, they were expected to conduct a life based on "watching others and being watched." In chapter 3, I explored male and female attachment to children. I wrote that, as decreed by ancestral lore, men had to keep limited contact with children until they grew to a certain size and that attachment grew as parents saw their children turning from food receivers into food providers. Such views might have facilitated what I have called the tremendous empathetic shift to be accomplished in the emplaced encounters of captives and raiders, both inside and outside the Bosmun world.

Let me now turn to the social configuration of the place called *taun*. In the first half of the last century, the "town" emerged in people's imaginations through what they were told by missionaries and colonial representatives. In the second half of the last century, people of Daiden began to travel to Madang and to other urban areas in the country. Ever since, life in town has served as a salient counterimage to local notions of self and place.

Life in Town

I mentioned that, in 2008, my "sister" and her husband stayed with me in Madang. In this context, I again became aware of the dualism permeating Bosmun assumptions about self and other, their place and places elsewhere. I briefly reflect on these assumptions before I present the case of a woman of Daiden who managed to maintain what she called proper social premises as based on local conventions while she lived in town.

'STINGY OTHERS'

The dualism that most people I talked to drew upon was made up of "generous selves" and 'stingy others' (*gridi lain*), the latter usually being described as "the people who eat only canned food." Furthermore, they distinguished between 'places that are full of food' (*ples i pulap long kaikai*) and 'places that lack food' (*ples i nogat kaikai*). In contemplating outsiders on a more global level, my conversation partners saw "white people" in general and the expatriates in Papua New Guinea in particular as stereotypically rich, selfish, and greedy. Urban Papua New Guineans were perceived similarly, though not as having deliberately chosen the lifestyle of what might be called an ideology of individualism; they were seen as having become involuntary victims of this ideology. Very often, people said that someone living in town cannot help but become selfish and greedy.

As our time together came to an end, my "sister" said that she was surprised at how generous I had been to them. I asked whether she had expected something else. She answered that she had not been sure since, after all, *Taun i no gutpela ples. Em ples bilong gridi* ('Town is not a good place. It is the place of greediness'). She added that in a familiar place such as Daiden, things were different, that everyone was supposed to be generous. It was as if she had conjectured that my being in Daiden had transformed my former "whiteness" or "townness" into "Bosmunness" and that once back in town I would fall back into my original behavior. I can imagine that my "sister" and her husband thought of me as openhanded. I shared with them what in their eyes was a luxurious urban house. I bought items in the stores and on the market with a regularity that impressed them. However, they also took notice of my own financial struggles. Every time before we went to a supermarket, I discussed with them what we would need to buy and what I could actually afford. I also told them that I had to save some money on which to subsist the following week when they would be gone, in the same way as I had saved some money prior to their arrival in order to be able to accommodate them. When they packed their bags for the departure, my "sister" said to her husband (so that I could hear it) that she was finally convinced that we were "real sisters" since I had shared my town life with them. In caring for me with food while I lived in Daiden, she had already substantiated the link between us. We had met in 2004, and this was my third visit to Papua New Guinea, but it was the first time that I heard her talking about our relationship so openly and so confirmatively.

Life in town is probably the worst form of social existence that my conversation partners could imagine, based on their local food-centered perception. During their lives, several of them had experienced life in town. Some had stayed a few years, some more than a decade in different places in Papua New Guinea, mostly in Madang, Lae, and Wewak. Most of the comments that I collected resembled the following objections: in town, there are no places to go and actively work as one would work at the Ramu, there are no swamps to plant and process sago palms, there are no waters where one can fish, there are no gardens to get bananas and other garden produce—only anonymous foods arriving in the stores in tins and plastic containers for horrendous prices. Consequently, there can be no generosity in town.

I observed that people who traveled to town and thought about staying with a relative there for a while usually took gifts of sago paste and dried fish with them to supply the relative's urban household. This was a common way to ask one's supposedly rich kin in town for shelter. In my impression, movement in town was always considered exciting at the outset. People bought the little items they needed and chatted with others gathering around the bus stop where PMVs to and from the Lower Ramu arrive and depart. Yet, apart from these achievements, I was told, moving through town becomes mere roaming, devoid of purpose-oriented and familiar social and embodied action. At least in the cases I knew of, staying in town with relatives actually meant that one left their house in the morning and returned only for the night. The food one carried to town was consumed quickly, too quickly it sometimes seemed, and food in stores is expensive. Since there are no wider fields of relatedness in town, one eventually wants to go back quickly. Two aspects of placial embodiment were uttered most frequently: people longed for eating and making sago, on the one hand, and for bathing in the river, on the other. Due to different bodily experiences and missing paths of social destination, town was seen as a place that caused people to become lazy.

TURNING SPACE INTO PLACE

I now present parts of an interview (recorded in January 2005) in which T., a woman of almost sixty years, told me about her experiences of life in town. T. had lived almost ten years in Lae, where her husband, S., had worked in a store. The couple then moved to Madang and stayed there for a few years before returning to the Ramu in 1988. During their time in Madang, T. and S. looked after three children. I invited T., a woman of high social repute who was said to have always "watched others carefully" and had years of outside experience in what people conventionalized as "unsocial" places, to come and tell me about her personal life. As mentioned in the Introduction, myths and stories, including life stories, were most fascinating when they were recounted in relational situations. This was the case with T., who accepted my invitation and who eventually came to me with her husband in tow. When we touched the subject of life in town, I asked T. to assess those years in comparison to local life:

A.: *Na yupela ting wanem ... yupela bin fesim disela laif long taun na long ples? Yupela ting wanem samting i gutpela long taun, wanem samting i nogut? ... Laif i bin isi long taun o ...?*

T.: *Mi yet, i no isi tumas!*

A.: *Nogat? Bilong wanem em i no isi tumas?*

T.: *Kaikai sait!*

A.: *Kaikai sait?*

T.: *Kaikai sait! Mani ... na yu gat femili, bikpela femili, bai no inap fit! Mi ... mi olsem ... mi stap long gutpela ples nau na mi yet mi save wok ... gaden ...*

S.: *long gaden ...*

T.: *... planim kaikai, kumu na gutpela. Na taim ... ol pikinini ... em ol i lus pinis long rais! Em disela tasol nau na i no gutpela!*

A.: *i no gutpela ...*

T.: *Na olsem na ... laki! Mi nogat planti pikinini! ... Ples mi stap long en, em wankain olsem as ples mi stap! Ol wail saksak i stap, mi save katim, wokim ... na gaden kaikai mi yet mi save wokim. Tasol, em kaikai bilong waitman tasol, em ... tingim ol pikinini na ... em i no gutpela tumas ...*

A.: *... em i no gutpela tumas?*

T.: *Tasol, disela taim em gutpela liklik long mani sait. I no bikpela mani tumas olsem ... na nau em i ... mani i go antap tru!*

A.: *Ah ... long bifo em i gutpela?*

T.: *Bifo tru, em i gutpela!*

S.: *Em i gutpela. Olsem man bilong yu wok, yu laki! Liklik mani long maket kaikai na long stua tu ... em liklik mani. Disela twentifaif keji em faif kina tasol long wanpela pek rais.*

A.: *Tru? Na nau em bikpela ...*

T.: *... na ten keji em tu fifti ...*

S.: *... kain olsem ...*

(A.: And what do [the two of] you think ... you have both been facing life in town and life at your place? Can you tell me what was good in town and what not? ... Did you cope with life in town easily or ...?

T.: According to my opinion, it was not that easy!

A.: No? Why was it not that easy?

T.: Because of food!

A.: Because of food?

T.: Because of food! [If everything depends upon] money ... and if you have a family, a big family, it will not be enough! I ... in my case ... I actually stayed at a good place and I used to make ... a garden... [this was when T. lived in Lae]

S.: in a garden ...

T.: ...[I] planted food, vegetables and this was good. And as ... the children ... they became addicted to rice! I was not happy about this situation!

A.: [this was] not good ...

T.: And so ... [I had] luck! [Because] I had not many children! ... The place were I lived [T. talks of Madang now] was like my home place! There were wild sago palms that I would cut and process ... and garden food that I would plant and harvest. Yet, this food of white people, this ... influenced the children and ... this was not very good ...

A.: ...this was not very good?

T.: Well, at that time it was not too bad as regards [our way to cope with a life based on] money. Things were not that expensive ... as it is now ... the prices have risen!

A.: Ah ... at that time it used to be good?

T.: In the past, it was good!

S.: It was good. If your husband had work, you were lucky! The prices for food at the markets and in the stores were fair ... fair prices. A rice bag of twenty-five kilograms was only five Kina [today, a twenty-kilogram rice bag costs up to eighty Kina, depending on the brand].

A.: True? Now, the prices are higher ...

T.: ... and ten kilograms was 2.5 [Kina] ...

S.: ... like that ...)

I also asked T. and S. about the local core ideal of *ramkandiar*, 'watching others and being watched.' In this context, I heard of another important term, *tuananiŋ ŋgar*, that is used to denote the thoughts and the actions typical to unsociable agents, people who respond harshly.

T.: *Ramkandiar ... ol wanwan manmeri i gat disela kain ...*

S.: *Olsem nau yu stap ... mi bai bihainim yu, mi bai no inap kam toktok wantaim yu, em hau yu wokabaut mi bai lukluk long yu. "Ey—trangu em sidaun olsem ... em mas ...*

T.: *nogat kaikai o ...?*

S.: *Em i nogat ... wanem samting o ...?" Mi bai go nating na apim wanpela trai-pela ... o banana mau o ... na bai kam givim yu! Nogut yu nogat kain samting olsem na yu sidaun olsem. Na yu bai kirap tok: "Nogat!"*

T.: *Na sampela bai tok: "Bilong wanem em sidaun sidaun nating?" Olsem tuananiŋ ŋgar ya ...*

A.: *tuananiŋ ... em wanem samting?*

T.: *Em olsem ...*

A.: *Mi raitim pastaim ...*

T.: [laughs] *tuananiŋ ... em olsem: "Bilong wanem yu sidaun nating stap? Yu mas wok!"*

S.: *Yu bai lukluk tasol na bai yu kisim disela kain tingting: "Em mas i wok na i gat kaikai! Mi bai no inap helpim em!" Em tuananiŋ.*

T.: *"Em bilong we na em sidaun nating?"*

S.: [laughs]

T.: *Em sampela i gat ol disela kain tingting, bai no inap givim yu! Na mipela, sampela lukim ... em bai mipela sori! "Aaah! Nogat!"*

S.: *Em ramkandiar ...*

T.: *em ramkandiar ...*

S.: *lukluk tasol long ai na bai yu sori gen ...*

T.: *... trangu em mas sot long kaikai o kain samting olsem o sol o saksak o ... disela kain ....*

A.: *Na long taun i nogat disela kain pasin?*

T.: *Taun tu!*

A.: *I gat?*

T.: *I gat! Tasol! Mipela! Olsem ples bilong mipela! Mipela gat disela kain! Man i no save long yu, yu yet yu bai pulim em i kam, kam nau, em nau yutupela meit nau! ... Ol save olsem: "Oh, dispela tupela marit ya, gutpela manmeri tru!" Na mi ya, taim mi stap long Sakalau ... olsem ol lain long ples i go ... ol bai kam bung tasol long hia! Kaikai bilong ol gutpela, slip bilong ol gutpela, ol stap amamas. Na ol i go long ol lain i stap long taun, bai ol i hangamap, nogat kaikai, bai stap. Ah Sakalau maket! Gutpela ples tru ya! Mi tok: "Mi no inap lusim kastam." Kastam em bikpela samting ... olsem* <u>ramkandiar</u>*. Maski em man yu no save: "Yu kam!" Na man ya, ya! Em longlong man ya! Em bai no inap toktok ... wanem samting em laik opim maus, mi tok: "Yu stop! Bai yu no inap givim mi tingting! Mi save!" Bikos mama papa bilong mi tupela i no kain manmeri olsem. Mama bilong mi, em ...*

A.: *... wanem kain meri?*

T.: *... no olsem, i no long pasim samting, gridi long kaikai o wanem samting. Nogat! Olsem nau na ... mipela, mipela disela femili, maski husait man yu no save ... kisim em i go givim kaikai long em pinis, lukautim em gut tru i stap, taim em i go bek na bungim yu long wanem hap, em bai tok: "Kam!" Em i gat mani, em bai givim long yu, baim kaikai bilong yu, em disela kain ... ol pasin. Na yu save lukluk nating: "Mi no save long disela man ya o mi no save long disela meri, mi bai lukluk tasol." Nogat! Yu traim! Ol gutpela manmeri tasol ol i wokabaut! ... Man ya, em bai no inap toktok, sidaun lukluk tasol long mi. Mi bai tok: "Yu stap! Em ya samting redi pinis ya kaikai ya!" bai ol i kaikai nau! ... "Mipela nogat mani, mipela nogat kaikai" Nogat! Helpim, trangu em tu em disela kain man! ...*

S.: *Wanpela samting ... sapos insait long taun yu laik sidaun gut nogat distebens, husait raskol manki yu bungim em, holim! Mitupela i holim ol top raskol stret!*

A.: *Ya?*

S.: *Bai nogat distebens.*

T.: *Olsem tok bilong Bikpela tu i stap olsem ... maski man nongut, yu ken holim em, em disela kain, na holim em. Kastam tu i gat disela kain toktok i stap. Kastam na tok bilong Bikpela, em wankain. Raskol man tu. Trangu em kamap long yu olsem wanem, lukautim em long kaikai, givim ples long em bilong slip na disela kain.*

(T.: <u>Ramkandiar</u> ... only a few people have this kind of ...

S.: Take you for example ... I will follow you, I will not come to you and talk to you [about it], I will watch the way you are roaming around. "Ey—this poor person's condition ... she probably ...

T.: is without food or ...?

S.: She is without ... whatever or ...?" I will go by myself and heap a huge ... or a bundle of ripened banana or ... and I will come to you and give it to you! Maybe you are empty handed or maybe not. And you will tell [to yourself]: "No!" ["I cannot leave it like this!"]

T.: And some will say: "Why is she in such a poor condition?" That is *tuaŋaniŋ ŋgar* ['to think about another one but without responding sociably' / 'to respond harshly'] ...

A.: *tuaŋaniŋ* ... what is this?

T.: It is like ...

A.: Let me write [this word] down first ...

T.: [laughs] *tuaŋaniŋ* ... is like this: "Why are you in this poor condition? You should work!"

S.: You will just watch that and develop such kinds of thoughts: "He / she should work so as to get food! I will not help him / her!" This is *tuaŋaniŋ*.

T.: "Where does this poor person come from?"

S.: [laughs]

T.: Some people have this kind of reasoning, [they] will not give you [anything]! But we, to see such [poor people] ... we will be worried! "Aaah! No!" [T. means that she cannot leave it like this]

S.: This is *ramkandiar* ...

T.: this is *ramkandiar* ...

S.: just watching [this] with your eyes will cause pity in you ...

T.: ... this poor person is obviously lacking food or something like that or salt or sago or ... this kind of ....

A.: And does this attitude also exist in town?

T.: Yes, also in town!

A.: It exists?

T.: It exists! But! With us! In [urban] places to where we came to live! We have this kind! You by yourself will drag a stranger to come to you, to come to you so that [the two of] you finally will become mates! ... Everybody will know: "Oh, these two who are married are really kind people!" In my case, at the time I stayed at Sakalau [a market place] ... whenever people of our home place went [to town] ... they would come and gather just here! They would have good food, a good place to sleep, they would be happy. But if they went to people living [directly] in town, they would hang around badly, they would be without food. Ah Sakalau market! Such a good place! I said [to myself]: "I will not abandon my custom." That custom is too important ... it is *ramkandiar.* No matter if it were a stranger: "You come!" But this man here! He was a crazy man! [T. is referring to her husband]. I would not let him discipline me in whatever way [but] I would say: "You stop! You cannot control my attitudes! I know [how to behave properly]!" Because my parents, both of them, were not that kind of people. My mother, she ...

A.: ... what kind of woman was she?

T.: ... well, I mean, she would not hide anything, would not be greedy for food or whatever. No! This is why ... we, we of this family did not bother if one was a stranger ... [we would] take him / her to us, give food to him / her, take pretty much care of him / her, and if he / she left and met you at whatever place, he / she would say: "Come!" If he /she had money, he / she would share it with you, would buy food for you, these would be the sorts of ... attitudes. [But] if you were ignorant: "I do not know this man or I do not know this woman, I just ignore [them]." No! You have to try it! Only good people are walking around! ... This man here [T. is again referring to S.], he would strike and just sit and stare at me. I would say: "Cool down! Look at what I have prepared here, the food here!" Now, they [people T. wished to care for] would have something to eat! ... "We have no money, we have no food!" No! [One must] help! He / she is also a human being! ...

S.: There is something else ... if you wished to live a safe life in town and without any disturbance you would have to persuade the rascals whenever you met them! The two of us, we persuaded the very top rascals!

A.: Really?

S.: So there was no disturbance.

T.: You know, the words of God say the same ... no matter if it is a bad person, you can persuade him / her, it is of this kind, [you can] persuade him / her. [Our] customs follow the same premise. [Our] customs and the words of God, they are the same. Even a rascal. If you meet such a poor person in whatever way, care for him / her with food, give him / her a place to sleep and so on.)

To assess a place is to assess the foodways of this place as T. did. In her thoughts about life in urban centers, she gave a rather unenthusiastic portrait. This she did by referring to rice. Although not apparent at first sight, T. made a thorough ideational statement when she talked about rice. Her linkage of a type of food (rice), a place (town), and, as her husband added, a type of effort (individual, cash-based work) was essential to Bosmun categorizations of physical environments, social worlds, and the emplacement of empathy. The linkage that T. and S. gave—of rice, town, and money—mirrors a frame of life that is diametrically opposed to local life where one engages in joint food production that takes place in familiar swamps. People in Daiden appreciated rice as a variation from traditional local starch foods. Rice has gained social value for those of my informants who were especially eager to seek a "modern life" (see Hess [2009] for the meaning of rice in Vanua Lava, Vanuatu). They would often link rice to the effort of *wokim bisnis* ('to engage in monetary enterprises'). Outside influence has introduced global ideas of poverty and backwardness to Daiden. It appeared to me that many people tried to acquire money to overcome feelings of inferiority. Men got money through the selling of copra, vanilla, and cocoa in Madang and women through the selling of fish on the coastal market in Bogia. Like elsewhere in Papua New Guinea (e.g., Foster 2008; Gewertz & Errington 1991: 46), batteries, nails, kerosene, soft drinks, salt, sugar, and rice have become important commodities. However, when my interviewees, including those favoring a "modern life," evaluated foods, they all stated that rice was nice but that it cannot really nourish as sago can.

Sakalau became a favorite place for T., since she even had wild sago from which to procure the food she had grown up with. The market known as Saka-lau and its adjacent dwelling areas are located next to the North Coast High-way, approximately ten kilometers away from the heart of Madang town. By means of identifiable social and even embodied practices, T. was able to turn this seemingly unfamiliar "space," where food provision was based on mon-etary income, into a familiar "place." Hirsch's (1995a) differentiation between "place" and "space" as implied in his notion of "landscape" is conceptually relevant here. "Place" denotes people's day-to-day experiences in a familiar environment, whereas "space" refers to rather irregular activities in this en-vironment and to the social and sensual perception of unknown landscapes (Hirsch 1995a: 4–5, 8, 13–16). With regard to experientially acquiring the world, the place Sakalau made T.'s body active in almost the same way as would her natal place, the place full of sago swamps. Although she also had to cut the palm, which is normally men's work but which her husband could not do since he worked in a store, this task created feelings of comfort and familiarity in a place previously foreign. Furthermore, T. offered a haven in town for visiting kin. In her understanding, the environs of Sakalau enabled her to make sago through which she was able to fulfill the conventional social obligations that she knew from Daiden. Other conversation partners spoke of relatives in town who were living in less benevolent surroundings and who therefore were too busy caring for their core families (see Gewertz & Errington [1999: 71, 82, 158] on reasons for the nuclearizing of families among urban Papua New Guineans). Such relatives were expected never to return home. In 2008 and 2010, I had more contact with Bosmun living in town. Some of my urban informants were indeed worried about returning. One reason was that land was becoming scarce. Another reason was that they felt misunderstood. With what seemed possible for them in town, they thought they had upheld the local value of reciprocity. However, visiting kin always complained that they had not been offered enough food. When talking to people who had visited T. in town, no one ever complained this way. Maybe it was due to the fact that Sakalau allowed T. to make sago that she had nothing to worry about when returning to Daiden.

The last interview passages indicate the power that T. ascribed to food in forming relationships. In retrospect, she obviously managed to create and maintain a field of relatedness via foodways not only with visiting kin but with foreigners, her urban neighbors, and people stemming from other places and provinces in Papua New Guinea. Sakalau market is a multicultural spot, clearly structured and occupied by different groups who sell different products that they bring to town from their distinct home areas or produce around settlements in the vicinity. Regarding her interpersonal encounters with adjacent town dwellers, T. said: "Only good people are walking around!" T. and S. even managed to live side-by-side with criminals running riots in both the center and the outer parts of Madang town, as is known in other urban areas of Papua New Guinea (see Goddard 2005). The couple applied a strategy of food-based appeal by inviting a few gang leaders to come and eat with them, and it worked well, as T. and S. concluded. Instead of becoming subjected to criminal enterprises, the couple made the rascals subject to their foodways. From time to time, they would come and sit around T.'s home hearth. After all, T. said, her ancestral customs, as exemplified by Semenbo in the Ropor myth, matched Christian ideals. People in Daiden were indeed very fond of the notion entailed in the "grace of charity." Frequently, premissionary forms of benevolent empathy were seen as correlating with the moral ideas brought in by the church (see Feinberg 2011: 161; Hermann 2011: 28–29).

T.'s affirmative perception of social strangers and her openness to establishing new relations was indeed prevalent in the views of many of my interviewees. People were inclined to deal positively with others and they expected positive rather than negative reactions. Approaching people with food is seen as a means of opening their feelings and thoughts. Once T. found a way to enact familiar foodways in a new locale, she started to radiate sociability among those who walked past her home in town. In my impression, people were convinced that positive foodways had the power to obliterate or, at least, mitigate the ill will and antisocial behavior of others, including strangers. Put in another way: someone I give food to will probably do no harm to me. Additionally, it appeared to me that the showing of positive foodways is deemed to depend on how places resonate with people, that is, how fertile or how inhospitable these places are.

Places themselves were accredited with empathetic resonance, since they were held to either enable or prevent people from exhibiting generosity. In the sago palm areas around Sakalau, T. found traces of a familiar landscape vested with emotion. Her way to maintain a food source in Sakalau was based on moral-ecological premises. As stated in chapter 2, living in an environment rich in food without using this food in sociable ways renders one's life immoral and leads to dietary scarcity, since food abundance is believed to cease if individuals fail to attune positively to each other. Stingy people cannot maintain the nurturing quality of the land, and in following paths of stinginess individuals not only bring harm to one another but to nurturing places—the very idea encoded in the myth of the sago spirit. Food abundance became the crucial sign for T. to positively attach to Sakalau, not just because it would guarantee her own subsistence and that of her close kin, but because she could give food to extended kin and town acquaintances. Whereas town was usually seen as a place of dietary scarceness and social hostility, Sakalau figured as a place in T.'s understanding that allowed and obliged her to cultivate social confidence in her new milieu, a confidence so typical of her home at the Ramu. From T.'s experience in a place like Sakalau and from what other people told me, I conclude that the cultivation and display of social trust is relative to one's actual emplacement in either a rich or scarce environment. Therefore, when thinking of relatives living in town who had become "murky faces," people almost always reasoned that this, of course, had to happen due to the "miserable" quality of this place, a place without swamps, waters, or gardens.

As I argued at the beginning of this chapter, social identity and agency are also grounded in a particular type of embodied experience. A physically productive body, the body that engages in sago making, hints, it seems, at a socially and morally sound being. According to her view, T. maintained this kind of embodied morality. Since her husband had to work in the store, T. had to cut and shred sago at Sakalau, work normally done by men in Daiden. In chapter 3, we heard of a woman who had to cut the palm. Since she had behaved indecently, her cutting the palm was taken as a sign of her ostracized state. T.'s case was different. She had to cut the palm because S. had to work in the store. In fact, S. acted selfishly according to T. As she emphasized openly, he wanted to restrain her from giving food to others. He brought home the money with which to buy rice, and in doing so, it seems, he brought home a different morality. Although T. did not say it this way when I recorded her story, she and others often interpreted people relying on money as people who follow a way of life opposed to local views of morality.

This showed up again in another case. A woman told me of her brother who had been away from home for more than thirty years and who had become stingy in town. The woman visited the brother and his family from time to time. The place where the family stayed was a good place, with a lake where fish and prawns could be caught in abundance. Catching fish was accomplished by the brother's wife and daughters, while he was confined to working in town. The woman told me how she came to be convinced that her brother had adopted the social demeanors of town, in which food is hidden from others. One day, the brother's daughter showed her a bag full of prawns. The girl complained that the father wanted to hide the food from the visiting sister. But the daughter and mother felt pity for the father's sister and decided to share the prawns with her. The woman concluded that her brother had changed since he was no longer engaging in the traditional methods of food procurement. He brought home the food that was obtained with money and therefore not to be shared.

Leaving Bosmun life experiences in town behind, I now return to the Ramu for the last time. It should have become clear that people who do not benevolently share food with kinsmen and kinswomen are believed to occlude their feelings and thoughts. Someone who shows a "murky face" is not only stingy and greedy, but has something to hide. In concealing one's states, individuals make themselves vulnerable to accusations of being selfish and unsociable— an image that no one really aspires to. To prevent such accusations, people not only continuously work at extending their individual fields of relatedness, but engage in a kind of transparent personhood, which, interestingly, includes the expression of negative feelings in public. Making one's states transparent to others is even ritually staged. In the final sections of this chapter, I describe Bosmun ritualized food appeals to the world of spirits and I close with remarks on sorcery and how people "solve problems."

Empathy—A Moral Command

As noted, people in Daiden were inclined to think of others as sociable and positively resonating, at least if a transmission of food was involved. Interestingly and it seems not without paradox, the "sociable person" in Daiden is someone who may show his or her anger to social consociates. For, if one does not show it, anger is said to turn into antipathy with the most serious consequences; one might become tempted to bring death to others. The tendency to perceive others as well-disposed agents is not necessarily a given in other social worlds. Also, the idea that publicly expressing one's anger is still inherent to what makes someone sociable might be alien to the configurations found in other social settings. In analyzing local understandings of empathy among the Highland Maya of Mexico, Groark (2008: 438), for example, applies Kluckhohn's (1944: 87) phrase of a "hypertrophy of social mistrust" to describe Maya intersubjective encounters. Mutual ascriptions of negative intentionality seem to be common. They must, however, not be uttered openly and remain hidden in the sought-after privacy of fenced households. As Groark (2008: 436) explains, Maya ways of interpersonal comportment are connected to exhibiting a "conventionalized positive politeness." This form of politeness serves to veil negative emotions and ill will, which are presumed to exist pervasively in the hearts of others (Groark 2008: 438). Moreover, "Maya ethnotheories of self posit a radical interiority, a largely occluded core of deep subjectivity that remains masked in everyday social life" (Groark 2008: 428).

I gained the impression in Daiden that people undoubtedly favored an atmosphere of benign interpersonality without propagating a form of shallow politeness behind which ill will and negative emotions hid. Rather, as I recurrently observed, individuals did not hesitate to express what they thought of others. They thus principally allowed others to assess their states, which according to Hollan (2008: 484) is an important, if not the most crucial, cue for empathetic processes to work. Being "never in anger," as Briggs (1970) had to learn as she lived with a Canadian Inuit family, was no obligation in Daiden. Interviewees acknowledged that people sometimes "eat the wrong food." If someone becomes angry, he or she is said to be in a state of *nduŋnduŋ aam*, which literally translates as 'to consume' (*aam*) 'a type of sea shell' (*nduŋnduŋ*) that, interestingly, is no part of local cuisine but is found in salt-water regions. Again, feelings that can lead to outbursts of unsociability are metaphorically emplaced—beyond Bosmun terrain. Two major forms of anger are recognized, a less harming form expressed by saying that "someone ate a sea shell," and a more serious form that involves the use of sorcery (*kook*). Someone caught up in antipathetic feelings of the latter kind is said to have consumed another improper substance. *Perŋa saaka aam* can be translated as 'to eat dog's flesh.' This is what happens when someone has decided to apply sorcery. This stage, however, is said to be prevented by revealing one's initial feelings of anger more or less immediately.

I now explore Bosmun spirit-human encounters. This is important for two reasons. First, the food appeals that T. made in town, for instance, cannot be fully comprehended unless I trace the persuasive power that food has in the communication with nonhuman, sentient entities. Second, the food appeals to the spirits encode a distinct model of how humans should manage feelings and feelings of anger in particular. Anger should not be occluded, suppressed, or ignored, but rather should be uttered in the presence of others so as to become altered through their reactions, ideally changed into its opposite. It is mutual openness that is encouraged in the formal display of spirit-human encounters, and this kind of display, I believe, gives ideational orientation to how humans should encounter one another.

Food Appeals to the World of Spirits

The world of Daiden is believed to be populated by a range of spiritual entities. Some are benevolent and some malevolent; some are helpful but dangerous at times. Despite the fact that several ritual practices with regard to the spirit world have been abandoned, the entities occupying this world still affect people's lives, mostly by bringing *ropuk* to them, that is, bodily or mental disorders that sometimes result in death. The spirits cause *ropuk* only if they have become angry with humans. Causing illness is the spirits' common mode of externalizing their negative empathetic stances toward humans. Humans' proper way to apologize and communicate that they understand the spirits' anger is by offering them food.

In the past, when men engaged in warfare, particular platforms were erected in honor of the *ŋgomndis*, spirits of rather malevolent character who helped the warriors win their battles. On a regular basis, plates of cooked food were placed on top of these platforms. It was commonly held that the 'war spirits' consumed this food. Humans were not allowed to sit on these platforms, nor were they allowed to eat from the gifts offered to the spirits. The war spirits were said to be ready to assist in a raid once the food had rotted away. If a raid proceeded successfully, people attributed feelings of positive resonance to the spirits. Since the time of warfare came to an end, people in Daiden have ceased to feed these spirits and platforms are no longer erected for them. But if a person gets ill or if a fire breaks out where such a platform once stood, people reason that it must be due to the anger of the war spirits. The fire mentioned at the outset of the book was said not to have been the first one to break out at exactly this spot. It started and ended where it had started and ended approximately ten years earlier. As I wrote, a woman had been drying fish at the spot where the fire broke out. Interestingly, no one really accused the woman of carelessness. Instead, people remembered that the powerful war spirits had dwelled at this spot. It was explained to me that the fire was a revenge of the war spirits who had been suffering from people's neglect recently. In the case of a newborn who had been crying too much, people also reasoned that it was because the birth-house stood where such a spirit platform had stood. Mother and child eventually moved to the birth-house of a kinswoman and the infant stopped crying. I remember a third case. On my second departure in 2006, a small food gathering was held for me to bid farewell. A woman had brought a particular delicacy, *kus*, cooked banana and breadfruit in a creamy coconut soup. After we had started to eat, a young man suddenly became infuriated. People had told me that the man was *rorer*, mentally disturbed, saying that he must have consumed an improper substance when visiting an uncle living in the Sepik region. Sometimes he talked to himself, undressed spontaneously, or attacked others physically. Since I had experienced the man's infuriation occasionally I did not take too much notice. He started to yell and scold and verbally insult other people standing close to him. Some of the men who attended our gathering had to calm him down. While they did so, several women around me whispered, *kus kus kus kus ya! Em kus ya wokim man ya na…* ('[It is this] *kus kus kus kus*! It is this *kus* which made the man become…'). I wondered what this gift of food had to do with the man's behavior until it was explained to me that *kus* traditionally was given to the war spirits. The man's state of bewilderment, mixed with aggression, was interpreted as a sign that the *kus* had aroused the war spirits who were continuing to intrude rather negatively into people's lives.

A further kind of spirit entity that people in Daiden empathized with was the *ngome*, the 'crocodile spirits.' Each section of the Ramu that runs through Bosmun terrain has its particular named crocodile spirit who has to be fed with cooked food. The crocodile spirits are also said to show anger toward people, although they are not perceived as malevolent entities. According to Bosmun views, they do not kill people, although crocodile attacks have been reported. Crocodile spirits express their anger by eroding the riverbanks or by holding back the seasonal freshwater mussels. Newly emerging sandbanks that harbor the mussels are said to be a gift from the crocodile spirits. If the sandbanks shift, people interpret this as a sign that a crocodile spirit feels offended in some way. The sandbank that I saw when I arrived in 2004 did not emerge at the same spot the following year, shortly before I had to leave. It appeared at a new spot further up the river. People worried that the residents in direct vicinity of the new position (still in Bosmun country) would not allow them to dive there. My elderly informants said to me that, according to ancestral lore, the sandbanks had been communally owned but that recently the attitude of *mi pasin* (which I translate as 'selfish behavior') had become strong, especially among the younger generations. While people were still seeking reasons for why the sandbank had shifted, it became apparent that the residents near the new sandbank would not forbid them to go and take their part. Eventually, a positive assessment of the spirit's motives to move could be made by referring to the image of a marriage as the basis for a continued relationship: the spirit of this river section had married the spirit of the other and hence had taken along the mussels.

One also has to be careful out in the forest. The beings called *ŋgaape* (tree-spirits) are said to have the tendency to fall in love with humans. They approach them with gifts of food and steal or disturb their *nyeroŋ*, their life-energy. Tree-spirits approaching humans with food is a common image in descriptions of spirit-human encounters as exemplified by the mythical characters of Nzari and Semenbo. A man told me of his brother, who was believed to have had a love affair with a female tree-spirit. I never asked the man himself. He now was married to another (human) woman, and I was not sure what my inquiries would ultimately uncover. As, likely, everybody else, I have had episodes in my life I do not wish to talk or think about anymore, and that I do not want others to ask me about. Perhaps it was this that made me decide not to ask the man directly. Now, I reckon, I could have asked him, since so much of what I regard as personal privacy was, in fact, public knowledge in Daiden. Still, in deciding as I did, I was able to gain information about how a man approximated the state of his brother who had changed his usual attitudes for unknown reasons. The brother had become less talkative and seemed unfocused. Instead of joining his siblings in the regular procurement of food, he roamed around in the forest, obviously spending his time procuring food with his spirit-wife, his family assumed. Since his parents did not want to have this tree-spirit marrying their son, the father took a plate of cooked food that the mother had prepared and went to find the spirit-woman. He was certain to have detected her by her smell and strange sounds that she produced at a certain spot and put the food down there. Then, he cast a spell that would make the tree-spirit lose interest in his son. The strategy worked, I was told. The brother readopted the attitudes that he had had prior to the ascribed meeting of the spirit woman.

I also observed what was explained to me as a spirit-human encounter, although it was not with a tree-spirit but with the spirit of a deceased (*ndom*). In fact, every dancing feast is an encounter with the ancestral spirits. Each time a feast starts, the dancers are welcomed with food. Coconuts are broken open in front of them (see figure 4.3); bananas, other garden produce, or lumps of sago are thrown in front of their feet. In welcoming the dancers, who always approach the dancing ground from the same direction (coming from where the sun sets), people also welcome the ancestors. Customary performances such as dancing feasts do not work without the goodwill of the ancestors whose spiritual remnants are believed to dwell in the direction of the sunset and who have to be invited to support the feasts.[6] Food and the practice of eating have a particular emotional significance even on a metaphysical level. During a *ndom taao* (the feast to honor the spirit of a deceased relative), I was able to witness an empathetic interaction between several elder men and women, on the one hand, and the deceased man's spirit on the other. Two pigs had been raised since the death of the man and were now fully grown. Domestic pigs are fed cooked food, which creates a bond of attachment between the cook and the animal that eats the food. Due to these bonds of attachment, individuals feel compelled to "ask" the pigs for their permission to be slaughtered. In an effort to solicit such permission, the pigs were lured with a gift of stirred sago. After two days of chanting and dancing that was intended to encourage them to come, however, the pigs were still missing, wandering around somewhere in the bush. Something was definitely wrong, and people began to wonder what possible reasons the pigs could have for refusing to give their permission for the slaughter. In an effort to discern the pigs' motives, several elders sat down together to eat. In this situation, I realized that consuming food is a medium that can also be used to make contact with the nonhuman realm. The elders started to discuss the matter over and over by directly addressing the deceased's spirit with questions about what kinds of transgressions each of them may have committed against him during his lifetime. Everyone considered actions that may have offended the deceased. The continuing absence of the pigs, however, was interpreted as a sign of the spirit's ongoing resentment. Finally, the spirit's sister, an old woman, admitted that she also should have provided yet a third pig for the feast—the two missing pigs had been provided by the spirit's children. The children must have felt insulted, the woman concluded, since in her role as the deceased's sister she, of course, should have given a particular sign of affection for her brother. Once the anger of the man's spirit had vanished, the two pigs returned from the bush, while a third one was bought in a neighboring area. The following day, three pigs were consumed

Figure 4.3: Welcoming the Dancers. Mian is breaking open a coconut in front of the dancers.

and the feast was finally able to come to an end. All of this was said to have resulted from the sister's critical self-reflection and the openness of all those who engaged in the empathetic discourse with the spirit.

The last category of important spirit entities in Daiden are the *mirip,* the 'flute-spirits,' widely known in the Ramu and Sepik regions (see Spearritt & Wassmann 1996; Tuzin 1980; Yamada 1997). I was told that whenever the flutes, which represent the voices of particular spirits such as that of Ropor, were played, loads of cooked food had to be prepared. Carved masks representing those spirits figuratively are also called *mirip.* Today, young men no longer spend the amount of time necessary to learn how to play these instruments.[7] According to my elderly informants, flutes were played on a regular basis in the past when, for instance, initiations took place or when a renowned person died. They were played inside the men's houses that were fenced on such occasions. Due to Nziŋgam's and Piatam's neglect of Ropor's order to play the flutes whenever bringing food to him, the instruments were irrevocably passed into the custody of the men. I was told that the flute-spirits are basically benevolent and admirable beings. People translated *mirip* also as 'something good / nice / beautiful.' Bodies in local attire and anointed with oils and herbal substances are *mirip.* Smiling faces are *mirip.* People who can concede to others that they have done wrong are *mirip.* Ropor was *mirip* too. He was a trader and he chose "the right woman," Semenbo, who was generous. Later, he gave Nziŋgam and

Płatam a good life by caring for them. These are the impressions I gained in listening to people's assessments of the sociomythical characters in the story of Ropor. Yet the flute-spirits also remind people of Ropor's final fate and what Nziŋgam and Płatam did to him. Interestingly, the sounds produced by the flute were framed as emotions. The changes in the rhythmic tempo of the sounds were imagined as the different feeling states of the spirits. The faster this tempo became, the more enraged and hungry the spirits were thought to be. This rage—mirroring Ropor's rage about the injury to his intestines—had to be calmed via donations of food, which women would throw over the fence. Cooked food had the power to reconcile the spirits. When flutes resounded, a collective atmosphere of anxiety and danger, based on the acoustic display of someone's anger, was evoked that could only be resolved by the medium of food donation. The end of a flute playing meant that the anger of the spirits had ceased, and it would only end after the food provisions planned for such an occasion were exhausted (such flute ceremonies lasted several days and nights). After that, players, spectators, and listeners would return to normalcy. The food appeals were considered to have been effective if no one became ill after such an occasion. Only then was it clear that the spirits had accepted people's attempts to soothe their anger. When the flutes were played, local morality became reaffirmed by performative acts of offering food to the flute-spirits. Moreover, the culminating scenario gave advice on how to ideally cope with feelings of anger regarding the realm of interhuman encounters. That the spirits revealed their anger / hunger was an integral part of the whole proce-dure, as was the fact that obviously powerful food appeals could equalize and mitigate this anger. In the flute ceremonies of Daiden, I believe, the ideal of psychological mutuality was staged.

From what has been said so far about the premise of *ramkandɨar*, of 'watch-ing others and being watched,' I hope to have provided some evidence for the idea that psychological aloneness does not fit into the relational scheme that people in Daiden have chosen to organize interpersonal life. In the remainder of this chapter, I argue that *ramkandɨar* is not just the vehicle to make and regulate the coexistence of kin in a social and emotional sense, but that it also protects individuals from becoming suspects and objects of sorcery.

SORCERY AND PEOPLE EATING AT OTHER HEARTHS

In Daiden, no one dies naturally. Illness and death are the products of what Keck (2005: 83, 117–119) has, in her medical-anthropological study about Yupno notions of illness, called "oppressing problems," sorcery being the worst. According to Bosmun explanations, even very old people die because of a sorcery attack and negative empathy imposed on them. It is mostly men who become suspects of sorcery, since they are the ones who contest land boundaries. Land and women, I was told, are the major reasons for men and their respective kin-groups to become opponents. The term for a 'sorcerer' is *kooko mot,* which implies the word for 'man / male' (*mot*). There was no specific term for a female with such capacities and no one confirmed that the word *kook* (for sorcery) could be combined with the word for 'woman / female' (*mes*). Women were said to be able to apply only one type of death magic: they can kill their husbands.

My interviewees on this subject emphasized that sorcery stems from elsewhere. I learned about a huge repertoire of magical spells for all kinds of matters, but the magic to kill someone was said to be brought in from outside. "Real sorcerers" have to be invited. I frequently heard sayings such as this one: *Sanguma em samting bilong ol narapela ples. Mipela nogat dispela kain samting.* ('Death sorcery is something that belongs to other places. We do not have this.')

Other groups seem to locate negative intentionality in similar ways. Kulick, for instance, writes of the people of Gapun that the "Ramu villages, which no one else in Gapun has ever seen, are feared for their powerful sorcery and *sangguma* [sic] men" (1992: 31). Dalton reports that for the Rawa living at the Finisterre Mountain slopes of Papua New Guinea, traditional sorcery became eradicated in the 1930s, but that other forms of sorcery have been introduced from other places. Sorcery itself is thus "not so much a thing or a person as it is a process and, moreover, an historical process" (Dalton 2007: 40). A similar process may have been at stake in the shifting of Bosmun ideas brought about by Christianity.

A person who has died because of a sorcery attack is said to have been bereft of his or her intestines; again a connection can be seen to the myth of Ropor, who lost his intestines because his wives did not approach him openly. If a person becomes ill, his or her spiritual energy (*nyeroŋ*) is hurt. The previously mentioned spirit entities attack people's spiritual frames, whereas a sorcerer attacks the belly. If someone dies very quickly and unexpectedly, his or her intestines (*moŋ*) are believed to have been irrevocably removed and injured. Another way to kill a human is to cast an evil spell on a poisonous snake or a crocodile, who will then attack the target. It was commonly held that snakes and crocodiles attack humans only when under the control of a sorcerer. Hence, someone who keeps his or her interpersonal relations in balance has nothing to fear when walking through the forest, the swamps, or the grasslands or when canoeing or bathing or diving in the river. This is what people said to soothe me when, in the beginning, I told them that I was afraid of snakes and crocodiles.

From Bosmun viewpoints, a sorcerer may be described as he is among the Rawa, who "speak of the typical sorcerer as someone unconstrained by social mores and unobliged in a community of relations based on mutual indebtedness and obligation.... [S]orcerers pursue their own desires for power in a nefarious manner which does not require them to provide for others. ... Sorcerers are also ungenerous and unsupportive of others in material exchange" (Dalton 2007: 41). My conversation partners believed that a sorcerer may also be detected based on his lack of sympathy when someone has died. Interestingly, this lack of sympathy is discerned through bodily empathy or, at least, through bodily projection. Put differently: people read a sorcerer's "skinscape." The sorcerer roams amid the mourners seemingly untouched. He appears well groomed, since he bathed in the river shortly before. He has shiny skin and appears agile, since he procured sago shortly before the funeral. Those who suffer, by contrast, have dusty skin and appear motionless. They abstain from food production and consumption during a funeral, as everyone should. Thus, when looking for a suspect, people also assess the embodied foodways of others. Accusations are supported by stories about suspects having been seen sneaking below the houses of victims in search of body substances such as hair, fingernails, or saliva in betel nut remains. To visit a household means to take the footpath that the household's residents have stamped into the ground. People who do not live or eat in this household should not take another path to approach it (see A.T. von Poser 2008a: 91). People should also make what may be called a "moral noise" when approaching a household; we recall Ropor, who asked Nziŋgam and Piatam to play the flutes whenever visiting him. LiPuma has made similar points about the movement of sorcerers in social space among the Highland Maring of Papua New Guinea. The Maring sorcerer is imagined in the following way:

> Greed overcomes him, envy "eats" him, and so he turns on his own kin. The sorcerer does not "walk on the road"—a description that is equally a metaphor of the public and visible paths that join residential hamlets. Rather, the sorcerer "walks in the bush" hidden and hiding from the comings and goings of everyday sociality. Where normal people make "noise" to announce their presence, the sorcerer treads silently to conceal his movements. ... [T]he sorcerer ... is the one type of person who may be killed, and killed justifiably, by his own close kin (LiPuma 1998: 70–71).

Among the Gebusi of Western Province in Papua New Guinea, sorcerers may even be killed instantly if the signs become apparent. A common situation in which such signs show up is when people come together at the corpse of the deceased. People try not to stay too long since the deceased is believed to be able to give signs by making gurgling noises or opening the eyes, for instance, and thereby point to the sorcerer (Knauft 1985: 38). In Daiden, sorcerers were thought to be too powerful to be killed through direct physical assault or countersorcery. The suspects I knew of were not considered sorcerers by a communal majority. Accusations were always based on the concretely observed quality of interaction that had defined the relationship between suspect and victim. Did they compete for land or a woman? Most importantly, did they eat together on a long-term basis, that is, did they have a kin-relation and to what degree? To turn against one's closest kin, one's parents, siblings, or children was said to be impossible since closest kin are those who have always shared food and have always sat around the same hearth. Ties established in this way cannot be disrupted unless they have been neglected right from the beginning. A man also will not consider his parents' siblings' sons aggressors since these people belong to the hearths to which he himself most often came. Long-lasting, shared foodways are believed to protect against malevolent magic attacks from all sides.

One's aggressor is usually a person who does not belong to one's direct kin, someone who lives beyond one's familiar households and hearths. If relatives turn against one another, it can only be those who stand at the borders of recognized kinship—one's second cousins (Ego's PPGCC) and their children. This should not happen, since this type of relationship is ideally marked by great mutual respect and occasional food exchanges. Such exchanges, however, are not as regular as are the exchanges with one's closest kin. People who do not share food do not really relate or feel obliged to one another. Outside one's kin sphere there are people who eat at other hearths, relying on trustful relations elsewhere, and who therefore might turn against one.

Feinberg states in the context of the Anuta in the Solomon Islands that "empathy is specially reserved for kin, and outsiders are kept at arm's length until they are incorporated into the kinship system. Thereafter, *aropa* [to be glossed as 'love / sympathy / pity / compassion / empathy'] becomes the order of the day" (Feinberg 2011: 161). Once accepted in a Bosmun household, affinal relatives, too, are offered good company, but they might more easily become suspicious of one another. A woman, for instance, was convinced that a child of hers had become the victim of sorcery by the brother of her sister-in-law since she had refused to marry him. There is also a myth that tells of a man called Out and his relationship with his daughter-in-law. Out tamed a crocodile by feeding it and named it Ndaame.[8] The daughter-in-law showed no respect for Out. Every time she returned from sago making, Out asked her for a piece of sago. Since she was a girl from another household, he wanted to examine her this way. After a while, she became tired and told him to go and get it himself. Therefore, he cast a spell on the crocodile he had tamed. When the daughter-in-law went to the rivulet to bathe her baby, the crocodile appeared and dragged the baby away.

Even between conjugal partners, ill will leading to death can occur. Earlier, I stated that a woman is able to kill her husband. He, of course, may do the same to her. We recall that Ropor was responsible for the death of his first two wives, but also that the women Nziŋgam and Pɨatam were responsible for his death. In this detail of the myth, men are made aware that female spouses can cause injury, even if Nziŋgam and Piatam did not intentionally kill Ropor. Sisters and daughters never bring harm to men but only their wives, I was told. In Bosmun food ideology, it is not unreasonable that partners who enter a basically positive relationship might still turn on each other. A couple has to build up what both have experienced separately in their respective house-holds—trustful, long-term relationships based on sitting amid one's kin and sharing food. A woman has been fed by her parents, she has shared food with her siblings, and she should at least feel obliged to feed her infant. A man has had similar experiences in his parental household. Wife and husband reach the level of highest mutual confidence once they have brought up their children together and see their children's children grow. This is also evidenced by the fact that a husband will lend his *siskum* to his wife only as the couple has grown old together. A man's *siskum* contains his strength. It is the inedible re-mains of a betel nut that the man chewed together with herbal substances. We have heard that whenever a man becomes father he has to restore his strength in the process called *rerak*—also by chewing a *siskum*. It is worth mentioning that a man's *siskum* stays with his mother, who stores it on a shelf hanging di-rectly above her hearth so that the steam from cooking food keeps it powerful. Once the mother has died, the man's sister continues to look after it. Only at a high age, when partners are still together, will a husband store his *siskum* on the shelf hanging over his wife's hearth.

'SOLVING PROBLEMS'
Kuehling has noted about sorcerers and witches on Dobu Island in southeast Papua New Guinea that their actions are considered as "antisocial ways of dealing with one's own negative emotions of 'anger' and 'envy'" (2005: 123). This has validity for Bosmun ideas of why individuals become tempted to apply sorcery. Sorcerers behave in antisocial ways because they elude what interviewees described to me as *miskindes rorte,* 'to solve a problem.' To solve a problem means to appease malevolent feelings. In that, *miskindes rorte* is a specific way of mutual empathy that seeks positive ends. It requires people to disclose their dispositions and allow others to understand them. I frequently listened to how people talked about existing problems to be dealt with. In-terestingly, such talks did not just focus on gossip over social outsiders, but hinted at the moral mistakes of one's own kin. According to local opinions, it is kin who should encourage one another to approach the world in benevolent ways. Therefore, from time to time everyone is likely to become subject of social revision by his or her own kin. Likewise, everyone might act as a social adviser from time to time. Members of a household who are known to solve problems regularly by engaging in open conflict are less likely to become suspects of sorcery. If people follow this type of acknowledged conflict reso-

lution, they save their "smiling faces." It is believed that only in reassessing one's feelings, including negative feelings, in the presence of one's kin and in allowing kin to critique and reshape one's feelings, can one avoid becoming a "murky face." The "smiling face" in Daiden is certainly different from Wikan's description of the Balinese virtue of the face that appears bright and happy: "Anger or offense, sorrow or fear—the injunction is the same: Be polite … and happy. … Laugh and joke. Do not care …, 'forget it' … and 'manage your heart' behind a clear … and cheerful … expression. Be *polos*: of one color, always" (1990: 50; original emphasis). To make Bosmun faces smile, feelings have to be disclosed and relationally negotiated. To examine the states of self and other in this way is the approved mode in Daiden that prevents people from developing severe distrust and hatred.

The tensions that I witnessed between individuals always occurred in the public places of familiar households. Several times, I observed someone arriving at a household in a hurry and shouting, *Ol i kros nau!* ('They just started to fight / verbally insult each other!'), followed by people running to see what was going on. Spectators always interfered by appeasing or gingering up their kin. To stay emotionally detached in view of commotion is a rather atypical reaction from Bosmun perspectives. To prevent problems from growing into serious conflicts that could cause illnesses among those involved, these problems must be discussed in the realm of one's own kin and in the realm of that of the opponent if it is clear that the problem has been caused because two people belonging to different families have been on bad terms. Both sides have to agree to arrange a meeting during which the tension must be unwound. It is not feelings of anger or envy as such that cause illness, but the failure to articulate these feelings in the appropriate way. In 2008, for instance, two men became suspects of sorcery. I asked why they qualified as sorcerers. My interviewees said that the two had been sitting together all the time, roaming around together, talking just to one another, excluding others, which meant that they had something to conceal. Not only overly individualistic behavior, but also excessive dyadic contact can cause suspicion. Therefore, it seemed to me, people felt more at ease in larger social gatherings.

Revisions of one another's moral, emotional, and embodied foodways were indeed an integral part of daily interpersonal encounters in Daiden. An example of how openly such revisions are made can be seen in T.'s life story, presented in this chapter. In an almost day-long, very detailed conversation in which her husband coparticipated, T. openly complained about him in front of me. S. listened to her complaints with a kind of equanimity I did not expect in view of the critique he received by T. However, I learned that he was aware of his wife's objections and knew that everyone else in their relational field knew about her objections, too. Hence, there was no reason to respond to it with either shame or anger. After all, the couple had been living for many years in a rather regular rhythm of breaking up and reuniting, of sharing and not sharing food. At one time, one would hear people saying "T. left S.," at another time, "S. left T.," and soon after, "T. and S. are reunited."

The relational way of speaking as well as acting in Daiden offers clues as to how people deal with the negative side of empathy. For instance, I observed how a father told someone that he was not happy about his daughter's marriage to a particular man. Interestingly, the father uttered his worry with his daughter sitting just two meters away. He talked as if she were not present. Yet, he knew she was there, listening closely to his complaints. Both had been particularly fond of each other and wished to be on good terms again. Another day, I saw the daughter doing the same, talking to someone else with her father sitting nearby and listening to what she had to say. This indirect way of talking things out eventually reunited them.

In another situation, a woman pretended to collect edible leaves in the bush as her sister sent a child to ask for prawns. The sister lived in town, but was currently visiting a brother in a nearby household. The woman did not want to send the prawns. In her view, the sister had broken the customary rules of reciprocity; living in town had turned her into a "murky face." The sister, however, had harbored the woman whenever she came to town and thus felt entitled to ask for the prawns. The woman told her husband and children to pretend that she was busy but in openly telling them about her anger she gave them the possibility to react in a way they thought to be suitable. Not wanting to inhibit any attempts to talk things out later, the husband eventually sent some prawns to his in-law.

While observing another case, I also learned how the use of empathy in the service of harming another person may be balanced by a third person who counterempathizes. N. and T. were sisters. T. was married to the brother of A.'s father. N. insulted A. by promising to bring her food and not keeping this promise. She admitted in the presence of others that she had failed to follow through with her pledge. What then happened was that T. came to A. with a plate of food. Being related to both A. and N., T. wanted to maintain a balance in her own relational surrounding. Since A. and T. were on good terms, T. reduced her sister's offense against A. by bringing A. food. One way to interpret this situation would be to say that although N. had not behaved according to the general moral code, equilibrium was upheld by T., who brought food to A. Another way, maybe more appropriate from Bosmun perspectives, would be to say that N. did behave according to the moral code since she immediately let others know that she had broken a food-related promise.

In yet another case, the children of a man took sides with the man's (classificatory) brother. The brothers, P. and D., had been debating the rightful ownership of a certain part of land. One day, P. saw how a son of D. climbed a coconut palm and he scolded him. An hour later, D. came to P. and they started to fight—visibly as usual in Daiden. In the evening, I saw P. sitting alone on a resting platform. I walked over to him. P. asked me whether I could help out with a tin of tuna. He told me that his wife had refused to cook for him and was to spend the night with a sister of hers and that his children were probably gathering with their (classificatory) siblings in the household of D. He told me that this was a common reaction whenever he got into a quarrel with this brother. Since he was the older brother, owning most of the clan land, he should have avoided scolding D.'s son because of a single coconut palm. In not supporting him, P.'s children counterbalanced his obviously greedy attempts. In so doing, they also demonstrated visibly that in this family negative intentions were subject to critical revisions.

To reveal one's states in the circle of food-sharing consociates is considered a constructive, and perhaps more importantly, a protective act. It is commonly assumed that individuals who make themselves transparent and thus allow others to shape their states cannot become sorcerers. But even if such accusations are made by social outsiders, kinsmen and kinswomen who "have been made" by means of shared foodways in familiar places will support the suspect. This support is understandable, for such accusations would mean that the suspect's entire relational field is under suspicion to have failed in the positive empathetic endeavor of "watching others and being watched."

Summary

The aim of this chapter has been to complement the preceding chapters by showing that foodways in Daiden also have an embodied dimension and that my conversation partners stressed the importance of foodways whenever making sense of "space" / social distance / unfamiliarity, on the one hand, and "place" / social closeness / familiarity, on the other. In the last section of this chapter, it became clear that close kin who relate on the basis of regular food exchange, joint sago labor, and consumption engage in relational mechanisms that they apply for the benefit of a macroemotional balance. Therefore, it is believed, they will not turn against one another in the case of suspected sorcery. Only social strangers and distant kin fall into the category of suspects. Distant kin, who are linked as "second cousins" at the borders of recognized kinship, should, however, avoid suspecting each other. In chapter 2, I described the "cooking scene" performed by Yombu und Nzenzema as they played. I said that the girls were related as second cousins 2 and that adults socialize their children into the "making of kin" by motivating them to imitate adult food-related behavior; the "cooking scene" was but one example of food-related socialization. As is now evident, parents thus also pursue a highly serious goal: they teach their children how to protect themselves from accusations of sorcery as well as from sorcery attacks in their future lives. Given that the girls (and their siblings and children) would be on good terms in the future through the perpetuation of food-sharing activities, they would probably help each other if one of them should become a suspect. After all, the children of second cousins are allowed to intermarry by ancestral convention and thus may reinforce the relations of past generations. If they do not intermarry, their respective fields of relatedness are likely to extend in different directions, thus rendering the ideal of transparent personhood as based on the moral, emotional, and embodied facets of *ramkandiar* no longer an obligation.

Notes

1. This fish, *kitpou*, has a thick belly and a short tail. It must not be eaten by men who are fathers of small children. Fathers are said to bring illness to their children if they consume this type of fish.
2. Ten years earlier, Tuzin (1980) proposed a similar theoretical stance when he described the felt experiences of Ilahita Arapesh novices in the initiatory phase of penis cutting, an impressive bodily experience. Tuzin spoke of individual experience as the locus for culture to emerge, yet an individual (or psychological) experience deeply tied to a bodily experience, that of a "young boy whose penis is being slashed by a savagely attired adult under conditions calculated to inspire maximum horror" (Tuzin 1980: 67). When substituting the word "individual" for "body / bodily" in the following quote, a theoretical equation becomes apparent similar to the one that can be found in Csordas's notion of the body as the origination point of culture: "One does not have to be a Freudian zealot to see that the special, subjective character of this experience, coming when it does in the life of the individual, could play a crucial role in instilling culturally approved attitudes and values on the part of impressionable novices. In this respect, then, we may say that culture is grounded in the experiences of individuals—even while affirming the obverse: that culture produces the very circumstances under which these experiences occur" (Tuzin 1980: 67).
3. Although Csordas (1994a: 7), like other scholars, deconstructs the body-mind dualism in the vein of Descartes, he nevertheless does not want to "vilify what is usually called 'Cartesian dualism' as a kind of moral abjection." He reminds us of the historical and political context of Descartes's times and the latter's methodological suggestion of a body-mind doctrine to counteract theological hegemony over the sciences (Csordas 1994a: 7).
4. Other terms or phrases such as the "mindful body" (Scheper-Hughes & Lock 1987) or "body thoughts" (A. Strathern 1996) have been coined to grasp the experiential approach that takes embodied experience as the foundation of any human existence and navigation in the world.
5. There are schedules for PMVs, but they are rather spontaneously moved up or postponed. Moreover, the ride often takes much longer than six hours due to the many stops along the road to drop off or take on passengers and to load copra, which is sold in town and makes up a vital source of income in this region.
6. Also, when people need help deciding where to build a new house or when to hold a communal ceremony, they ask the ancestors by offering them food. Interestingly,

receiving advice from the ancestors is a bodily act. People stand or sit in a canoe, raise questions, and wait for the kinetically perceived movements of the canoe. These canoe movements are believed to be instigated by the ancestral spirits. From a purely phenomenological standpoint, one might equally say that people listen to the decision that their bodies express.

7. In 2005, for example, when a new men's house in Ndoŋon was opened, men from Manam Island had to be invited to play the flutes. Two of the last elder Bosmun flute players were supposed to perform it. They did not, however, perform since they had had a dispute going on for a while. One had accused the other of having used sorcery to kill a relative. A reunion as a performing group was thus not possible. Several men said to me that this probably would have been the last chance to hear a wonderful flute playing by skilled players who had learned it traditionally in the secret subterranean caverns.

8. Ndaame's descendants are said to still live in the rivulet where Out raised the crocodile. Interviewees reasoned that since Out had fed Ndaame, the crocodiles of this rivulet did not attack people. I was told that approximately thirty years ago a girl had been attacked at this rivulet by a crocodile. When I asked (already knowing of Out's story) why this had happened, everyone said that it had been a "crocodile from outside," probably a saltwater crocodile that had entered the Ramu at its mouth. The girl fortunately survived the attack (which left her with a disabled leg) because a courageous brother of hers, then a youngster of fifteen, had pulled her away.

Conclusion

In this book, I have discussed Bosmun notions of relatedness as they were revealed to me in Daiden during a particular stretch of time. I contemplated Bosmun ethnography by connecting it to recent anthropological thoughts about kinship as a creative, processual phenomenon (see Carsten 1997, 2000; Leach 2003). Following this perspective, I hope to have offered evidence for the idea that, although kin-ties in Daiden are considered to have genealogical roots, they need to be engendered through locally meaningful social exchange in order to become truly binding. Dwelling on important steps in people's life cycles, I have attempted to unfold a deeply interdependent mode of life and show how interdependencies are made and unmade on various levels of social connectedness.

The people who committed their time to working with me taught me that, from Bosmun perspectives, meaningful social exchange is grounded on a paramount precept that they referred to as _ramkandiar_ and that I translated as 'watching others and being watched.' I showed that the precept of _ramkandiar_ is linked to a complex set of recognized foodways, on the one hand, and a distinct social configuration of empathy, on the other. I used the term "foodways" to describe actions, practices, and views relating to the production, distribution, and consumption of sago, the staple diet in the Bosmun area. Based on emic assumptions that shared foodways allow as well as oblige individuals to inquire into one another's states, the study at hand combined a rather conventional theme in anthropology, that of food exchange, with a more novel one, that of empathy. Food's role with regard to the making of social identities and social relationships has been addressed variously in the anthropological study of human lives (e.g., Alexeyeff, James & Thomas 2004; Counihan & van Esterick 1997; Fajans 1997; Manderson 1986b). The interpretations that I have given in this book of Bosmun ethnography, however, show that more research could be done in order to uncover the conceptual convergence of foodways with empathy, a subject that only recently has gained more focused attention in anthropology (e.g., Hollan 2012; Hollan & Throop 2008, 2011; Robbins & Rumsey 2008).

My considerations of Bosmun foodways were based on observations of interpersonal life in Daiden, on the examination of food-related idioms and statements and the analysis of mythical stories, and on reflections concerning sociality beyond Daiden. In describing people's foodways throughout the chapters, also in relation to the foodways of mythical ancestors, I touched on Bosmun notions of morality, gender, and emotion, feeding, nurturing, and growing, movement, embodiment, and placial incorporation, and the ascription of benevolence / malevolence to persons and places.

I used the following arguments in order to convey a Bosmun sense of relatedness: First, I argued for a conceptual merging of morality and sago making. Based on the taboo that one must not eat the sago one has planted, I showed that people in Daiden constantly have to build good relations in order to obtain sago for the purpose of consumption. Second, I proposed a conceptual merging of empathy, gender, and age. In pursuing the idea that empathy in Daiden is rendered a moral obligation to be fulfilled by opposite-sex agents who jointly produce sago, I argued that the most successful empathetic assessments are believed to be accomplished by men and women who, as food reciprocators, are at the prime of life, and who are no longer and not yet _rorer_ ('insane' / 'immature' / 'unsociable') as are children and old people. Third, I argued that in Daiden trust and mutual openness are shaped through long-term, food-based relations and that feeling states are articulated through food-related enactments. Fourth, I claimed that, in pondering the states of a person, one always ponders the moral, emotional, and embodied foodways of this person: is a person inclined to share food? In what ways does a person engage in the sago-making ventures of his or her family? Does a body bear the signs of sago labor? In what kinds of food-related ways does a person express his or her feelings, and, most importantly, does he or she express them loudly enough for others to hear? Fifth, related to the marked expression of feelings in public, I argued that it is not only appropriate to estimate the states of others but to be open to the attempts of others to estimate one's own states and to offer the necessary hints for understanding. Finally, I argued that, in adhering to this kind of "transparent personhood," people in Daiden constantly seek to create shields against accusations of sorcery. I began this book by recounting that I was constantly given information about a household's current food situation. As should be evident now, I was being given clues as to the processes of making and protecting kin-relations in these households.

In my concluding remarks, I wish to address ideas about empathy and relatedness of rather recent origin in Daiden; these were presented by the middle-aged and younger people who spoke with me. To do this, I first recount what a woman in her mid thirties told me in early 2008 as we were discussing what my conversation partners called *gridi pasin* ('the way of greediness') or *mi pasin* ('selfish behavior'), a kind of self-centeredness ranging, according to Bosmun perspectives, among the ultimate social values of "white people." Keeping in mind the expositions presented especially in chapters 2, 3, and 4, we find in the statement below a forecast relating to changing notions of empathy and relatedness. In speculating about Daiden's future, the woman stated: *Mipela bihainim disela kastam yet! Saksak yu yet yu planim yu no inap kaikai! Tasol mipela i no klia! Bihain ... long taim bilong ol pikinini bilong mipela ... disela kastam bai stap yet o nogat?* ('We [our generation] still keep to this custom! You must not eat the sago you planted! However, we are not certain! Later ... when it is up to our children ... is this custom going to prevail or not?')

To not eat the sago one has planted was a pervading directive of Bosmun sociality during my stays at the Ramu. I gained the impression, however, that people were evoking "a more disciplined, orderly, and relational era" (Wardlow 2006: 35) when talking about the past, while thinking of the present and future as a more chaotic, unsteady time. This compares to the situation in Tari, in the Southern Highlands of Papua New Guinea, where people have begun to impose on their lives a "brand of 'auto-orientalism'—representing themselves as excessively desirous, too easily failing each other, and too easily embittered by others' similar failures" (Wardlow 2006: 35). In other words, positive empathetic qualities such as trust, amity, and sympathy are seen as having been lost.

Empathy is indeed a historical process. This is also underlined by Mageo, who argues that "enacted empathy" seems to prevail in more group-oriented, face-to-face settings whereas empathy thought of "as an imaginative identification of self with another, ... as an inner state in which one imagines another's inner state" (2011: 76) has grown large in societies ruled by Western capitalism and the ideal of individualism. Hermann (2011) makes a similar point in her analysis of the politicohistorical embeddedness of empathy and the emergence of a notion of "pity" in the relocation process of Banaba Islanders to Fiji; ideas of empathy as they exist today among Banaba Islanders are not based on "timeless notions that have been transported unchanged and in unbroken continuity from the past to the present" (Hermann 2011: 26). From such dynamic views of empathy, it follows that in the same way that particular forms of empathy emerge under certain societal conditions, they may equally change or even disappear.

In my accounts of Bosmun mythology, for example, I showed how the precept of *ramkandiar* evolved as the product of local history at a particular point in time. In the contemporary social context, which is to be seen as having been tremendously reshaped by religious and economic upheavals in the region since approximately the middle of the last century, local facets of empathy also have taken new shape. As noted in chapter 3, the Christian value of the "grace of charity" has been seen as corresponding to the ancestral paramount value of *ramkandiar*. This is what I learned from most of the middle-aged and older people in Daiden. Among the younger people, however, a category of the *bisnis man / bisnis meri* ('business man' / 'business woman') was becoming more and more important, and was vested with personal traits opposed to local ideals of benevolent empathy. Too occupied with making money, my interviewees reasoned, younger "business people" also attended the local church services less regularly.

In 2010, when I explored Bosmun notions of aging (see A. von Poser 2011b), a woman described her situation as a senior member of her family: *Mi trangu ... mi mama blo bisnis man ya. Em sa tingim meri wantaim ol pikinini blo em tasol. Em i no wari moa lo mi. Em lusting pinis lo olgeta kastom blo ples.* ('I am [a] poor [woman] ... I am the mother of a business man. He only takes care of his wife and his children. He no longer takes care of me. He has forgotten about all the customs of this place.')

Several other women and men in Daiden wondered in my presence whether the customary foodways they had grown up with would live on in what they perceived as an increasingly changing world. My younger interviewees would tell me: *Pasin blo ai i wok lo daiaut ... em ova* ('[Our] way of observing is coming to an end ... it is over').

In view of rapid population growth, people indeed have begun to anticipate problems arising from the resulting land scarcity, leading them to rethink the model of relatedness as decreed by ancestral lore. Especially with regard to emerging land scarcity, the younger generations have lately been stressing the biological kin-ties, thereby undermining the social mechanisms that have been at work in the "making of kin" as I observed during most of my time in Daiden. These younger generations also showed particular interest in how I mapped their kin-ties in a kinship diagram. This is different from what Gow describes for the Piro in Western Amazonia; he writes: "I found the famous 'genealogical method' rather embarrassing to use, for my informants were either insulted or aggrieved by my objectification of their kinship relations.... I learned about kinship through what people told me about the land, and through observing how they used the land in their relations with other people" (1995: 48). As shown in this book, I mostly learned about kinship in Daiden through observing people's foodways. But there were cases that made me aware that, if I were to conduct research in Daiden in the future, I certainly would have to pay closer attention to how relatedness would be reconfigured by those who had told me that the time of *ramkandiar* was coming to an end.

On my last visit, I increasingly recognized the rise of a "biological world-view." A man around thirty years of age, for instance, told me that he was currently thinking about returning his personal name to his mother's family, who, following the practice of *roosingar* (in which the firstborn is given to the mother's parents so as to replace her), had cared for him and were supposed to provide him with a piece of land. Recently, though, fights over land rights had been increasing in the family and thus one of his "brothers" had raised the issue that he should be provided with a piece of land by his "real father." The man got upset and asked his supposed "real family" to reintegrate him. Since, according to customary lore, biological parents are allowed to take back the child they gave away, if they see that he or she is being treated badly, the man anticipated his reintegration positively. In other cases of land disputes, I heard younger people opposing their opponents' rights to land by saying that their ancestors had been _tum tasol,_ that is, 'just captives' (children taken during raids), and therefore did not really belong to this place. According to the opinions of the elder generations, adoptions were considered customary; adopted children, classificatory siblings, and _tum_ were considered "true kin" as long as they learned to reciprocate in the conventional food-based way.

In comparing Euro-American understandings of descent and procreation based on a biological framework with Kamea understandings of relatedness that posit a radically different, nonbiological framework, Bamford makes us aware of the "implications of extending biology as a worldview to other parts of the globe," underpinning that "an emerging form of biological imperialism ... will fundamentally alter how many indigenous and Fourth World peoples conceptualize self, sociality, and processes of life more generally" (2007: 11–12). After reading this, I asked myself: was I wrong in showing people the kinship diagrams that I had made? In using this method, which, of course, is based on a Western frame of thought, did I help augment the younger generations' move toward a "biological worldview," thus taking part in the undoing of what was so vividly and generously shown to me by Ndombu, Kose, and many others? Or was I just part of the general processes of making, unmaking, and remaking of kin that were going on in Daiden anyway?

Burning a Tattered Rice Bag

Let me finish by telling of an encounter in 2008 with Ndoor, a woman in my closest circle of female consociates. Before I left Daiden, not yet knowing when I would return, Ndoor came to say goodbye. We sat on a resting platform near my house, looked at the Ramu, smoked, and chewed betel nut. Several children surrounded us. Ndoor pulled an old plastic bag out of her net bag, showed it to me and told me that she would burn the plastic once the children around us were gone. The children drew me into a chat and therefore I paid no further attention to what she had told me. When all the children except for Ndoor's granddaughter had left, she told me once more that she would light the plastic and that I should watch carefully. I could also take a photo if I wanted (see figure 5.1).

I then asked her what the plastic bag was all about. It was one of the bags of rice that I had distributed among all families for my farewell party in 2005. Back then, we had agreed that I would buy rice and canned tuna in town and that the women of Daiden would provide local foods. Ndoor had kept this old rice bag as a memento of me (see Lohmann [2010] for Asabano mementos that evoke memories of past relationships), and now she wanted to let me

Figure 5.1: Burning a Tattered Rice Bag.

know that, whenever she had looked at this old tattered rice bag, she had thought of me and of the last meal that we had shared. Before she eventually lit the bag on fire, she smiled at me and said: *Mi no save ... bai yu lukim mi gen o nogat ... mi bai dai pinis o ...*? ('I am not sure ... are you going to see me again or not ... will I be dead or ...?')

While participating in parts of *ndom taao* (the complex ritual to 'honor a deceased'), I had learned that bidding farewell to a deceased person is marked by the burning of his or her belongings. Ndoor's burning of the rice bag that she had imbued with meaning relating to me appears to me—in retrospect—as an altered version of *ndom taao*. We were both alive but we did not know whether we would be meeting again in the future and thus Ndoor chose a food-based action to mark our parting, to anticipate my leaving and the mourning she felt. I replied to her that we would definitely meet again. I remember that, at that moment, I was also hoping that more tattered rice bags had been stored away somewhere to commemorate my presence in Daiden. Fortunately, this was not our last meeting. We saw each other in 2010, and this time, interestingly, she showed me a *laplap* ('waistcloth') that I had left with her in 2008 as a reminder that I would return and that we would eat together again. The point I wish to make with this short episode toward the end of my narrative is that again, through Ndoor's burning of the rice bag, I was given a glimpse into a world in which social relationships, empathy, and expressions of amity were engendered by the use of unique foodways.

Notes

1. After more than seventy years of mission and several decades of the aid post system in the area, I was hardly the first person to bring Western biomedical ideas to Daiden.

Glossary

aam	to consume food.
aamarees	cooked food (literally: something cooked that can be eaten).
aaok	small water stream.
eimi pur	yam sprouts.
eis	male genitals.
eisi mɨmɨk	sexual intercourse (literally: to enclose the penis).
eŋ	scent.
erok	sago pudding.
kaakos	person of social renown.
kaam	1. sound / language, 2. boundary marker.
kan	female genitals.
kaŋgat	1. husband, 2. female Ego's sister's husband.
kaonzo nduan	umbel of the breadfruit tree.
karvi	1. moon, 2. moiety name.
kaut (or *kout*)	traditional hair tube worn by men.
kɨnɨr	1. sadness / emotional distress, 2. bodily numbness.
koku taka xorpe	to find consent.
kom	type of bamboo.
kook	sorcery.
kookomot	sorcerer.
kosir	customs of a widow / a widower.
kuit (singular of *kuvi*)	type of plant (*abelmoschus manihot*).
kus	cooked banana and breadfruit in a creamy coconut soup.
maame	Ego's biological and classificatory mother.
mak	Ego's biological and classificatory opposite-sex sibling's son.

makanmoŋ	Ego's biological and classificatory opposite-sex sibling's daughter.
mbaak	eating spoon.
mbaaŋ	to care for.
mbairim raaŋ	to replace spoons (idiomatic expression).
mbakmbak	1. color term (referring to darker colors), 2. whitish layer that makes sago starch inedible, 3. negative / unsociable intentionality.
mbi	1. male Ego's biological and classificatory sister, 2. male Ego's opposite-sex "second cousin 1."
mbiermba	type of vine.
mbikit	male semen.
mbimbit	wrinkles in the forehead.
mbin	Ego's biological and classificatory grandchildren.
mbiŋ	wooden slit-drum.
mbitit	broken.
mbook	betel nut palm.
mbu	wild sago palm.
mbuki	menarche.
memkor	human beings (plural).
memok	human being.
mes	1. woman, female, 2. wife, 3. male Ego's brother's wife.
mesndaŋ	Ego's son-in-law.
mimiŋ	1. mother's milk, 2. substance of human brains.
miaŋ	1. sexual desires / sexual awakening, 2. female personal name.
mir	1. to deliver, 2. breast.
mirip	1. type of spirit being, 2. spirit mask.
miriri tomuŋ	birth-house.
mirpi nzit	secret flute.
mirpi tomuŋ	spirit house.
moke	1. Ego's father's sister, 2. paternal cousin, 3. maternal in-law, 4. mother-in-law.
mono	your.

moŋ	1. to do, 2. intestines.
mooŋ	Ego's biological and classificatory daughter.
moptiŋ	1. baby crayfish, 2. girl prior to menarche.
mormes	female "second cousin 2."
mormot	male "second cousin 2."
mot	man, male.
muon (*mbaŋ*)	opposite / other (side).
nanmakae	stick for the stirring of sago.
nda	group of people.
ndaare	type of rat.
ndaaremes	female messenger.
ndaaremot	male messenger.
ndair mbɨmbɨt	teeth pain.
ndakanmes	1. woman's brother's wife, 2. husband's sister.
ndakanmot	1. man's sister's husband, 2. wife's brother.
ndei	Ego's biological and classificatory grandmother.
nden / *ndennden*	grasslands.
ndene tomuŋ	secret cult-place (built underground).
ndɨar	the willingness to make peace / to mediate.
ndɨara xonom	platform of the peace-makers.
ndom	spirit of the deceased (spiritual entity detached from the human body).
ndombo	spirits of the deceased (plural).
ndombok	1. to play, 2. to joke.
ndom taao	to honor a deceased (literally: to decorate a deceased).
ndoor	1. love magic, 2. female personal name.
nduaŋ	1. female Ego's biological and classificatory brother, 2. female Ego's opposite-sex "second cousin 1."
nduŋnduŋ aam	to be angry (literally: to consume a type of sea shell).
neŋ	type of palm tree containing starch-like substance (similar to sago starch).
nimbit	blood.
ninkut	dead.
nis	1. inside, 2. womb.

nisnisi xonom	men's house.
nis tak	to become pregnant (literally: to put into the womb).
nit	body skin.
niŋ	a pair.
nɨŋ	bottom of a tree.
nɨŋɨn	ability of talking.
nɨŋ koku	one's descent (literally: one bottom of a tree).
nuok	Ego's biological and classificatory son.
nyeroŋ	spiritual (embodied and body-animating) entity.
nzit	type of bamboo.
nzokumbu	"friend" (child of "second cousins 2") of the same moiety.
ŋaamŋaam	not tasty.
ŋaas	to be lazy.
ŋanzi	1. to be jealous, 2. to be envious, 3. to distrust.
ŋas	banana (generic term).
ŋaspakmes	girlfriend.
ŋaspakmot	boyfriend.
ŋgaam	1. young, 2. new.
ŋgaaŋgo	1. to imitate, 2. to practice.
ŋgaape	tree-spirit.
ŋgaaper	tree-spirits (plural).
ŋgangɨr	adopted child.
ŋgɨambar	urine.
ŋgɨanmes	female "friend" (child of "second cousins 2") of the opposite moiety.
ŋgɨanmot	male "friend" (child of "second cousins 2") of the opposite moiety.
ŋgɨanxaam mbaŋ	this side.
ŋgome	1. crocodile, 2. crocodile spirit.
ŋgomndis	type of spirit beings.
ŋgoris	1. birds (plural), 2. type of spirit beings.
ŋgu	fish (generic term).
ŋguarak	bird (generic term).

ŋgum	1. face, 2. nose.
ŋgumu mbakmbak	murky face / stingy, greedy, lazy, selfish person (idiomatic expression).
ŋguŋguru aam	to eat in secrecy (idiomatic expression).
ŋguruk	to hide.
ŋgusuŋgu	euphoria.
ŋoi	to upset / to insult.
osnis	sago swamps (planted by humans).
outut	1. sorrow / grief / anguish, 2. strong physical pain.
paar mbɨtɨt	a broken hand (idiomatic expression).
pak	several.
perŋa saaka aam	to apply sorcery (literally: to eat dog's flesh).
peskete	tasty.
poŋ	bad temper / anger / aggression.
raao	1. sun, 2. moiety name, 3. male personal name.
raaraŋ	creator-being.
raarŋa ma taka	established by an ancestral being.
raarŋanini	ancestral story.
raarŋaosnis	sago swamps (wild growing / spiritually empowered).
ramak	eye.
ramakniŋ	a pair of eyes.
ramkandɨar	to watch / feel into others, to empathize benevolently.
ramka vaas	to appreciate (literally: to perceive via the visual organ).
reŋepak	garden (literally: several plots).
rerak	1. to reconstitute, 2. to transform / to change.
rimsi	eyes (plural).
roŋe	type of flute.
roŋgo maankat mes / mot	knowledgeable, sociable person (literally: someone looking through bamboo).
roombuŋ	type of tree (with mythological significance).
roosiŋgar	to return a firstborn to his or her mother's parents.
ropuk	bodily or mental disorder caused by spiritual entities.
rorer	1. crazy, 2. unreasonable, 3. sound and deep sleep.

rupaam	to beg (literally: to ask for food).
rupaama xonom	platform of the beggars.
saamoŋ	Ego's daughter-in-law.
saane	chant (generic term).
saar	ladder.
saate	Ego's biological and classificatory father.
sae	magical powers.
sak	flesh of humans and animals.
se	1. to visit, 2. to look after.
serap	hearth / fireside.
sim	1. individual character, 2. chain of hills.
simando	word used to indicate lament in song.
simbir	Calophyllum tree (*callophyllum inophyllum*).
siskum	inedible part left from a betel nut that was chewed with herbal substances.
sokve	type of bird (onomatopoetically derived).
sombit	saliva.
soŋgae	1. to love, 2. to long for.
suak	fire.
suruvok	1. to appreciate a food-gift, 2. to lift a food-taboo.
taan	1. public, 2. open.
taana tak	to disclose (literally: to put outside).
taana xonom	public platform (without a roof).
taao	to honor (literally: to decorate).
tak	to put.
tei	scout.
tip	behavior.
toŋ	Ego's biological and classificatory grandfather.
toup	1. walking track, road, 2. male personal name.
toupmbi ŋgimŋginir	the time between November and February (literally: paths are muddy and hardly accessible).
toupu motor	exchange partners (literally: men with the right to walk on certain paths).

tuaɲaniɲ ŋgar	to think about another one but without responding sociably / to respond harshly.
tum	child or adult captured during raids.
vaam	1. raft, 2. moiety.
vai	1. elder, 2. to hear / to listen.
vaiyap	1. Ego's biological and classificatory same-sex sibling, 2. Ego's same-sex "second cousin 1."
ve	1. to process sago, 2. to dance.
vees	1. planted sago palm, 2. sago starch (unprocessed and processed).
veesenyeroŋ	sago palm spirit.
veŋ	type of ginger (used as a banner of peace).
viur	type of flute.
viaraŋ	coconut palm.
voke	Ego's father-in-law.
vout	1. stone, 2. plateau.
vumbu	1. ill, 2. solid edge of something.
vumbusak	body.
vunis	place / residential space / space where social action takes place.
vunsi mes / mot	woman / man of the place.
vut	1. heart, 2. pulse.
xaam	1. eating spoon, 2. type of tree, 3. male personal name.
xaame	wind (generic term).
xaarak	1. to know, 2. to understand.
ximir	raw food.
xoaam	river (generic term).
xonom	1. platform, 2. clan / clan-association.
xorpe	gathering / discussion with the aim of gaining consent.
xue	same-sex friend.
xuop	happy, content.
xur	old.

yaakak	bad, unsociable.
yaam	1. to know, 2. to understand, 3. clan-specific knowledge, 4. male personal name.
yaaoŋ	good, sociable, virtuous.
yae	1. Ego's mother's brother, 2. maternal cousin, 3. paternal in-law.
yaka / *yake*	exclamation of astonishment.
yap	younger.
ye	to cry.
yepsi xonom	platform of the warriors.
yimyɨt	vegetables (generic term).
yɨmbɨn	type of inedible fruits.
yuxur	feces.

Appendix

The appendix contains a version of the myth, which I summarize in chapter 3, that tells of the cultural heroine Nzari. I collected the story that the men M., K., and Ŋ. told me at an early stage of my fieldwork (24 October 2004). I recorded it in Tok Pisin and it is presented this way here. If one looks at the recorded story in terms of a speech act, one will see (even without necessarily understanding Tok Pisin) that M., the speaker who contributes most in terms of quantity, regularly pauses and takes up utterances by either K. or Ŋ. and that K. or Ŋ. regularly interrupt or add to M.'s telling. My questions and utterances (indicated by A.) are also included. A few details to which I refer in the analysis that accompanies my summary of the myth in chapter 3 are missing in this version. It was only later that people provided me with further particulars. As I said in the Introduction to this book, Bosmun storytelling does not serve the purpose of revealing the "full story."

M.: *Nzari em ... stat ... stori bilong em i go olsem. Taim em i stap wantaim mama bilong em insait long wanpela hul bilong diwai* <u>roombuŋ</u> [particular type of tree] *na wanpela man ol kolim ...*

K.: *Soŋe!*

M.: *Soŋe! Em i go na katim wanpela diwai kanu ... i wok long sapim. Em sapim i stap, disla meri Nzari i wok long lukluk long em. Na em i tingting: "Man ya, ating, i nogat meri bilong em!" Olsem nau na taim em i kam wok ... em save wok pultaim long san, na meri bilong em i no sa bringim kaikai i kam na em i no save kam painim em long ples bilong wok. Nogat! Em wan yet, em save mekim wok i stap. "Ating, bai mi kamap long en!" Oke ... na mama bilong em i tokim em, em tok: "Ey, lukaut! Em i gat meri ya! Nogut yu mekim olsem nau na bai yutla sidaun stap meri bilong em i kam lukim, bai yutla pait." Na em tok: "Nogat mama! Em i gat meri olsem, em bai meri bilong em bai bihainim em long wok ya!" Oke i stap. Wanpela de nau, em i kisim buai na daka ...*

K.: *mekim marila*

M.: *mekim marila long em pinis. Em godaun ... na mekim hap singsing.*

K.: *mekim singsing*

M.: *na bilong winim em nau na em i slip. Em i slip dai pinis i stap nau na em i go putim buai daka nau na oke, bihain gen, em i mekim hap singsing gen na kirapim em bek. Na em i go hait sanap lukluk i stap. Nau em ... man ya kirap lukim buai*

daka na em i tok: "Samting bilong kaikai na mi kaikai buai nau. Husait i putim, em
gutpela tru!" Na em kisim disla buai, daka na em kaikai. Kaikai nau i wok go go go
go abinun, em go long ples. Lusim hap wok i stap na em go long ples. Neks de em
i kambek gen, nau, meri ya lukluk i stap na em i kisim banana mau, kisim sampela
banana mau, na … godaun, mekim olsem bifo em i mekim ya, em i slip. Nau em i
go putim banana mau, lusim na i go sanap longwe na kirapim em bek. Na em kirap
lukim na em tok: "Samting bilong kaikai nau na banana mau mi kaikai nau! Husait
i putim, em gutpela tru!" … Em kisim kaikai pinis, em wok long kanu i go go go
go go abinun nau em i go. Nau, meri ya em i save pinis disla man em i nogat meri
bilong em! Yu save, em devol meri ya! Em save lukluk long olgeta hap.

K.: *ŋgaape mes* [a female tree-spirit]

M.: *mmh, nau em i neksde moning em i kambek nau, em lukluk i go, em taimim em*
yet bilong em bai tanim saksak olsem nau mipela kaikai ya! Em tanim pinis.

K.: *long sel, bikpela sel*

M.: *bikpela sel ya. Sel, drai ya, kokonas, em klinim gut nau na em i putim …*

K.: *saksak*

M.: *saksak i go long disla, pinis, em putim sup antap long saksak. Nau, em kisim*
em i godaun. Em bai hait yet. Soŋe i no lukim em yet. Oke, em i godaun mekim
disla hap singsing, winim em nau na em slip pinis nau, em i go putim disla saksak,
lusim nau i go sanap longwe na mekim narapela hap singsing gen, kirapim em bek.
Na Soŋe kirap lukim na i tok: "Oh sori, samting bilong kaikai na mi kisim kaikai
nau. Husait putim long mi, em gutpela tru!" Nau em kisim disla saksak, kaikai
pinis, putim gut sel bilong em na em wok i go go abinun nau na em i laik go na
em i tok: "Sel … plet sel bilong yu ya—yu husait i putim yu kambek na kisim, mi
go nau." Oke, na Nzari em wok long harim harim i stap. Nau, em i go long ples.
Na mama bilong em i tokim em, em tok: "Ey, Nzari, yu lukaut!" Mama bilong em
snek, bikpela moran.

K.: *moran …*

M.: *yea. Nau … na Nzari tok: "Em i nogat meri." Nau, em i … tingting bilong en i*
go olsem em bai maritim disla man nau. Neksde moning, em kambek nau long wok,
nau em … i tekim taim bilong en i go go go go taim bilong kaikai nau, em i kuk nau.
Kuk pinis, em i sutim long bikpela …

K.: *plet*

M.: *… plet nau, limbum, ol samapim long em. Putim long disla limbum pinis, putim*
sup pinis …

K.: *em yet bilas pinis …*

M.: *Em yet em i bilasim em yet nau. Em i bilasim em pinis, em kaikai buai pinis,*
buai i stap yet long maus, em i kisim disla saksak limbum nau na em i wokabaut i

go. I go nau ... na smel bilong en i go na Soɳe i smelim nau na em i ..." Ey! Wanem gutpela smel ya!" Olsem ...

K.: *olsem ... spray ... kain olsem.*

M.: *Na em laik tanim lukim ... em Nzari i stap. Ah, em lukim nau na tok: "Em i no meri, em wanem kain nau? I naismoa long olgeta narapela meri!" Nau em i ... kirap, holim pasim em na i tok: "Tsea! ... Yu no ken holim pasim mi ... Em ...*

K.: *kaikai ... saksak bilong yu ...*

M.: *Em saksak bilong yu, yu kaikai! Kaikai kwik na bai mi go."... Em traim em nau: "Nogut meri bilong yu bai kam lukim mitla wantaim na em bai paitim mi." Em tok: "Mi nogat meri, mi singel man ya!" "Oh." "Mi ting long yu, nogut man bilong yu bai kam lukim mi na ... em bai paitim mi." Em tok: "Mi nogat man ya, mi singel ya." Oke nau, tupela i promis nau.*

A.: *Oke.*

M.: *Tupela marit nau. Marit nau, em lus ting long ol lain long ples nau. I no tulait yet, em tekof ... long bus, long meri bilong em na em kisim ol lain dok bilong en i go long bus, kilim wanpela pik em bai kam lusim long meri bilong em. Em bai kukim na katim pinis bai ol i kuk kaikai i stap i go abinun em bai go. Na long ples, em tambu bilong en wantaim susa bilong en i save lukautim em.*

K.: *Em i nogat meri*

M.: *Em i nogat mama ... papa em dai ... bifo*

A.: *Tambu bilong ...? ... Sori, bilong husait?*

M.: *Tambu bilong Soɳe.*

A.: *Ah oke.*

M.: *Em nau. Mekim olsem i go, em kilim tupela [pik], wanpela bai lusim long meri na narapela bai em bai karim long tambu wantaim susa bilong em. Olgeta taim em save mekim olsem. I go go nau na kanu em i pinis nau. Oke, em wantaim meri bilong en, Nzari, tupela kukim disla kanu pinis, subim i godaun ...*

K.: *long wara ...*

M.: *long wara ... na kanu em i godaun sidaun long wara nau. Oke nau, em i go na tambu bilong en i askim em: "Olsem wanem, bai mi kam halvim yu o?" Em tok: "Nogat! Em liklik wok, longtaim mi putim kanu i godaun long wara pinis." Em tok: "Ah, yu rong tru! Mipela i no halvim yu na yu wan yet i pinis olgeta wok." Nau, em i tingting nau, em laik kisim meri bilong em i go long ples nau. Oke. Neksede em i go bek nau, em i tokim Nzari nau: "Inap bai mitupela i go long ples nau?" Em tok: "Ya, bai mi go!" Nau em i redi pinis, em tokim mama bilong em: "Yu ken i stap. Mi bai kam ... go i stap, kam visitim yu, luksave yu stap olsem wanem, yu gat sik, mi ken i stap wantaim yu." Em mekim disla ol toktok pinis, em i lusim na bihainim man i go long ples. Go long ples, ol i lukluk long disla meri na ol i tingting: "Mipela i nogat disla kain meri long wanpela ples long insait bilong mipela. Em i kisim disla meri long wanem hap? Em i naispela moa long olgeta meri." Nau i stap, em i stat lusim mun nau long kisim bebi nau. I go, nambawan pikinini bilong em i Mbobot. Em nem bilong en. Nau em i karim. Em karim nau em i stap long haus karim i go …* *inap long taim em i go antap long bikpela haus. Olsem long pastaim mipela stori pinis long kol ya, em long disla* [the Tok Pisin term *kol* is used by speakers to refer to the debilitating influence that women's fluids have on male bodies].

A.: *Oke.*

M.: *Nau em i go antap long bikpela haus i stap. Nau, pikinini em i kamap bikpela pinis, em save lukim mama na papa i lap i lap nabaut nau …*

K.: *olsem tri mun, fo mun*

M.: *fo mun, faif mun samting*

A.: *Ya.*

M.: *Nau, em pikinini i bikpela pinis.*

K.: *Em i save sidaun …*

M.: *… Sidaun na wokabaut long tupela skru nau, muvmuv long as bilong em. Nau em i … man bilong em i tokim em:*

K.: *"Mitla go wok saksak!"*

M.: *"Mitla go wok saksak nau! Mipela i no gat saksak." Oke, nait tasol, em i go tokim mama bilong en: "Tumoro … nau bai mitupela go wantaim nau na … tumoro moning bai yu was long tumbuna bilong yu na i stap. Mitupela man bilong mi i laik go wok saksak ya." Mama bilong em tok: "Oke, bai mi kam." Na traipela snek i godaun na i bihainim bilong pikinini bilong en i go. I go…*

K.: *Masalai snek ya …*

M.: *Moran ya bilong diwai. Nau em i go nau na tulait moning nau em putim piki-nini insait long bikpela sospen wantaim snek em i stap insait long bikpela sospen. Nau karamapim long sospen nau. I stap nau na snek ya wok long raunim namel bilong em na …*

K.: *em kis long em …*

M.: *… na longpela tang bilong em i wok long kis long fes bilong em, maus bilong em na … pikinini ya wok long krai krai krai. Na … disla anti meri bilong disla pi-kinini ya, em wok long brum. Na em i wok long harim na tok: "Ey! Pikinini i stap we nau na em wok long krai krai?" Em go antap nau. Em i go antap opim basket … bifo ol i save slip long basket* [woven tents in which people traditionally spent the nights to protect themselves from mosquitoes].

A.: *Ya.*

M.: *Nau, em opim lukluk pinis, bilong mama bilong en em opim lukim pinis, tok: "Em i no stap yet." Na em krai gen nau na em harim nau. "Oh!" Em krai insait long sospen ya na em go apim sospen na em lukim traipela moran i stap raunim em. Em tromoim sospen i godaun! Em ronowe go autsait nau na i go singaut i go long ples nau.*

K.: *"Eee!"*

M.: *"Noh!" Tok: "Traipela moran snek ya i kam nau na bagarapim pikinini ya i stap long ... insait long pot ya." Na ol i ron nau, kisim ol stik bilong paitim em, kilim em dai, supia, ol ron i kam i go antap lukim em nau, na em i lukim olsem ol i birua long em nau. Em lusim pikinini i stap.*

K.: *Nogut kilim wantaim pikinini ...*

M.: *Nogut bai ol paitim nau na bai kilim indai pikinini. Em kamap nau na slip i stret long floa bilong haus olsem. Na ol i no luksave olsem ol tok: "Em harim ... na em gat save tu ya, maski, mipela i no ken kilim." Nogat! Ol i kilim nau!*

K.: *Meri ... pikinini bilong em i tok: "Sapos ...*

M.: *taim ol i kilim yu na ...*

K.: *kukim ...*

M.: *... kukim yu long paia, sit bilong paia mas flai i go go go na kamdaun stret long susu bilong mi. Bai mi save." Na mama bilong em tok: "Yes." Na taim ol i kilim em pinis, i go wokim bikpela paia nau na kukim em long paia nau, sit bilong paia na em flai nau. Flai i go go go na i godaun antap long susu bilong pikinini bilong em. Na em lukim nau na em save, tok: "Oh, ol kilim mama bilong mi pinis."*

K.: *Em giaman tok, tokim man bilong em: "Susu bilong mi, pikinini i krai na susu bilong mi i solap."*

M.: *Nau em i ... em i ... em i sori tru long mama bilong en, em wok sik nau. Na man ... em i tokim man bilong em: "Soŋe! Yu kam na halvim mi na pinisim disla hap pipia na mipela bai go kwik long ples. Pikinini, ating, i krai long susu na susu bilong mi i wok long solap na pulim pulim mi i go antap." Nau, man bilong em, Soŋe, i halvim em long ...*

K.: *wasim ...*

M.: *pipia ya, wasim saksak pinis, hariap tupela kukim pinis, karim na i go long ples nau. Em krai wantaim wokabaut, em i stap baksait long man bilong em. Na man bilong em i no tanim na luksave long en. Na man ya, man bilong em, em tu i no save long mama bilong Nzari i kam na stap. Em i no save olsem. Em i no lukim tu mama bilong em. Na olsem na, na em i longlong ya. Tupela wokabaut i go kamap long ples nau, las haus i tokim em: "Traipela snek ya bagarapim pikinini bilong yu na i stap i stap nau na ol lain i go antap, mama bilong em i go antap lukim em nau na singaut i go na ol i kilim na mipela kauntim na katikatim na mipela i laik kaikai nau. Em tok: "Gutpela! Yupela kaikai na olsem bikpela samting bihain bai gat stori bilong em. Stat long tel na i go pinis long het bilong en, olgeta bun kam long mi, bai mi bungim. Bihain bai mipela stori." Na em tok: "Oke." Em i joinim tok i go olgeta meri man pinis. Ol i kaikai, ol i bringim bun i go bek. Em i go tasol, putim bilum bilong em i stap, em i go kisim tupela mambu i go pulimapim wara … i kam, sanapim, brukim paiawud i go antap putim. Nau wokim paia pinis, putim pot antap long paia nau, kapsaitim mambu wara i godaun pinis, na smuk bilong paia nau em i save bihainbihainim smuk bilong paia …*

K.: *nogut ol i save em krai bilong …*

M.: *… save em i krai. Smuk bilong paia i go olsem, em bai go sidaun long disla sait. Na win i kam gen na nau sakim i go long narapela sait, em bai bihainim gen smuk bilong paia i go sidaun.*

K.: *Olsem … em bai giaman …*

M.: *giaman bai aiwara bilong en bai godaun bai ol i save olsem smuk bilong paia i mekim na aiwara i godaun. Na man bilong em i no luksave long disla. Na ol bun bilong mama bilong en, em i bungim pinis lusim i stap na em i wok long hariap long tanim saksak bilong ol. Nau, em i tanim saksak pinis, mekim sup, putim pinis, dilim ol saksak pinis, na ol kaikai i stap, em i go krai insait long haus na i stap. I stap i go, ol plet samting ol bringim i kambek, em wasim pinis, putim gut ol samting pinis i lusim i stap, tudak nau, em kisim wanpela limbum i kamdaun na joinim disla ol bun nau. Joinim disla ol bun pinis, putim pen long em pinis, bilasim pinis, disla bun ya, em krai i go klostu tulait nau, em i go mekim hul nau na planim. Planim pinis nau, em kam antap long haus giaman slip na harim harim i stap. Long disla nait yet, ol man i pasim tok bilong go kukim wanpela kunai … bilong raunim ol pik na bai sutim. Nau moning, em kamap nau, tokim Nzari nau: "Yu lukluk long paia … long kunai. Paia i go antap sanap i stret tru i stap nau na i laik pinis, yu godaun katim disla banana bilong mi na … arere long haus tasol ya, kam antap na boilim pinis nau na larim i stap. Taim mi kambek, bai mi kaikai pinis na mi go waswas. Na Nzari tok: "Yes. Em gutpela." Na em nau, man bilong en i go long … paia long kunai nau, Nzari i wok long lukluk i stap. Nau, paia i sanap i stret i stap klostu em i laik pinis nau, Nzari i godaun katim banana, kam antap, putim wara long pot, mekim paia pinis, sidaunim em antap long paia, kisim ol banana putim sampela i godaun. Oke, na em kisim pikinini nau i wok long katikatim nau. Pikinini i wok long krai. Em wok long katim ol han lek bilong em …*

K.: *katim hia, katim hia* [K. points to the joints of his arms and legs]

M.: *… ol join bilong em, em bihainim ol join na katim … na putim insait long pot pinis.*

K.: *boilim wantaim ol banana*

M.: *na pikinini i dai pinis. Em wok long krai nau na narapela anti mama bilong em i askim em na em tok: "Em krai long kisim basket bilong papa bilong em na bilasim em." Em tok: "Oke, kisim na bilasim! Em ol samting bilong papa bilong em." Na em bilasim pinis disla bodi nating, nogat han lek bilong en. Bilasim pinis, putim pen long em pinis, putim long wanpela hap limbum, putim subim em i go insait long basket bilong papa i save slip long en. Pinis nau, em i lukluk long pot banana i stap em boil pinis nau. Em rausim na putim insait long stov yet, karamapim long sel. Nau, em kisim olgeta samting bilong em na putim insait long bel bilong em.*

K.: *Paia tu, olgeta samting*

M.: *paia, olgeta samting em kisim nau putim insait long bel bilong em pinis. Em redim em yet pinis, em godaun nau, kisim bilum. I go autsait na i tokim tambu meri bilong em: "Soŋe i kam, oke, tokim em, em banana bilong em ya i stap long pot yet, na mi go kisim pangal bilong kokonas ya. Nogut em kisim ol sampela mumut i kam, bai mi hat long painim paia. Olsem nau na mi go kisim na i kam na bai wet long em. Em go long ailan nau, go long as bilong ol kokonas na painim ol pangal bilong kokonas. Nau, em go long basis nau*

K.: *brukim ol …*

M.: *brukim olgeta kanu nau na wanpela gutpela tasol em i larim bilong en. Em nau, em kalap long disla kanu i go sanap—ah—sidaun long namel long wara nau holim het bilong diwai na lukluk i stap. Ol pinis nau … na ol i kam, ol man i kambek long ples. Na Soŋe, longtaim em save, em banana bilong em i stap.*

K.: *Nzari i no stap.*

M.: *Nau, em i kam tasol nau na sanapim tupela supia i stap, askim susa bilong em: "Na meri ya i go we?" "Em go kisim liklik paiawud bai kam na yu holim sampela mumut i kam na em bai kukim … long ailan ya. Na banana bilong yu em i stap long pot yet. Yu go antap lukim." Em go insait lukim nau na rausim sel na kamautim nil long het bilong en … olsem wanpela supia nil ya ol save kaikai long en ya. Na em kamautim tasol long* kaut *[or* kout, *'traditional hair tube'] bilong en. Nau, em i wok long sutsutim banana na kaikai. I go go go nau na em i sutim hap bilong pikinini bilong en na apim i go antap. Han bilong pikinini. Em lukluk nau na em tok: "Ey, kapul ah?" Na em i no kaikai, em i lusim i stap nau na i go autsait gen na i go askim susa: "Na pikinini em putim we na i go?" Em tok: "Em slip nau na putim insait long basket bilong yu na em i go nau. Em tokim mi olsem, tok: "Em krai, oke, yu go antap na kisim." "Nau em i ron i go insait, opim basket bilong en na lukim, holim disla limbum nau na pulim i kam autsait na lukim pikinini em indai pinis. Em i no moa stap laif. Tromoim tasol olsem i stap, ron i kam autsait, kalap i godaun. Na susa bilong en i tok: "Olsem wanem?" "Ey, meri ya bagarapim pikinini bilong mi ya, em dai pinis." Na em kisim tupela supia bilong em ron i go long basis. Em let ya. Em i go lukim Nzari i sidaun i stap. Nau em i go sanap long wanpela kanu, em wara longtaim pulap pinis. I go long narapela kanu, olsem tasol i go, olgeta kanu i pinis. Na em lusim nau disla belhat bilong em na em go antap long graun na singaut: "Nzari, maski, kambek! Bihain bai mitla karim narapela gen." Na Nzari tok: "No! Mi, mi no inap kambek! Bilong wanem mama bilong mi, em mi tokim em na i kam hia na was long tumbuna bilong em." Nau … em tok: "Ah, yu no toksave long mi olsem nau na ol i ting em snek nau na i kilim em pinis. I orait, maski, yu kambek!" "Nogat. Mama em bikpela samting tru! I no yu i lukautim mi inap mi kamap bikpela meri. Em mama i lukautim mi na mi kamap bikpela meri. Trangu, sindaun! Mi go nau!" Em kirap tekof. Em bai pul i go, lukim wanpela basis, em bai lapun nogut tru. Em senisim em yet. Bai lapun nogut tru, kus i pulap long en. Ol bai lukim bai tok: "Lukim wanpela lapun meri nogut tru ya!" Em go nau. Em harim tasol na abrusim ol i go. I go long narapela basis, em bai olsem man. Putim paspas, kaut, em dresap gut tru! Sanap long stia bilong kanu, em tekof olgeta i go! Pul i go! Na ol lukim tok: "Ey!"*

K.: *"Wanpela yangpela man!"*

M.: *"Wanpela yangpela man tru em i pul i go nau!"*

Ŋ.: *Em senis insait!*

M.: *"Aja! Lukim! Smel bilong em ya! Nais moa long olgeta man!" Nau em bai lukluk i go lukim narapela basis, em bai kamap yangpela meri. Em bai pul i go. Ol bai tok: "Ey! Meri ya! Man! Kam insait ya!" Nogat, Nzari tekof. I go long narapela basis gen, em bai kamap olsem bikmeri, namel … namel meri nau. Em bai pul i go. Olsem tasol i go go go go go na klostu i laik kamap long wanpela ples meri i gat bel bai ol brukim … na kisim pikinini, na meri bai ol planim. Em bai dai.*

A.: *Ol i brukim na …?*

M.: *Brukim long bel na kisim bebi!*

A.: *Ah, na ol i dai?*

M.: *Ol i dai. I nogat senis i stap. Sapos yu … mi, olsem mi gat wanpela pikinini man tasol. Em disla pikinini man tasol bai stap na kamap pikinini meri, em bai ol i brukim, em tu bai dai. Man tasol em bai stap yet.*

K.: *Wanpela pikinini i go waswas long wara long basis*

M.: *nau ol i go waswas long basis i stap na meri ya em i senisim kanu, senisim em yet. Nongut tru! Ai bilong em tu i no lukluk. Tasol ai pekpek i pulap long pes bilong em, kus i pulap long nus bilong em na i bun nating tru. Na pulpul bilong em tu brukbruk nabaut na rop nating. Nau, em trangu, em pul i go insait, kanu bilong en i bagarap olgeta. Kisim graun na putim long hul bilong kanu nogut wara i go insait. Ol i lukim em nau na ol i kirap ronowe go antap. Na wanpela pikinini meri tasol em sanap nau na krosim ol, tok: "Ey! Bilong wanem yupela ronowe long em? Em man tu ya!" Ol tok: "Eee, mipela … pastaim mipela i no lukim wanpela kain meri olsem. Olsem na mipela i no laik, em samting bilong yu." Ol i ronowe pinis! long ples! Nau, em i holim kanu bilong en i go insait long basis, em i holim strong, kanu klostu i laik bruk. Em tok: "Ey ey ey! Yu no ken holim samting bilong mi em nogut pinis ya." Em tok: "Ah, sori tru!" Na taim em i laik kirap em bai guria nogut tru. Na ol ting olsem em lapun tru. No, em yangpela meri ya!*

Ŋ.: *Roombuŋ roombuŋ* [the *roombuŋ* tree, the *roombuŋ* tree]

M.: *em disla liklik diwai ya, em disla <u>roombuŋ</u> ya … i stap long baksait bilong kanu. I gat liklik graun ol i putim long en nau na disla liklik diwai i godaun long disla hap graun na i stap. Long kanu.*

A.: *Insait long kanu?*

M.: *Insait long kanu.*

A.: *Insait long kanu … wanpela … diwai i gro?*

M.: *Yes. Em gro insait long kanu. Nau em i …*

K.: *em i <u>roombuŋ niŋ</u>* [the bottom of the <u>roombuŋ</u> tree].

A.: *Ya.*

M.: <u>*Roombuŋ*</u> *diwai ya. Na em i askim disla yangpela meri:*

K.: *"Ol i mekim wanem?"*

M.: *"Ol i mekim wanem na krai? Wanpela man dai?" "Nogat, pasin bilong mipela! Nau mipela laik brukim bel bilong en na kisim pikinini na ol i bung krai na stap. "Oh? Na inap bai mi go antap lukim?" Em tok: "Ya, i nogat tambu!" Oke, em i laik kirap nau, skin bilong em guria. Trangu, em i lukim em olsem na em holim han bilong em. Em tok: "Ee ee ee! Disla han bilong mi pen ya, yu no ken holim mi strong. Yu yangpela ya!" Em tok: "Oh, sori tru, sori tru." Em holim em isi i go antap, sanap long graun nau, em tok: "Pasim gut kanu nogut bilong mi, nogut bai tait kisim na i go. Em tok: "Oke, yu sidaun pastaim." Em pasim kanu pinis, rop bilong kanu pinis. Em go antap holim em, kirapim em, kisim rabis umben—a—bilum bilong em. Em yet karim nau na holim em nau na go. Ol manki ron i go pastaim, ol kirap lukim em na tok: "Ey! Bilong wanem yu holim samting nogut bilong yu kam long mipela?" Em tok: "Tsss, yupela pasim maus na lukluk tasol long mi!" Nau em tok: "Olgeta manmeri ol bung i stap." Em tokim em, tok: "Mi no inap go antap long leta, em longpela haus tumas." "Bai mi holim yu go antap o nogat bai mi karim yu go antap." Nau, em i holim em isi isi tasol i go antap, sidaunim long blok, na em i muv long as bilong em i go na em i lukluk long meri ya. Em i lukluk pinis. Em tanim bek na askim disla yangpela meri: "Haus bilong husait?" Nau meri ya tokim em: "Haus bilong man bilong en." "Ah? Yu holim mi na go insait klostu long meri ya." Nau, em i kisim … disla lapun meri Nzari ya i go insait na ol kirap tok: "Tsss, mipela krai long man ya, yu no ken kisim samting nogut bilong yu kam klostu long mipela!" Na em kirap nau na tokim ol, tok: "Tsss, pasim maus na lukluk tasol! Samting bilong mi, em bai mi wokim wok bilong em." Em i go sidaun klostu na lukluk pinis long kain join olsem ya* [M. shows me the ties in the floor of a house] *na em tokim em: "I gat tamiok i stap?" Em i tok: "I gat tamiok bilong man i stap go kisim i kam!" Em i go daun kisim tamiok i kam na em go i muv sidaun longwe liklik na em tok: "Katim of disla ol limbum." Nau em katim of disla limbum pinis. Ol kirap tok: "Ey, bilong wanem ol i bagarapim haus?" Na yangpela meri ya tokim ol, tok: "Pasim maus! Lukluk tasol!" Nau, i kam joinim gen em lukim em i stap olsem bifo yet. Nau em i askim em, em tok: "I gat sampela mambu long hia i stap?" Em tok: "Man bilong em i gat ol mambu bilong em i stap." "Oke, yu tokim sampela ol yangpela long katim sampela na i kam wantaim wanpela sotpela stik." Kam nau, na ol i wokim banis insait long disla ... andanit long haus nau. Em tok: "Hariap long wokim!" Na ol i wokim banis pinis.*

K.: *Hul ...*

M.: *Nau, ol ... ol wokim liklik hul nau bilong bebi i godaun long en. Olsem pasin kastam bilong mipela. Nau em i olsem yet i stap i stap. Nau i stap yet. Sampela i go long klinik ....*

A.: *Na sampela i go long haus karim?*

M.: *Em. Em bai wokim long disla kain we.*

A.: *Oke.*

M.: *Em nau, redim pinis na bringim wara, pulimapim long mambu na i kam putim pinis. Em tokim em: "Yu go na yu lukim wanpela liklik diwai i stap baksait long kanu bilong mi, long hap graun ya. Kisim tupela lip tasol. No ken brukim. Nau, na em tok: "Mi no save long disla diwai." "Yu go kisim na liklik tasol na yu smelim. Em i gat smel bilong em." Oke, meri ya ron i go na lukim disla liklik diwai ya i stap. Tupela lip em kisim nau na em smelim, em tok: "Em tasol." Na kisim i go antap, nau em i tokim em: "Yu go benim long paia." Em benim long paia pinis i kam nau na ...*

K.: *em mekim singsing ...*

M.: *em givim long lapun meri ya, Nzari, i no lapun, yangpela meri em tanim em yet na i stap olsem. Em mekim hap singsing pinis na winim long disla lip pinis. Em tokim em: "Yu go na rapim bel bilong em na baksait bilong em, disla olgeta hap bilong bodi bilong en." Pinis nau, em tokim disla liklik meri: "Yu i stap klostu wantaim mitupela." Em tokim ol man: "Olgeta, go long haus bilong yupela!" Na meri ya kirap na ... yangpela meri ya i tokim ol: "Yupela olgeta man klia long disla haus!" "Bilong wanem? Mipela i laik ...*

K.: *krai olgeta*

M.: *krai long meri ya wantaim man bilong em." Na em i tokim yanpela meri: "Yu go tokim man bilong em olsem: namel pos ya em i mak bilong yu, yu no ken kam long disla sait. Yu i stap long sait bilong yu tasol!" Na yu tu, yu go autsait. Yu no ken stap insait long haus!" Nau ... em nau ... em i ... em i tokim meri ya nau, yangpela meri ya: "Holim mi godaun pas. Long ... insait long banis ya, oke, na tokim meri ya i kamdaun, meri ya karim pikinini." Olgeta i gat kros nau na ol i go nabaut long ol haus bilong ol. Meri ya godaun long andanit long haus nau. I stap liklik, em i kisim bebi nau. Bebi i kamap pinis. Em bebi krai nau na, em tokim yangpela meri ya: "Kapsaitim kwik wara na wasim em na katim hap bel bilong em na putim hap bel i godaun long disla hul na graunim wantaim disla hap mambu em i katim bel bilong em." Nau, bebi i krai nau, man bilong en harim, tok: "Ey! Wanpela bebi i krai ya!" Nau ol tok:"Meri ya em i karim bebi pinis." Na man bilong en i laik ron i kam. Em tokim em, tok: "Yu stap … namel long disla pos ya inap, na yu go bek! No ken kam insait hia!"*

K.: *As bilong kol ya.*

M.: *Em nau. I go nau. Na man bilong en i no amamas. Em laik lukim bebi wantaim mama bilong em. Yu save bikpela laik bilong em i go lus nating. Em i go long hap bilong em i stap nau na olgeta man ron i kam lukim! Ol i tingim meri bilong ol i wok long krai. Wanpela tu bai sidaun olsem wantaim pikinini bilong em bai krai na i stap. Na ol i … disla yangpela meri i kirap na tokim ol, tok: "Lukim, yupela wok long rausim mitupela, rausim em na nau senis i kamap. Na bai mipela stap amamas nau. Na man ya, man bilong disla meri ya, em i amamas nogu tru, bilong wanem meri bilong em i no lusim laif! Em i stap! I stap i go go go go, pikinini ya i wok long lukim mama na … mipela save sutim nus bilong em long neil nau na tupela iau tu. Wokim disla ol samting pinis, bilasim em long lip tanget na i stap. Ol sua i drai pinis, nau em man i wokim hotwara nau. Nzari tokim em, tokim disla yangpela meri ya: "Kisim disla hatwara nau na givim man bilong em na yu boilim na givim em nau na em bai kapsaitim kam insait long hap bilong meri." Na meri tu bai kapsaitim bilong en i go long man. Na tupela senis nau na em fri nau. Nau tupela wokabaut long go i kam go i kam.*

K.: *kol i pinis nau.*

M.: *Em kol i pinis nau. Nau em i stap pikinini bikpela pinis, ol i bilasim em long bilas tru tru nau, putim ol paspas bilong em, bilasim tupela paspas long lek. Nau, i stap nau meri i laik go long bus nau bai wokim festaim bilong em long wokim saksak na em bai waswas long wara bilong saksak. Nzari tok: "Oh mi laik go bek nau." Na man bilong disla meri i tokim em, em tok: "No! Yu mekim gutpela samting tru na mipela bai amamasim yu pastaim, mi bai redim olgeta samting bilong yu na bai yu go." Na meri ya, Nzari ya, em i wok long traim traim ol, nogat. Nau em i stap. Man bilong em i wok saksak pinis, em i … festaim em i katim kanu, sapim kanu pinis, sapim pul bilong em pinis, sapim ol plet bilong em pinis. Nau, putim daun kanu long wara na em tok: "Yu no ken hariap, mi redim ol samting bilong yu pastaim, kisim sampela gaden kaikai i kam, kilim pik i kam, ol i sidaun wantaim em, amamas wantaim em pinis. Moning nau, bringim olgeta samting long kanu bilong em. Em meri ya, Nzari ya kirap tok: "Ah, kanu nogut bilong mi i stap, maski, em nogut pinis." Em kanu ya i no nogut! Em senisim ya! Nau em godaun long disla nupela kanu nau. Pinis, ol i sekanim em pinis, em tekof i go nau. Em go bek gen long disla hap em i kam long en.*

K.: [In the local vernacular, K. points out a mistake in the narrative sequence of events]

M.: *Em mitupela abrusim pinis!* [M. says that to K.] *Em i no bungim Kaamndoŋ yet. Em rong pinis nau! Em mitupela kalapim nau na mekim stori i go namel pinis.*

Ŋ.: *Wanpela pat bilong stori ol i no bin … toktok …*

M.: *i no stori.*

A.: *Bai mi stopim pastaim o?*

M.: *Yes.*

Ŋ.: *Stopim pastaim!*

A.: *Mi statim gen.* [I have stopped the recorder for a few minutes and now we continue].

M.: *Yes.*

A.: *Oke, nau yu tokim mi gen … wantaim Kaamndoŋ …*

M.: *Em lusim Soŋe nau na em pul i kam na em lukim Kaamndoŋ. Kaamndoŋ i wok long sidaun long han bilong diwai na sapos pis i kam nau na mekim nois long wara na i laik godaun bek, em kalap i godaun, save holim long han bilong em i go antap, putim long san. Olgeta san em save wok long disla na i stap i stap. Nait san! Em i nogat ples bilong slip, em ples we em i stap long em long han bilong disla diwai mangro ya … em tasol em i stap long en. Na Nzari pul i go go na em lukim em.*

K.: *Wanpela man i stap.*

M.: *Wanpela man ya i sidaun long han bilong mangro na i stap. Nau em i go. Taim em kalap i go daun long wara na go longtaim em i go antap pinis long … antap long het bilong mangro. Em kisim ol liklik liklik ston na i go antap sidaun. Na em laik traim trikim Kaamndoŋ nau! … Em sidaun i stap na Kaamndoŋ i godaun, holim pis i kam antap, putim long san nau, i go sidaun gen long sem hap ples em i sidaun long em. Nau em i lukluk i stap. Ai bilong en bai no inap lukluk nabaut. Em bai lukluk stret long wara na i stap. Pis i kam nau na paitim tel bilong em antap long wara, i laik godaun, Kaamndoŋ tu i kalap i go antap long en. Em save wok olsem. Nau em i kalap i godaun, Nzari bai troim wanpela ston i go daun paitim em. "Ee ee eee!! Wanem samting paitim het bilong mi ya? Bifo mi no save mekim olsem nau na kisim ol pis. Em nau tasol disla kain pasin i kamap!" Em Nzari sidaun lukluk long em i stap. Em nau, em disla san em mekim olsem tasol i go … klostu i laik belo nau … olsem twelf oklok, nau em i luksave long sedo bilong en i kamap long wara ya … long san i sutim em nau na … em i lukim nau na lukluk i go antap: "Ey! Yu wanem meri ya? Bilong wanem yu kam na i stap long antap nau na yu bagarapim gutpela wok bilong mi ya? Kamdaun! Kamdaun hariap!" Nau, em Nzari i godaun nau. Godaun nau na … olsem … bai mi tok wanem? Em holim em nating nau! Na … lovim em nabaut! Em tok: "Ey, yu klia! Yu nogat disla ol kain samting ya! Yu wanem kain man ya?" Na em askim em: "Na yu stap yet na mekim wanem?" "Em ya, mi kisim ol pis!" "Na paia we?" "Ey, wanem samting yu kolim? Nogut mi dai? Mi no save long disla samting!" "Na yu save kukim pis long wanem paia na kaikai?" "Em ya, mi smukim long san tasol na mi save kaikai." Em tok: "Em i no stret!" Em i no tokim em. Nau em tokim em: "Yu go antap sidaun long han bilong mangro!" Nau, em i go antap sidaun long han bilong mangro nau, em putim wanem ya bilong en i go antap long ples bilong pekpek i kamap. Pekpek ya i sut nating, simel nogut tru!! "Ey!" Kaamndoŋ kisim win nau na kalap i godaun na em tok: "Oh sori! Tenkyu tru! Nau mi kisim bikpela win tru nau!" "Ah!" Em holim pasim Nzari na kis long em! Na em tok: "Tsss, yu klia! Skin bilong yu i smel nogut tru! I no olsem smel bilong man!" Em tok: "Ah! Bilong wanem yu mekim mi disla kain?" Em tok. Nau ...*

Ŋ.: *Em wok long ...*

M.: *Nau em i tokim em, tok: "Yu go antap sidaun antap long bed ya i stap." Nau, Nzari tu i go antap sidaun, sidaun nau em bai mekim paia pundaun long ... klostu long na i lait long Kaamndoŋ nau. Nau, tupela i go antap sidaun long bed nau na ...*

Ŋ.: *olgeta ...*

M.: *kisim disla stik bilong sel kambang bilong em long kaikai buai em troimoim em godaun. "Ah! Kaamndoŋ! Mi ... samting ya stik bilong kaikai buai ya kisim kambang ya i pundaun pinis yu godaun na kisim!" Em tok: "Eh! Wanem samting yu kolim nem bilong em? Nogut mi kisim na bai mi dai!" Em tok: "Yu godaun na kisim! Nogat samting bai mekim yu na yu dai!" Nau em i godaun. Em i godaun ya, Nzari go sidaun long kain hul olsem nau na paia pundaun i godaun. Em kirap ronowe nauuu! Kaamndoŋ i no laik go insait nau na lukim em. Em tok: "Yu noken ronowe! Em paia ya yu kisim!" "Em bai mi kisim olsem wanem?" "Kisim, brukim wanpela hap mambu nau na brukim olsem sisis na holim long em na kam autsait na mekim bikpela paia." Nau, Nzari godaun mekim paia pinis, putim pot long paia, kisim ol pulpul, diwai, smel nabaut ya, boilim pinis, i laik wasim Kaamndoŋ nau!*

K.: [I do not understand what K. says since his voice is too low]

M.: *Na disla diwai <u>roombuŋ</u> tu em i kisim, putim i godaun wasim pinis, eh ... boil pinis nau em kisim em na wasim em nau. Kisim hatwara na wasim Kaamndoŋ pinis. Nau, em i go long bus kisim disla plaua bilong kapiak, narapela kapiak i no-gat nil long en. Na wantaim tupela pikinini bilong wanpela wel plaua. Bus bilong mi i gat planti i stap! Kisim tupela tasol. I kam nau na traim fiksim pispis bilong Kaamndoŋ nau. Fiksim pispis bilong Kaamndoŋ pinis na em i kamap pispis bilong ol man nau! Na em tokim Kaamndoŋ: "Em ya, yu man nau!" Bifo yu no man, yu olsem wanpela hap diwai nating!" Na em nau, em pispis ya em bilong man! Na tupela i gat wanpela dok mama ... meri stap. Em Nzari yet holim na i go. Em i stap insait long bel bilong em na i go autsait. Kakaruk, dok, paia, ol kaikain bilas ... bilong tumbuna. Nau, em nau tupela i go long bus! Na em i laik teistim! Tupela i go long bus nau, em tokim Kaamndoŋ ... wanpela tok sem tu ya ... olsem stori na mi toktok nau ...*

K.: *Em i orait ...*

M.: *Nau, tupela i go long bus nau na Nzari tokim, tok: "Yu traim!" Na em i teistim nau … Kaamndoŋ teistim nau na i tok: "Eeyy! Swit moa! Nais olgeta!" Em tok …*

K.: *na dokmama tu i slip lukim …*

M.: *Em tok: "Man ya! Em man! Em wok bilong man ya! Nau yu kamap olsem man nau!" "Oh Nzari, em gutpela samting tru!" Bifo em mi no save long disla, pasin bilong pren." Em i no save!*

A.: *Ah! Nogat?*

M.: *Nogat tru! Nogat, em i nogat disla save long em! Na dokmeri bilong tupela tu, slip arere long tupela na lukluk i stap. Disla taim, ol dok i save tokples wantaim ol man.*

A.: *Ya …*

M.: *Nau em tupela i kambek long ples nau. Kaamndoŋ i go waswas pinis kam sidaun long bed i stap. Na ol lang na ol natnat i kam mekim bodi bilong em nau, em i wok long rausim … han … rausim long han nau na em i lukluk nabaut nau. "Ey, Nzari! Brum bilong mi i stap we?" Nzari tok: "Mi no save! Na yu putim we?" Tupela wok long toktok nau, dok i kirap na tokim tupela: "Ples … yutupela … ples yutupela i stap long em ya … yu lusim antap long disla ol lip … limbum ya yutupela wokim bed nau na slip antap long em ya. Yutupela lusim long disla hap, brum bilong yu i stap long disla hap."*

K.: *Tupela sem …*

M.: *Tupela sem nau! Em tok: "Ah! Nzari! Yu harim disla tok ya, dok i mekim ya. Brukim tok bilong mitupela pinis, planti manmeri bai harim nau." Na Nzari tok: "Wet, bai mitupela katim tang bilong em."*

A.: *Ah, oke.*

M.: *Nau em i tanim saksak pinis, ol i kaikai nau, ol i kaikai pinis, putim bilong dok nau, i godaun, em i brukim hap mambu nau, sapim gut pinis, i go nau na dok i laik kaikai saksak nau, subim tang bilong em i kam autsait nau, Nzari holim pasim tang bilong em nau na katim of. Na dok i kirap nau na singaut olsem i go:*

K.: *"Auauau …*

M.: *"Auauauauauauauau" em i no moa toktok nau.*

A.: *Oke …*

M.: *Tang bilong em i go sot pinis.*

Ŋ.: *Faulim tokples pinis.*

A.: *Oke.*

M.: *Nogut em bai … bihain gen, bai nekstaim tupela wokim olsem bai dok brukim tok gen.*

A.: *Ya.*

M.: *Olsem nau na em katim of. Nau em nau, tupela stap amamas tasol. Nzari sapim ol supsup bilong em long sutim ol pis, wokim pul. Kanu Nzari go long em, em wok long yusim. Olgeta taim, Kaamndoŋ save … moning, apinun … save sutim pis.*

Ŋ.: *painim ol pis*

M.: *painim pis i go i kam, tupela wok long kaikai stap, Kaamndoŋ amamas! "Bifo mi no man olsem na nau mi kamap man tru nau!" I stap. Nau, Nzari kisim tupela mambu na go pulimapim wara.*

K.: *Kisim basket … mambu*

M.: *mambu olsem baket nau. Nau, em i … tupela meri i stap namel—tupela sin meri!*

A.: *Ya …*

M.: *Tupela meri nogut tru!*

A.: *Ya?*

M.: *Tupela i stap namel na tupela godaun long wara nau na pilai pilai long wara i kam kam na lukim Nzari na Nzari pasim traipela nupela pulpul nau na i go pulimapim wara. Na tupela tromoi wara long em … long Nzari, na Nzari tok: "Ey, Kaamndoŋ! Disla ol pis ya i kam nau na pilai pilai ya, na lukim pulpul bilong mi ya wara wara pinis." Kaamndoŋ kirap! Ron i go long basis, kisim tupela supsup bilong em wantaim pul i godaun long kanu. Sutsut long disla ol pis i go nau. I go i go … Nzari go antap, sanap antap na lukluk na tokim em: "Kaamndoŋ! Maski na kambek!" Em tok: "Nogat! Gutpela supsup bilong mi ya! Disla meri ya i giaman long sutim skin bilong em. Em holim long han bilong em na pulim pulim supsup bilong em i go. Na Kaamndoŋ bihainim supsup tasol na pul i go i laik kisim bek supsup bilong em. Na Nzari em i save, em i singautim em: "Maski, lusim na kambek! Bai mitupela sapim narapela!" Na Kaamndoŋ tok: "Nogat, disla supsup ya mi save … save gut tru long holim em na sut yet. I no save popaia! Mi sutim wanpela pis nau na em pulim pulim i go na bihainim em ya. "Maski! Lusim na kam!" Nogat. Kaamndoŋ sakim tok bilong em! I go brukim poin nau, i godaun long narapela sait nau, i go stret long basis bilong tupela meri nau, tupela kirap tasol, apim kanu wantaim Kaamndoŋ insait long haus bilong tupela. Na Kaamndoŋ bai mekim wanem? Nzari wet wet wet i go tudak, tok: "Oh, Kaamndoŋ go pinis." Nau, em wanpela i stap, wetim Kaamndoŋ. Em i go antap tasol, tupela meri ya holim holim em pinis. I stap. Disla pispis bilong em, tupela wok long pilai pilai long em. Olgeta man long disla hap ol i pret long disla tupela meri na ol i ranawe nabaut na i stap long ol busples. Nau, Kaamndoŋ i mekim em i go solap olgeta. Na em i les tru, em i filim olsem: "Bai mi dai." Na em kirap na tokim tupela … disla tupela meri ya, Min wantaim Ngoar, ah?*

K.: *Mindu … Ngoirpak.*

M.: *Mindu … Mindu wantaim Ngoirpak.*

A.: *Ŋgoirpak?*

M.: *Ŋgoirpak! Nau, em tokim tupela: "Yutupela lusim mi liklik! Ol wok long kai-*
kaim mit bilong pik na mipela bai olsem wanem? Bai i stap olsem tasol?" Tok:
"Oke." Nau em tupela tokim em: "Taim yu laik kisim ol dok i go, i noken go insait
long bikbus. Bihainim tasol ol bus, ol yangpela bus long gaden, i go go na kambek.
I noken i stap longpela taim. … Nau em, man ya go insait em bai wokabaut long
laik bilong ol. Raun malolo na i go. I go go go go kambek na em i pilim pispis, em
bai tokim tupela: "Lusim mi na mi laik go pispis!" Tok: "Sindaun tasol hia na pis-
pis i go!" Mekim em olsem, kalabusim em gut tru i stap i stap. Wanpela de nau, em
i kisim ol dok na i go long bus. I go na harim pairap bilong wanpela man em wok
long sapim kanu i stap. Wanpela ŋgaape *mot* [male tree-spirit].

K.: *dewel*

M.: *dewel man. Nau em i bihainim i go. I go kamap long em na tok: "Eh!" Disla*
dewel man ya i tokim em, tok: "Yu kam olsem wanem?" "Eh … yu noken tok, lu-
kim." Em i wokabaut olsem lek bilong i no inap go pas long pispis bilong em, solap
olgeta. "Yu lukim, mi bagarap pinis." "Lukim! Olsem wanem na mipela olgeta i
pret long em na … tupela nau na olsem na mipela ronewe nabaut i stap long bus
nabaut. Tupela i no gutpela meri." Nau em tok: "Bai mi halvim yu! Kanu ya mi
sapim ya bai mi halvim yu. Bai mi redim olgeta samting bilong yu. Em bai yu lusim
tupela nau na bai yu go." Nau em i go kilim tupela pik bai lusim wanpela long disla
ŋgaape mot *nau. Oke wanpela em bai karim i go long tupela meri ya." Wanpela bai*
kukim pik, wanpela bai holim pasim em na i stap. Oke, meri ya kukim pik pinis bai
lusim i kam antap holim i stap. Bai narapela i go wasim pik. Em man ya nogat wok,
wok bilong em ya em sidaun tasol na tupela i wok long holim holim sem bilong em
i stap. Olsem tasol i go, katim pik pinis, wanpela holim i stap, wanpela bai kuk.
Kambek, narapela i holim i stap, narapela bai go na skelim kaikai. Olsem tasol,
kaikai i pinis i go insait long … taim bilong slip, bai tupela wantaim holim pas na i
stap tulait. Kaamndoŋ i mekim les pinis. Em nau, em i … olgeta moning em save go
long bus i go lukluk long luksave long wok ya man i mekim. Na man ya tu i hariap
long katim kanu. Pinis, em kukim pinis, sidaunim tasol i stap, em redim ol supsup
nau, supsup bilong sutim dispela tupela meri. Pinis, wokim ol paspas long ol sup-
sup pinis, nau em i redim ol pent, blakpela pent, retpela pent, waitpela pent olsem
kambang, karamapim planti bilong ol. Redim bilong Kaamndoŋ nau. Oke, kara-
mapim ol binatang nabaut ya, ol binen na, wanem kain kain binen, ah, binatang

K.: *kurakum*

M.: *kurakum na disla ol kain samting. Karamapim pinis, olgeta i kam putim insait*
long kanu. Ol supsup tu, em putim insait long kanu.

K.: *Ol stik …*

M.: *Na ol pul tu. Hamaspela pul, em pul long wanpela … i bruk, em bai kisim*
narapela gen. Olsem na, em redim planti. Na man ya, em i givim pe bilong kanu

olsem ol pik em save kilim, em save kam lusim long em. Oke, na dispela dewel man tu i gat bikpela amamas long Kaamndoŋ. Na halvim em.

K.: *Sampela hap ...*

M.: *sampela hap diwai em i katim, putim i go insait long kanu bilong em i kisim na sutim dispela tupela meri. Tupela salim pisin na em kam, em bai kisim dispela on na sut! Pinis, olgeta samting i setim pinis, narapela de em tokim em: "Nau yu go na yu redim wanpela banana na i stap. Long nait, mi laikim bai tumoro yet bai yu go." Em tok: "Yes, mi gat laik olsem!" Kisim wanpela hap rop, redim bilong pasim ...*

Ŋ.: *dua*

M.: *dua ... na long maus bilong basket bilong slip. Yu klinim gut. Redi. Olgeta samting i redi. Banana tu redi. Katim na olsem makim yu yet nau na bai putim i go insait namel long tupela na tupela ting em man ya i slip na holim pasim banana na i slip i stap. Man ya kam autsait tasol, samapim maus bilong basket ya pinis, i go pasim strong dua pinis—tekof! I go. Dispela dewel man i halvim em subim kanu bilong em i go daun long wara. Kaamndoŋ tekof nau! Pul i go go go go go em lusim longpela hap pinis. Nau, emtupela meri ... i tulait pinis, tupela kirap luksave, tok: "Eeeh! Man ya i go pinis. Mi yet ... mitupela holim pasim banana na i slip ya." Tupela i kirap nau na godaun long wara tanim tupela pis nau na swim i go—nogat! Tupela go antap gen tanim long pisin. Olsem dispela balus pisin ya, tanim long dispela tupela balus pisin na flai i go lukim Kaamndoŋ. "Ah, mitupela i ting yu go pinis." Na Kaamndoŋ tok: "Kam. Mi go nau!" Tupela laik holim em. Em bai kirap, kisim dispela karamap, kambang o wanem kain sit bilong paia, bai sutim tupela nau bai ai bilong tupela i tudak nau na faul nau na godaun sanap long graun na rausim dispela samting i stap. Kaamndoŋ tekof gen. Mekim olsem tasol i go go go go, dispela ol samting i pinis. Ol binatang i pinis, em i stat long sutim long supsup nau. I go go go go go ... brukim dispela point nau na laspela point em lukim basis bilong em nau. Tupela sanap ya na i tok: "I orait, yu go. Planti taim bai mitupela lukim yu gen!" Kaamndoŋ pul tasol i go na Nzari em kisim olgeta samting bilong em putim insait long bel bilong em pinis, paia tasol em i larim bilong em, haus tasol em i larim bilong em. Oke, na ol narapela samting, em putim insait long bel bilong em pinis. Nau, em i go hait long basis na lukluk i stap. Kaamndoŋ i go tasol, putim kanu i go antap, ron i go na tok: "Ah!! Nzari!! Nzari!! Yu stap we?" Nzari kamap isi tasol, kisim kanu bilong em i go sidaun autsait long ... namel long wara holim het bilong diwai na lukluk i stap. Kaamndoŋ i go painim long haus—no-gat—tanim bek gen. Tanim bek ron i kam em lukim Nzari em sidaun long kanu i stap. "Ey, Nzari yu kam insait! Mi kam pinis." "Ah? Kaamndoŋ—sori tru! Yu no save kukim long paia na kaikai, yu no save boilim long hatwara na kaikai. Yu save putim long san na smukim long san na yu kaikai. Yu nogat we bilong pispis, yu nogat we bilong pekpek. Mi ... mi mekim dispela ol samting i kamap na yu kamap olsem man! Nau yu man, bifo yu piksa bilong ol man! Trangu, i stap. Haus bilong yu, paia bilong yu em i stap. Mi go nau!" Em tok: "Ah Nzari!! Maski!! Kambek!"*

Em tok: "No! Tenkyu!" Em nau, em go! Pastaim mipela go long en ya, stori pinis ya, em go nau long dispela nau.

A.: *Ah, oke, oke.*

K.: *Olsem ...*

M.: *Oke, Em bai kambek gen.*

A.: *Oke.*

M.: *Em, em nau. Inap olsem nau na mi go long ples we ol i brukim ol meri na kisim. Na ol i amamasim wantaim em pinis, na em kambek nau. Em kamap olsem wankain gen. Em i kam long wanpela basis, bai yangpela tru. Abrusim dispela basis i go long narapela basis gen, bai traipela yangpela man. Putim* kaut, *paspas, putim nupela malo, kaikai buai, smel bilong em bai olsem narapela ... wanem kain samting. Ol smelim tok: "Ey, yangpela yangpela man i go!" Ol wok long sapim ol kanu long basis na i save lukluk. I go go nau i kamap long tupela brata. Nau, tupela ... tupela wok long banis ... ol i wok insait long wara, na insait blokim ol pis insait long dispela banis nau na taim draiwara nau, tupela bai godaun na kisim. Tupela wok olsem i stap nau na Nzari ya em tanim em yet na lapun nogut tru! I go stret long basis bilong tupela. Na bikpela bilong en i lukim em na i tok: "Ehhh! Lukim dispela samting nogut ya! Bilong wanem em i kam insait long hia?" Na liklik brata i lukim em tok: "I orait, trangu, mi hatwok long kukim kaikai ya, bai mi holim bilong mi na i go antap na em bai kukim kaikai bilong mi. Ol moning mi save hat tru long kuk, mi hangre mi wok long kuk." "Ah? Larim dispela rabis samting nogut em i go!" Em tok: "No no no! Mi no inap harim tok bilong yu." Liklik brata i godaun holim em, kisim ol samting bilong em. Bilum bilong em tu bruk bruk nabaut. Kanu bilong em tu nogut. Em senisim olgeta samting! Nau, em i kirap tok: "Mmh! Smel bilong dispela lapun meri i nogut tru ya! Bilong wanem yu holim na em kam antap? Mi no amamas tru." I tok: "I orait. Hap bilong yu, yu wanpela i stap na long hapsait bilong mi em bai mi stap wantaim em." Na em holim em i go long hapsait bilong em nau, kisim em i go antap sidaunim em long haus. Na ... em i sori tru long em! Em tok: "Sapos yu hangre, oke yu ken brukim paiawud i kam antap putim, kisim wara i kam putim. "Mi no inap long kisim wara, yu lukim mi lapun nogut tru," em tok. Man ya tok: "Sori tru, olgeta bikpela wok bai mi mekim, yu ken lukautim samting insait long paia tasol. Samting hevi, bai mi halvim yu." Nau, tupela i stap na bikbrata bilong en tokim em: "Wanem kaikai yutupela kuk nau na kaikai i noken tingim mi. Mi no laikim kain ol kaikai nogut olsem han nogut i wok na kuk." Na em tok: "I orait. Yu yet yu kuk na kaikai. Mi bai wantaim lapun meri nogut bilong mi, bai mitupela yet kuk na kaikai." Na em i no wari moa. Em tok: "Bai mi wari long wanem? Lapun meri ya i stap long haus ya. Em yet kuk bai mi kaikai na yu ... yu yet yu hat wok long kuk."*

K.: *Ai pekpek i pudaun*

M.: *Planti ai pekpek bilong em ... olsem kus tu pulap. I stap nau i go go go go go nau tupela wok long sapim kanu nau. Liklik brata tu katim bilong en. Na bik brata tu em i katim bilong en. Tupela wok long sapim kanu i stap nau, na em tokim man bilong em: "Yu redim ol samting bilong mi pinis na yu lusim nau na yu go wok long kanu. "Em tok: "Yes, bai mi mekim." Olgeta samting em redim pinis. Nau em tok: "Mi laik go nau." Tok: "Oke, yu halvim mi na putim pot long paia pastaim." Em las wok bilong em nau! Nau em i ... man bilong em i go antap redim olgeta samting, putim pot long paia pinis, kisim wara putim insait long pot pinis na em tokim em: "Taim yu laik rausim pot long paia, singaut! Bai mi harim, mi kam bai mi rausim pot na putim nau na bai tanim saksak pinis, lusim, na bai mi go." Em tok: "Yes!" Tasol em i no mekim! Man ya i go i stap nau wok long kanu i stap, Nzari wan tu pinisim dispela olgeta samting, senisim em yet pinis, em kamap yangpela tru olsem em i nogat pikinini—em yangpela meri stret! Nau em bilasim em yet nau. Bilasim em yet pinis, kaikai buai pinis, nau em kisim saksak bilong man bilong em, putim long het bilong em, em tait i go nau! Nupela pulpul na yangpela meri tru! Smel longtaim i go pinis! Na tupela wantaim smelim nau na i laik tanim lukim, em Nzari em wokabaut i kam! Man ya em kirap ron i go holim pasim meri bilong em na tok ... brata bilong em, bik brata bilong em i tok: "Ah! No! Yu liklik manki nating, em meri bilong mi!" Em tok: "No! Longtaim yu no laikim em na mi yet kisim em i go antap nau na ... na em meri bilong mi!" Tupela wok long pait long toktok i go nau na holim hap hap, pulim nau! Na Nzari kirap tok: "Eh! Lusim mi! Mi laik go putim saksak pastaim." Nogat, saksak i stap yet long het bilong em yet nau na tupela wok long pulim pulim nau ...*

K.: *ŋ̯ianxaam mbaŋa* [this side] *pulim pulim ...*

M.: *Pulim pulim na em i bruk namel!*

A.: *Nzari i bruk?*

M.: *Aa! Nzari bruk namel nau. Wanpela kisim hap bilong het wanpela kisim hap bilong as! Na em pinis bilong Nzari nau.*

A.: *Oke, em pinis.*

M.: *Em pinis nau.*

A.: *Na nem bilong tupela brata?*

M.: *Em ... nem bilong tupela i no kamap.*

A.: *I no kamap ... oke ...*

M.: *Yes.*

A.: *Orait, mi stopim.*

References

Aisa, Joseph A. 1971/72. *Patrol Report Bogia No.13 of 1971/72 (Situation Report)*. Sub-District Office, Bogia, Madang District. Port Moresby: National Archives.

Alexeyeff, Kalissa. 2004. "Love Food. Exchange and Sustenance in the Cook Islands Diaspora." *The Australian Journal of Anthropology,* Special Issue 15 (1): 68–79.

Alexeyeff, Kalissa, Roberta James, and Mandy Thomas, eds. 2004. "Taste This! An Anthropological Examination of Food." *The Australian Journal of Anthropology,* Special Issue 15 (1).

Anderson, Astrid. 2003. "Landscapes of Sociality. Paths, Places and Belonging on Wogeo Island, Papua New Guinea." In *Oceanic Socialities and Cultural Forms. Ethnographies of Experience,* ed. Ingjerd Hoëm and Sidsel Roalkvam. New York and Oxford: Berghahn Books, pp. 51–70.

———. 2011. *Landscapes of Relations and Belonging. Body, Place and Politics in Wogeo, Papua New Guinea.* New York and Oxford: Berghahn Books (Person, Space and Memory in the Contemporary Pacific, Volume 3).

Anonymous. 1885. "Aus den Berichten des Dr. Finsch über die im Auftrage der Compagnie nach Neu Guinea ausgeführten Reisen." *Nachrichten über Kaiser Wilhelms-Land und den Bismarck-Archipel* 4: 3–19.

———. 1887. "Aus dem Schutzgebiet." *Nachrichten über Kaiser Wilhelms-Land und den Bismarck-Archipel* 2: 32–71.

———. 1896. "Ergebnisse der Kaiser Wilhelmsland Expedition." *Nachrichten über Kaiser Wilhelms-Land und den Bismarck-Archipel*: 36–53.

———. 1897. "Ramu-Expedition." *Nachrichten über Kaiser Wilhelms-Land und den Bismarck-Archipel*: 52–55.

———. 1898. "Die Ramu-Expedition." *Nachrichten über Kaiser Wilhelms-Land und den Bismarck-Archipel*: 51–59.

———. 1899. "Deutsch-Neu-Guinea. Ein unbekannter Weißer." *Deutsches Kolonialblatt* 10: 565.

Bamford, Sandra, ed. 1998. "Identity, Nature and Culture. Sociality and Environment in Melanesia." *Social Analysis,* Special Issue 42 (3).

———. 2007. *Biology Unmoored. Melanesian Reflections on Life and Biotechnology.* Berkeley, Los Angeles and London: University of California Press.

———. 2009. "'Family Trees' among the Kamea of Papua New Guinea. A Non-genealogical Approach to Imagining Relatedness." In *Kinship and Beyond. The Genealogical Model Reconsidered,* ed. Sandra Bamford and James Leach. New York and Oxford: Berghahn Books, pp. 159–174.

Barber, Elizabeth W. and Paul T. Barber. 2004. *When They Severed Earth from Sky. How the Human Mind Shapes Myth.* New Jersey and Oxfordshire: Princeton University Press.

Barker, John. 2008. *Ancestral Lines. The Maisin of Papua New Guinea and the Fate of the Rainforest.* Peterborough et al.: Broadview Press.

Barlow, Kathleen. 1995. "Achieving Womanhood and the Achievements of Women in Murik Society. Cult Initiation, Gender Complementarity, and the Prestige of Women." In *Gender Rituals. Female Initiation in Melanesia,* ed. Nancy C. Lutkehaus and Paul B. Roscoe. New York and London: Routledge, pp. 85–112.

————. 2001. "Working Mothers and the Work of Culture in a Papua New Guinea Society." *Ethos* 29 (1): 78–107.

Barnett, Douglas, and Hilary Horn Ratner. 1997. "Introduction. The Organization and Integration of Cognition and Emotion in Development." *Journal of Experimental Child Psychology* 67: 303–316.

Bateson, Gregory. 1972. *Steps to an Ecology of Mind. Collected Essays in Anthropology, Psychiatry, Evolution and Epistemology.* San Francisco et al.: Chandler.

Battaglia, Debbora. 1990. *On the Bones of the Serpent. Person, Memory, and Mortality in Sabarl Island Society.* Chicago and London: University of Chicago Press.

Bell, Sandra, and Simon Coleman 1999. "The Anthropology of Friendship. Enduring Themes and Future Possibilities." In *The Anthropology of Friendship,* ed. Sandra Bell and Simon Coleman. Oxford and New York: Berg, pp. 1–19.

Bender, Barbara, ed. 1993. *Landscape. Politics and Perspectives.* Oxford: Berg.

————. 1996. "Landscape." In *Encyclopedia of Social and Cultural Anthropology,* ed. Alan Barnard and Jonathan Spencer. London and New York: Routledge, pp. 323–324.

Black, Peter W. 1985. "Ghosts, Gossip, and Suicide. Meaning and Action in Tobian Folk Psychology." In *Person, Self, and Experience. Exploring Pacific Ethnopsychologies,* ed. Geoffrey M. White and John Kirkpatrick. Berkeley, Los Angeles, and London: University of California Press, pp. 245–300.

Blackwood, Beatrice. 1950. "Reserve Dyeing in New Guinea." *Man* 50: 53–55.

————. 1951. "Some Arts and Industries of the Bosmun, Ramu River, New Guinea." In *Südseestudien. Gedenkschrift zur Erinnerung an Felix Speiser,* ed. Museum für Völkerkunde und Schweizerisches Museum für Volkskunde Basel. Basel: Museum für Völkerkunde, pp. 266–288.

Boskovic, R.M. 1996. *Madang Resource Atlas.* Madang: Planning and Co-ordination Branch, Department of Madang.

Braun, Max. 1916. "Die Gogol-Ramu-Expedition in Kaiser-Wilhelmsland. September und Oktober 1913. Bericht über die Ergebnisse der Landerkundung zwischen Gogol- und Ramu-Fluß in Deutsch-Neuguinea." *Mitteilungen aus den Deutschen Schutzgebieten* 29: 51–81.

Briggs, Jean L. 1970. *Never in Anger. Portrait of an Eskimo Family.* Cambridge, MA and London: Harvard University Press.

————. 2008. "Daughter and Pawn. One Ethnographer's Routes to Understanding of Children." *Ethos* 36 (4): 449–465.

Browne, R.C. 1968/69. *Patrol Report Bogia No.7 of 1968/69.* Sub-District Office, Bogia, Madang District. Port Moresby: National Archives.

Buchheimer, Arnold. 1963. "The Development of Ideas about Empathy." *Journal of Counseling Psychology* 10 (1): 61–70.

Cahill, J. 1949/50. *Patrol Report Angoram No.9 of 1949/50.* Ambunti Patrol Post, Angoram Sub-District, Sepik District. Port Moresby: National Archives.

Calderwood, B.R. 1970/71. *Patrol Report Bogia No.20 of 1970/71 (Situation Report).* Sub-District Office, Bogia, Madang District. Port Moresby: National Archives.

Capell, Arthur. 1951/52. "Languages of the Bogia District, New Guinea." *Oceania* 22: 130–147, 178–207, 317.

———. 1954. *Un Inventaire Linguistique du Pacifique Sud-Ouest.* Nouméa: Comission du Pacifique Sud (Document Technique No.70).

Carrier, James G. 1999. "People Who Can Be Friends. Selves and Social Relationships." In *The Anthropology of Friendship,* ed. Sandra Bell and Simon Coleman. Oxford and New York: Berg, pp. 21–38.

Carrithers, Michael, Steven Collins, and Steven Lukes, eds. 1985. *The Category of the Person. Anthropology, Philosophy, History.* Cambridge et al.: Cambridge University Press.

Carsten, Janet. 1997. *The Heat of the Hearth. The Process of Kinship in a Malay Fishing Community.* Oxford: Clarendon Press.

———. 2000. "Introduction. Cultures of Relatedness." In *Cultures of Relatedness. New Approaches to the Study of Kinship,* ed. Janet Carsten. Cambridge: Cambridge University Press, pp. 1–36.

———. 2004. *After Kinship.* Cambridge: Cambridge University Press.

Ciompi, Luc. 1997. *Die emotionalen Grundlagen des Denkens. Entwurf einer fraktalen Affektlogik.* Göttingen: Vandenhoeck and Ruprecht.

Colchester, Chloë, ed. 2003. *Clothing the Pacific.* Oxford and New York: Berg.

Counihan, Carole M. 1998. "Introduction—Food and Gender. Identity and Power." In *Food and Gender. Identity and Power,* ed. Carole M. Counihan and Steven L. Kaplan. New York and London: Routledge, pp. 1–10.

———. 1999. *The Anthropology of Food and Body. Gender, Meaning, and Power.* New York and London: Routledge.

Counihan, Carole M., and Penny van Esterik, eds. 1997. *Food and Culture. A Reader.* New York and London: Routledge.

Counihan, Carole M., and Steven L. Kaplan, eds. 1998. *Food and Gender. Identity and Power.* New York and London: Routledge.

Crapanzano, Vincent. 1986. "Hermes' Dilemma. The Masking of Subversion in Ethnographic Description." In *Writing Culture. The Poetics and Politics of Ethnography,* ed. James Clifford and George E. Marcus. Berkeley, Los Angeles and London: University of California Press, pp. 51–76.

Crocombe, Ron. 2001. *The South Pacific.* Suva, Fiji: University of the South Pacific.

Csordas, Thomas J. 1990. "Embodiment as a Paradigm for Anthropology." *Ethos* 18 (1): 5–47.

———. 1994a. "Introduction. The Body as Representation and Being-In-The-World." In *Embodiment and Experience. The Existential Ground of Culture and Self,* ed. Thomas J. Csordas. Cambridge: Cambridge University Press, pp. 1–24.

———. 1994b. "Self and Person." In *Handbook of Psychological Anthropology,* ed. Philip K. Bock. Westport, Connecticut, London: Greenwood Press, pp. 331–350.

Dalton, Doug. 2007. "When is it Moral to be a Sorcerer?" In *The Anthropology of Morality in Melanesia and Beyond,* ed. John Barker. Hampshire and Burlington: Ashgate, pp. 39–55.

Damasio, Antonio R. 1994. *Descartes' Error. Emotion, Reason, and the Human Brain.* New York: Grosset / Putnam.

Douglas, Mary. 1966. *Purity and Danger. An Analysis of Concepts of Pollution and Taboo.* London and New York: Routledge.

————. 1997. "Deciphering a Meal." In *Food and Culture. A Reader,* ed. Carole M. Counihan and Penny van Esterik. New York and London: Routledge, pp. 36–54.

Douglas, M.A. 1970/71. *Patrol Report Bogia No.4 of 1970/71 (Situation Report).* Sub-District Office, Bogia, Madang District. Port Moresby: National Archives.

Dundon, Alison. 2005. "The Sense of Sago. Motherhood and Migration in Papua New Guinea and Australia." *Journal of Intercultural Studies* 26 (1–2): 21–37.

Durkheim, Emile. (1893) 1933. *The Division of Labor in Society.* London: Collier Macmillan.

Dyer, K.W. 1952/53. *Patrol Report Bogia No.8 of 1952/53.* Sub-District Office, Bogia, Madang District. Port Moresby: National Archives.

Ellen, Roy, and Katsuyoshi Fukui, eds. 1996. *Redefining Nature. Ecology, Culture and Domestication.* Oxford: Berg.

Engelen, Eva-Maria, and Birgitt Röttger-Rössler. 2012. "Current Disciplinary and Interdisciplinary Debates on Empathy." *Emotion Review* 4 (1): 3–8.

Eves, Richard. 1998. *The Magical Body. Power, Fame and Meaning in a Melanesian Society.* Australia et al.: Harwood Academic Publishers.

Fairbairn, Andrew, and Pamela Swadling. 2005. "Re-Dating Mid-Holocene Betelnut (Areca Catechu L.) and other Plant Use at Dongan, Papua New Guinea." *Radiocarbon* 47 (3): 377–382.

Fajans, Jane. 1985. "The Person in Social Context. The Social Character of Baining 'Psychology.'" In *Person, Self, and Experience. Exploring Pacific Ethnopsychologies,* ed. Geoffrey M. White and John Kirkpatrick. Berkeley, Los Angeles, and London: University of California Press, pp. 367–397.

————. 1997. *They Make Themselves. Work and Play among the Baining of Papua New Guinea.* Chicago and London: University of Chicago Press.

Feinberg, Richard. 2011. "Do Anutans Empathize? Morality, Compassion, and Opacity of Other Minds." In *The Anthropology of Empathy. Experiencing the Lives of Others in Pacific Societies,* ed. Douglas Hollan and C. Jason Throop. New York and Oxford: Berghahn Books, pp. 151–167.

Feld, Steven. (1982) 1990. *Sound and Sentiment. Birds, Weeping, Poetics, and Song in Kaluli Expression.* Philadelphia: University of Pennsylvania.

Feld, Steven, and Keith H. Basso, eds. 1996. *Senses of Place.* Santa Fe / New Mexico: School of American Research Press.

Finnegan, Ruth. 2005. "Tactile Communication." In *The Book of Touch,* ed. Constance Classen. Oxford and New York: Berg, pp. 18–25.

Finsch, Otto. 1888. *Samoafahrten. Reisen in Kaiser Wilhelms-Land und Englisch-Neu-Guinea in den Jahren 1884 u. 1885 an Bord des Deutschen Dampfers "Samoa."* Leipzig: Ferdinand Hirt und Sohn.

Fisher, Bernard S.V.D., ed. 1992. *The Grace Lit Memories of Father Hilarion Morin S.V.D. Missionary to Papua New Guinea 1905—1992 (and Counting).* Alexishafen: Stella Press.

Foley, William A. 2005. "Linguistic Prehistory in the Sepik-Ramu Basin." In *Papuan Pasts. Cultural, Linguistic and Biological Histories of Papuan-Speaking Peoples,* ed. Andrew Pawley et al. Canberra: Pacific Linguistics, Research School of Pacific and Asian Studies, Australian National University, pp. 109–144.

Foster, Robert J. 2008. *Coca-Globalization. Following Soft Drinks from New York to New Guinea.* New York: Palgrave MacMillan.

Fox, James J., ed. 1997a. *The Poetic Power of Place. Comparative Perspectives on Austronesian Ideas of Locality.* Canberra: Research School of Pacific and Asian Studies, Australian National University.

———. 1997b. "Place and Landscape in Comparative Austronesian Perspective." In *The Poetic Power of Place. Comparative Perspectives on Austronesian Ideas of Locality,* ed. James J. Fox. Canberra: Research School of Pacific and Asian Studies, Australian National University, pp. 1–21.

Frawley, J.W. 1953/54. *Patrol Report Bogia No.10 of 1953/54.* Sub-District Office, Bogia, Madang District. Port Moresby: National Archives.

Fuchs, Thomas. 2008. *Das Gehirn—ein Beziehungsorgan. Eine phänomenologisch-ökologische Konzeption.* Stuttgart: Kohlhammer.

Gallese, Vittorio. 2003. "The Roots of Empathy. The Shared Manifold Hypothesis and the Neural Basis of Intersubjectivity." *Psychopathology* 36: 171–180.

Gassner, Burghard. 2006. *Empathie in der Pädagogik. Theorien, Implikationen, Bedeutung, Umsetzung.* Doctoral Thesis, University of Heidelberg. http://www.ub.uni-heidelberg.de/archiv/7224/.

Geertz, Clifford. 1972. "Deep Play. Notes on the Balinese Cockfight." *Daedalus* 101: 1–37.

———. 1973. *The Interpretation of Cultures. Selected Essays.* New York: Basic Books.

———. (1974) 1984. "'From the Native's Point of View.' On the Nature of Anthropological Understanding." In *Culture Theory. Essays on Mind, Self, and Emotion,* ed. Richard A. Shweder and Robert A. LeVine. Cambridge: Cambridge University Press, pp. 123–136.

Gehrmann, Karl. 1916. "Die Gogol-Ramu-Expedition in Kaiser-Wilhelmsland. September und Oktober 1913. Tagebuch über die Gogol-Ramu-Expedition." *Mitteilungen aus den Deutschen Schutzgebieten* 29: 2–30.

Gewertz, Deborah B., and Frederick K. Errington. 1991. *Twisted Histories, Altered Contexts. Representing the Chambri in a World System.* Cambridge et al.: Cambridge University Press.

———. 1999. *Emerging Class in Papua New Guinea. The Telling of Difference.* Cambridge et al.: Cambridge University Press.

Goddard, Michael. 2005. *The Unseen City. Anthropological Perspectives on Port Moresby, Papua New Guinea.* Canberra: Pandanus Books.

Godelier, Maurice. 1986. *The Making of Great Men. Male Domination and Power among the New Guinea Baruya.* Cambridge: Cambridge University Press / Paris: Editions de la Maison des Sciences de l'Homme.

Goodale, Jane C. 1995. *To Sing with Pigs is Human. The Concept of Person in Papua New Guinea.* Seattle and London: University of Washington Press.

Gow, Peter 1995. "Land, People, and Paper in Western Amazonia." In *The Anthropology of Landscape. Perspectives on Place and Space,* ed. Eric Hirsch and Michael O'Hanlon. Oxford: Clarendon Press, pp. 43–62.

Groark, Kevin P. 2008. "Social Opacity and the Dynamics of Empathic In-Sight among the Tzotzil Maya of Chiapas, Mexico." *Ethos* 36 (4): 427–448.

Hagen, Bernhard. 1899. *Unter den Papua's. Beobachtungen und Studien über Land und Leute, Thier- und Pflanzenwelt in Kaiser-Wilhelmsland.* Wiesbaden: C.W. Kreidel's Verlag.

Haines, Helen R. and Clare A. Sammells, eds. 2010. *Adventures in Eating. Anthropological Experiences of Dining from Around the World.* Boulder: University Press of Colorado.

Halpern, Jodi. 2001. *From Detached Concern to Empathy. Humanizing Medical Practice.* Oxford: Oxford University Press.

Harris, Grace G. 1989. "Concepts of Individual, Self, and Person in Description and Analysis." *American Anthropologist* 91: 599–612.

Harris, Kyle, and Kathy Harris. 2002. "Our First Visit to the Bosman Language Group." *Ramu Ramblings* 16 (1). http://www.flyingfox.org/cms/archives/spring2002.pdf.

———. 2004. "Sorcery, a Crocodile Attack, Death, and the Peacemaker." *Ramu Ramblings* 18 (2). http://www.flyingfox.org/cms/archives/spring2004.pdf.

Harrison, Simon. 1990. *Stealing People's Names. History and Politics in a Sepik River Cosmology.* Cambridge et al.: Cambridge University Press.

Healy, J.P. 1951/52. *Patrol Report Bogia No.6 of 1951/52.* Sub-District Office, Bogia, Madang District. Port Moresby: National Archives.

Herbst, Franziska. n.d. *Person, Health, and Illness among the Giri, Papua New Guinea.* Doctoral Thesis in Preparation, University of Heidelberg.

Hermann, Elfriede. 2011. "Empathy, Ethnicity, and the Self among the Banabans in Fiji." In *The Anthropology of Empathy. Experiencing the Lives of Others in Pacific Societies,* ed. Douglas Hollan and C. Jason Throop. New York and Oxford: Berghahn Books, pp. 25–41.

Hess, Sabine C. 2009. *Person and Place. Ideas, Ideals and Practice of Sociality on Vanua Lava, Vanuatu.* New York and Oxford: Berghahn Books (Person, Space and Memory in the Contemporary Pacific, Volume 2).

Hickok, Gregory. 2009. "Eight Problems for the Mirror Neuron Theory of Action Understanding in Monkeys and Humans." *Journal of Cognitive Neuroscience* 21 (7): 1229–1243.

Hirsch, Eric. 1995a. "Landscape. Between Place and Space." In *The Anthropology of Landscape. Perspectives on Place and Space,* ed. Eric Hirsch and Michael O'Hanlon. Oxford: Clarendon Press, pp. 1–30.

———. 1995b. "The Coercive Strategies of Aesthetics. Reflections on Wealth, Ritual and Landscape in Melanesia." *Social Analysis* 38: 61–71.

Hirsch, Eric, and Michael O'Hanlon, eds. 1995. *The Anthropology of Landscape. Perspectives on Place and Space.* Oxford: Clarendon Press.

Höltker, Georg. 1937a. "Die Kinder der Kopfjäger." *Wochenpost* 9 (50): 1570–1571.

———. 1937b. "Vorbericht über meine ethnographischen und anthropologischen Forschungen im Bogia-Distrikt (Neuguinea)." *Anthropos* 32: 963–967.

———. 1940. "Drei Jahre ethnologische und anthropologische Forschungen in Neuguinea, 1936 bis 1939." *Verhandlungen der Schweizer Naturforschenden Gesellschaft* n.v.: 187.

———. 1947. "Die Maritime Ortung bei einigen Stämmen in Nordost-Neuguinea." *Geographica Helvetica* 2 (1): 192–105.

———. 1960. "Der Schutzgeisterglaube in Neuguinea." *St. Michaelskalender* 81: 75–77.

———. 1961. "Leichenbrand und Anderes vom Unteren Ramu (Neuguinea)." In *Beiträge zur Völkerforschung. Hans Damm zum 65. Geburtstag,* ed. Dietrich Drost and Wolfgang König. Berlin: Akademie-Verlag (Veröffentlichungen des Museums für Völkerkunde zu Leipzig, Volume 11), pp. 285–301.

———. 1962. "Aus dem Kulturleben der Kire-Puir am Unteren Ramu (Neuguinea)." *Jahrbuch des Museums für Völkerkunde zu Leipzig* 19: 76–107.

———. 1964. "Die Nubia-Awar an der Hansa-Bucht in Nordost-Neuguinea." *Jahrbuch des Museums für Völkerkunde zu Leipzig* 20: 33–70.

―――. 1965a. "Töpferei und irdene Spielpuppen bei den Bosngun in Nordost-Neuguinea." *Jahrbuch des Museums für Völkerkunde zu Leipzig* 21: 7–22.

―――. 1965b. "Mythen und Erzählungen der Monumbo- und Ngaimbom-Papua in Nordost-Neuguinea." *Anthropos* 60: 5–107.

―――. 1966. "Das Geisterhaus bei den Bosngun am unteren Ramu River, Neu-Guinea." *Jahrbuch des Museums für Völkerkunde zu Leipzig* 22: 17–39.

―――. 1969. "Der Frauenkampf bei den Kopfjägern am Ramufluß." *Steyler Missions-Chronik* n.v.: 70–73.

―――. 1975. "Die Knaben-Jugendweihe bei den Bosmun am unteren Ramu (Nordost-Neuguinea)." *Abhandlungen und Berichte des Staatlichen Museums für Völkerkunde Dresden* 34: 555–579.

Hogbin, Ian. (1970) 1996. *The Island of Menstruating Men. Religion in Wogeo, New Guinea.* Long Grove, Illinois: Waveland Press.

Hollan, Douglas. 2008. "Being There. On the Imaginative Aspects of Understanding Others and Being Understood." *Ethos* 36 (4): 475–489.

―――. 2011. "Vicissitudes of 'Empathy' in a Rural Toraja Village." In *The Anthropology of Empathy. Experiencing the Lives of Others in Pacific Societies,* ed. Douglas Hollan and C. Jason Throop. New York and Oxford: Berghahn Books, pp. 195–214.

―――. 2012. "Emerging Issues in the Cross-Cultural Study of Empathy." *Emotion Review* 4 (1): 70–78.

Hollan, Douglas, and C. Jason Throop. 2008. "Whatever Happened to Empathy? Introduction." *Ethos* 36 (4): 385–401.

―――, eds. 2011. *The Anthropology of Empathy. Experiencing the Lives of Others in Pacific Societies.* New York and Oxford: Berghahn Books.

Holtzman, Jon D. 2006. "Food and Memory." *Annual Review of Anthropology* 35: 361–378.

Howard, F.J. 1957/58. *Patrol Report Bogia No.3 of 1957/58.* Sub-District Office, Bogia, Madang District. Port Moresby: National Archives.

Howes, David. 2005. "Skinscapes. Embodiment, Culture, and Environment." In *The Book of Touch*, ed. Constance Classen. Oxford and New York: Berg, pp. 27–39.

Ingold, Tim. 2000. *The Perception of the Environment. Essays in Livelihood, Dwelling and Skill.* London and New York: Routledge.

Jahoda, Gustav. 2005. "Theodor Lipps and the Shift from 'Sympathy' to 'Empathy.'" *Journal of the History of the Behavioral Sciences* 41 (2): 151–163.

Jebens, Holger, ed. 2004. *Cargo, Cult, and Culture Critique.* Honolulu: University of Hawai'i Press.

―――. 2005. *Pathways to Heaven. Contesting Mainline and Fundamentalist Christianity in Papua New Guinea.* New York and Oxford: Berghahn Books.

Johnston, W.J. 1957. *Comments to the Patrol Report Bogia No. 9 of 1956/57.* Sub-District Office, Bogia, Madang District. Port Moresby: National Archives.

Jorgensen, Dan. 1998. "Whose Nature? Invading Bush Spirits, Travelling Ancestors and Mining in Telefolmin." *Social Analysis* 42 (3): 100–116.

Josephides, Sasha. 1990. "Seventh-Day Adventism and the Boroi Image of the Past." In *Sepik Heritage. Tradition and Change in Papua New Guinea,* ed. Nancy Lutkehaus et al. Durham, North Carolina: Carolina Academic Press, pp. 58–66.

Kahler, S.P. 1959/60. *Patrol Report Bogia No.3 of 1959/60.* Sub-District Office, Bogia, Madang District. Port Moresby: National Archives.

Kahn, Miriam. 1986. *Always Hungry, Never Greedy. Food and the Expression of Gender in a Melanesian Society.* Cambridge: Cambridge University Press.

——. 1990. "Stone-Faced Ancestors. The Spatial Anchoring of Myth in Wamira, Papua New Guinea." *Ethnology* 29 (1): 51–66.

——. 1996. "Your Place and Mine. Sharing Emotional Landscapes in Wamira, Papua New Guinea." In *Senses of Place,* ed. Steven Feld and Keith H. Basso. Santa Fe / New Mexico: School of American Research Press, pp. 167–196.

Kaniku, John W.T. 1975. *The Epic of Tauhau.* Port Moresby: Institute of Papua New Guinea Studies.

Kapferer, Bruce. 1997. *The Feast of the Sorcerer. Practices of Consciousness and Power.* Chicago and London: University of Chicago Press.

Katz, Robert L. 1963. *Empathy. Its Nature and Uses.* London: The Free Press of Glencoe.

Keck, Verena. 1994. "Die 'Was' und die 'Warum.' Zur Benennung ethnischer und linguistischer Gruppen in Papua New Guinea." In *Geschichte und mündliche Überlieferung in Ozeanien,* ed. Brigitta Hauser-Schäublin. Basel: Wepf (Basler Beiträge zur Ethnologie, Volume 37), pp. 301–321.

——. 2005. *Social Discord and Bodily Disorders. Healing among the Yupno of Papua New Guinea.* Durham: Carolina Academic Press.

Keck, Verena et al. 2008. "Hochschulpartnerschaft Heidelberg—Madang (Papua-Neuguinea)." *Mitteilungen der DGV* 39: 95–98.

Keesing, Roger M. 1982. "Introduction." In *Rituals of Manhood. Male Initiation in Papua New Guinea,* ed. Gilbert H. Herdt. Berkeley, Los Angeles, and London: University of California Press, pp. 1–43.

Kirmayer, Laurence J. 2008. "Empathy and Alterity in Cultural Psychiatry." *Ethos* 36 (4): 457–474.

Kirsch, Stuart. 2006. *Reverse Anthropology. Indigenous Analysis of Social and Environmental Relations in New Guinea.* Stanford, California: Stanford University Press.

Kirschbaum, Franz. 1927. "Ein neuentdeckter Zwergstamm auf Neu-Guinea." *Anthropos* 22: 202–215.

Kluckhohn, Clyde. 1944. *Navaho Witchcraft.* Boston: Beacon.

Knauft, Bruce M. 1985. *Good Company and Violence. Sorcery and Social Action in a Lowland New Guinea Society.* Berkeley, Los Angeles, and London: University of California Press.

Knowles, Chantal. 2000. "Reverse Trajectories. Beatrice Blackwood as Collector and Anthropologist." In *Hunting the Gatherers. Ethnographic Collectors, Agents and Agency in Melanesia, 1870s–1930s,* ed. Michael O'Hanlon and Robert L. Welsch. New York and Oxford: Berghahn Books, pp. 251–271.

Köpping, Klaus-Peter, Michael Welker, and Reiner Wiehl, eds. 2002. *Die autonome Person—eine europäische Erfindung?* München: Wilhelm Fink Verlag.

Krieger, Maximilian. 1899. *Neu-Guinea.* Berlin: Alfred Schall.

Kuehling, Susanne. 2005. *Dobu. Ethics of Exchange on a Massim Island, Papua New Guinea.* Honolulu: University of Hawai'i Press.

Kulick, Don. 1992. *Language Shift and Cultural Reproduction. Socialization, Self, and Syncretism in a Papua New Guinea Village.* Cambridge et al.: Cambridge University Press.

Lambek, Michael, and Andrew Strathern, eds. 1998. *Bodies and Persons. Comparative Perspectives from Africa and Melanesia.* Cambridge: Cambridge University Press.

Lawrence, Peter. 1964. *Road belong Cargo. A Study of the Cargo Movement in the Southern Madang District New Guinea.* Victoria: Melbourne University Press.

Laycock, Donald, and John A. Z'graggen. 1975. "The Sepik-Ramu-Phylum." In *New Guinea Area Languages and Language Study. Vol. 1: Papuan Languages and the New Guinea Linguistic Scene,* ed. Stephen Wurm. Canberra: Pacific Linguistics, pp. 731–763.

Leach, James. 2003. *Creative Land. Place and Procreation on the Rai Coast of Papua New Guinea.* New York and Oxford: Berghahn Books.

Lepowsky, Maria. 2011. "The Boundaries of Personhood, the Problem of Empathy, and 'the Native's Point of View' in the Outer Islands." In *The Anthropology of Empathy. Experiencing the Lives of Others in Pacific Societies,* ed. Douglas Hollan and C. Jason Throop. New York and Oxford: Berghahn Books, pp. 43–65.

Lévi-Strauss, Claude. (1964) 1969. *The Raw and the Cooked. Introduction to a Science of Mythology: I.* New York et al.: Harper and Row.

———. 1997. "The Culinary Triangle." In *Food and Culture. A Reader,* ed. Carole M. Counihan and Penny van Esterik. New York and London: Routledge, pp. 28–35.

Levy, Catherine. 2005. "Language Research in Papua New Guinea. A Case Study of Awar." *Contemporary PNG Studies: DWU Research Journal* 2: 79–92.

Lipps, Theodor. 1903a. *Ästhetik. Psychologie des Schönen und der Kunst. Erster Teil: Grundlegung der Ästhetik.* Hamburg and Leipzig: Voss.

———. 1903b. "Einfühlung, innere Nachahmung und Organempfindungen." *Archiv für die gesamte Psychologie* 1 (1): 185–204.

———. 1906. *Ästhetik. Psychologie des Schönen und der Kunst. Zweiter Teil: Die ästhetische Betrachtung und die bildende Kunst.* Hamburg and Leipzig: Voss.

Lipset, David. 1997. *Mangrove Man. Dialogics of Culture in the Sepik Estuary.* Cambridge: Cambridge University Press.

LiPuma, Edward. 1998. "Modernity and Forms of Personhood in Melanesia." In *Bodies and Persons. Comparative Perspectives from Africa and Melanesia,* ed. Michael Lambek and Andrew Strathern. Cambridge: Cambridge University Press, pp. 53–79.

Lohmann, Roger I. 2003. "Turning the Belly. Insights on Religious Conversion from New Guinea Gut Feelings." In *The Anthropology of Religious Conversion,* ed. Andrew Buckser and Stephen Glazier. Boulder: Rowman and Littlefield, pp. 109–121.

———. 2008. "Sexual Snakes Strike Again. Immortality Expressed and Explained in a New Guinea Myth." In *Sexual Snakes, Winged Maidens and Sky Gods. Myth in the Pacific. An Essay in Cultural Transparency,* ed. Serge Dunis. Nouméa: Le Rocher-à-laVoile / Pape'ete: Haere Po, pp. 113–125.

———. 2010. "In the Company of Things Left Behind. Asabano Mementos." *Anthropological Forum* 20 (3): 291–303.

———. 2011. "Empathic Perception and Imagination among the Asabano. Lessons for Anthropology." In *The Anthropology of Empathy. Experiencing the Lives of Others in Pacific Societies,* ed. Douglas Hollan and C. Jason Throop. New York and Oxford: Berghahn Books, pp. 95–116.

Lord Moyne. 1936. *Walkabout. A Journey in Lands Between the Pacific and Indian Oceans.* London and Toronto: William Heinemann LD.

Lord Moyne and Kathleen Haddon. 1936. "The Pygmies of the Aiome Mountains, Mandated Territory of New Guinea." *The Journal of the Royal Anthropological Institute of Great Britain and Ireland* 66: 269–290.

Lutkehaus, Nancy C. 1988. "Beatrice Mary Blackwood (1889–1975)." In *Women Anthropologists. A Biographical Dictionary,* ed. Ute Gacs et al. New York, Connecticut, and London: Greenwood Press, pp. 17–22.

———. 1995. *Zaria's Fire. Engendered Moments in Manam Ethnography.* Durham, North Carolina: Carolina Academic Press.

Lutkehaus, Nancy C., and Paul B. Roscoe, eds. 1995. *Gender Rituals. Female Initiation in Melanesia.* New York and London: Routledge.

Lutz, Catherine. 1985. "Ethnopsychology Compared to What? Explaining Behavior and Consciousness among the Ifaluk." In *Person, Self, and Experience. Exploring Pacific Ethnopsychologies,* ed. Geoffrey M. White and John Kirkpatrick. Berkeley, Los Angeles, and London: University of California Press, pp. 35–79.

Lutz, Catherine, and Geoffrey M. White. 1986. "The Anthropology of Emotions." *Annual Review of Anthropology* 15: 405–436.

Lyon, M.L., and J.M. Barbalet. 1994. "Society's Body. Emotion and the 'Somatization' of Social Theory." In *Embodiment and Experience. The Existential Ground of Culture and Self,* ed. Thomas J. Csordas. Cambridge: Cambridge University Press, pp. 48–66.

Mageo, Jeannette. 2011. "Empathy and 'As-If' Attachment in Samoa." In *The Anthropology of Empathy. Experiencing the Lives of Others in Pacific Societies,* ed. Douglas Hollan and C. Jason Throop. New York and Oxford: Berghahn Books, pp. 69–93.

Malinowski, Bronislaw. 1922. *Argonauts of the Western Pacific. An Account of Native Enterprise and Adventure in the Archipelagoes of Melanesian New Guinea.* London: Routledge and Kegan Paul.

Manderson, Lenore. 1986a. "Introduction. The Anthropology of Food in Oceania and Southeast Asia." In *Shared Wealth and Symbol. Food, Culture, and Society in Oceania and Southeast Asia,* ed. Lenore Manderson. Cambridge: Cambridge University Press, pp. 1–25.

———, ed. 1986b. *Shared Wealth and Symbol. Food, Culture, and Society in Oceania and Southeast Asia.* Cambridge: Cambridge University Press.

Mauss, Marcel. (1925) 1966. *The Gift. Forms and Functions of Exchange in Archaic Societies.* London: Routledge and Kegan Paul.

———. (1938) 1985. "A Category of the Human Mind. The Notion of Person; The Notion of Self." In *The Category of the Person. Anthropology, Philosophy, History,* ed. Michael Carrithers, Steven Collins, and Steven Lukes. Cambridge et al.: Cambridge University Press, pp. 1–25.

May, Patricia, and Margaret Tuckson. (1982) 2000. *The Traditional Pottery of Papua New Guinea.* Honolulu: University of Hawai'i Press.

McCallum, Cecilia. 2001. *Gender and Sociality in Amazonia. How Real People are Made.* Oxford and New York: Berg.

McCarthy, Jack D. 1967. "Tambaran." *Walkabout. Australia's Way of Life Magazine* 33 (9): 19–22.

McCarthy, Jack D., and Kurt Pfund. 1973. *Legends of Papua New Guinea.* Adelaide et al.: Rigby Limited.

Meigs, Anna. 1984. *Food, Sex, and Pollution. A New Guinea Religion.* New Brunswick, New Jersey: Rutgers University Press.

Meinerzag, Angella. 2006. *Being Mande. Personhood, Land and Naming System among the Hinihon in the Adelbert Range / Papua New Guinea.* Doctoral Thesis, University of Heidelberg.

Meiser, Leo. n.d. *The Meiser Manuscript.* Unpublished Transcript from 1979 by John Z'graggen from a now lost collection of material on the Kayan people. Madang: Archbishop Noser Memorial Library.

Mennis, Mary R. 2006. *A Potted History of Madang. Traditional Culture and Change on the North Coast of Papua New Guinea.* Aspley: Lalong Enterprises.

Merleau-Ponty, Maurice. (1945) 1962. *Phenomenology of Perception.* London: Routledge and Kegan Paul.

Metcalf, Peter, and Richard Huntington. (1979) 1991. *Celebrations of Death. The Anthropology of Mortuary Ritual.* Cambridge et al.: Cambridge University Press.

Mihalic, Francis S.V.D. (1971) 1986. *The Jacaranda Dictionary and Grammar of Melanesian Pidgin.* Papua New Guinea: Web Books.

Mintz, Sidney W., and Christine M. Du Bois. 2002. "The Anthropology of Food and Eating." *Annual Review of Anthropology* 31: 99–119.

Morris, Brian. 1994. *Anthropology of the Self. The Individual in Cultural Perspective.* London and Boulder, Colorado: Pluto Press.

Murphy, Greg. 1998. *Fears of Loss, Tears of Joy. Raun Raun Theatre and its Role in the Construction of a National Culture in Papua New Guinea.* Doctoral Thesis. University of Papua New Guinea.

Obrist, Brigit. 1990. "The Study of Food in Its Cultural Context." In *Sepik Heritage. Tradition and Change in Papua New Guinea,* ed. Nancy Lutkehaus et al. Durham, North Carolina: Carolina Academic Press, pp. 455–463.

Papua New Guinea Tok Pisin English Dictionary. 2008. Oxford et al.: Oxford University Press in Association with *Wantok Niuspepa.*

Parkin, Robert, and Linda Stone, eds. 2004. *Kinship and Family. An Anthropological Reader.* Malden, Oxford, and Carlton: Blackwell Publishing.

Paulsen, Rune. 2003. "Fighting Hierarchy. Relations of Egality and Hierarchy among the May River Iwam of Papua New Guinea." In *Oceanic Socialities and Cultural Forms. Ethnographies of Experience,* ed. Ingjerd Hoëm and Sidsel Roalkvam. New York and Oxford: Berghahn Books, pp. 29–49.

Poirier, Sylvie. 2005. *A World of Relationships. Itineraries, Dreams, and Events in the Australian Western Desert.* Toronto, Buffalo and London: University of Toronto Press.

Pollock, Nancy J. 1986. "Food Classification in Three Pacific Societies. Fiji, Hawaii, and Tahiti." *Ethnology* 25 (2): 107–117.

Quanchi, Max. 2003. "Contrary Images. Photographing the New Pacific in *Walkabout* Magazine." *Journal of Australian Studies* 79: 77–92, 230–233.

Radcliffe-Brown, A.R. 1940. "On Joking Relationships." *Africa* 13 (3): 195–210.

―――. 1964. *The Andaman Islanders.* New York: The Free Press of Glencoe.

Rannells, Jackson. (1995) 2001. *PNG. A Fact Book on Modern Papua New Guinea.* Melbourne, Oxford and New York: Oxford University Press.

Reddy, William M. 2001. *The Navigation of Feeling. A Framework for the History of Emotions.* Cambridge: Cambridge University Press.

Rizzolatti, Giacomo, and Michael R. Arbib. 1998. "Language Within Our Grasp." *Trends in Neuroscience* 21 (5): 188–194.

Robbins, Joel. 2004. *Becoming Sinners. Christianity and Moral Torment in a Papua New Guinea Society.* Berkeley, Los Angeles and London: University of California Press.

Robbins, Joel, and Alan Rumsey. 2008. "Introduction. Cultural and Linguistic Anthropology and the Opacity of Other Minds." *Anthropological Quarterly* 81 (2): 407–420.

Rosaldo, Michelle Z. 1980. *Knowledge and Passion. Ilongot Notions of Self and Social Life.* Cambridge et al.: Cambridge University Press.

———. 1984. "Toward an Anthropology of Self and Feeling." In *Culture Theory. Essays on Mind, Self, and Emotion,* ed. Richard A. Shweder and Robert A. LeVine. Cambridge: Cambridge University Press, pp. 137–157.

Rosaldo, Renato I. (1984) 1988. "Grief and a Headhunter's Rage. On the Cultural Force of Emotions." In *Text, Play, and Story. The Construction and Reconstruction of Self and Society,* ed. Edward M. Bruner. Prospect Heights, Illinois: Waveland Press, Inc., pp. 178–195.

Rumsey, Alan, and James F. Weiner, eds. 2001. *Emplaced Myth. Space, Narrative, and Knowledge in Aboriginal Australia and Papua New Guinea.* Honolulu: University of Hawai'i Press.

Sahlins, Marshall. 1972. *Stone Age Economics.* New York: Aldine.

Schegloff, Emanuel A. 2000. "Overlapping Talk and the Organization of Turn-Taking for Conversation." *Language in Society* 29 (1): 1–63.

Scheper-Hughes, Nancy, and Margaret M. Lock. 1987. "The Mindful Body. A Prolegomenon to Future Work in Medical Anthropology." *Medical Anthropological Quarterly (N.S.)* 1 (1): 6–41.

Schieffelin, Edward. 1976. *The Sorrow of the Lonely and the Burning of the Dancers.* New York: St. Martin's Press.

Schindlbeck, Markus. 1980. *Sago bei den Sawos (Mittelsepik, Papua New Guinea). Untersuchungen über die Bedeutung von Sago in Wirtschaft, Sozialordnung und Religion.* Basel: Ethnologisches Seminar der Universität und Museum für Völkerkunde (Basler Beiträge zur Ethnologie, Volume 19).

Schneider, David. 1984. *A Critique of the Study of Kinship.* Ann Arbor: University of Michigan Press.

Schuster, Meinhard, and Gisela Schuster. 1974. "Aibom (Neuguinea, Mittlerer Sepik). Sago-Gewinnung. Film E 1375." In *Encyclopaedia Cinematographica,* ed. Gotthard Wolf. Göttingen: Institut für den Wissenschaftlichen Film.

Schwab, Johann. 1970. "Klan-Gliederung und Mythen im küstennahen Inland-Gebiet zwischen Sepik und Ramu (Nordost-Neuguinea)." *Anthropos* 65 (1/2): 758–793.

Sheekey, D.P. 1962. *Comments to the Patrol Report Bogia No.6 of 1961/62.* Sub-District Office, Bogia, Madang District. Port Moresby: National Archives.

Shweder, Richard A., and Robert A. LeVine, eds. 1984. *Culture Theory. Essays on Mind, Self, and Emotion.* Cambridge: Cambridge University Press.

Sillitoe, Paul. 1998. *An Introduction to the Anthropology of Melanesia. Culture and Tradition.* Cambridge: Cambridge University Press.

Silverman, Eric K. 2001. *Masculinity, Motherhood, and Mockery. Psychoanalyzing Culture and the Iatmul Naven Rite in New Guinea.* Ann Arbor: University of Michigan Press.

Sodian, Beate, Christian Hülsken, and Claudia Thoermer. 2003. "The Self and Action in Theory of Mind Research." *Consciousness and Cognition* 12 (4): 777–782.

Souter, Gavin. 1963. *New Guinea. The Last Unknown.* Sydney et al.: Angus and Robertson.

Spearritt, Gordon, and Jürg Wassmann. 1996. "Myth and Music in a Middle Sepik Village." *Kulele* 2: 59–84.

Stamenov, Maxim I., and Vittorio Gallese, eds. 2002. *Mirror Neurons and the Evolution of Brain and Language.* Amsterdam and Philadelphia: John Benjamins.

Stanek, Milan. 1983. *Sozialordnung und Mythik in Palimbei. Bausteine zur ganzheitlichen Beschreibung einer Dorfgemeinschaft der Iatmul, East Sepik Province, Papua New Guinea.* Basel: Ethnologisches Seminar der Universität und Museum für Völkerkunde (Basler Beiträge zur Ethnologie, Volume 23).

Stasch, Rupert. 2002. "Joking Avoidance. A Korowai Pragmatics of Being Two." *American Ethnologist* 29 (2): 335–365.

———. 2009. *Society of Others. Kinship and Mourning in a West Papuan Place.* Berkeley, Los Angeles, and London: University of California Press.

Steffen, Paul. 1995. *Missionsbeginn in Neuguinea. Die Anfänge der Rheinischen, Neuen-dettelsauer und Steyler Missionsarbeit in Neuguinea.* Nettetal: Steyler Verlag (Studia Instituti Missiologici Societatis Verbi Divini, Sankt Augustin, Nr. 61).

Stewart, Pamela J., and Andrew Strathern. 2000. "Naming Places. Duna Evocations of Landscape in Papua New Guinea." *People and Culture in Oceania* 16: 87–107.

———. 2001. "Origins versus Creative Powers. The Interplay of Movement and Fixity." In *Emplaced Myth. Space, Narrative, and Knowledge in Aboriginal Australia and Papua New Guinea,* ed. Alan Rumsey and James F. Weiner. Honolulu: University of Hawai'i Press, pp. 79–98.

Strathern, Andrew J. 1996. *Body Thoughts.* Ann Arbor: University of Michigan Press.

Strathern, Andrew J., and Pamela J. Stewart. 1998. "Seeking Personhood. Anthropological Accounts and Local Concepts in Mount Hagen, Papua New Guinea." *Oceania* 68 (3): 170–188.

———. 2000. *Arrow Talk. Transaction, Transition, and Contradiction in New Guinea Highlands History.* Kent, Ohio, and London: The Kent State University Press.

———. 2007. "Morality and Cosmology. What Do Exemplars Exemplify?" In *The Anthropology of Morality in Melanesia and Beyond,* ed. John Barker. Hampshire and Burlington: Ashgate, pp. xiii–xxi.

Strathern, Marilyn. 1988. *The Gender of the Gift. Problems with Women and Problems with Society in Melanesia.* Berkeley, Los Angeles, and London: University of California Press.

Strauss, Claudia. 2004. "Is Empathy Gendered and, If So, Why? An Approach from Feminist Psychological Anthropology." *Ethos* 32 (4): 432–457.

Stürzenhofecker, Gabriele. 1998. *Times Enmeshed. Gender, Space, and History among the Duna of Papua New Guinea.* Stanford: Stanford University Press.

Sutton, David E. 2001. *Remembrance of Repasts. An Anthropology of Food and Memory.* Oxford and New York: Berg.

Swadling, Pamela. 1990. "Sepik Prehistory." In *Sepik Heritage. Tradition and Change in Papua New Guinea,* ed. Nancy Lutkehaus et al. Durham, North Carolina: Carolina Academic Press, pp. 71–86.

———. 1997. "Pacific Prehistory." *World Archaeology* 29 (1): 1–14.

Swadling, Pamela, et al. 1988. *The Sepik-Ramu. An Introduction.* Boroko: PNG National Museum.

Swadling, Pamela, and Robin Hide. 2005. "Changing Landscape and Social Interaction. Looking at Agricultural History from a Sepik-Ramu Perspective." In *Papuan Pasts. Cultural, Linguistic and Biological Histories of Papuan-Speaking Peoples,* ed. Andrew Pawley et al. Canberra: Pacific Linguistics, Research School of Pacific and Asian Studies, Australian National University, pp. 289–327.

Telban, Borut. 1998. "Body, Being and Identity in Ambonwari, Papua New Guinea." In *Common Worlds and Single Lives. Constituting Knowledge in Pacific Societies,* ed. Verena Keck. Oxford and New York: Berg, pp. 55–70.

Throop, C. Jason. 2008. "On the Problem of Empathy. The Case of Yap, Federate States of Micronesia." *Ethos* 36 (4): 402–426.

———. 2011. "Suffering, Empathy, and Ethical Modalities of Being in Yap (Waqap), Federate States of Micronesia." In *The Anthropology of Empathy. Experiencing the Lives of Others in Pacific Societies,* ed. Douglas Hollan and C. Jason Throop. New York and Oxford: Berghahn Books, pp. 119–149.

Tiesler, Frank. 1969. "Die intertribalen Beziehungen an der Nordküste Neuguineas im Gebiet der kleinen Schouten-Inseln (I)." *Abhandlungen und Berichte des Staatlichen Museums für Völkerkunde Dresden* 30: 1–122.

———. 1970. "Die intertribalen Beziehungen an der Nordküste Neuguineas im Gebiet der kleinen Schouten-Inseln (II)." *Abhandlungen und Berichte des Staatlichen Museums für Völkerkunde Dresden* 31: 111–195.

Tietjen, Anne Marie. 1985. "Infant Care and Feeding Practices and the Beginnings of Socialization among the Maisin of Papua New Guinea." In *Infant Care and Feeding in the South Pacific,* ed. Leslie B. Marshall. New York et al.: Gordon and Breach (Food and Nutrition in History and Anthropology, Volume 3), pp. 121–135.

Tilley, Christopher. 1994. *A Phenomenology of Landscape. Places, Paths and Monuments.* Oxford and Providence: Berg.

Titchener, Edward B. 1909. *Lectures on the Experimental Psychology of the Thought-Processes.* New York: MacMillan.

Townsend Patricia K. 1982. "A Review of Recent and Needed Sago Research." In *Sago Research in Papua New Guinea,* ed. Papua New Guinea Institute of Applied Social and Economic Research. Boroko, Papua New Guinea (IASER Discussion Paper Nr. 44).

———. 2003. *Palm Sago. Further Thoughts on a Tropical Starch from Marginal Lands.* Canberra: Research School of Pacific and Asian Studies (Resource Management in Asia-Pacific, Working Paper No. 49).

Tuzin, Donald F. 1980. *The Voice of the Tambaran. Truth and Illusion in Ilahita Arapesh Religion.* Berkeley, Los Angeles, and London: University of California Press.

———. 1992. "Sago Subsistence and Symbolism among the Ilahita Arapesh." *Ethnology* 31 (2): 103–114.

———. 1997. *The Cassowary's Revenge. The Life and Death of Masculinity in a New Guinea Society.* Chicago and London: University of Chicago Press.

———. 2001. *Social Complexity in the Making. A Case Study among the Arapesh of New Guinea.* London and New York: Routledge.

Ubl, Bettina. 2007. *Die "Theory of Mind" im interkulturellen Vergleich. Eine Feldstudie zum Verständnis falscher Überzeugungen bei den Bosmun in Papua Neuguinea.* Diploma Thesis, University of Heidelberg.

Ucko, Peter J., and Robert Layton, eds. 1999. *The Archaeology and Anthropology of Landscape. Shaping Your Landscape.* London and New York: Routledge.

van Helden, Flip. 1998. *Between Cash and Conviction. The Social Context of the Bismarck-Ramu Integrated Conservation and Development Project.* Boroko: The National Research Institute (NRI Monograph 33).

Vischer, Robert. 1873. *Ueber das optische Formgefühl. Ein Beitrag zur Aesthetik.* Leipzig: Hermann Credner.

von Poser, Alexis T. 2008a. *Inside Jong's Head. Time, Person, and Space among the Kayan of Papua New Guinea.* Doctoral Thesis, University of Heidelberg.

———. 2008b. *Tuning in and Out of Kayan Personhood. Male Initiation and Mortuary Rites in Northern Papua New Guinea.* Paper delivered at the ASAO Meetings, Canberra, Australia.

von Poser, Anita. 2009. "Spracherhalt bei den Bosmun im Nordosten Papua-Neuguineas. Wortdokumentation und praktischer Einsatz auf lokaler Ebene." *GBS Bulletin* 15: 10–12.

———. 2011a. "Bosmun Foodways. Emotional Reasoning in a Papua New Guinea Lifeworld." In *The Anthropology of Empathy. Experiencing the Lives of Others in Pacific Societies,* ed. Douglas Hollan and C. Jason Throop. New York and Oxford: Berghahn Books, pp. 169–192.

———. 2011b. "Ageing and Taking Care of the Elderly in Contemporary Daiden (Northeast Papua New Guinea)." *Max Planck Institute for Social Anthropology Working Paper* No. 129.

von Poser, Anita, and Adam K. Saŋgam. 2008. *Bosmun—Tok Pisin—English Dictionary.* Unpublished Typescript.

von Poser, Anita, and Bettina Ubl. Forthcoming. "Investigating the Understanding of False Belief among the Bosmun of Northeast Papua New Guinea." In *Theory of Mind in the Pacific. Reasoning across Cultures,* ed. Jürg Wassmann, Birgit Träuble, and Joachim Funke. Heidelberg: Universitätsverlag Winter.

Vriens, A., and J. Boelaars. 1973. "An Overview of the Primitive Economy of the Auwju People of the Mappi Area along the Bamgi and the Ia Rivers." In *An Asmat Sketch Book No. 3* (A Publication of the Asmat Museum of Culture and Progress), ed. Frank A. Trenkenschuh. Hastings: Crosier Missions, pp. 43–74.

Wagner, Roy. 1996. "Mysteries of Origin. Early Traders and Heroes in the Trans-Fly." In *Plumes from Paradise. Trade Cycles in Outer Southeast Asia and Their Impact on New Guinea and Nearby Islands until 1920,* ed. Pamela Swadling. Boroko: Papua New Guinea National Museum, pp. 285–298.

Walter, Henrik. 2012. "Social Cognitive Neuroscience of Empathy. Concepts, Circuits, and Genes." *Emotion Review* 4 (1): 9–17.

Wardlow, Holly. 2006. *Wayward Women. Sexuality and Agency in a New Guinea Society.* Berkeley, Los Angeles, and London: University of California Press.

Wassmann, Jürg. 1991. *The Song to the Flying Fox. The Public and Esoteric Knowledge of the Important Men of Kandingei about Totemic Songs, Names and Knotted Cords (Middle Sepik, Papua New Guinea).* Boroko: National Research Institute, Cultural Studies Division (Apwitihire: Studies in Papua New Guinea Musics, 2).

———. 1993. "When Actions Speak Louder Than Words. The Classification of Food among the Yupno of Papua New Guinea." *The Quarterly Newsletter of the Laboratory of Comparative Human Cognition* 15 (1): 30–40.

———. 2001. "The Politics of Religious Secrecy." In *Emplaced Myth. Space, Narrative, and Knowledge in Aboriginal Australia and Papua New Guinea,* ed. Alan Rumsey and James F. Weiner. Honolulu: University of Hawai'i Press, pp. 43–70.

Wassmann, Jürg, and Katharina Stockhaus, eds. 2007. *Experiencing New Worlds.* New York and Oxford: Berghahn Books (Person, Space and Memory in the Contemporary Pacific, Volume 1).

Watson, James L., and Melissa L. Caldwell, eds. 2005. *The Cultural Politics of Food and Eating. A Reader.* Malden, Oxford and Victoria: Blackwell Publishing.

Weiner, James F. 1991. *The Empty Place. Poetry, Space, and Being among the Foi of Papua New Guinea.* Bloomington / Indianapolis: Indiana University Press.

Weismantel, Mary. 1995. "Making Kin. Theory and Zumbagua Adoptions." *American Ethnologist* 22 (4): 685–704.

White, Geoffrey M., and John Kirkpatrick, eds. 1985. *Person, Self, and Experience. Exploring Pacific Ethnopsychologies.* Berkeley, Los Angeles, and London: University of California Press.

Whitehead, Harriet. 2000. *Food Rules. Hunting, Sharing, and Tabooing Game in Papua New Guinea.* Ann Arbor: University of Michigan Press.

Wikan, Unni. 1990. *Managing Turbulent Hearts. A Balinese Formula for Living.* Chicago and London: University of Chicago Press.

———. 1992. "Beyond the Words. The Power of Resonance." *American Ethnologist* 19 (3): 460–482.

World Health Statistics. 2012. http://www.who.int/countries/png/en/.

Worsley, Peter. 1957. *The Trumpet Shall Sound. A Study of 'Cargo' Cults in Melanesia.* London: MacGibbon and Kee.

Wurm, Stephen A. 1982. *Papuan Languages of Oceania.* Tübingen: Gunter Narr Verlag.

Yamada, Yoichi. 1997. *Songs of Spirits. An Ethnography of Sounds in a Papua New Guinea Society.* Boroko: Institute of Papua New Guinea Studies (Apwitihire: Studies in Papua New Guinea Musics, 5).

Young, Michael W. 1971. *Fighting with Food. Leadership, Value and Social Control in a Massim Society.* Cambridge: Cambridge University Press.

Z'graggen, John A. 1972. *Comparative Wordlist of the Ramu Language Group, New Guinea.* Alexishafen, Madang Province, PNG: Anthropos Institute.

———. 1975. *The Languages of the Madang District, Papua New Guinea.* Canberra: Australian National University (Pacific Linguistic Series B, No. 41).

———. 1992. "The Myth of Daria." In *The Language Game. Papers in Memory of Donald C. Laycock,* ed. Tom Dutton, Malcom Ross and Darrel Tryon. Canberra: Pacific Linguistics, pp. 553–565.

———. 1996. *And Thus Became God.* Edinburgh et al.: The Pentland Press Limited.

Index